Indigenous Borderlands

Indigenous Borderlands

NATIVE AGENCY, RESILIENCE, AND POWER IN THE AMERICAS

Edited by

JOAQUÍN RIVAYA-MARTÍNEZ

UNIVERSITY OF OKLAHOMA PRESS : NORMAN

Chapters 5, 6, 8, and 9 are published with the generous support of The Americas Research Network. Publication of this book is also made possible through the generous support of Texas State University and Edith Kinney Gaylord.

Library of Congress Cataloging-in-Publication Data

Names: Rivaya-Martínez, Joaquín, editor.
Title: Indigenous borderlands : Native agency, resilience, and power in the Americas / edited by Joaquín Rivaya-Martínez.
Description: Norman : University of Oklahoma Press, [2023]. | Includes bibliographical references and index. | Summary: "In the essays collected here, twelve scholars explore how Native peoples, despite the upheavals caused by the European intrusion, often thrived after contact, preserving their sovereignty, territory, and culture and shaping indigenous borderlands across the Americas, from the sixteenth-century U.S. South to twentieth-century Bolivia. The book defines borderlands as spaces where diverse populations interact, cross-cultural exchanges are frequent and consequential, and no polity or community holds dominion"—Provided by publisher.
Identifiers: LCCN 2022045933 | ISBN 978-0-8061-9183-6 (hardcover) | ISBN 978-0-8061-9193-5 (paperback)
Subjects: LCSH: Indigenous peoples—America—History. | Indigenous peoples—America—Social conditions. | Indigenous peoples—America—Government relations. | Cultural relations. | BISAC: HISTORY / Latin America / General | HISTORY / Indigenous Peoples of the Americas
Classification: LCC GN562 .2023 | DDC 305.80097—dc23/eng/20221202
LC record available at https://lccn.loc.gov/2022045933

The paper in this book meets the guidelines for permanence and durability of the Committee on Production Guidelines for Book Longevity of the Council on Library Resources, Inc. ∞

Contents

List of Illustrations   ix

Acknowledgments   xi

List of Abbreviations   xiii

Introduction: Problematizing Indigenous
Borderlands   1
Joaquín Rivaya-Martínez

PART I. MULTIDISCIPLINARY APPROACHES

CHAPTER 1   Indigenous Borderlands: State of the
Field and Prospects   15
Joaquín Rivaya-Martínez

CHAPTER 2   Reading Cultural Landscapes through
Interdisciplinary Perspectives: The Yoreme
and Neighboring Peoples in Northwestern
New Spain   35
Cynthia Radding

CHAPTER 3   Beeswax and Borderlands in the
Seventeenth-Century Northern Maya Lowlands   54
Geoffrey H. Wallace

PART II. INDIGENOUS POWER AND CHARIS-MATIC LEADERSHIP

CHAPTER 4   When Giants Walked the Earth: Chief Tascalusa,
Hernando de Soto, and the Precolonial
Mississippian Borderlands of the
Sixteenth-Century US South   81
Robbie Ethridge

CHAPTER 5   Picax-andé Ins-tisle and the Llaneros:
             Apache Power in the Indigenous Borderlands
             of the Late-Eighteenth-Century Southern Plains   110
             *Cuauhtémoc Velasco Ávila and
             Antonio Cruz Zárate*

             PART III: IMAGINED BORDERLANDS:
             COLONIAL DISCOURSES AND
             INDIGENOUS REALITIES

CHAPTER 6   The Hows and Whys of Naming Indios:
             The Case of the Bolsón de Mapimí   141
             Chantal Cramaussel

CHAPTER 7   Fearing Apaches into Existence: The Discursive
             Borderlands of Nueva Vizcaya and Cuba in the
             Late Eighteenth and Early Nineteenth Centuries   158
             Paul Conrad

CHAPTER 8   Guaraní Territorialization: State Narratives and
             Indigenous Logics in South America's
             Eighteenth-Century Borderlands   185
             Guillermo Wilde

             PART IV. INDIGENOUS SOVEREIGNTY
             IN UNEXPECTED PLACES

CHAPTER 9   The Chaco de Jujuy: An Indigenous
             Borderland in Sixteenth- and
             Seventeenth-Century Colonial Tucumán   207
             Enrique Normando Cruz

CHAPTER 10   Pueblo and Genízaro Agency in the Preservation
             of Indigenous Land: New Mexico, 1815–1825   221
             Gary Van Valen

CHAPTER 11   Do Indians Have Land Rights? The Case of
             Tierras Baldías and Chiriguano Integration
             in the Bolivian Lowlands in the Nineteenth
             and Early Twentieth Centuries   242
             Erick D. Langer

Epilogue: Ongoing Indigenous Struggles 272
Joaquín Rivaya-Martínez

Bibliography 275
List of Contributors 327
Index 333

Illustrations

FIGURES

4.1. Artistic rendering and photograph of Moundville
Archaeological State Park   84, 85
4.2. Graphic reconstruction of de Soto's route through
central Alabama   91
4.3. Late Mississippian Timucuan chief and his wife   93
11.1. Map of San Ramón de Ñaguambaruzú   255
11.2. Map of Caraparirenda   258
11.3. Map of Caipipendi   261
11.4. Map of San Miguel   263
11.5. Map of Iti and Itimiri   265

MAPS

0.1. Indigenous borderlands discussed in this volume   5
2.1. Northwestern New Spain   37
3.1. Trans-frontier trade in the northern Maya lowlands   55
3.2. Maximum annual wax repartimiento per town   60
3.3. Availability of wax in Yucatán   61
4.1. US South and the Mississippian World, showing route of
Hernando de Soto   87
6.1. Bolsón de Mapimí and its periphery   142
8.1. Frontier outposts and ethnic dispersion   195
9.1. Major settlements in Jujuy and the surrounding region   211
11.1. Tierras baldías in the Andean foothills of southeastern Bolivia   246

Acknowledgments

This book is the result of the sum of many efforts and the support of many people and institutions over the course of several years. The Indigenous Borderlands project began with a two-day symposium that I organized, sponsored by the Center for the Study of the Southwest and the Department of History at Texas State University, and held at the university's main campus in San Marcos, Texas, in April 2018. This seminar benefited from the participation of many of the scholars contributing to the present volume, who have remained engaged with the project since its inception. At that first meeting, apart from discussing the first drafts of many of the chapters now in this volume, we conceptualized the project and established the foundation of our collaborative effort.

The Instituto de Investigaciones Históricas of the Universidad Nacional Autónoma de México (UNAM) sponsored a second seminar in Mexico City, which I co-organized with UNAM's Gerardo Lara Cisneros, in January 2019. Many thanks to Gerardo and to Ana Carolina Ibarra González, then director of the instituto, for facilitating the seminar. This second meeting permitted us to enlist additional scholars and sharpen our analyses.

I am very grateful to the staffs of the Texas State University Center for the Study of the Southwest and the UNAM Instituto de Investigaciones Históricas, whose hard work made the two seminars possible. Many thanks as well to all the scholars who participated in those seminars: Shawn Austin, Paul Conrad, Chantal Cramaussel, Enrique Normando Cruz, Erick Langer, Gerardo Lara Cisneros, Cynthia Radding, Carlos Manuel Valdés, Gary Van Valen, Cuauhtémoc Velasco Ávila, Geoff Wallace, and Jesse Zarley. Their valuable feedback on their colleagues' essays helped refine these contributions and confirm that our project would elicit wide interest. I am particularly indebted to Gerardo, Cynthia, and Geoff for going beyond expectations in their commitment to the project. Many thanks also to our other contributors, Robbie Ethridge, Guillermo Wilde, and Antonio Cruz Zárate.

A subvention from the Americas Research Network (ARENET) funded the translation into English of several chapters originally written in Spanish. A grant from the History Department at Texas State University provided funding for the cartography. Special thanks to Terry Rugeley for his excellent translation work, to Kirsteen Anderson for her superb copyediting, to Geoff Wallace for his exceptional cartographic work, and the whole team at the University of Oklahoma Press for their professionalism and efficiency. The Center for the Study of the Southwest, the History Department, and the College of Liberal Arts at Texas State University jointly provided a generous publication subvention. The directors of the Center for the Study of the Southwest at Texas State University, Frank de la Teja and John McKiernam-González, provided invaluable help, as did Angie Murphy and Jeff Helgeson, chairs of the History Department, and Mary Brennan, dean of the College of Liberal Arts.

Coordinating an international, multilingual project like this has been no easy task. The persistent COVID-19 pandemic brought about unexpected delays and complications. Therefore, I extend my most sincere gratitude to all the contributors to this volume and my other collaborators for their trust and patience. Finally, I thank my wife, Yasmine, and our children, Shane and Olaya, for their unfailing support despite the many hours that this project has deprived them of my company and attention.

Abbreviations

AACh	Archivo del Ayuntamiento de Chihuahua
ABNB	Archivo y Biblioteca Nacionales de Bolivia
AGES	Archivo General del Estado de Sonora
AGES TP	Archivo General del Estado de Sonora, Títulos Primordiales
AGI	Archivo General de Indias
AGN	Archivo General de la Nación (Mexico City)
AHJ-ARR	Archivo Histórico de Jujuy, Archivo Ricardo Rojas
AHPM	Archivo Histórico de la Provincia de México
AOJ	Archivo del Obispado de Jujuy
ARENET	Americas Research Network
ATJ	Archivo de Tribunales de Jujuy
BL	Bancroft Library
BNFR AF	Biblioteca Nacional Fondo Reservado Archivo Franciscano
BPEJ	Biblioteca Pública del Estado de Jalisco
FGD	Fondo Gerardo Decorme
GIS	Geographic Information System
MANM	Mexican Archives of New Mexico
PI	Provincias Internas
SANM	Spanish Archives of New Mexico
UNAM	Universidad Nacional Autónoma de México

Introduction

PROBLEMATIZING INDIGENOUS BORDERLANDS

Joaquín Rivaya-Martínez

The romantic masterpiece on the cover of this book, *La vuelta del malón* (The Return of the Indian Raid), represents an indigenous raiding party returning victorious with its loot, presumably in the Pampa region of nineteenth-century Argentina. Its author, Ángel Della Valle, painted it for the World's Columbian Exposition, held in Chicago in 1893 to commemorate the fourth centenary of Columbus's first arrival in the Western Hemisphere. There the painting obtained a medal. Evocative of the pretended confrontation between indigenous "barbarism" and European "civilization," the canvas has often been interpreted as legitimizing the infamous Desert Campaign of 1879, which brought an end to native resistance in southern Argentina. It certainly resonates with some of the themes that have been the staple of Euro-American expansionist propaganda along many frontiers: native fierceness and heathenism, the plundering of settlements, the desecration of sacred objects, the theft of livestock, and the kidnapping of Christian women. Intentionally or not, however, the painting admits an alternative reading. The white female captive and the Christian ritual objects carried by the raiders symbolize indigenous power and dominance. The natives ride horses and carry iron-tipped lances, evincing the incorporation of European-introduced species and objects into Amerindian cultures. The raiders are spread all over the landscape in a way that suggests symbiosis with and occupation of the land. Implicitly, this work of art thus conveys indigenous

1

agency, adaptiveness, resilience, sovereignty, and power, all key themes in this book.

Recent scholarship on the Americas has dispelled once-pervasive myths of European domination and indigenous submission and disappearance, showing instead that, despite the initial upheavals caused by the European intrusion, Amerindians often thrived after contact. It is now widely accepted in academic circles that European expansion depended fundamentally on the participation of Indian allies, that the immediate and long-term outcomes of initial encounters were neither predictable nor unavoidable, instead, often those outcomes hinged on native understandings and actions. Building on that scholarship, this book explores the manifold ways in which Amerindians adapted to the intrusion of people of European descent to preserve their sovereignty, their land, and their culture, thus shaping indigenous borderlands across the Americas.[1]

Covering a wide chronological and geographical span, from the sixteenth-century US South to twentieth-century Bolivia, this volume expands our knowledge in innovative ways, challenging conventional wisdom about what supposedly happened to native peoples across the Western Hemisphere after contact and pointing out alternative approaches and potential avenues for further research. Often drawing on previously untapped or underutilized primary sources, the contributors to this book manifest the incompleteness of imperial and state conquests; the resilience and relative success of indigenous communities decades or even centuries after they are commonly and wrongly thought to have been subordinated to nonnatives, made dependent on colonial forces, or even vanished; and the rhetorical creation of imagined borderlands through the discursive construction of indigenous "others." They also underscore the persistence of internal indigenous borderlands within territories claimed by Europeans or Euro-Americans, implicitly challenging the traditional dichotomy between center and periphery that underlies much borderlands scholarship.[2]

INDIGENOUS BORDERLANDS:
A WORKING DEFINITION

The meaning of "borderlands," once restrictively applied in US historiography as a synonym for the "Spanish" (then "Mexican") frontiers in North America, has expanded considerably in the last decades, becoming a pervasive catchall expression in English-language scholarship.[3] Hence, it is pertinent to clarify up front what we mean by it. A borderland can be defined simply as any territory near a border, characterized by a set of topographic, environmental, and sociodemographic features.[4] The notion of borderland that we espouse, however, has both material and nonmaterial components: a borderland is a geographic or ideological space (frequently both) of vague contours where discrete and ethnically diverse human populations meet and interact, where cross-cultural influences and exchanges (both physical and intellectual) are relatively frequent and consequential, and over which no polity or community can de facto exercise full jurisdiction or domination. It is precisely the fluidity of the interethnic relationships and the lack of political and cultural control that confer upon a borderland its distinct nature, setting it apart from other spaces. Contrary to some definitions advanced by other scholars, our notion of borderland does not presume the existence of a state, empire, or marked border.[5] Like Danna Levin Rojo and Cynthia Radding, we consider borderlands as "lived spaces rather than boundaries."[6] Such spaces may exist within or beyond states and empires.[7]

Similarly, "indigenous borderlands" has both geopolitical and sociocultural connotations. The expression refers to those borderlands, within and beyond colonial frontiers and state boundaries, where indigenous groups interact(ed) in significant ways with one another, with nonnatives, or with both prior to the displacement, extermination, or incorporation of the natives into modern states. In indigenous borderlands, independent or semiautonomous native peoples exert(ed) considerable power, often retaining control of the land and remaining paramount agents of historical transformation after the European intrusion. Conversely, European conquests and colonization were typically slow and incomplete, as the newcomers, often operating in a climate of mistrust and violence that hindered peaceful coexistence, struggled to assert their authority and implement policies designed to subjugate aboriginal societies and change native beliefs and practices. In indigenous borderlands, people, plants, animals, pathogens, technologies, and ideas moved across ethnic boundaries that blurred often as cultural traditions intertwined and merged. Yet, numerous indigenous groups in the Americas and around the world remain culturally distinct and politically autonomous (or at least partially unincorporated) to this day. Thus, although the essays in this book focus on the period prior to 1920, "indigenous borderlands" is still a valid category for studying the modern world.[8]

Recent years have witnessed growing academic interest in "urban Indians"; that is, natives who resided, often in separate enclaves, in metropolitan settings where they sometimes interacted extensively with nonnatives.[9] Indeed, much of the most influential literature on Amerindians produced in the last decades deals with indigenous communities established according to colonial models under European auspices and domination, albeit often in ways that partially conformed to aboriginal practices and expectations.[10] Such developments typically occurred in regions that cannot be easily classified as borderlands or that did not maintain a borderland configuration for very long. Conversely, we cast Amerindians as pivotal historical agents in long-lasting borderlands defined by the presence of independent or semiautonomous indigenous peoples.[11]

Even though the essays in this book focus on the period after 1492, it is important to remember that the history of the Western Hemisphere began several millennia earlier with the arrival of the first human populations from Asia. The last few centuries are just the terminal period of a much deeper and richer history that archaeologists across the Americas are still unearthing. Indeed, the existence of borderlands in the Western Hemisphere predates the arrival of Europeans. By 1492, the Americas had long been the scene of migrations, conquests, mergers of peoples, and the rise and spread of countless beliefs and practices, as cultures, polities, and borderlands formed, evolved, coalesced, and disappeared over time. This dynamism gave rise to the enormous ethnic and linguistic diversity and the complex political mosaic that Europeans encountered. In fact, the nature of precontact borderlands and intergroup relations fundamentally conditioned the speed and thoroughness of European conquests and colonization.[12]

ORGANIZATION OF THIS BOOK

The book is organized into four parts and an epilogue. Part I, "Multidisciplinary Approaches," consists of three chapters. In chapter 1, I provide a state-of-the-field survey of the historiography, identify some under-researched areas, and discuss the benefits of interdisciplinary approaches, thus introducing a central idea of this volume: that historians can partially compensate for the lack of Amerindian written records by studying archival documents in combination with nonwritten evidence to reconstruct indigenous perspectives and experiences. Such a strategy requires borrowing concepts, research questions, and methodologies from archaeology, cultural anthropology, linguistics, geography, ecology, and other disciplines.

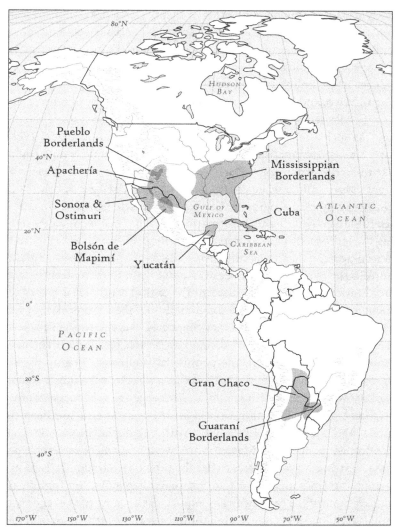

Map 0.1. Indigenous borderlands discussed in this volume.
(Map © G. Wallace Cartography & GIS)

As Cynthia Radding demonstrates in chapter 2, reading archival sources in light of nontextual evidence permits scholars to reconstruct and interpret the entwined processes of colonial encounter and cultural re-creation in indigenous borderlands. She discusses the historical construction of cultural landscapes in Ostimuri, a province of northwestern New Spain bounded by the Yaqui, Mayo, and Fuerte Rivers. Radding reads a variety of sources in dialogue with selected archaeological, ecological, and ethnographic themes to explore the formation of that region as a series of cultural spaces evolving through time. This multidisciplinary approach permits her to bring to light the secular resilience of the Yoreme and neighboring native peoples despite their apparent vulnerabilities when confronted with the exigencies of colonialism.

Canadian historical geographer Geoffrey Wallace demonstrates in chapter 3 the usefulness of geographic information system (GIS) technology in reassessing the indigenous past. Through examining GIS-generated maps in light of environmental data and quantitative analyses of Spanish documents, Wallace unveils the relevance of the beeswax industry in the seventeenth-century Yucatec Maya borderlands and discerns the critical roles Mayas played in the production and trade of that coveted commodity. Wallace painstakingly reconstructs the overland trade routes that connected Yucatec towns in the outer edges of the Spanish province of Yucatán to Yucatec refugee settlements and independent Maya polities in the peninsula's southeast. Beginning in the late sixteenth century, large quantities of beeswax flowed along those Maya networks toward the Spanish colony in exchange for salt, metal tools, and other goods. The proliferation of bees in the central and southern Maya lowlands, and the ease and reliability with which the wax could be bartered, afforded independent Mayas both a livelihood and considerable political clout, enticing Maya refugees to flee the province. Paradoxically, beeswax extraction and trade made Yucatán Spaniards dependent on fugitive communities for one of the province's key exports at the same time as they sought to eradicate independent Maya communities and curb the flow of refugees out of the colony.

Part II, "Indigenous Power and Charismatic Leadership," consists of two chapters that reassess power relations in two well-studied indigenous borderlands by situating the focus squarely on the natives and highlighting the political power and diplomatic acumen of two little known yet very influential indigenous leaders. In chapter 4, the anthropologist Robbie Ethridge examines documentary and archaeological evidence in unison to reveal the deeply rooted indigenous social, political, and cultural norms that shaped native responses to the Spanish intrusion into the Mississippian borderlands of today's US South in the 1540s. Ethridge cogently proposes to parse Hernando de Soto's entrada for its numerous encounters with discrete native polities, instead of conceptualizing the whole expedition as a single episode. She discusses de Soto's encounter with Chief Tascalusa, grand cacique (chief) of the paramount chiefdom of Tascalusa in present-day central Alabama. Spaniards described Tascalusa as a giant of a man, and Ethridge's analysis corroborates the physical and political stature of this native leader whose military might and political acumen enabled him to manipulate and resist the Spanish.

In chapter 5, Mexican scholars Cuauhtémoc Velasco Ávila and Antonio Cruz Zárate discuss a series of diplomatic contacts between Juan de Ugalde, commander in chief of the eastern Internal Provinces of New Spain, and the little-known Llanero (also Lipiyan) Apaches between 1787 and 1789. Drawing partly on untapped sources, Velasco and Cruz shed light on the identity of the Llaneros; their culture, customs, and political organization; and the preeminence of their main leader, Picax-andé Ins-tinsle. Their analyses reveal that, in the last decades of the eighteenth century, Spaniards recognized the Llaneros as a powerful indigenous group capable of preserving their independence from the Spanish while confronting the expanding Comanches. Llaneros ranged over a vast territory centered between the Pecos River in New Mexico and the Colorado River of Texas. Picax-andé's military and religious ascendancy extended to the Lipan and Mescalero Apaches. Llanero influence spread thus over an enormous territory on both sides of the Rio Grande.

Part III, "Imagined Borderlands: Colonial Discourses and Indigenous Realities," explores different ways in which uncritical acceptance of colonial sources may blur scholars' comprehension of indigenous realities and lead to unwarranted interpretations.[13] In chapter 6, French historian Chantal Cramaussel discusses the historical contexts and the criteria that Spaniards followed to designate native groups from the Bolsón de Mapimí, a vast region of present-day north-central Mexico that remained an internal indigenous borderland after the colonial period. She cautions scholars against credulously reproducing the Spanish system of designations. Even though Spaniards sometimes adopted indigenous terms to label native groups, the main purpose of the terminology they used, Cramaussel argues, was to show the Indians' place within colonial society, classifying them as "friends," "enemies," "mission/encomienda/hacienda Indians," and so on. Hence, the common assumption that Spanish designations for indigenous groups refer only to their territory or ethnicity is misleading.[14]

Another potential problem derived from historians' unquestioning reliance on Euro-American sources is the risk of perpetuating cultural misunderstandings, fabrications, and discursive fictions. In chapter 7, Paul Conrad compares Spanish documents from eighteenth-century Nueva Vizcaya and Cuba, arguing that the suspected presence of indigenous people deemed dangerous to colonial society exercised a historical influence that outsized their actual demographic or military power. In both regions, the presence of Apaches, real or imagined, took on a discursive life of its own. In Nueva Vizcaya, Apaches were singled out as perpetrators of numerous crimes, even though investigations suggested the participation of various individuals of diverse ethnic heritage.[15] Anxieties about the allegiance of mission Indians and other Spanish subjects, and about their sympathies for *indios bárbaros* (independent, unacculturated Indians), compelled colonial authorities to wage war on Apaches and deport those captured as far away as Cuba, where similar apprehensions eventually emerged.[16] After some of the prisoners fled to the island's countryside, killings and depredations began to be blamed on Indian fugitives and runaway African slaves, despite scarce and inconclusive evidence. Thus, the Apache borderlands of Nueva Vizcaya and Cuba were, at least in part, a discursive construct. As Conrad concludes, historians need to be aware that the perceived threats posed by indigenous people to colonial society did not have to be proven to be consequential to Spanish policy.

Euro-American sources may also be deceiving in other ways. In chapter 8, Argentinian historian Guillermo Wilde cautions against accepting official colonial narratives at face value, as they tend to obscure indigenous logics and realities. Beginning in the late eighteenth century, amidst the renewed Spanish and Portuguese impetus to colonize the fringes of their South American dominions and control the peoples there, officials, travelers, and jurists endeavored to refine classifications, descriptions, measurements, and cartographic representations, and to establish boundaries. In the Guaraní borderlands of today's Brazil, Paraguay, and Argentina, colonial agents attempted to assimilate native populations into colonial society through homogenizing practices and formal discourses, progressively circumscribing indigenous territories as a continuous space distributed among ethnic "nations" or imperial domains. As Wilde shows, however, indigenous territorial logics structured in dynamic networks of families and *cacicazgos* (chiefdoms) betray the porousness of those supposed ethnic and imperial boundaries. Indeed, some of the kinship networks and cacicazgos persisted even after the dissolution of the *pueblos de misión* (mission villages) and the fall of the Iberian empires.

Colonial authorities often claimed domination in regions where a careful scrutiny of the documents reveals native agency and autonomy. That is the overarching theme of Part IV, "Indigenous Sovereignty in Unexpected Places," which consists of three chapters. Despite the disproportionate historiographic emphasis on imperial frontiers that tend to be seen as outlying and marginal from a Eurocentric colonial perspective, stories of native survival, resistance, and domination also abound at the heart of territories claimed by European empires and American republics—what we refer to as internal indigenous borderlands. Like the aforementioned Bolsón de Mapimí, the Jujuy region of today's northwestern Argentina provides a case in point. As Enrique Normando Cruz, a native of the area, explains in chapter 9, the jurisdiction of Jujuy, a city founded by the Spanish in 1593 in the district of Tucumán, became an internal borderland and remained so until the first decades of the nineteenth century. The Indians in the region successfully resorted to a variety of strategies to resist foreign domination and, ultimately, incorporate themselves into the colonial system on their own terms.

The ability of indigenous peoples under the nominal jurisdiction of foreign polities to retain their land in the face of external encroachment is the subject of the other two chapters in this section. In chapter 10, Gary Van Valen examines the oft-successful efforts of Pueblo Indians and Genízaros (Hispanized descendants of ransomed Indians) to resist spoliation in late Spanish and early Mexican New Mexico. Between 1815 and 1825, members of the Hispanic elite, drawing partly on new liberal theories of private landownership advanced at the Cortes of Cádiz, implemented various strategies to privatize communal and common land at the expense of people of indigenous descent.[17] Pueblos and Genízaros actively resisted those land acquisitions and usurpations. Thus, the initially successful attempts at privatizing public land on the New Mexican frontier came to a halt in 1825.

In chapter 11, Erick Langer challenges the widespread idea that frontier land grants in Latin American republics favored only settlers of European descent to the detriment of indigenous people. Examining land grant records and documents kept by landlords, Langer shows that the Chiriguano and Chané Indians from the lowlands of southeastern Bolivia managed to use the land grant process, meant to take away Indian land, to preserve some of their communities.[18] Chiriguanos succeeded in this endeavor through alliances with powerful Euro-American landlords and local authorities whom they provided with indigenous labor. Where agricultural labor was needed and scarce, landlords had an interest in maintaining the territorial integrity of the indigenous communities for their own benefit—and Chiriguanos took full advantage of the situation.

The epilogue reflects briefly on some of the challenges that native communities still face. Social and political discrimination, usurpation of land and resources, cultural loss, and other infringements of individual and communal rights continue to afflict many indigenous peoples across the Americas. In every instance, though, natives remain active in defense of their lands, their rights, their autonomy, and their culture.

NOTES

1. We use "Americas" synonymously with "Western Hemisphere." Contributors refer to the aboriginal inhabitants of the Americas and their descendants in various ways, as "indigenous/native people(s)," "natives," "Amerindians," or simply "Indians," without any other implications. Although all of these generic terms are exonyms (designations coined by outsiders) and can be problematized in different ways, all are used by academics and, more importantly, by indigenous peoples themselves.

2. For an approach to the dichotomy between center and periphery that prioritizes ideological and power relations over geographical distance, see Bushnell and Greene, "Peripheries, Centers," 1–14. In contrast, TePaske, "Integral to Empire," 29–42, has defended an integrative approach to the study of the fringes of Spanish America.

3. Herbert Bolton first used the expression "Spanish Borderlands" in 1921 in reference to the Spanish frontiers in the present-day United States. See Bolton, *Spanish Borderlands*. Originally, the term was narrowly limited to studying the presence of Spaniards in the United States during the colonial period, but Bolton's successors gradually increased the scope of their interests geographically to encompass northern Mexico and territories beyond the Spanish frontiers, chronologically into the present, and ethnically to incorporate non-Spaniards into their analyses. Considering recent scholarship highlighting indigenous power, "Spanish" and "Mexican" seem reductionistic epithets. Hence, the current preference is simply to use "borderlands" by itself or accompanied by some geographic qualifier, as in "Southwest Borderlands." For discussions of the historiographic influence of Bolton and his intellectual successors, see Bannon, *Bolton*; Hanke, *Do the Americas Have a Common History?*; Worcester, "Significance of the Spanish Borderlands"; Weber, "John Francis Bannon"; Thomas, "Columbian Consequences"; Weber, "Spanish Borderlands of North America"; Weber, "Spanish Borderlands, Historiography Redux"; Hämäläinen and Truett, "On Borderlands."

4. According to the online Merriam-Webster dictionary, "borderland" refers to "a territory at or near a border," a "fringe" in the sense of "something that is marginal, additional, or secondary to some activity, process, or subject" or "a vague intermediate

state or region." See "Borderland," *Merriam-Webster.com*, accessed June 10, 2020, https://www.merriam-webster.com/dictionary/borderland. Our usage of "borderland" retains only some aspects of that formal definition and presupposes neither the existence of a formal border nor marginality.

5. For other definitions of borderlands that presuppose the existence of states or geopolitical boundaries, see Clifford, "Diasporas," 304; Baud and van Schendel, "Comparative Approach," 7; Readman, Radding, and Bryant, "Introduction," 3.

6. Levin Rojo and Radding, "Introduction," 1.

7. Scholars often understand borderlands as spaces *outside* states or empires. See, for instance, Hämäläinen and Johnson, "What Is Borderlands History?" 1–2. Considering borderlands as "the contested spaces between colonial domains," Adelman and Aron argued that, as European empires declined, the expansion of nation-states ended the existence of borderlands in North America during the nineteenth century. "From Borderlands to Borders," 16.

8. Our notion of indigenous borderland shares with Boccara's idea of "border/frontier complex" (*complejo fronterizo*) the emphases on political autonomy, cultural diversity, and interwoven sovereignties (*soberanías imbricadas*). Our definition does not presuppose however that indigenous groups necessarily "initiate relatively stable relations in a colonial context of struggles between imperial powers." See Boccara, "Génesis y estructura," 47.

9. On urban Indians, see Castillo Palma, *Cholula*; Castro Gutiérrez, *Los indios y las ciudades*; Ramos, *Death and Conversion*; Connell, *After Moctezuma*; Velasco Murillo, Lentz, and Ochoa, *City Indians*; Rosenthal, *Reimagining Indian Country*; Velasco Murillo, *Urban Indians*; Corbeil, *Motions Beneath*; Miller, *Indians on the Move*.

10. Stern, *Peru's Indian Peoples*; Castro Gutiérrez, *Los tarascos*; Yannakakis, *Art of Being In-between*; Lamana, *Domination without Dominance*; Talavera Ibarra, *Historia del pueblo de indios*; Martínez Baracs, *Un gobierno de indios*; Ruiz Medrano and Kellogg, *Negotiation within Domination*; Pizzigoni, *Life Within*; Mumford, *Vertical Empire*; Brown, *Pueblo Indians*; Brosseder, *Power of Huacas*; Penry, *People Are King*.

11. Among the extensive English-language scholarship on borderlands, several important precedents to this volume stand out for their hemispheric approach and their attention to native peoples: Guy and Sheridan, *Contested Ground*; Weber, *Bárbaros*; Barr and Countryman, *Contested Spaces*; Levin Rojo and Radding, *Oxford Handbook of Borderlands*. *Bárbaros* deals mostly with the development and implementation of Spanish policies toward independent Indians during the late colonial period. *Contested Ground*, in turn, focuses on the remotest fringes of the Spanish Empire, as do most of the relevant Spanish-language edited volumes published in the last decades: Pinto Rodríguez, *Araucanía y pampas*; Mandrini and Paz, *Las fronteras hispanocriollas*; Mandrini, *Vivir entre dos mundos*; Giudicelli, *Fronteras movedizas*; Quijada, *De los cacicazgos a la ciudadanía*; Medina Bustos and Padilla Calderón, *Indios, españoles y mestizos*; Medina Bustos and Padilla Calderón, *Violencia interétnica*; De Jong, *Diplomacia, malones y cautivos*; Gallardo Arias and Velasco Ávila,

Fronteras étnicas. See also the relevant chapters in Landavazo, *Territorio, frontera y región.*

12. On the Americas' deep history see, for instance, Carballo, *Collision of Worlds.* For an eloquent example of the formation of borderlands in the fluid precontact milieu of the US Southwest, see Clark et al., "Resolving the Migrant Paradox."

13. A topic also explored in Giudicelli, *Fronteras movedizas.*

14. For a similar argument regarding the natives of the Southern Cone, see Nacuzzi, *Identidades impuestas.*

15. See also Ortelli, *Trama de una guerra.*

16. On the forced relocation of Apaches and other natives from the continent to the Caribbean, see Yaremko, "Indigenous Diaspora," 817–39.

17. The Cortes of Cádiz was an independent legislative body formed by Spanish patriots, including representatives from the Americas, during the Napoleonic invasion. Most famously, the liberal-dominated Cortes produced the influential Spanish Constitution of 1812, which established a constitutional monarchy and abolished several Old Regime institutions and privileges. See, for instance, Pérez Garzón, *Las Cortes de Cádiz;* Eastman and Sobrevilla Perea, *Rise of Constitutional Government.*

18. For a compelling analysis of how urban Indians adapted to this process in the department of Beni, in the Bolivian Amazonia, see Guiteras Mombiola, "Los indígenas benianos," 67–89.

PART I

Multidisciplinary Approaches

CHAPTER 1

Indigenous Borderlands

STATE OF THE FIELD AND PROSPECTS

Joaquín Rivaya-Martínez

Indigenous peoples have played crucial roles in the history of the Western Hemisphere ever since the earliest human populations colonized it more than fifteen thousand years ago. Beginning in the 1490s, the aboriginal peoples of the Americas endured military conquest, enslavement, coerced labor, cultural deprivation, land encroachment, and many other forms of colonial oppression, frequently during or in the wake of extremely deadly epidemics of diseases imported from the Old World that caused tremendous population declines.[1] Europeans and their descendants wreaked such havoc on indigenous peoples that their actions have often been branded as "ethnocide," "ethnic cleansing," or "genocide."[2] Irrespective of what labels we choose, as James Merrell and Colin Calloway have argued, after 1492, the Western Hemisphere truly became a "New World for all," natives included.[3] Far from being passive victims, though, Amerindians implemented a myriad of strategies to cope with the formidable challenges the newcomers brought about, giving rise to indigenous borderlands throughout the hemisphere. Indeed, despite the ambitious territorial claims of European empires and the independent republics that succeeded them, indigenous peoples often remained autonomous and retained control over vast expanses of the Western Hemisphere long after their initial contact with Europeans. These statements, now widely accepted among specialists, stand in stark contrast with the Eurocentric views forged and perpetuated by generations of scholarly assumptions and misinterpretations, some of which are still common among the general public. In this chapter, I offer a panoramic overview of the historiography (referenced mostly in the notes) and propose ethnohistorical perspectives and interdisciplinary approaches as the most promising avenues to expand our knowledge about the indigenous borderlands of the Americas.

INDIGENOUS RESPONSES TO EUROPEAN COLONIZATION

Confronted with colonialism, most Amerindians sooner or later put up a fight.[4] Some opted for outright warfare, which often led to long-lasting conflicts, as in the cases of the so-called Chichimecas of north-central Mexico; the Chiriguanos and other natives of the South American Gran Chaco; the Pijaos of present-day Colombia; and many of the natives in the Orinoco and Amazon Basins, southern Chile, and Tucumán.[5] Even groups generally portrayed as "peaceful," such as the Guaranís of Paraguay, confronted the Spanish initially.[6] In the long term, the introduction of livestock (and in some cases firearms) turned plundering into an essential aspect of the political economy of many independent native peoples. Some, like the Guaycuruans of the Gran Chaco, the Apaches of the US Southwest, and several nomadic groups of the North American Great Plains, thrived as equestrian raiders.[7] Comanche and Kiowa riders, for instance, launched large-scale looting expeditions deep into Mexico as late as the mid-nineteenth century, often journeying more than one thousand miles in a single campaign.[8]

Other indigenous groups simply fled, under different degrees of coercion, to shelter in regions that did not necessarily offer better prospects, frequently encroaching on the territories of other natives—an extant pattern in the Amazon Basin.[9] The Kickapoos, for instance, migrated repeatedly. Originally from the Great Lakes area, some Kickapoos ended up as far south as present-day Coahuila, Mexico, where a number of their descendants still live today.[10] Other natives, such as the Hopis of Arizona, attempted passive resistance.[11] The Pueblos of New Mexico, the Tepehuanes of northwestern Mexico, the Wayuu of the Guajira Peninsula, and many others rebelled, sometimes long after having been nominally subjugated, a recurrent phenomenon in colonial times that sometimes continued into the national period, as exemplified by the so-called Caste War of Yucatán.[12] Other Amerindians practiced resistance more surreptitiously. After the Spanish reconquest of New Mexico, the Pueblos of the upper Rio Grande Basin covertly subverted the colonial order through secrecy and a selective incorporation of Catholic elements into their ritual world, but on Pueblo terms.[13] Mobility afforded many indigenous communities a degree of autonomy rarely enjoyed by fully sedentary peoples under colonial rule.[14]

Throughout the hemisphere, countless native groups capitalized on the arrival of Europeans to diverse degrees, using them as political allies and economic partners, sometimes dictating the terms of their relations from a position of dominance, and often retaining their sovereignty and their territory intact for prolonged periods. In North America, some groups remained so powerful throughout the colonial period that scholars now use expressions such as indigenous "masters of empire," indigenous maritime power, "Native Ground," "native New Worlds," and "reversed colonialism" to describe their territorial, demographic, economic, or political preponderance.[15]

So-called European conquests typically depended on the support of indigenous allies as combatants, porters, guides, and interpreters. Totonacs, Tlaxcallans, and many others helped Hernán Cortés defeat the Mexicas (Aztecs).[16] Following the fall of Tenochtitlan, Tlaxcallans, Mexicas, and other Nahuatl speakers, Otomís, Purépechas (Tarascans), Zapotecs, and Mixtecs were instrumental in the Spanish expansion north and south of Central Mexico.[17] Similarly, analyses of indigenous agency in many Andean regions reveal that pre-Hispanic interethnic feuds and rivalries within and between indigenous polities motivated a multitude of "Indian conquistadors" to ally themselves with the newly arrived Spaniards against the Inca overlords.[18]

While some Amerindians facilitated "European" conquests, others became conquerors in their own right, boosting their political clout and territorial reach considerably after contact. During the so-called Beaver Wars of the seventeenth century, for instance, the Iroquois of northeastern North America ranged over an expanding land base to collect furs for European markets, to the territorial and demographic detriment of many of their native neighbors.[19] In the eighteenth and nineteenth centuries, Blackfoots, Comanches, Osages, and Lakotas made the most of the introduction of horses and firearms, spreading their hegemony over immense areas of the Great Plains and beyond.[20] After pushing the Spanish back north of the Biobío River between 1598 and 1604, the Mapuches of the Southern Cone expanded across the Andean range into what is today Argentina between the seventeenth and nineteenth centuries.[21]

To defend their sovereignty, many Amerindians built alliances with former native foes, with some of the European newcomers, or with both (see chapters 4 and 5). Charismatic political and religious leaders typically fostered and directed such interethnic alliances.[22] Thus, in 1680, Popé, a Tewa shaman from Ohkay Owingeh (San Juan Pueblo), New Mexico, united the culturally diverse Pueblos to push the Spanish temporarily out of the upper Rio Grande Basin.[23] Similarly, the Shawnee brothers Tecumseh and Tenskwatawa led a multiethnic confederacy that included Wyandots, Mingos, Odawas (Ottawas), Miamis, Pottawatomis, and many other groups then residing northwest of the Ohio River against the United States in the early nineteenth century.[24] Later in that century, powerful leaders such as Red Cloud and Sitting Bull galvanized the resistance of the different Lakota divisions and their Cheyenne and Arapaho allies against US encroachment.[25] Likewise, cunning Apache leaders including Mangas Coloradas, Cochise, and Victorio extended their political sway beyond their original people to defend their land from Euro-American intruders.[26] In the Andean region, charismatic figures such as Túpac Amaru II (born José Gabriel Condorcanqui Noguera) and Túpac Katari (born Julián Apasa Nina) managed to enlist the support of large numbers of nonnatives despite the decidedly pro-indigenous stance of many of their claims in the early 1780s.[27]

Indians under colonial rule were frequently essential to the defensive systems of European colonies and frontiers, as was true with the Ópatas and Pimas of Sonora, the Pueblos of New Mexico, the Guaranís of interior South America, and many others.[28] Sometimes, European frontier defense relied fundamentally on independent indigenous groups, as in the cases of the Spanish alliances with Wichitas and Comanches in northern New Spain in the 1770s and 1780s, and a similar coalition between Spaniards and Pehuenches in the southern Andes, also in the 1780s.[29] In nineteenth-century North America, prolonged conflicts such as the Plains Wars and the Apache Wars were finally brought to an end with the decisive participation of Native Americans enlisted by the US Army as scouts and fighters.[30]

Mutual adjustments between Amerindians and Europeans were often crucial to both. In indigenous borderlands, the safety and welfare of the latter depended crucially on their capacity to attract native allies. To this end, European conquerors, missionaries, traders, military men, and officials frequently had to adapt to indigenous expectations, practices, and rituals.[31] The missions of the Californias, the Guaycuruan Chaco, and the Guaraní borderlands of South America, as well as the Apache *establecimientos* (settlements) provide abundant examples of reciprocal accommodation.[32] Indigenous elites often maintained part of their ascendancy by strategically collaborating with or resisting their European overlords.[33] After the nominal conquest of indigenous lands and peoples, European colonial systems frequently adapted to or incorporated, at least in part, aboriginal patterns of landownership, labor extraction, and more generally, sociopolitical organization.[34]

In indigenous borderlands, natives remained important agents of historical and cultural change, selectively absorbing elements from colonial society and often imbuing it with elements from their own intellectual tradition; diplomatic rituals, kinship relationships, food habits, spiritual beliefs and practices, and linguistic loans are examples. In the Guaraní borderlands, for instance, Spaniards adopted the practice of *cuñadazgo*, a reciprocal relationship between brothers-in-law established when a native woman married a Spaniard, thus becoming the link between her Guaraní brother and her Spanish husband.[35] Catholic missionaries strove to spread the Gospel in autochthonous languages throughout the Americas, with unequal success. Some Protestant pastors would replicate this model on US reservations in the late nineteenth and early twentieth centuries. Perhaps such efforts were nowhere as consequential as in the *reducciones* (mission settlements) of Paraguay, where Jesuits worked hard to translate Catholic theological concepts into Guaraní, creating in the process a "new Christian language."[36] In an analogous development, Dominican friars in colonial Oaxaca relied on the autochthonous Zapotec language for an evangelization project whose cornerstone was the participation of members of the indigenous elite as translators and parish administrators, turning the effort into a native enterprise that resulted in the creation of a distinctly indigenous church.[37] In the Yucatán Peninsula, in turn, Maya remained the lingua franca throughout the eighteenth century.[38]

Native societies sometimes enjoyed prolonged periods of prosperity by judiciously absorbing and adapting those European elements that suited them best. Upon becoming acquainted with some domesticated species of Old World plants and animals, many Amerindians modified their subsistence patterns. Formerly nomadic hunter-gatherers typically preferred animal husbandry over sedentary agriculture, as did the Diné (Navajos) of the US Southwest and the Wayuu (Guajiros) of Colombia and Venezuela.[39] Others, like the Guahibos (or Sikuani) of the Orinocan Llanos never became full pastoralists, but instead gradually adopted agriculture as they raided Euro-American settlements for cattle, a way of life that helped them remain independent into the twentieth century despite the environmental damage caused by the introduction of livestock.[40] Still others, including the Pueblos,

Tohono O'odhams, and Yaquis of the US Southwest and northwestern Mexico, incorporated colonially imposed political forms to exercise sovereignty based on their own political, economic, and social needs.[41]

Indigenous societies' selective absorption of European elements typically gave rise to new, hybridized cultural norms and syncretic praxes that colonizers often found unintelligible.[42] Indigenous healing rituals and unorthodox pseudo-Christian religious practices frequently attracted the attention of colonial authorities, with women of mixed descent becoming the favorite scapegoats of male officials.[43] As Susan Deeds has recently argued for Nueva Vizcaya (today's Mexican states of Chihuahua, Durango, and parts of Coahuila), in many areas of the Americas, extant populations are indeed the result of centuries of intense biological and cultural mestizaje (mixing) despite a tendency among contemporaries to whiten their history by assuming the early vanishment of indigenous cultures and genes.[44]

All the violence and turmoil brought about by Euro-American expansionism notwithstanding, Amerindians often interacted with the newcomers through diplomacy, trade, and kinship.[45] Indigenous women and captives played leading roles in such interactions.[46] In the Southern Cone, diplomatic encounters known as *parlamentos* (parleys or peace talks) became the primary setting for exchanges between Hispanics and independent natives.[47] In the Northern Hemisphere, Caddos, Wichitas, Comanches, and other independent groups willingly allied themselves with the Spanish in the Internal Provinces of northern New Spain in the late eighteenth century.[48]

After contact, some indigenous peoples entered the global economy by supplying colonial markets with coveted commodities, freely or under coercion: examples are furs and hides throughout North America, horses on the southern Great Plains, rubber in the late nineteenth- and early twentieth-century Amazon, cochineal in colonial Oaxaca and Central America, and beeswax in Yucatán.[49] Over time, indigenous participation in the global economy spread through most of the hemisphere.

Europeans' unremitting demand for labor enticed many Amerindians to enslave massive numbers of their native neighbors for profit, often giving up ancestral practices of interethnic captivity and incorporation in the process.[50] The aboriginal peoples of the Colorado River Basin—Apaches, Utes, Navajos, Comanches, and others—contributed significantly to human trafficking across the US Southwest and the Great Plains.[51] Intertribal slave wars caused probably the greatest havoc among the indigenous societies of the US South, where, in less than two centuries, the once-thriving Mississippian chiefdoms disappeared into what Robbie Ethridge and her collaborators have described as a desolate "shatter zone."[52] Paradoxically, some members of the so-called Five Civilized Tribes of the US South (Cherokees, Chickasaws, Choctaws, Creeks, and Seminoles) had adopted the plantation model of slavery by the time the US government forcibly removed them to Indian Territory in the 1830s.[53]

Contrary to the passive victims of colonial oppression depicted in traditional historiography, nominally conquered indigenous peoples typically strove to preserve their sovereignty, defend their rights, and retain their homeland—an ongoing struggle in many parts of the Americas. Numerous native communities and individuals under colonial domination learned to operate within the legal system to fight for their rights and defend their autonomy, land, and resources, and they frequently did so effectively (see chapters 10 and 11).[54] Some Andean and Mesoamerican native subjects of the Spanish monarchy even traveled to the Iberian Peninsula to assert their claims at the Hapsburg court, often fruitfully.[55] Across the hemisphere, natives adapted maximally to their environment to form long-lasting internal indigenous borderlands, including the Calchaquí Valleys of northwestern Argentina and much of the Eastern Andes, the Chaco region of interior South America (see chapter 8), and the Sierra Gorda and Bolsón de Mapimí in Mexico (see chapter 6), as well as most of the Amazon Basin, parts of which remain indigenous borderlands today.[56]

We must not forget that, like natives, communities of runaway African slaves (known in Spanish as *cimarrones*; that is, "maroons") carved out spaces of sovereignty in numerous parts of the Caribbean and elsewhere in the Americas, notwithstanding European colonial claims of domination. In many instances, the ability of those communities to preserve their autonomy and exert de facto control of their land over prolonged periods warrant the denomination "maroon borderlands."[57] Sometimes, maroons and indigenous people allied, as was suspected in the Cuban cases Paul Conrad presents in chapter 7. Other times, fugitives of African descent intermarried with natives and merged culturally, giving rise to mixed communities, such as the so-called Black Caribs (Garinagu) of Saint Vincent and the Grenadines, and the Black Seminoles removed from Florida in the 1830s.[58]

AVENUES FOR FURTHER RESEARCH

In the last decades, scholars have undoubtedly made substantial progress in reconstructing the history of the Western Hemisphere in a more balanced and nuanced way than earlier generations did. Because of the nature of the sources, however, scholars of the indigenous past in the Americas and elsewhere will continue to confront long-standing challenges, the most severe one being the general lack of documentary sources produced by natives themselves. In some parts of the Western Hemisphere, the adaptation of the Roman alphabet to indigenous languages after the European arrival permitted Amerindians to generate records in new, literary forms—most notably in Mesoamerica, where natives had already developed a sophisticated pictographic tradition before Spaniards arrived.[59] Up to the twentieth century, however, the types of textual evidence that most historians of the New World depended on were produced by the bearers of European culture, mostly male colonial agents. Therefore, pre-1900 documentary sources seldom recorded female or native perspectives, understandings, or interests, which often turns the reconstruction of indigenous/women's contexts and the interpretation of indigenous/women's actions into a misgiving.

As the essays in this volume (and the long and fecund trajectory of the journal *Ethnohistory*) show, using an ethnohistorical methodology can help scholars overcome the challenge posed by the absence of indigenous-produced written sources and reach more balanced interpretations of the past. Such methodology involves situating the focus on the natives, incorporating indigenous sources and testimonies whenever possible, and trying to comprehend indigenous actions and perspectives through multidisciplinary approaches that often rely on nondocumentary archaeological, linguistic, ethnographic, environmental, or other sources.[60]

Research on indigenous borderlands stands to benefit enormously from interdisciplinary perspectives. Fortunately, a growing number of historians are adopting this approach; the result is often first-rate scholarship. Elizabeth Fenn's masterful work on the Mandans of the upper Missouri River provides a case in point. Fenn creatively utilizes recent geological, climatological, environmental, archaeological, anthropological, epidemiological, and nutritional findings to show how farming and commerce allowed the Mandans to thrive in the challenging environment of the northern Great Plains until they were almost eradicated by smallpox in the 1830s.[61]

The reinterpretation of the documentary record in light of archaeological, linguistic, and ethnographic evidence has yielded other important insights in recent years. For instance, Carl Henrik Langebaek has recently challenged the views that the Muiscas of the eastern Colombian Andes shared the type of nuclear/cellular organization James Lockhart identified among the peoples of Central Mexico, and that they waged war to extract tribute and labor. Draw-ing on ethnographic and archaeological data, he argues that the primary function of war among the Muiscas was instead symbolic legitimization of their caciques.[62] In another exemplary instance of interdisciplinary collabo-ration, Frances Berdan, John Chance, and other scholars have approached the complicated and oft-controversial issue of ethnic identity through documen-tary, ethnographic, and archaeological lenses, unveiling diverse processes of continuity and change among the Nahuatl-speaking peoples of Mesoamer-ica from pre-Hispanic times to the present.[63]

Because archaeology offers a unique window into the material worlds of the past, it is an essential tool when reconstructing precontact and post-contact indigenous contexts (see chapter 4).[64] As Matthew Liebmann's work on the Pueblo Revolt and its aftermath demonstrated, archaeological research can be particularly helpful in reconstructing the materiality of social movements and institutions.[65] Archaeology can also be illuminating when (re-)inter-preting early encounters between natives and Europeans. Recently, David Carballo revisited the Spanish-Aztec war of 1519–21, using a long-term archae-ological perspective to trace the origins of that encounter in the deep pasts of Mesoamerican and Iberian cultures and to explain its outcome in light of the parallels and divergences between them.[66] Reassessment of the docu-mentary evidence against archaeological, linguistic, and genetic data has also permitted scholars to challenge Western assumptions about the formation of ethnic identities in ancient Amazonia.[67]

Within the multidisciplinary approach that we advocate, the use of new technologies offers opportunities to formulate novel queries and look at old problems through new lenses. The combination of GIS and statistical analyses, and the utilization of genetic variables in demographic history, are two prom-ising avenues for research in the short term. Digital mapping, for instance, opens immense analytic possibilities (see chapter 3).[68] An in-depth study of geographic patterns can refine long-held historical interpretations and develop alternative ones. GIS technology permits us to superimpose layers of spatial data on a map so that selected variables (both conceptual and quanti-tative) and the relationships among them can be explained geographically. It also allows us to manipulate strictly spatial features such as coordinates, dis-tance, direction, elevation, dispersal, relative location, density, scale, bound-aries, and so forth, as well as to tabulate and conduct quantitative analyses of data associated with spatial and chronological variables. GIS-generated maps can thus help scholars gain a better understanding of the geographic distribution of individuals, human groups, territorial claims, resources, cultural traits, and institutions, as well as to identify habitats, settlement and mobility patterns, migration and trade routes and, generally, connections among individuals and communities. They also allow us to visualize change over time and space through animation, to construct accurate spatial representations of historical processes, and to identify patterns that would likely go unnoticed otherwise. Furthermore, such maps can also be useful tools to decolonize empirical approaches to space typically based on historical maps and documents produced almost exclusively by people of European descent.

Genetic research can also shed light on aspects of indigenous history obscured by the documentary record. Analysis of mitochondrial DNA haplogroup frequencies indicates, for instance, that the pre-Hispanic Tainos of the Greater Antilles were genetically related most closely to extant Arawakan-speaking Amazonian populations. Ongoing genetic research has rebuffed the widespread popular belief in the early disappearance of the native inhabitants in areas of Puerto Rico, the Dominican Republic, Cuba, Panama, and Argentina where the genetic markers of extant populations reveal a long history of interracial and interethnic mixing. At least three pre-Hispanic (presumably Taino) mitochondrial genomes are present in contemporary Puerto Ricans, more than 60 percent of whom can trace their ancestry to aboriginal peoples. The fact that the largest concentration of Amerindian genes occurs in the mountainous regions of the Greater Antilles suggests the persistence of clusters of indigenous people in refuge zones that likely became internal borderlands like the ones discussed in this volume.[69] Similar results are to be expected as indigenous genetic research spreads to other parts of the Americas. Meaningfully, more than 43 percent of the more than five million US citizens who self-identified as Native American in the 2010 US census acknowledged being of mixed descent.

Linguistic studies can also contribute substantially to the research on indigenous borderlands. Of the numerous ways in which language can be profitably applied in historical studies, I will single out just three. First, there is a pressing need for scholarly annotated transcriptions and English translations of non-English-language primary sources related to the indigenous peoples of the Western Hemisphere. Anglophone scholars who specialize in certain areas of the Americas (such as the US Southwest) tend to rely overwhelmingly on published English translations. In many cases, those translations were done more than fifty years ago by well-meaning individuals who—not being professional linguists or historians and lacking familiarity with the indigenous cultures mentioned in the documents—were not well equipped to capture the subtle nuances of the original texts or the rich ethnic diversity they described. Ideally, translators should be bilingual specialists with the necessary philological and historiographic skills, and their translations should include digital images or meticulous transcriptions of the original text. This is the approach of, among others, the Cibola Project, an initiative to produce accurate, open-access transcriptions and translations of original Spanish documents from the US Southwest, administered by the Research Center for Romance Studies at the University of California–Berkeley and directed by Jerry Craddock.[70] Ideally, translations and transcriptions of original documents would also be produced by scholars with a proficient historical-anthropological knowledge of the relevant cultures. This approach characterizes the praiseworthy transcriptions published since 2011 in the online journal *Corpus: Archivos virtuales de la alteridad americana.*[71] The tremendous void of reliable scholarly transcriptions and translations, combined with the increasing online availability of primary sources through virtual repositories such as PARES (the Spanish Ministry of Culture database that provides free access to digitized documents from Spanish archives) make this undertaking as desirable as it is feasible.[72]

Second, historians of the indigenous Americas can also gain important insights by borrowing some concepts, research questions, and methodologies from historical linguistics. How (and how effectively) did Europeans communicate with the speakers of (to them) completely unintelligible Amerindian tongues that lacked formal grammars, dictionaries, and an alphabetic script? How did the newcomers cope with indigenous phonetic and syntactic systems whose complexity far outstripped that of their own language? How did Europeans and natives bridge the seemingly unsurmountable semantic gaps that separated their respective lexicons and conditioned the way each society conceptualized and experienced the material and spiritual world? Further, to what extent can theories developed by specialists in language contact be applied to analyze the effects of the transatlantic encounter on other cultural realms? Nancy Farriss's recent book *Tongues of Fire*, focusing on the contact between Spanish missionaries and the native speakers of Otomanguean languages in colonial Oaxaca, answers these and similar questions.

Farriss reveals that the language contact and indoctrination processes intertwined. Unlike Spanish, Zapotec and related tongues are tonal, meaning that the pitch of the speech carries significance for word meanings.

Sixteenth-century Dominicans partly overcame this problem by producing written Zapotec-language texts for evangelization (as other missionaries did for Nahuatl and Mixtec). They also relied on bilingual mediators fluent in Nahuatl, the language of the Aztecs and their neighbors, which enjoyed a prestige comparable to that of Latin in the European Middle Ages and had become the lingua franca of pre-Hispanic Mesoamerica, including Oaxaca, the region with the greatest linguistic diversity. Most importantly, missionaries relied on a literate, polyglot native elite to convert the rest of the autochthonous population. Farriss concludes that the translations of theological concepts and Catholic doctrine utilized in early Zapotec religious texts still influence the Oaxacan belief system today.

Lastly, the identification and interpretation of indigenous names may help scholars make important inferences about the culture and history of the name-givers. Specifically, many toponyms contain abundant information about native land usage and territoriality, as well as mythical and historical episodes deemed important enough to be inscribed in topographic names.[73] To most indigenous peoples "wisdom sits in places," to quote Keith Basso's famous adage.[74] Toponyms may also help determine the dispersion of indigenous peoples. For instance, the identification of Nahuatl, Zapotec, Purépecha, Otomí, and other Mesoamerican-language place-names beyond the aboriginal boundaries of their respective speech communities may help track the migrations of Indian conquistadors whose participation in "Spanish" conquest and colonization enterprises European chroniclers sometimes neglected to mention.

As we have seen, recent decades have witnessed a spike in the scholarship on indigenous agency, power, dominance, territoriality, sovereignty, involvement in the global economy, and similar topics. While there is room to expand the study of those subjects in multiple directions, other topics remain underresearched. Indigenous women, for instance, are clearly underrepresented in the literature. We know much more about females who were cultural brokers and intermediaries or played domestic roles than we do about women who were political leaders or held other public responsibilities.[75] This is partly a reflection of androcentric biases in the documentary and early ethnographic records, but the now-expansive gender and feminist scholarship points out different strategies to overcome those biases—by, for instance, recovering the critical public roles women once played in many indigenous societies, challenging Western epistemologies and exposing the colonial origins of the patriarchal and heteronormative ideologies of race and gender that came to dominate the Americas. Tai Edwards's recent work on the Osages constitutes a good example of what an interdisciplinary approach can achieve through the lens of gender.[76] As Margaret Conkey has argued, the combined use of feminist theory and indigenous epistemologies (including folktales and oral traditions) can yield important findings in the archaeological study of space and gender.[77] At the same time, the incorporation of archaeological evidence into the study of indigenous borderlands can be particularly fruitful given that material remains are free of the androcentric biases implicit in the documentary and ethnographic records.

The study of indigenous borderlands can also benefit from the insights of Chicana feminist writer Gloria Anzaldúa. As she argued for the US-Mexican frontier region, there often remains an intellectual and emotional space where people can resist and redefine their identity on their own terms in spite of all the violence and oppression inherent in conquest, colonization, and the eradication of a physical borderland. A borderland can thus be understood metaphorically as "a vague and undetermined place created by the emotional residue of an unnatural boundary."[78] In other words, the disappearance of the (indigenous) borderland as a physical space does not necessarily entail the disappearance of the (indigenous) borderland as a liminal state of being, since individuals and communities may retain a consciousness of their distinctiveness and enact it in different contexts. This acknowledgment draws attention to the study of emotions and emphasizes the importance of personal narratives and oral testimonies in the study of past and present (indigenous) borderlands.

Other under-researched areas include Euro-American populations' absorption of native cultural schemas, the extension of indigenous meanings to foreign introductions, and the contribution of traditional Amerindian knowledge to (early) modern science, to name but a few. Lopsidedly, scholars have paid considerable attention to indigenous assimilation into Western societies and modern states, but much less to the processes of transculturation through which natives often appropriated and reinterpreted foreign beliefs and practices in culturally meaningful ways.

Another promising area for future research is comparative studies. Fortunately, there is an abundance of high-quality case studies on borderlands and indigenous communities susceptible to comparison. Comparative works on indigenous borderlands across the Americas, however, are still rare.[79] Comparisons across continents can also be fruitful. In a thought-provoking essay, James Scott has argued that much of the culture of the indigenous peoples

of the Southeast Asian mainland massif "can be read as strategic position-
ing designed to keep the state at arm's length." In his view, a process of
"self-barbarization" permitted those peoples successfully to resist state incorporation until at least 1945.[80] To what extent are the adaptations Amerindians developed to tackle colonialism equivalent to the process Scott has
described?

Despite repeated appeals from indigenous scholars, intellectuals, activ-
ists, and leaders for a paradigm shift that takes into consideration native
voices and perspectives from both the present and the past, many historians
remain skeptical of Amerindian sources.[81] Conversely, some scholars who
use such sources do so uncritically, as if the indigenous provenance of a testimony were a guarantee of authenticity and veracity. Despite widespread
claims to tell the story "from a native perspective," relatively few academics
have taken the trouble to reach out to extant indigenous communities and
familiarize themselves with their history. Fearful of unwarranted upstream-
ing, scores of historians are still reluctant to incorporate oral traditions,
family histories, folklore, and testimonies from living indigenous people into
their analyses of the past. Whether or not one believes that contemporary
Amerindians should set the scholarly agenda, an awareness of indigenous
ways of remembering and recording history can only enlighten professional historians' interpretations.

Finally, scholars need to be mindful that there exist different ways of "being
indigenous." Many still tend to assume, for instance, that the disappearance
of a spoken language inevitably leads to the extinction of its associated culture and identity. The revival of supposedly long-lost cultural elements demonstrates that incorporation does not necessarily entail a loss of inherited
community consciousness.[82] At the same time, the strong communion that
Amerindian peoples generally show when threatened by outsiders reveals
that ancestral ethnic-political identities are now compounded across the
Americas by a sense of indigeneity that extends across and beyond distinct,
state-recognized native communities.

NOTES

1. On the lethal effects of Old World germs on Amerindian populations see
Crosby, *Columbian Exchange*; Crosby, "Virgin Soil Epidemics"; Thornton, *American
Indian Holocaust*; Dixon, "Furthering Their Own Demise"; Rivaya-Martínez, "Inci-
dencia de la viruela"; Cameron, Kelton, and Swedlund, *Beyond Germs*; Cramaussel,

"Population and Epidemics." For a succinct overview and assessment of indigenous slavery and other forms of coerced labor in the Americas, see Reséndez, "Borderlands of Bondage."

2. Adams, *Education for Extinction*; Anderson, *Conquest of Texas*; Anderson, *Ethnic Cleansing*; Madley, *American Genocide*; Ginzberg, *Destruction of the Indigenous Peoples*; Ostler, *Surviving Genocide*.

3. Merrell, *Indians' New World*; Calloway, *New Worlds for All*.

4. See, for instance, Beckerman, *Datos etnohistóricos*; Whitehead, *Lords of the Tiger Spirit*; Taylor and Pease, *Violence, Resistance, and Survival*; Vitar, *Guerra y misiones*; Barba, *Frontera ganadera*; Fernández C., *Historia de los indios ranqueles*; Barrera Monroy, *Mestizaje, comercio y resistencia*; Langfur, *Forbidden Lands*; West, *Last Indian War*; Ramsey, *Yamassee War*; Stratton, *Buried in Shades of Night*; Medina Bustos and Padilla Calderón, *Violencia interétnica*; Lipman, *Saltwater Frontier*; Santiago, *Bad Peace*; Carballo, *Collision of Worlds*.

5. Obregón Iturra, Paz, and Roldán, *Revers de conquête*. On the so-called Chichimecas, see Powell, *Soldiers, Indians, and Silver*, 211–59; Powell, *Mexico's Miguel Caldera*; Altman, *War for Mexico's West*; Sheridan Prieto, *Fronterización*; Álvarez, "La guerra chichimeca." On the Chiriguanos, also called Ava Guaraní, see Pifarré, *Los Guaraní-Chiriguano*; Saignes, *Ava y Karai*; Combès, *Etno-historias del Isoso*; Saignes and Combès, *Historia del pueblo chiriguano*; Langer, *Expecting Pears*. On the Pijaos, see Ortega Ricaurte, *Los inconquistables*.

6. On the initial Guaraní resistance to the Spanish, see Roulet, *La resistencia de los guaraní*.

7. These processes are amply discussed in Weber, *Bárbaros*. On the Guaycuruans, see Saeger, *Chaco Mission Frontier*; Mendoza, "Bolivian Toba." On the Apaches, see Moorhead, *Apache Frontier*; John, *Storms Brewed in Other Men's Worlds*; Anderson, *Indian Southwest*; Blyth, *Chiricahua and Janos*; Babcock, *Apache Adaptation*. On Plains Indians, see Mishkin, *Rank and Warfare*; Secoy, *Changing Military Patterns*; Hämäläinen, "Rise and Fall"; Gelo, *Indians of the Great Plains*.

8. On Comanches and Kiowas, see John, *Storms Brewed in Other Men's Worlds*; Anderson, *Indian Southwest*; Kavanagh, *Comanche Political History*; DeLay, *War of a Thousand Deserts*; Hämäläinen, *Comanche Empire*; Rivaya-Martínez, "Trespassers."

9. La Vere, *Contrary Neighbors*; Shuck-Hall, *Journey to the West*.

10. Gibson, *Kickapoos*.

11. Adams, "Passive Resistance."

12. See, for instance, Stern, "Age of Andean Insurrection"; Reff, "'Predicament of Culture'"; Robins, *Native Insurgencies*; Folsom, *Yaquis and the Empire*; Medina Bustos, "Cambio político y las rebeliones"; Thomson, "Sovereignty Disavowed"; Svriz Wucherer, *Un levantamiento indígena*; Paz Reverol, *El pueblo Wayuu*; Mirafuentes Galván, *Movimientos de resistencia*, vols. 1–2. These authors document hundreds of indigenous revolts in northern New Spain alone. On the famous Pueblo Revolt of 1680, see Knaut, *Pueblo Revolt*; Kessell, *Pueblos, Spaniards*; Liebmann, *Revolt*. On the Tepehuanes and their neighbors, see Deeds, *Defiance and Deference*; Gradie, *Tepehuan Revolt*; Álvarez, "De 'zacatecos' y 'tepehuanes'"; Álvarez, *El indio y la sociedad*.

On the Caste War of Yucatán, see Rugeley, *Yucatán's Maya Peasantry*; Reed, *Caste War*; Rugeley, *Rebellion Now and Forever*; Gabbert, *Violence and the Caste War*.

13. McComb Sanchez, "Resistance through Secrecy."

14. Radding, *Wandering Peoples*; Roller, *Amazonian Routes*; Warren, *Worlds Shawnees Made*; Valdés, *Los bárbaros*.

15. DuVal, *Native Ground*; Witgen, *Infinity of Nations*; McDonnell, *Masters of Empire*. On reversed colonialism, see Hämäläinen, *Comanche Empire*. On indigenous maritime power, see Bahar, *Storm of the Sea*.

16. Hassig, *Mexico and the Spanish Conquest*; Carballo, *Collision of Worlds*.

17. Escalante Arce, *Los tlaxcaltecas*; Asselbergs, *Conquered Conquistadors*; Matthew and Oudijk, *Indian Conquistadors*; Levin Rojo, *Return to Aztlan*; Levin Rojo, "'Indian Friends and Allies'"; McEnroe, "Indian Garrison Colonies"; Lovell, Lutz, and Kramer, *Strike Fear in the Land*.

18. Stern, "Rise and Fall of Indian-White Alliances"; Spalding, *Huarochirí*; Lamana, *Domination without Dominance*; Zuloaga Rada, *La conquista negociada*; Mikecz, "Beyond Cajamarca"; Covey, *Inca Apocalypse*. For a thorough (up to its date of publication) historiographic review of the participation of various indigenous peoples in the Inca and Spanish conquests of the Andes, see Heaney, "Conquests of Peru."

19. On the Iroquois, see Jennings, *Ambiguous Iroquois Empire*; Richter, *Ordeal of the Longhouse*; Viau, *Enfants du néant*; Taylor, *Divided Ground*; MacLeitch, *Imperial Entanglements*.

20. On the Blackfoot, see Lewis, *Effects of White Contact*; Dempsey, "Blackfoot." On the Lakotas, see White, "Winning of the West;" Ostler, *Plains Sioux and U.S. Colonialism*; Ostler, *Lakotas and the Black Hills*. On the Osages, see Din and Nasatir, *Imperial Osages*; Rollings, *Osage*. On the Comanches, see Kavanagh, *Comanche Political History*; Hämäläinen, *Comanche Empire*; DeLay, *War of a Thousand Deserts*; Velasco Ávila, *La frontera étnica*.

21. On the Mapuches, see Villalobos R., *Relaciones fronterizas, Los pehuenches*, and *Vida fronteriza en la Araucanía*; Pinto Rodríguez, *Araucanía y Pampas*; Boccara, *Guerre et ethnogenèse Mapuche*; Pinto Rodríguez, *La formación del estado*; Boccara, *Los vencedores*; Zavala Cepeda, *Los mapuches*; Urbina Carrasco, *La frontera de arriba*; Obregón Iturra, *Des Indiens rebelles*; Montanez-Sanabria and Urbina Carrasco, "Spanish Empire's Southernmost Frontiers."

22. On indigenous charismatic leaders, see, for instance, the classic Wallace, *Death and Rebirth*.

23. On the 1680 Pueblo Revolt, see note 12.

24. On the confederacy led by Tecumseh and Tenskwatawa, see Edmunds, *Shawnee Prophet*; Edmunds, *Tecumseh*; Warren, *Worlds Shawnees Made*.

25. On the Lakota leaders of the Sioux Wars, see Price, *Oglala People*; Ostler, *Plains Sioux and U.S. Colonialism*; Ostler, *Lakotas and the Black Hills*; Drury and Clavin, *Heart of Everything*.

26. On the Apache leaders, see Sweeney, *Mangas Coloradas*; Chamberlain, *Victorio*; Sweeney, *From Cochise to Geronimo*.

27. Stern, "Age of Andean Insurrection"; Stavig, *World of Túpac Amaru*; Robins, *Native Insurgencies*; Walker, *Tupac Amaru Rebellion*; Thomson, *We Alone Will Rule*; Thomson, "Sovereignty Disavowed."

28. Jones, *Pueblo Warriors*; Ruiz-Esquide Figueroa, *Los indios amigos*; John, *Storms Brewed in Other Men's Worlds*; Weber, *Bárbaros*; McEnroe, "Sleeping Army"; McEnroe, *From Colony to Nationhood*; Güereca Durán, *Milicias indígenas*. On the Ópatas and Pimas, see Radding, *Wandering Peoples*; Yetman, *Ópatas*; Yetman, *Conflict in Colonial Sonora*; Borrero Silva and Velarde Cadena, "Los indios auxiliares"; Medina Bustos and Almada Bay, "Inter-Ethnic War in Sonora." On the Guaraní militias, see Melià, *El guaraní conquistado*; Austin, *Colonial Kinship*.

29. On the Spanish alliance with Wichitas and Comanches, see Navarro García, *Don José de Gálvez*; Moorhead, *Apache Frontier*; John, *Storms Brewed in Other Men's Worlds*; Kavanagh, *Comanche Political History*; Anderson, *Indian Southwest*; Smith, *From Dominance to Disappearance*; Barr, *Peace Came*; Hämäläinen, *Comanche Empire*; Rivaya-Martínez, "Diplomacia interétnica." On the Pehuenches, see León Solís, *Los señores de la cordillera*.

30. On the Plains Wars, see Dunlay, *Wolves for the Blue Soldiers*; van de Logt, *War Party in Blue*; Ostler, *Plains Sioux and U.S. Colonialism*; West, *Contested Plains*. On the Apache Wars, see Jacoby, *Shadows at Dawn*; Sweeney, *From Cochise to Geronimo*; Lahti, *Wars for Empire*.

31. León Solís, *Maloqueros y conchavadores*; White, *Middle Ground*; Ruiz-Esquide Figueroa, *Los indios amigos*; Brooks, *Captives and Cousins*; Nacuzzi, *Funcionarios, diplomáticos, guerreros*; Mandrini, *Vivir entre dos mundos*; Havard, *Histoire des coureurs de bois*; Havard, *Empire et Métissages*; Austin, *Colonial Kinship*. See also Medina Bustos and Padilla Calderón, *Indios, españoles y mestizos*; Conrad, "Empire through Kinship."

32. There is an ample literature on indigenous collaboration with (and resistance to) missionaries and other clergy, particularly among the Nahuas. See Pardo, *Origins of Mexican Catholicism*; Díaz Balsera, *Pyramid under the Cross*; Lara, *Christian Texts for Aztecs*; Crewe, *Mexican Mission*. On missions in the Californias, see Magaña Mancillas, *Población y misiones*; Jackson, *From Savages to Subjects*; Hackel, *Children of Coyote*; Newell, *Constructing Lives*. On the Guaraní missions, see Melià, *El guaraní conquistado*; Melià, *La lengua guaraní*; Ganson, *Guaraní under Spanish Rule*; Wilde, *Religión y poder*; Sarreal, *Guaraní and Their Missions*; Austin, *Colonial Kinship*. For missionary-indigenous relations in other borderlands, see Bruno, *La evangelización*; Block, *Mission Culture*; Santamaría, *Del tabaco al incienso*; Hahn, *History of the Timucua*; Vitar, *Guerra y misiones*; Saeger, *Chaco Mission Frontier*; Tomichá Charupá, *La primera evangelización*; Jackson, *Missions and Frontiers*; Wade, *Missions, Missionaries, and Native Americans*; Langer, *Expecting Pears*; Charles, *Allies at Odds*; López Castillo, *El poblamiento en tierra de indios cáhitas*; Wilde, *Saberes de la conversión*; de la Torre Curiel, *Twilight of the Mission Frontier*; Wilde, "Frontier Missions." For indigenous collaborations with nonclergy see, for instance, Skinner, *Upper Country*; Shapard, *Chief Loco*.

33. Ramírez, *World Upside Down*; Krippner-Martínez, *Rereading the Conquest*; Martínez Baracs, *Convivencia y utopía*; Chipman, *Moctezuma's Children*; Brosseder,

Power of Huacas; Muñoz Arbeláez, *Costumbres en disputa*; Villella, *Indigenous Elites*; Benton, *Lords of Tetzcoco*.

34. On the incorporation of indigenous notions, practices, and institutions into Euro-American colonial systems see, for instance, Lockhart, *Nahuas after the Conquest*; DuVal, *Native Ground*; Greer, *Property and Dispossession*.

35. Austin, "Guaraní Kinship." For an in-depth discussion of interethnic kinship in the Guaraní borderlands, see also Austin, *Colonial Kinship*.

36. Melià, *La lengua guaraní*.

37. Farriss, *Tongues of Fire*.

38. Lentz, "Castas, Creoles."

39. On the Diné, see Iverson, *Diné*; Weisiger, *Dreaming of Sheep*. On the Wayuu, see Picon, *Pasteurs du Nouveau Monde*; Paz Reverol, *El pueblo Wayuu*.

40. Morey and Morey, "Foragers and Farmers."

41. Crandall, *These People*.

42. On religious syncretism see, for instance, Lara Cisneros, *El cristianismo en el espejo indígena*; Lara Cisneros, *¿Ignorancia invencible?*; Maroukis, *Peyote Road*; Smoak, *Ghost Dances*; McComb Sanchez, "Resistance through Secrecy."

43. Few, *Women Who Live Evil Lives*; Lewis, *Hall of Mirrors*; Ebright and Hendricks, *Witches of Abiquiu*.

44. Deeds, "Labyrinths of Mestizaje."

45. Levaggi, *Paz en la frontera*; Levaggi, *Diplomacia hispano-indígena*; Metcalf, *Go-Betweens*; Ruiz Medrano and Kellogg, *Negotiation within Domination*; Velasco Ávila, *Pacificar o negociar*; Rindfleisch, *George Galphin's Intimate Empire*.

46. On the key roles of indigenous women as culture brokers, laborers, and intermediaries, see Van Kirk, *Many Tender Ties*; Shoemaker, *Negotiators of Change*; Schroeder, Wood, and Haskett, *Indian Women*; Sleeper-Smith, *Indian Women and French Men*; Greer, *Mohawk Saint*; Graubart, *With Our Labor and Sweat*; Barr, *Peace Came*; Sousa, *Woman Who Turned into a Jaguar*; Delgado, *Laywomen*. On captives, see Brooks, *Captives and Cousins*; Bernabéu, Giudicelli, and Havard, *La indianización*; De Jong, *Diplomacia, malones y cautivos*.

47. Zavala Cepeda, *Los mapuches*; Zavala Cepeda and Dillehay, "El 'Estado de Arauco'"; Quijada, *De los cacicazgos a la ciudadanía*; Zarley, "Between the Lof and the Liberators."

48. See note 29.

49. MacLeod, *Spanish Central America*; Isenberg, *Destruction of the Bison*; Baskes, *Indians, Merchants, and Markets*; Van Valen, *Indigenous Agency in the Amazon*. On beeswax production in Yucatán, see chapter 3 in this volume.

50. Reséndez, *Other Slavery*, contains an excellent overview of the literature and many thoughtful insights on the enslavement of Amerindians. See also the relevant essays in Gallay, *Indian Slavery*; Martin and Brooks, *Linking the Histories of Slavery*. On the Indian captive traffic in various regions of North America, see Ekberg, *Stealing Indian Women*; Shefveland, *Anglo-Native Virginia*; Rushforth, *Bonds of Alliance*.

51. On the captive traffic in the US Southwest, see Brooks, *Captives and Cousins*; Blackhawk, *Violence over the Land*; Smith, *Captive Arizona*; Zappia, *Traders and Raiders*.

52. Ethridge and Shuck-Hall, *Mapping the Mississippian Shatter Zone*. On the effects of the slave traffic in the southeastern United States, see also Gallay, *Indian Slave Trade*; Snyder, *Slavery in Indian Country*; Ramsey, *Yamassee War*.

53. On the shift toward European-style slavery and its effects among the Five Civilized Tribes, see Perdue, *Slavery*; Saunt, *New Order of Things*; Yarbrough, *Race and the Cherokee Nation*; Naylor, *African Cherokees*; Krauthamer, *Black Slaves, Indian Masters*; Miles, *Ties That Bind*. On Indian removal in the United States, see Anderson, *Conquest of Texas*; Anderson, *Ethnic Cleansing*; Heidler and Heidler, *Indian Removal*; Bowes, *Exiles and Pioneers*; Bowes, *Land Too Good for Indians*; Denson, *Monuments to Absence*.

54. On Amerindian use of colonial and state legal systems to protect their interests see, for instance, McMillen, *Making Indian Law*; Owensby, *Empire of Law*; Romero Frizzi, "Power of the Law"; Cunill, *Los defensores de indios*; Castro Gutiérrez, "Los ires y devenires"; Yannakakis and Schrader-Kniffki, "Between the 'Old Law' and the New"; Dueñas, "Indian Colonial Actors"; and relevant chapters in Ross and Owensby, *Justice in a New World*.

55. Van Deusen, *Global Indios*; de la Puente Luna, *Andean Cosmopolitans*.

56. Langer, "Eastern Andean Frontier"; Lara Cisneros, *El cristianismo en el espejo indígena*; Lucaioli, *Abipones*; Cipolletti, *Sociedades indígenas*; Giudicelli, "Indigenous Autonomy"; Langfur, "Native Informants."

57. On what I have termed "maroon borderlands," see, for instance, Schwaller, "Contested Conquests." See also the relevant sections in Landers, *Black Society*; Din, *Spaniards, Planters, and Slaves*.

58. Bateman, "Africans and Indians"; Mulroy, *Seminole Freedmen*; Mulroy, "Mixed Race."

59. On the pre-Hispanic Mesoamerican pictographic tradition and its persistence during colonial times, see Lockhart, *We People Here*; León Portilla, *Visión de los vencidos*; Restall and Asselbergs, *Invading Guatemala*; Terraciano, "Three Texts in One"; Townsend, *Annals of Native America*; Hidalgo, *Trail of Footprints*; Diel, *Codex Mexicanus*; Townsend, *Fifth Sun*; Peterson and Terraciano, *Florentine Codex*. The philological approach espoused by Lockhart and others has considerably enriched our understanding of Mesoamerican indigenous societies under Spanish rule. See, for instance, Lockhart, *Nahuas after the Conquest*; Terraciano, *Mixtecs of Colonial Oaxaca*.

60. On the ethnohistorical method and the use of nontextual sources to reconstruct indigenous contexts, see Barber and Berdan, *Emperor's Mirror*; Brown and Vibert, *Reading Beyond Words*; Galloway, *Practicing Ethnohistory*; McMillen, *Making Indian Law*.

61. Fenn, *Encounters at the Heart of the World*.

62. Langebaek Rueda, *Los muiscas*; compare Gamboa Mendoza, *El cacicazgo muisca*. On the Indians of Central Mexico, see Lockhart, *Nahuas after the Conquest*.

63. Berdan et al., *Ethnic Identity in Nahua Mesoamerica*.

64. For an excellent and classic example of the combined study of archaeological and documentary evidence, see Spielmann, *Farmers, Hunters, and Colonists*.

65. Liebmann, *Revolt*.

66. Carballo, *Collision of Worlds*.

67. Hornborg and Hill, *Ethnicity in Ancient Amazonia*.

68. For additional examples of the fruitful use of spatial analysis and digital mapping to study indigenous borderlands, see Erbig, "Borderline Offerings"; Erbig and Latini, "Across Archival Limits"; Mikecz, "Beyond Cajamarca."

69. Siegel, *Ancient Borinquen*; Perego et al., "Decrypting," e38337; Moreno-Estrada et al., "Reconstructing the Population," e1003925; Marcheco-Teruel et al., "Cuba," e1004488; Benn Torres, "Prospecting the Past," 21–41; Benn Torres et al., "Genetic Diversity," e0139192; Hannes et al., "Origins and Genetic Legacies."

70. Find the Cibola Project website at https://escholarship.org/uc/rcrs_ias_ucb_cibola.

71. The *Corpus* journal website is at https://journals.openedition.org/corpus archivos/.

72. The PARES website is at https://pares.culturaydeporte.gob.es/inicio.html.

73. See, for instance, Meadows, *Kiowa Ethnogeography*.

74. Basso, *Wisdom Sits in Places*.

75. Two recent exceptions that study indigenous females in leadership roles are Sousa, *Woman Who Turned into a Jaguar*; and Ochoa and Guenguerich, *Cacicas*.

76. Edwards, *Osage Women and Empire*. See also Stern, *Secret History of Gender*; Twinam, *Public Lives, Private Secrets*; Few, *Women Who Live Evil Lives*; Gauderman, *Women's Lives*; Mihesuah, *Indigenous American Women*; Powers, *Women in the Crucible of Conquest*; Jaffary, *Gender, Race, and Religion*; Murray and Tsuchiya, *Unsettling Colonialism*.

77. Conkey, "Dwelling at the Margins." See also several scholars' responses to Conkey's arguments and Conkey's own rebuttal in *Archaeologies* 1, no. 1 (2005).

78. Anzaldúa, *Borderlands/La Frontera*, 25.

79. Some significant exceptions are Guy and Sheridan, *Contested Ground*; Langer, "Eastern Andean Frontier"; Mandrini and Paz, *Las fronteras hispanocriollas*; Jackson, *Missions and Frontiers*; Weber, *Bárbaros*; Radding, *Landscapes of Power*.

80. Scott, *Art of Not Being Governed*, x.

81. An exemplary exception is Jacoby, *Shadows at Dawn*. Indigenous scholars who have called for academics to hear indigenous voices include Blackhawk, "Currents"; Deloria, *Custer Died for Your Sins*; Taiaiake, *Peace, Power, and Righteousness*. Perhaps the most forceful adjuration has been that of Maori scholar Linda Tuhiwai Smith in *Decolonizing Methodologies*.

82. An example is southern Plains Indians' revival of military societies. See Meadows, *Kiowa, Apache, and Comanche*, 251–368.

CHAPTER 2

Reading Cultural Landscapes through Interdisciplinary Perspectives

THE YOREME AND NEIGHBORING PEOPLES IN NORTHWESTERN NEW SPAIN

Cynthia Radding

The peoples of the Yaqui, Mayo, and Fuerte river basins shaped cultural landscapes over two millennia through their settlement patterns, productive labor, and creative adaptations to the ecological conditions of watered river valleys, coastal plains, and upland thorn forests. Their histories wove together subsistence strategies with complex spiritual cosmologies for centuries before Europeans approached these northwestern borderlands of Mesoamerican trade networks and urban centers. Indigenous polities that created and defended clusters of villages in the intermontane valleys often engaged in intraregional rivalries, revealing a complex mosaic of resource procurement and territorial boundaries. They became entwined with the commercial economies and the religious and political institutions of the Spanish Empire only gradually, demonstrating their capacity to set the terms of colonial expansion in this semiarid region. The peoples of these indigenous borderlands in the provinces that became known as Sinaloa, Ostimuri, and Sonora, developed the art of negotiation through successive stages of colonial encounters with Jesuit missionaries, military officers, and Hispano-criollo settlers. They defended ancestral croplands along the streams and arroyos as well as the uncultivated spaces of coastal wetlands and forested ranges that sustained their communities. At the same time, they sought entry into the colonial economy as independent laborers and producers. The cultural landscapes they created and defended emerge through not only the words and images of colonial archives but also the archaeological record, ethnographic testimonies, and the geographical terrain.

ECOLOGICAL AND CULTURAL BORDERLANDS IN NORTHWESTERN NEW SPAIN

The region that became the colonial provinces of Sinaloa and Ostimuri constituted a series of overlapping borderlands radiating northward from the tropical environs of the Gran Nayar, Chiametla, and Culiacán to the arid lands of the Sonoran Desert.[1] What the Spaniards first called Petatlán (the land of reed houses) was shaped by four major river valleys—the Sinaloa, Zuaque (Fuerte), Mayo, and Yaqui—and their tributaries, which flowed through slopes and canyons to water the coastal plains leading from the sierra to the Gulf of California. Alluding to the houses built of carrizo stalks (*Arundo donax*) and palm thatch throughout the region, Petatlán reflected the production of culturally crafted spaces through mixed practices of food procurement and dwelling in the land. The material landscapes the natives created through their labor, knowledge, and ceremonial cycles encompassed different ecological zones that extended eastward from the Gulf of California through coastal beaches and brackish wetlands, networks of streams and floodplains, and the uncultivated *monte* (mixed forests) of thorn scrub, cacti, and hardwood trees in the sierra.[2]

The indigenous peoples of this region shaped the territories they defended as "our world" (*itom ania*) through their relationship to nature. These mosaics of distinctive geographical features based on elevation, rainfall and moisture, soils, and vegetation were further inscribed with meaning by the spiritual power emanating from nature.[3] The life-giving monte sustained game animals, medicinal plants, fruits, seeds, and building materials. The indigenous world of Petatlán embraced the sierras—with hills and ranges whose names evoke stands of vegetation, boulders, and small, seasonal settlements known as *rancherías*—the cultivable farmland in the river valleys; the villages that mark their domestic spaces, the *enramadas* (arbors) for their rituals, and the centers of local governance; the streams and arroyos that flow into the main river channels; and the maritime estuaries and open waters of the Gulf of California.[4]

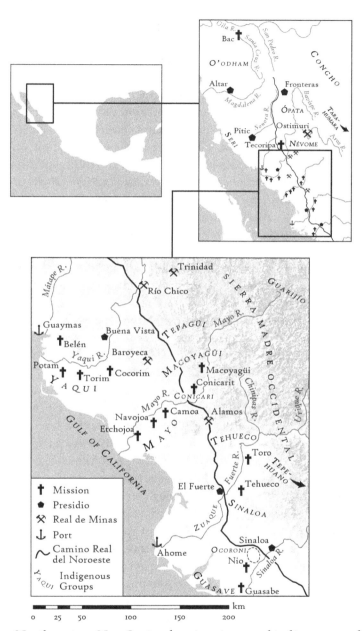

Map 2.1. Northwestern New Spain, showing rivers and indigenous and colonial settlements bordering the desert. (Map by Javier Etchegaray and G. Wallace Cartography & GIS)

The peoples of all four river basins practiced different techniques of floodplain farming to adapt Mesoamerican cultigens to this semi-arid climate. They developed local varieties of maize, cucurbits, beans, chiles, amaranth, cotton, and tobacco, as well as root crops such as camotes (*Ipomoea batatis*). Beyond the floodplains, along the ephemeral arroyos and in small clearings throughout the monte, the Yoreme and neighboring peoples, including the Guarijíos, Tepagüis, Conicaris, Macoyagüis, and Rarámuris (Tarahumaras), planted milpas in shifting cycles of cultivation and fallow. Their combined practices of planting, harvesting, and gathering redistributed different species of herbaceous plants, agaves, and cacti. Furthermore, all the indigenous communities of the highlands and river valleys cultivated and gathered numerous varieties of edible and fibrous plants.[5] The rivers, coastal mangrove forests, and estuaries provided an abundance of fish, clams, freshwater shrimp, mollusks, and amphibians, as well as salt. Indigenous peoples lived in these spaces and moved seasonally through the different biomes to practice a mixed livelihood of farming, foraging, and trade. The Yoreme/Mayos, Yoeme/Yaquis, Guarijíos, and Rarámuris/Tarahumaras represent living peoples whose cultures endure to the present day. The Tepagüis, Macoyagüis, and Conicaris no longer exist as separate ethnic groups, though they maintained their languages and distinct identities well into the nineteenth century.

Indigenous landscapes were not timeless or unchanging, however, and the cycles of planting, hunting, and foraging produced ecological spaces in a series of evolving and shifting borderlands. Over centuries that extended at least through the first millennium CE, indigenous survival skills and techniques learned through experimentation created funds of knowledge that passed from one generation to the next through quotidian practices, oral traditions, and rituals of dance and song.[6] Archaeological evidence is uneven for different portions of the region; nevertheless, it supports a broad vision of the chronological depth of cultural development and ecological management of the streams, vegetation, and wildlife that sustained the worlds of the Yoreme and neighboring native peoples. Their ancestors crafted landscapes through farming and foraging. Recent archaeological findings suggest that the cultural roots of the historical communities in the region ran deep through changing environments from the Mocorito Valley in the south to the Yaqui Valley in the north. Analyses of ceramic, lithic, and processed shell remains for different sites in the Sinaloa, Fuerte and Mayo drainages support the hypothesis of continuous settlement extending to European contact. As ecological transformations occurred in these fluvial borderlands over a millennium, ethnic boundaries shifted within networks of chiefly alliances and rivalries among different ranchería and village bands.[7]

Throughout their millennium of development, the peoples of Sinaloa and Ostimuri exhibited discernible livelihood and political organization patterns that scholars have been able to distinguish from the urbanized settlements of Culiacán and Acaponeta to the south and from the villages of the Sonoran highlands and the hunter-gatherers of the Sonoran Desert to the east and north. Archaeological surveys and selective site excavations carried out in present-day central and southern Sonora point to common cultural traditions in the valleys and ranges leading eastward to the Sierra Madre Occidental, based on common cultivation practices, terracing, methods for manufacturing ceramic and lithic artifacts, and local and regional variations in temporal ranges and settlement sizes.[8] Agriculture and long-distance trade networks fostered a complex of villages known as Huatabampo in the coastal marshes of southern Sonora and in the Mayo and Fuerte river valleys between about 200 BCE and the mid-fifteenth century CE.[9] On the northern boundary of Ostimuri in the midsection of the Yaqui drainage and its tributaries, archaeological surveys of the Ónavas Valley have found evidence of trade with areas as distant as Huatabampo to the south, and the Casas Grandes complex centered in Paquimé, Chihuahua, to the northeast.[10]

The urban ceremonial and trade centers of Huatabampo, Paquimé, Chalchihuites (in present-day Durango), and Hohokam in the Gila and Santa Cruz river valleys (present-day Arizona) reached their height circa 800–1200 CE. They began to disperse a century before initial European contact due to causes attributed variously to climate change, internal dissension, and external invasions.[11] Clusters of agricultural villages continued to thrive throughout the alluvial valleys and piedmont, producing food surpluses, tools, and prestige insignia such as pearls, shells, obsidian, and cloth that maintained the regional trade networks Spaniards would encounter in the sixteenth century. Well-storied expeditions led by Nuño Beltrán de Guzmán, Álvar Núñez Cabeza de Vaca, Marcos de Niza, Francisco Vázquez de Coronado, and Francisco de Ibarra passed through portions of Sinaloa and Ostimuri, led by multilingual indigenous guides who had traveled among the provinces along trails that linked coastal routes, highland ravines, and mountain passes.[12] Enduring Spanish settlement, however, would await the turn of the seventeenth century.

COLONIAL BORDERLANDS

Spanish colonialism came to the Yoreme borderlands in the early seventeenth century through Jesuit missions and the mining industry. The Society of Jesus founded a network of mission districts extending through the river valleys of Sinaloa, Ostimuri, and Sonora from its base in the Colegio de San Felipe y Santiago in the presidio and villa of Sinaloa. In mid-century the frontiers of mission evangelization advancing northward from the Villa de Sinaloa met the mining frontier proceeding westward from Parral in Nueva Vizcaya. Mining began in Ostimuri in the 1660s with silver strikes at San Miguel Arcángel on the headwaters of the Yaqui River, and San Ignacio and San Ildefonso de Ostimuri, deep in the sierra between the Yaqui and Mayo drainages.[13] From the late seventeenth to the early eighteenth centuries, new mines opened in the Reales de los Alamos, Río Chico, Tacupeto, Piedras Verdes, and Baroyeca. Alamos, with extraction and processing works nearby in Los Frailes, Promontorios, and La Aduana, became the principal commercial and administrative center for indigenous pueblos and Spanish settlements in the Mayo River basin.[14]

The parallel development of missions and mining centers created layered conflicts involving labor and resources. The mines and surrounding settlements became markets for mission produce and livestock, while the missions simultaneously became labor repositories for the mines through the supply of rotational workers recruited for specific places and time periods. This system of labor, known as *repartimiento*, became an important conduit of labor for the mines in Ostimuri and Nueva Vizcaya, where mine operators often abused the time limits and required pay.[15] The Real de los Alamos drew heavily from the Mayo pueblos even as Yaquis, Mayos, and other indigenous groups worked in Parral.[16] Parallel to the repartimiento labor drafts Indians traveled to the mines of their own volition, incorporating paid labor into their patterns of seasonal migration. Over time colonists and pueblos competed ever more rigorously for indigenous workers and for the productive resources of croplands, pasturage, and woodlands in the monte, and sources of water in streams and springs.

Colonial boundaries were negotiated over more than three centuries through different concepts and practices of defining space and allocating resources in a mixed thorn forest and riparian environment, extending from the basin-and-range topography of the Sierra Madre Occidental to the deltas, wetlands, and estuaries of the Gulf Coast. The nucleated towns that

Jesuits congregated to bring scattered indigenous settlements into permanent villages became in practice an interface between the rancherías that supported the Indians' seasonal movements through different biomes and the ceremonial and political centers in the missions. As the Spanish population grew with the expansion of mining and livestock ranching, the institutional status of the missions under colonial law protected indigenous agricultural lands and portions of the monte, where native shepherds and cowhands tended mission herds. Yet, mission lands were not necessarily contiguous or clearly defined. Instead, both indigenous and Spanish cultivators, pastoralists, and foragers occupied distinct parcels of temporal croplands, dependent on rainfall or the seasonal flow of intermittent streams, and grasslands mixed with thorn forest. Called *parajes*, which translates simply to "places," these irregularly shaped stretches of monte were named—often with indigenous toponyms—thus revealing locally recognized histories of occupation and use.[17]

Over the course of the eighteenth century, colonial authorities in Nueva Vizcaya, Sinaloa, and Sonora pressured Spanish *vecinos* (Hispanic heads of households) to regularize their occupation of *realengas* (public lands nominally owned by the Crown). This procedure was called *composición*, a legal process involving the payment of royal fees to carry out their measurement, public auction, and issuance of title and turn them into discretely bounded parcels of private property.[18] Realengas referred to lands that were not alienated to a private owner. Vecinos were Hispanic subjects, identified as residents of a given city or town, with potential landholding rights and duties to contribute to the local defense.

The provinces of Sinaloa, Ostimuri, and Sonora were under the administration of the Kingdom of Nueva Vizcaya until 1734, when the governorship of Sonora-Sinaloa was established; after 1786, the western provinces from Chiametla to Sonora came under the authority of the Intendancy of Arizpe. Private landholdings evolved from conventional use rights negotiated through verbal agreements and informal arrangements for sharing pasturage and water or transferring use rights through purchase and inheritance to demarcated properties defined by local authorities—alcaldes mayores, subdelegados, or other commissioned officers—under the procedures of composición.[19] Formal landownership with measured boundaries and property markers ran counter to indigenous practices of land use and access, derived from seasonal or temporary occupation of the monte and the resources of water, forests, and wildlife located within it.

The thick web of relationships that bound together indigenous communities, Hispanic settlements, and the cultural landscapes they created emerges through a wide range of archival holdings, from local correspondence among missionaries, military officers, and magistrates to formal reports, mission and parish censuses, maps, land measurements, and judicial hearings for contested claims to land and water rights. Colonial sources with diverse origins and purposes reveal the mixed strategies for physical survival and social well-being that the Yoreme and other indigenous groups practiced in the highland and lowland environments of Sinaloa and Ostimuri. Of these abundant manuscript collections, the following section analyses three sets of documents within the genre of missionaries' letters and reports, dating from the sixteenth to the eighteenth centuries and originating in the Sinaloa, Mayo, and Yaqui river valleys. Their content and the circumstances under which they were produced illustrate ways to read landscapes through the observations recorded in these texts and, thereby, to infer the contrasting worldviews of their authors and the peoples who had sculpted these borderlands.

INDIGENOUS-JESUIT ENCOUNTERS IN SINALOA AND OSTIMURI

Jesuit missionaries penned the earliest descriptions of these frontier provinces in the 1590s, soon after their arrival in the Villa de Sinaloa. In the *cartas anuas* (annual letters) directed to the padre provincial of the Society of Jesus in Mexico, the missionaries provided a chronicle of significant events that had occurred during the year, always oriented to promoting their evangelizing mission in terms of the numbers of baptisms, the congregation of Indians into villages, the missionaries' progress in learning the indigenous languages in order to preach to the neophytes and hear their confessions, and the initial construction of ramadas, living quarters, and chapels for conducting the liturgy. The missionaries' annual reports also took note of the obstacles and setbacks they had suffered, due to disease episodes, local rebellions, or crop failures that impelled their indigenous charges to leave the villages and return to the monte. To explain both their advances and reverses, the Jesuits invoked the blessings of divine intervention and the machinations of the devil to thwart the salvation of Amerindian souls.[20]

The Sons of Loyola assigned to the province of Sinaloa arrived as strangers in a new land, dependent upon the indigenous peoples for their very survival and for knowledge about the natural environment and the constellation of native communities distributed throughout its valleys and upland ranges. For this reason they were attentive to the flora and fauna; to the contours of the river valleys, sierras, and canyons; and to the ways the native peoples farmed, hunted, fished, and gathered in the coastal estuaries and the inland monte. The earliest carta anua, dated 1592 and signed by P. Pedro Díaz, incorporates a copy of a letter he had received from P. Martín Pérez, who opened the Jesuit mission in Sinaloa. His report communicated an initial moment of mutual curiosity between Jesuits and the *sinaloas* of this fertile valley, and it described in detail the ways in which both women and men moved through the land and drew a livelihood from it. Pérez reported that upon his arrival at the Villa of Sinaloa with P. Gonzalo de Tapia, they heard long-overdue confessions by the Spanish vecinos who lived there without benefit of a priest. At the same time, with the help of two Nahua interpreters, they began to learn two of the local languages that were spoken by the indigenous groups who had most readily welcomed the missionaries to their villages and built them houses of wood frames covered with *"petates* as they call them." The utility of Nahuatl in these northern provinces illustrates the relative linguistic proximity of Nahuatl and the languages of Petalán, as well as the extent of travel and trade among different groups along both the coastal and mountainous routes that connected central, western, and northwestern Mexico. Pérez and his companion were able to speak to these pueblos in their languages, in order "to attract them [to our faith] and with our Lord's help, to teach them the catechism [because] in the time that it took us to learn their languages, they could learn the things of our holy faith and begin to benefit from them."[21]

Pérez went on to state that these were the easiest people to get to know of any that he had yet seen, "extraordinarily affable, for all day long we could not be alone in our houses, and even at night they did not leave us, asking us many things and telling us about themselves."[22] Pérez described the ways in which the *sinaloas* worked the land, asserting that they sowed two crops each year, gathering copious harvests of "maize, beans, squashes, melons, and other seed plants that they eat and store, especially the squashes, which they cut into strips, dry in the sun, and then rehydrate and conserve, and these are very good to eat." Pérez observed that in addition to farming, the Indians hunted deer and rabbit; the women were equally hardworking, he affirmed, as they "helped their husbands in the fields" and spun and wove cloth from the large quantities of cotton fiber they harvested (*Gossypium hirsutum*).[23] Subsequent cartas anuas repeated the assertion that the communities settled in the valleys harvested two crops annually, supplementing these foodstuffs with the bounty of the monte and rivers through hunting, fishing, and gathering.

This stage of reciprocal curiosity and exchange of knowledge did not last long. In 1594, the Jesuits claimed their first martyr in the mission field of Sinaloa, Gonzalo de Tapia, who was murdered in Tovoropa, a pueblo de visita of the mission of Ocoroni, northwest of the Villa of Sinaloa.[24] The cartas anuas of the following years reported in detail the consequences of his unexpected, violent death and Spanish military reprisals, leading to the flight of Indians deeper into the sierra and northward to the upper Fuerte River drainage. These events signaled divisions among different indigenous groups, notably the Zuaques, Tehuecos, and Ocoronis, and equally significantly, the mounting pressures of Spanish demands on native communities for food and labor. As the Jesuits were made keenly aware, they operated in cultural borderlands marked by disputed claims to power that they only poorly understood.

The missions endured, nevertheless, with advances and setbacks, and by the close of the second decade of the seventeenth century, the Jesuits had begun working among the Yoreme/Mayos and Yoeme/Yaquis in the central portions of these river valleys north of Sinaloa and in the mountainous region of the upper Mayo and Cedros drainages in the province of Ostimuri. An anonymous Jesuit report, probably dating from the second half of the seventeenth century, signaled the Jesuits' dependence on the indigenous caciques for their admittance to indigenous rancherías and villages to begin preaching, baptizing, and building the physical spaces and governing framework for establishing mission communities. Although incomplete, this document provides excellent insight into the Jesuits' perspective on their new mission field, complementing the cartas anuas and the *Historia de Sinaloa* in the Archivo Histórico de la Provincia de México (AHPM). The manuscript is undated, but the author cites Andrés Pérez de Ribas's *Historia [de los triunfos de nuestra santa fe]* and, thus, it would date after the 1640s, when Pérez de Ribas's monumental history was in circulation. The author's hagiographic language extolling the Jesuits' good deeds, when read critically, opens the way to view these early contact histories as evolving from initiatives taken by indigenous caciques to secure peace and comparative advantage vis-à-vis other tribes and nations, working through the Jesuits as intermediaries.[25]

The author of this report made it clear that the Çinaloas (agricultural villagers from the central valleys of the Sinaloa River basin) became the anchor for Jesuit operations in the region, opening the missionaries' access to itinerant tribes deeper in the sierra, like the Huites, Chínipas, Temoris, Ilhíos, Guarijíos, Guazapares and Yoes/Choix. In particular, he extolled the governor of the Çinaloas, identified only as Baptista, "whose industry made possible the entire reducción [missionization] of these mountainous peoples, for his prestige and authority went before him among his own people and the surrounding nations."[26] Acknowledging that captive-taking and enslavement were motives for conflict and simmering warfare in the region—but without admitting Spanish involvement in these networks of forced labor, captive ransoming, and exchange—the author credited Governor Baptista for arranging the return of Huite captives taken by the Chínipas. In response to the missionary's "persuasion," Baptista accepted in marriage one of the ransomed Huite women, thus cementing an alliance between the Çinaloas and the Huites. Governor Baptista and his wife brought the Huites into the Christian fold through their visits into the highland rancherías, their persuasive language, and their own pious conduct.[27]

Extending his gaze some forty leagues (approximately 160 miles) northward from the Sinaloa Valley, the author of this mid-seventeenth-century report dedicated chapter 16 to an encapsulated history of the "conversion to Christ" of the peoples of the Mayo Valley and the upland Conicaris and Tepagüis. "Like the other rivers," he wrote, "the Mayo has its source in the Sierra Madre, emptying its waters into the Sea of California. It is not the largest river of the province, but it is heavily settled, its population said to reach 30,000 souls and, for this reason, they are called the Mayo nation."[28] Having observed the rudiments of mission life among the Çinaloa and Zuaque villages, the Mayos repeatedly petitioned Governor Diego Martínez de Hurdaide at the Villa de Sinaloa for missionaries to live in their valley and lay the foundations of mission life. In response to the Indians' initiative and with the approval of Viceroy Álvaro Manrique de Zúñiga, the Jesuit padre provincial assigned the veteran missionary Pedro Méndez to begin congregating the Mayos into mission towns, recognizing his experience of more than twenty-four years' service in the missions of the Ocoronis and Tehuecos. The governor provided a military escort for Méndez from the Villa de Sinaloa to the southern bank of the Mayo River; however, they were met by a number of Mayo *principales* (leaders), who advanced "many leagues" beyond their rancherías to intercept Méndez and his party, "having erected crosses along the way. All of them displayed such a favorable disposition that in a fortnight some four thousand adults and children gathered into seven pueblos and

[were] baptized."[29] In this affirmation of the Mayos' fervor and dedication to the "new law of Christ," expressed spatially, the author suggests that the indigenous leaders took the initiative to bring missionaries to their territory and create the conditions necessary for evangelization and resettlement of several thousands of their people in nucleated villages. Furthermore, through their halting of Méndez, Martínez de Hurdaide, and his militias at a calculated distance from their pueblos, the principales established a clear boundary that no stranger could enter their dwelling places without their permission.

The Jesuit author affirmed that by the 1620s, the conversion of the Mayos was complete, observing that women and men among the Mayos had developed the skills to preach to their kinsmen and persuade them to take up the new religious observances. The Lord had blessed them with abundant harvests, he noted, and the Mayos remained faithful through the Guazapares rebellion of 1632 that engulfed the Chínipas and other upland tribes.[30] Some three thousand Conicaris and Tepagüis joined the Mayos' turn to Christendom, under the tutelage of their own baptized leaders and additional Jesuit missionaries sent to the province.[31] *Conversion*, as employed in this passage, comes from the language of the documents and signifies a turning away from or toward spatial practices and rituals of spirituality that implies a process of creativity and deliberate choice. In the Mayo traditions of religious rituals, conversion does not mean a rejection of their ancient concepts of spirituality linked to the monte in favor of Catholic orthodoxy; rather, it combines the notions of spiritual power and renewal to create a new, composite cosmology. This is observed dramatically in the communal and household *pajko*, ceremonial dances that reenact the diurnal solar cycle in tandem with the Catholic liturgical calendar, and in the theatrical but deeply religious annual rituals observed for Lent and Easter Week in nearly all Yaqui and Mayo traditional villages and modern settlements.[32] "Their numbers were diminished, however, because of repeated disease episodes and the inherent 'curiosity' that led them to migrate to the pueblos of other nations in the Jesuit mission field and even to those of other religious orders, thus forming new population clusters. In addition, they were attracted to opportunities for paid labor in the mining centers [*reales de minas*] and many new villas, ranchos, and haciendas that proliferated in their environs."[33] In this passage the author recognized the longstanding mobility of the indigenous peoples, notwithstanding their agricultural base in the well-watered central valleys of Sinaloa and Ostimuri, and the undeniable pressures of Spanish colonial settlements. These increasingly complex and imbricated borderlands traced new footpaths and roads across ethnic lines, through the economic webs linking indigenous landscapes with the expanding shadows of the colonial mining economy. Their consequences for the cultural resilience of the peoples of Sinaloa and Ostimuri and their territorial base became starkly apparent through the economic and demographic developments of these provinces over time.

In the mid-eighteenth century, Jesuit Patricio Imaz, who served for more than two decades in the mission of San Andrés de Conicari, penned a report that provides a detailed description of the ecological and economic conditions that framed the livelihood of indigenous peoples in the midst of the colonial mining economy. Composed in 1744, Padre Imaz's history of Mission Conicari and its four villages responded to the information requested of him by the Jesuit provincial and Padre Visitador Juan Antonio Balthasar in the wake of a province-wide uprising in 1739–41 that threatened to shatter Spanish dominion in Sinaloa and Ostimuri.[34] This uprising of Yoeme, Yoreme, and neighboring peoples signaled a crisis in the colonial governance of the provinces of Sinaloa and Ostimuri stemming from the contradictory pressures that bore on indigenous communities from the religious and material demands of mission life, labor recruitment to mines and haciendas, and encroachments by Spaniards on native territories. Padre Imaz situated his history of the mission in a colonial landscape that was framed by the geological formations of the Sierra Madre and its coursing river channels, but transformed by colonial settlements, livestock raising, and the mining industry.[35]

Located at the juncture of the Mayo and Cedros rivers, Conicari marked a transitional zone between the watered valleys of the lower Mayo River and the steep slopes and canyons of the Sierra Madre Occidental. The mission began in 1621, bringing together various dialect groups into three pueblos: the head village of Conicari and the visitas of San Miguel de Macoyagüi and Nuestra Señora de la Asunción de Tepagüi. The fourth village, San Bartolomé de Batacosa, was founded later under conditions that show how the missionaries followed the Tepagüis' cultural practices and knowledge of the terrain.

> Several native families of Tepagüi lived some eight leagues distant from the village, in a place called Batacosa with good lands for planting in the summer rainy season and a beautiful spring that waters a few tablelands where they can sow wheat, *vaviris* (a kind of squash), and melons. In some years, however, due to poor rains and to the damage caused by the vecinos' livestock that trample the edges and stream flow of the spring that surfaces in soft soil, the water becomes scarce.[36]

Worried that the Tepagüis would not have adequate religious instruction and the sacramental ministry they needed while living at such a distance from the mission, their missionary founded a formal pueblo in Batacosa, some fifteen leagues distant from the head village of Conicari, where wheat could be planted with irrigation and maize sown and harvested *de temporal* (according to the seasons), when rainfall was adequate. Imaz added a pointed observation that "since each Indian clears and plants his milpa individually, [the area planted] cannot be large, because the soil produces many weeds . . . which they remove manually, thus one laborer can only tend a small planted field."[37]

Padre Imaz stressed throughout his report the hardships that the families of all four pueblos faced because of the generally poor soils and small patches of land adequate for planting, as well as the inconstant rainfall, which limited agricultural yields even for the more productive lands surrounding Batacosa. In addition, Imaz underscored the commercial disadvantages that the Indians of his mission faced when bartering with Spanish vecinos to exchange their meager harvests for cloth. In a province where currency was scarce, Imaz observed, indigenous peasants who engaged in trade were forced to sell cheap and buy dear, victims of an arbitrary pricing system that worked against them. These conditions, he argued, forced many of the indigenous residents formally registered in the mission to work outside their villages for the vecinos, in mining reales or haciendas, where they were paid in kind.[38]

Padre Imaz's candid observations of the problems that beset the widely separated villages of his mission emerged from his long acquaintance with the material conditions of the pueblos and their natural surroundings. His descriptions of daily life and the economic relations between Indians and vecinos—enriching the latter at the expense of the former—are closely detailed, creating a portrait of this mission that had endured for more than a century in the highlands where streams ran but arable lands were scarce. Possibly because of the scattered plots of land available for farming in this mountainous terrain, and consequently the heightened importance of the monte for sustenance, the native commoners and village officers of Conicari, Macoyagüi, and Tepagüi proved to be tenacious in their defense of their pueblos' woodlands and water in the face of the vecinos' expanding landholdings and livestock herds. Indigenous council members from all three pueblos appear frequently in the proceedings for measuring and titling realengas, and in land disputes heard in the local courts of Sinaloa and Ostimuri throughout the eighteenth century and even into the national period.[39]

Two decades after Padre Imaz sent his report to the Jesuit provincial in Mexico, the royal order to expel the Society of Jesus from all the Spanish dominions forced the departure of Jesuit missionaries from northern New Spain in 1767–68. The Sons of Ignatius were replaced in Sonora and the Pimería Alta with Franciscan missionary-friars from the province of Xalisco and the Colegio de Propaganda Fide of Querétaro, in Baja California with Dominican friars and, in Nueva Vizcaya with secular clergy. The missions of Sinaloa and Ostimuri came under the purview of the Diocese of Guadiana, with its seat in Durango, until the creation of the bishopric of Sonora in 1779. Formally speaking, these missions were secularized and turned into parishes, although the indigenous parishioners did not pay a tithe or fees for the sacraments (nor did many of the Hispanic vecinos whom the clergy served).

In the Yaqui Valley, the eight mission pueblos gathered together under Jesuit auspices in the early seventeenth century had constituted a bastion of the mission system in northwestern New Spain, due to the fertility of the river's floodplains and the demographic strength of its pueblos. The Yaqui pueblos famously supplied surplus foodstuffs and livestock to the missions of Baja California and the Pimería Alta, where arid conditions made agriculture more tenuous. Furthermore, Yaqui laborers spread throughout Nueva Vizcaya as mineworkers, and they were recruited as divers and oarsmen for pearl harvesting along the shores of the Gulf of California even as they sustained their pueblos in the valley. Despite the crisis that erupted with the uprising of 1739–41, revealing the pressures of the colonial economy and leaving permanent fissures in the institutional and social structures of the missions, the pueblos endured through the transition from Jesuit to secular administration.

Curate Br. Francisco Joaquín Valdez entered the Yaqui Valley to assume responsibility for the pueblos in 1767, the very year of the Jesuits' departure. By the time he sent a detailed report on the missions to the intendant-governor of Sonora, Enrique Grimarest, in August 1790, Valdez had served in the Yaqui missions for twenty-three years. Fluent in the language, Valdez expressed considerable knowledge of the complex ecology of the river valley and of Yoeme cultural management of the floodplain and the surrounding monte. Responding to a set of structured questions, Valdez addressed the themes of language, modes of settlement, administration of communal patrimony, modes of agriculture, and trade with the Spanish vecinos.[40] Valdez identified the dominant language in the valley as *lengua chuíta*, explaining that although many of the Yoeme knew Spanish, they did not speak it "in their own country," so Valdez and the priests who assisted him heard confessions, preached, and delivered the sacraments in the indigenous tongue.[41] Valdez qualified his reference to the eight pueblos of the Yaqui Valley by saying that they were not truly consolidated villages but numerous rancherías dispersed along the banks of the river. The curate estimated the total population of the missions at sixteen thousand. Despite their dispersed settlement pattern, the Yoeme managed the missions' communal property, largely quantified in herds of livestock—cattle, horses, sheep, goats, and mules—belonging to each of the eight pueblos and totaling some twenty-three thousand head in all.

Turning to agriculture and the productivity of the land, Padre Valdez revealed the necessary complementarity of the resources of the monte and floodplain cultivation. He identified the main crops as native maize and frijoles and, of European origin, garbanzos, lentils, and wheat. In this short list of cultigens, like other Europeans, he seemed to privilege seed crops— granos—and perhaps neglected to mention the wide variety of cucurbits (squashes), root crops, and amaranth, the last both cultivated and gathered for its seeds and leaves. Valdez despaired of what he considered the Yaquis' refusal to dedicate their labor systematically to agriculture and their willingness to sell their harvests even before they had fully ripened, observing that the Yoeme gathered wild fruits, seeds, and herbs from the monte to satisfy their medicinal and nutritional needs, including different varieties of agave and pitahaya. At the same time he recognized that floodplain agriculture was unreliable for regularly spaced seasonal crops: in some years rainfall and streamflow were insufficient, and in other years, the floodwaters washed away soils, leaving sandy deposits leached with salts that took several years to restore for cultivation. Valdez related these ecological limitations to his explanation that no formal distribution of lands among households had taken place in the Yaqui pueblos; rather, families cleared and planted their milpas "where they pleased" in different seasons, for if they were held to a fixed plot of land, the river might destroy it. In this sense, Valdez observed philosophically, "even as the river provides the maintenance and livelihood of its inhabitants, it brings equally their suffering and travail."[42]

READING LANDSCAPES IN THE ARCHIVES

Historical documents from a great variety of sources offer eloquent observations and direct evidence of the cultural landscapes that were created over centuries in the indigenous borderlands of northern New Spain. Rhythms of continuity and innovation marked both the ecological and cultural dimensions of the landforms, river courses, and plant communities that constituted the transitional biomes of Petatlán—between the tropical zones of Aztatlán and the Sonoran Desert—both before and after Spanish contact and colonization. The missionary reports analyzed throughout this chapter provide abundant descriptive material that is intrinsically valuable and permits "reading against and across the grain" to detect cultural disjunctures as well as transcultural processes of adaptation and change.[43] The Jesuits' annual letters and ecclesiastical reports from the secular clergy read alongside the documents generated during land measurement and titling procedures, recorded land disputes, military reports, and indigenous petitions provide traceable evidence of ecological changes and cultural transformations in the landscapes of Sinaloa and Ostimuri. Unquestionably, the proliferation of mines, livestock ranches, and mixed haciendas throughout the highlands of both provinces accelerated processes of deforestation, altering the stream flow of arroyos and leading to greater aridity. As the reports by Padre Imaz (1744) and Curate Valdez (1790) express, indigenous livelihoods were increasingly entwined with colonial commerce and extractive economies. The mission pueblos that were formed out of the model for Jesuit evangelization endured, but these nucleated towns coexisted with indigenous rancherías that were dispersed away from the floodplains and closer to the monte. Over time, the spatial composition of mission towns became the nuclei for the political and ritual life of Yoreme and Yoeme communities observed in the present day.

These multilayered meanings of the archival texts become even clearer when read in conjunction with ethnographic, linguistic, geographic, and ethnohistorical studies, and in light of archaeological research focused on the material remains of past societies in the region. The literatures produced in these fields open a fulsome range of interpretations, stemming from ceremonial cycles, spatial distribution of settlements, permanent and ephemeral constructions of enramadas, household dwellings, and crosses to mark ceremonial routes and pueblo boundaries, as well as seasonal patterns of foraging and cultivation. In turn, historical analysis of texts for their content and the languages they employ enhance the research findings from cultural geography and the diverse fields of anthropology. These multidisciplinary approaches are necessarily complementary even as they deepen the palimpsest of meanings for indigenous borderlands in greater northwestern Mexico.

NOTES

1. Sauer, *Aboriginal Population*. Sauer coined the term Aztatlán for the pre-Hispanic frontier of Mesoamerica in western Mexico, extending from Acaponeta to Culiacán. Sauer, *Aztatlán*.

2. Ingold, *Perception of the Environment*; Crumrine, *Mayo Indians*; Camacho Ibarra, "El sol y la serpiente," 18–19; Gentry, *Río Mayo Plants*, 27–41.

3. Crumrine, *Mayo Indians*, 98; Shorter, *We Will Dance*; Moctezuma Zamarrón, López, and Harriss, "Los territorios del Noroeste," 253–55; Camacho Ibarra, "El sol y la serpiente," 312.

4. Lerma Rodríguez, "*El nido heredado*," 53–72.

5. Bañuelos, "Etnobotánica," 403–7; Harriss Clare, "*Hasta aquí son todas las palabras*," 27, 72–73.

6. Shorter, *We Will Dance*; Yetman and Van Devender, *Mayo Ethnobotany*.

7. Carpenter, "Pre-Hispanic Occupation."

8. Pailes, "Archaeological Reconnaissance"; Pailes, "Relaciones culturales"; Doolittle, *Pre-Hispanic Occupance*.

9. Álvarez Palma, "Huatabampo," 9–93.

10. Gallaga Murrieta, "Archaeological Survey," 105–252.

11. Webster, McBrinn, and Gamboa Carrera, *Archaeology without Borders*; Berrojalbiz, *Paisajes y fronteras*.

12. Sauer, "Road to Cíbola"; Pailes, "Archaeological Perspective"; Obregón, *Historia de los descubrimientos*.

13. West, *Sonora*, 44–55.

14. West, *Sonora*, fig.18: "The Alamos mining district, southern Sonora."

15. Biblioteca Nacional Fondo Reservado Archivo Franciscano (BNFR AF), caja 32, 650.1, 1698, fojas 1–44v.

16. Cramaussel, "Poblar en tierras."

17. On the institutional practices for formalizing land tenure, see López Castillo, *Composición de tierras*; Radding, *Wandering Peoples*, 171–206; Archivo General del Estado de Sonora (AGES), Títulos Primordiales Tomo LX 800, tomo XXI, 286.

18. López Castillo, *El poblamiento*; López Castillo, *Composición de tierras*; Radding, *Wandering Peoples*; Radding, *Landscapes of Power*. Also see the interesting discussion of *realengos* and *real* in BNFR AF, caja 32, 650.1, 1698, f. 44.

19. Numerous examples of land titles conferred through composición, often called *títulos primordiales*, are preserved in the Archivo General del Estado de Sonora, Títulos Primordiales (AGES TP); in the Archivo Histórico General del Estado de Sinaloa, Ramo de Tierras; in the Archivo Histórico de Jalisco; and in the Archivo General de la Nación (AGN), Ramos de Tierras and Indiferente Virreinal.

20. The cartas anuas consulted for this study are preserved in the Archivo Histórico de la Provincia de México, Fondo Gerardo Decorme, Antigua Compañía, Mexico City (AHPM, FGD).

21. AHPM FGD, caja 1, carpeta 1, Antigua Compañia, #6. Anua de la Provincia de Nueva España, p. 18.

22. AHPM FGD, 1, 1, #6. Anua de la Provincia de Nueva España, pp. 19–20.

23. AHPM FGD, 1, 1, Antigua Compañia, #6, p. 19.

24. AHPM FGD, 1, 1, Antigua Compañia, #10, pp. 14–15; Bayne, *Missions Begin with Blood.*

25. BNFR AF, 32/648, ff. 27–36. I thank Brandon Bayne for bringing this document to my attention.

26. BNFR AF, 32/648, f. 27r.

27. BNFR AF, 32,648, ff. 27v–28r.

28. BNFR AF, 32,648, ff. 29r–30r; quotation on 29r.

29. BNFR AF, 32,648, f. 29v.

30. BNFR AF, 32,648, f. 28; Pérez de Ribas, *Historia*, libro 4, capítulo 1.

31. BNFR AF, 32,648, f. 30.

32. See Crumrine, *Mayo Indians*; Camacho Ibarra, "El sol y la serpiente," 73–140, who link these concepts with human sexuality. On conversion as a religious concept with an ethnohistorical sensibility, see Bayne, "Willy-Nilly Baptisms," 9–37.

33. BNFR AF, 32,648, f. 30. "permanece hasta lo presente esta christiandad, aunque muy disminuida de número porque las epidemias que a tiempos han sobrevenido han hecho grandes estragos, y siendo el genio de esta nación muy curioso, muchos de ellos se han extraviado a otras partes, y con el número crecido de gentes que se hallaron en nuestras misiones y en las doctrinas de otros religiosos se han formado las poblaciones, los reales de minas con muchas nuevas villas, y se ha proveído un número casi infinito de ranchos, estancias, y haciendas populosas de que antes el reino carecía." (Translation by the author.)

34. Bancroft Library (BL) M-M 1716. V-25. Padre Imaz's "Historia de Conicari" is part of a corpus of Jesuit mission histories written during the same years that provide important demographic and economic information and a wide range of perspectives on northwestern New Spain.

35. Radding, *Wandering Peoples*, 283–85; Folsom, *Yaquis and the Empire*, 150–81; Hu-Dehart, *Adaptación y resistencia*; Spicer, *Yaquis.*

36. BL M-M 1716. V-25, f. 2.

37. BL M-M 1716. V-25, ff. 4–6.

38. BL M-M 1716. V-25, f. 8.

39. See AGN Indiferente Virreinal and Tierras, AGES TP, and Hermosillo Casa de la Cultura Jurídica, Ramo Civil.

40. BNFR AF, 35/775, 12 ff., 1790.

41. *Chuíta* may be a variant spelling of *cáhita*; however, the Yoeme refer to their language as *hiak nooki.* Moctezuma Zamarrón and Aguilar Zeleny, *Los pueblos indígenas*, 16; Lerma Rodríguez, "El nido heredado," 16. Yaqui derives from *hiaqui*, and this spelling commonly used in colonial documents, may come from *jiak*, "to speak."

42. BNFR AF, 35/775, ff. 8–9, 1790. "en el concepto que del mismo río proviene la utilidad y provecho de sus habitantes; como igualmente las miserias y trabajos." (Translation by author.)

43. For reading with the grain, see Stoler, *Along the Archival Grain*, 1–15.

CHAPTER 3

Beeswax and Borderlands in the Seventeenth-Century Northern Maya Lowlands

Geoffrey H. Wallace

In the autumn of 1602, five Yucatec Maya men were apprehended in the town of Chiná, just south of the city of Campeche in the Spanish colonial province of Yucatán. Juan Chan, Francisco Mis, Antonio Tun, Francisco May, and one other, who went unnamed, had entered the province from the unconquered forested region to the east known as the *montaña* (see map 3.1), bearing wax that they had intended to sell in Chiná. Arrested for the offenses of contraband trade, fleeing Spanish rule, and abandoning the Catholic Church, the four named men—what happened to the fifth is unknown—were imprisoned in Campeche and interrogated by one of its magistrates, Francisco Sánchez Cerdán.[1]

The resulting document offers a glimpse into the province's growing contraband trade in beeswax and some details about its participants.[2] The captives had all come into the Campeche region from an independent community called Tucolahmexmo (the location and proper transcription of which are unclear), but their prior origins were diverse. Juan Chan was an orphan from the northwestern town of Conkal who had worked as a household servant in both Mérida and Campeche.[3] Francisco Mis was from Oxkutzcab, a town in the central-southern district of Sierra. Francisco May was born and married in Maní, also in Sierra. Antonio Tun did not remember where he

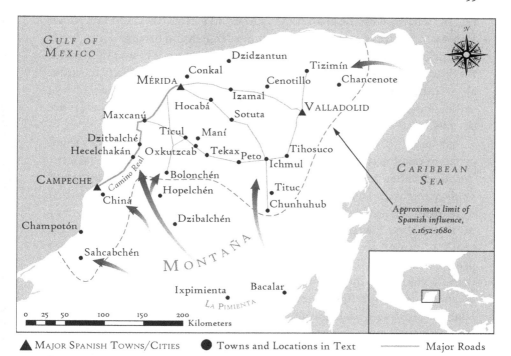

Map 3.1. Transfrontier trade in the northern Maya lowlands, ca. 1600–1697.
(Map © G. Wallace Cartography & GIS)

was born, but he was married in Dzitbalché, a large town along the camino real, the highway between the port city of Campeche and the Spanish provincial capital of Mérida. The men had been living in the montaña—three of them with their families—for between six and fourteen years.

Thus, the four men had come from all over Yucatán, fled colonial rule, and eventually ended up in the southern interior, where they had taken up beeswax trading from Tucolahmexmo to make a living. It was, in fact, the wax trade that had enticed Juan Chan to flee the province in the first place; while he was working as a servant in Campeche for a man named Antón Julián, four or five Yucatec Mayas came out of the forest selling wax, and Chan decided to leave with them. He told Sánchez "that he went to the montaña to sell wax both to the Spaniards and the indios."[4] They peddled wax across the Campeche region, "buying with the proceeds . . . knives, machetes, axes, and salt, which is that which is lacking in the interior forests."[5] Chan and his fellow merchants essentially told Sánchez that there was a black-market trade in wax right under the Spaniards' noses, one which was lucrative enough to lure participants from all over the province and provide supplies to refugee and independent Maya settlements that colonial authorities had been trying to stamp out for six decades.

The interrogation of Juan Chan and his fellow merchants is part of a small group of documents detailing the contraband trade in beeswax across the Yucatec frontier. In this chapter I use it and a number of other archival and published primary sources to shed some light on the complex relationship that developed between beeswax and borderlands in the seventeenth-century northern Maya lowlands. As we shall see, wax extraction in seventeenth-century Yucatán was concentrated at the province's margins, where greater precipitation and thicker forests afforded better habitats for stingless bees. Demand for the commodity drove a widespread clandestine trade, wherein merchants like Juan Chan—many of them refugees from the Spanish province—took advantage of the limited Spanish presence on the edges of the province to barter wax for salt and metal tools that could not be obtained in the interior. My overarching argument is that this transfrontier wax trade was a historically significant but somewhat contradictory phenomenon. On one hand, by bringing large amounts of wax into the province, Yucatec Mayas living in and around the peninsula's borderland regions underpinned the Spanish province's wax industry. On the other, many Mayas on both sides of the frontier turned demand for the commodity to their own economic or political gain. In short, beeswax and borderlands significantly influenced and shaped each other in the northern Maya lowlands of the seventeenth century. I make three smaller points within that framework, each addressed in its own section: first, that the wax industry was concentrated along the Yucatecan frontier; second, that the contraband wax trade was a complex and lucrative business that Yucatec Mayas on both sides of the frontier sought to access and protect; and third, that at times beeswax was used as a tool of active resistance against Spanish rule.

Here, I pull on a thread that Yucatán's colonial historiography has left dangling. The field's canonical works have touched on the subject of beeswax, but only a few pages in Grant D. Jones's *Maya Resistance to Spanish Rule* have examined its significance in the region's borderlands.[6] In many ways I deepen and expand on Jones's conclusions, especially his description of beeswax as a commercial tool that gave Yucatec Mayas who had fled the colony continued access to the Mesoamerican economy and made it easier for them to retain the autonomy that they had sought by migrating south.[7] I also take several further steps by proposing that the wax industry as a whole was largely isolated from Spanish control and by exploring the different ways in which Yucatec Mayas on both sides of the frontier participated in and protected their interests in transfrontier wax trade.

More germane to this volume, the Yucatecan wax industry and the transfrontier trade it drove are illustrative of the complex ways in which European-driven natural product extraction was articulated in spaces of limited European influence in the colonial-era Americas. Spanish demand, transmitted through extractive institutions and practices, was the prime mover of beeswax commerce in colonial Yucatán. However, before being pocketed by Europeans and reported in Spanish documents, much of the wax wound its way through a lengthy and obscure network of Maya gatherers, middlemen, merchants, elites, and commoners. Not unlike the early fur and brazilwood trades elsewhere in the colonial Americas, or the later chicle industry in Yucatán, the commodity became entangled in indigenous contexts of trade, politics, and migration playing out in forested landscapes at and beyond the fringes of European control or knowledge.[8] I seek to shed some light on that process and to gain a better understanding of beeswax's historical significance to the history of both the Maya lowlands and of indigenous borderlands in the colonial-era Americas.

THE WAX INDUSTRY IN COLONIAL YUCATÁN

From its conquest and founding in the 1540s until the mid-eighteenth century, the province of Yucatán's second most important export product (after cotton textiles) was wax derived from the nests of domestic and wild meliponines, or stingless honeybees.[9] Spaniards extracted it from Yucatec Maya villages through a variety of means then exported it to Mexico and beyond, where candles made from Yucatecan wax provided illumination for liturgies, baptisms, and processions.[10] It came from the nests of the sixteen or so different species of meliponine found in the Yucatán Peninsula and was either harvested from domestic beehives or, far more commonly, gathered from wild nests in the patchwork forests surrounding most Yucatec Maya towns and beyond. The domesticated variety of stingless honeybee is the *xuna'an ka'ab* ("regal lady bee," *Melipona beecheii*), which has been kept in Yucatec Maya house gardens for at least fifteen hundred years and continues to produce honey and wax for beekeepers.[11] The rest are *k'aaxil ka'abo'ob* ("forest bees" or "wild bees"). Six of these species nest in trees, building large, conspicuous hives with substantial quantities of honey and wax.[12] The other ten are diminutive bees called trigonids, which build small nests in a mix of trees, caves, and underground cavities.[13]

Tribute payments leveed through the *encomienda* system (by which individual Spaniards in Yucatán were given the right to tax one or more Yucatec Maya villages) were the main tools of wax extraction during the province's earliest years. From 1549 to 1561 each tributary (a married adult male) owed his *encomendero*, or the Crown in some cases, one pound of wax (0.45 kg). Payment was tripled to three pounds (1.36 kg) per year in 1561, and remained at that level until wax was struck from the tribute rolls in 1583.[14] Thereafter, wax extraction came to be dominated by the Yucatecan *repartimiento de efectos*, a controversial system of dubious legality wherein Yucatec Maya communities sold goods to Spaniards (especially the governor) and their middlemen who, wielding or backed by state power, paid in advance at below-market rates in return for future repayments in kind.[15] While encomienda tribute was a homogenously applied head tax, repartimiento was a considerably more flexible apparatus. Payments ranged from just a few ounces of wax to more than twenty pounds per tributary, depending on the place and time.[16] On top of *repartimientos*, most Yucatec Mayas living in the province also owed between one and three pounds to their local parish or Franciscan mission, collected as compulsory alms known as *limosnas* or as surcharges for baptisms, marriages, funerals, and even confessions.[17] Between repartimientos and limosnas, a typical Yucatec Maya household in the second half of the seventeenth century was responsible for collecting between five and eight pounds of wax per year.[18] Exact numbers are scarce, but a few documents suggest that the province's annual output in the seventeenth century was in excess of 100,000 pounds.[19] Within the province, wax was extracted exclusively by males. In the heavily gendered world of commodity extraction in colonial Yucatán, women were responsible for weaving thread and textiles, while the outfield tasks of growing cotton and gathering wax fell to men.[20]

Regional discrepancies in the availability of wax began to manifest as extraction increased in the late sixteenth and early seventeenth centuries.[21] In general, wax was in poorer supply in the northwestern part of the province than it was to the south and east. The immediate cause of this gradient was environmental: meliponine species are not uniformly distributed across the Yucatán Peninsula, and many are notoriously picky about their habitats. In particular, the larger varieties that produce the most wax usually nest only in trees with trunk diameters of at least twenty centimeters, which are scarcer in the thin soils and scrub forests of the northern and northwestern Yucatán Peninsula.[22] To the south and east, a combination of thicker soils and increased precipitation makes for larger trees and more abundant forage for bees in the form of flowering plants. There were human causes as well; the second half of the seventeenth century saw a rise in the Yucatec Maya population and a gradual increase in the number of cattle-raising estates around the province's three Spanish towns (especially the provincial capital of Mérida), leading to both deforestation and the reorientation of the regional workforce toward livestock and agriculture.[23] The combination was so potent that by 1700 most wax repartimientos in northwestern Yucatán had ceased altogether.[24]

Beginning in the late sixteenth century and accelerating in the first half of the seventeenth, wax extraction in Yucatán became heavily concentrated in the province's outlying regions to the south and east.[25] Map 3.2, derived from testimony on repartimientos collected by the bishop of Yucatán during a partial tour of the province in 1669–70, affords a glimpse of the industry's spatial distribution at the time. The features on the map represent the maximum annual beeswax repartimiento collected from 97 of the province's 275 official towns in the years between 1665 and 1669.[26] Bishop Luis de Cifuentes's tour was cut short by the rainy season, so much of the province's northern and western regions are unaccounted for. Fortunately, the report captured the province's key wax-producing areas: Sierra, Beneficios Altos, and (to a lesser extent) Tizimín.[27] Despite constituting a mere third of the province's total Yucatec Maya population, these three regions produced nearly three-quarters of the total output shown in map 3.2 (59,906 lbs. out of 78,218.75 lbs.), and likely around 60 percent of the province's annual intake of wax through repartimiento. Sierra's significant population of around thirty thousand, combined with generally available wax, made it the province's single greatest source of wax, but the southeasternmost district of Beneficios Altos also stands out. This region contained three small parishes (Peto, Ichmul, and Tihosuco) and was home to at most eight thousand Yucatec Mayas in 1670, or about 5 percent of the provincial total.[28] Yet, it was responsible for nearly a quarter of the wax shown in map 3.2. The hamlet of Tituc, far to the south, was so specialized in wax that it was exempt from all other

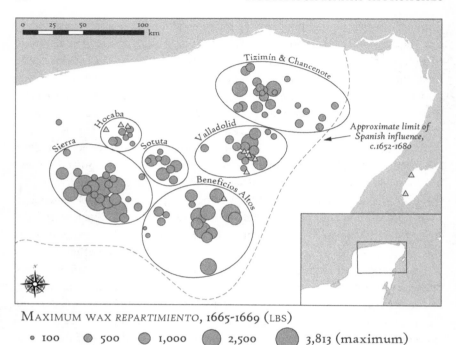

MAXIMUM WAX *REPARTIMIENTO*, 1665–1669 (LBS)

- 100   500   1,000   2,500   3,813 (maximum)

△ Towns included in visita, but no data recorded   ◯ Regions discussed in text

Map 3.2. Maximum annual wax repartimiento per town, 1665–1669, according to the Cifuentes visita; from AGI, Escribanía 318; also available in García Bernal, "La Visita de Fray Luís de Cifuentes." Some locations have been shifted by up to twelve kilometers to facilitate data visibility. (Map © G. Wallace Cartography & GIS)

repartimientos (cotton, textiles, dye, and so on); apparently, each married man in the town was instead responsible for the collection of twelve pounds of wax each year.[29] Away from Beneficios Altos, repartimientos decreased gradually toward the northwest, with the Hocabá region producing hardly any wax at all despite being one of the largest urban agglomerations in the province.

If anything, the data in map 3.2 underrepresent the proportion of wax coming from Yucatán's frontier regions, especially Sierra and Beneficios Altos. A second document—a tour by a different bishop in 1678—shows that Yucatec Mayas in northern Yucatán depended on their counterparts to the south for much of their wax, even if on paper they were the purveyors.[30]

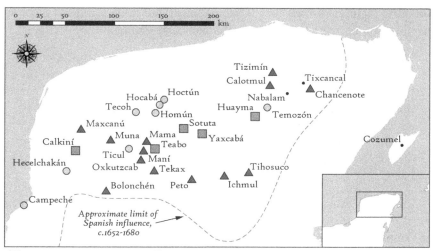

Testimony from the Escalante *visita*, 1678-1679

▲ Sufficient wax available   ◯ Insufficient wax available

▣ Sufficient wax available, but   • No information about wax
  textiles took priority   in testimony

Map 3.3. Availability of wax in Yucatán, according to testimony from the
Escalante visita, 1678–1679; AGI, Escribanía 326A, ramo 3, pieza 2, ff. 9v–66r.
(Map © G. Wallace Cartography & GIS)

Among a slew of other questions, Bishop Escalante asked witnesses whether
"the items being demanded exist in this town or region" in sufficient quantities
to meet repartimiento requirements.[31] Simplified versions of their responses on
the subject of wax—most from Yucatec Maya leaders and officials—are represented in map 3.3. This cartographical representation closely mirrors the distribution of repartimientos in map 3.2: abundant wax in the far southeast, general
availability in the Tizimín and Sierra regions, and scarcity in the northwest.
The document also adds the Camino Real region from Campeche to Max-
canú, where wax was apparently in short supply to the south but easier to
find in the north.

The testimony in Escalante's report offers a look at the wax industry's inner
workings, particularly the difficult position of towns whose local wax supplies fell short and the vital role that wax-rich regions in southern and southeastern Yucatán played in shoring them up. A number of witnesses painted

sobering pictures of their local circumstances, but none stand out quite so much as a letter from the town of Temozón, near Valladolid:

> The people have gone from the center of the forest to the shores of the sea to search for wax, and they do not find it because neither in the trees nor in the cracks in the ground nor in the hives of the land are there bees, because for having drained them so much they have died and fled from their combs and for this [reason] the wax is lacking . . . we are thinking of this day and night and we do not have time to rest or sleep because we are in the forests all the days except Sunday and Easter.[32]

There were essentially two options for people in towns like Temozón whose local wax supplies fell short. They could either buy the wax from the repartimiento contract holder at an inflated rate and sell it back at a loss (a roundabout way of forcing payment in cash while preserving the facade of commerce), or they could gather or buy wax elsewhere.[33] Judging from the testimony, "elsewhere" was Sierra and Beneficios Altos. Pedro Canche, the batab of Mamá in Sierra, told Escalante that "many indios from all of the province come to this district to search for wax, some to search for it and others to buy it," and an ecclesiastical official in the southeastern town of Peto said that "[so many] had come to the forest unto the point of killing one another for three pounds of wax . . . generally there is no wax in all of the province and generally it is [nevertheless] contracted to all of the indios so that they all come to the districts that have it."[34]

On paper, most towns in the province were responsible for procuring some amount of beeswax, but the Escalante testimony shows how much of the wax extracted from Yucatán's northwest was actually sought out or bought in the southeastern regions of Sierra and Beneficios Altos. These two regions stood head and shoulders above others in the reports, although Tizimín was also an important contributor. We shall see in the next section that these outlying regions were endpoints for widespread and complex commercial networks that brought even more wax into the province. For now, the key takeaway from the Cifuentes and Escalante reports is that much of Yucatán's wax industry was squarely in the hands of Yucatec Mayas who were as far as one could get from the centers of Spanish power without leaving the province. In these regions, Yucatec Maya refugees, commoners, elites, and merchants could take advantage of the limited Spanish presence to participate in the lucrative business of wax on their own terms.

THE TRANSFRONTIER WAX TRADE

Environmental conditions in southern and southeastern Yucatán made for better wax gathering than in the north, but those areas were not solely responsible for the commodity's availability there. A great deal of the wax flowing out of Sierra, Beneficios Altos, and other wax-rich regions was not gathered there at all but was instead hauled into the province from beyond its borders. For the first 150 years of the colonial period, overland trade routes connected Yucatec Maya towns in the Spanish province to refugee settlements in the montaña, and from there on to the independent Lacandón, Acalan, Kejach, and Itzá regions that lay between Yucatán and the Kingdom of Guatemala.[35] Salt and metal tools were the articles that most commonly left the colony, while a large number of forest and agricultural products were transported in the other direction, including cacao, annatto, dyewood, textiles, and vanilla.[36] Beeswax, however, dominated the transfrontier trade, reaching such a scale and ubiquity that one mid-seventeenth-century chronicler described the entire phenomenon as a matter of "wax and other things . . . those of this province communicate with them regularly, bringing machetes, axes, salt, and other things that they do not have there, and redeeming wax and other things they collect there. The short distance offers opportunity for this, and [so does] the indios being naturally inclined to penetrate the forests."[37]

Although archival fog obscures much of the transfrontier wax trade, the extant sources indicate that it was widespread, complex, and significant in scale during the seventeenth century. To my knowledge, the earliest specific example of wax being smuggled into the province and sold is the aforementioned arrest of Juan Chan and his fellow merchants in 1602, though Chan's story of being lured into the montaña by a different group of wax merchants suggests that the practice dated to at least the final decade of the sixteenth century.[38] The true origins of this commerce, however, likely lay in the late Postclassic Period (ca. 1200–1521 CE) when similar overland trade routes brought salt, textiles, and slaves into the southern interior of the Yucatán Peninsula in exchange for cacao, feathers, and obsidian, among other goods.[39] Conquest and colonization disrupted those trade patterns through violence, epidemics, and displacements. It also introduced new commodities and altered the economic importance of others (beeswax, for instance, was of little consequence prior to contact, and iron tools did not exist). But in the early colonial era as much as in the Postclassic, people in the northwest and southeast still each possessed things the other needed, and according to Spanish estimates, at any given time there were anywhere from twenty thousand to fifty thousand Yucatec Maya refugees living in the montaña who had access to wax and other forest products but lacked local sources of salt or iron tools.[40]

In terms of mechanics and configuration, the most commonly reported way for wax to enter Yucatán from the montaña was for male Yucatec Maya refugees to carry it in, barter it for salt and metal tools, then make the return trip. In addition to the 1602 example of Juan Chan, we know from Grant D. Jones's research that during the first half of the seventeenth century refugees from the enclave of Ixpimienta and the surrounding region (just west of present-day northern Belize) were bringing large quantities of wax into the Sierra and Camino Real regions, passing through the borderland town of Hopelchén along the way.[41] Jones also found evidence of a group of wax merchants being arrested in Chancenote in 1624, indicating the presence of another route in the northeast of the province.[42]

Yucatec Maya refugees did not always have to risk entering Spanish-controlled regions to sell wax, as many Mayas from colonial towns made the trip to the montaña themselves. Seven men from Hecelchakán journeyed to Ixpimienta in 1620, for example, bearing hatchets, machetes, knives, and salt and coming back with seventy-five pounds of wax.[43] Yucatán's bishop complained to the Crown about Yucatec Maya wax hunters engaging in similar activities around Bacalar in 1643.[44] At times, a Yucatec Maya batab would dispatch salt- and tool-bearing merchants from inside the colony. In 1663 Diego de la Cámara, the batab of Oxkutzcab, sent a merchant with several mules south toward La Pimienta with the explicit goal of trading machetes and axes for wax, a trip that was apparently not the merchant's first.[45] Cámara's intent in dispatching the trader was mostly likely to accumulate wax that he could then resell to other Yucatec Mayas in Oxkutzcab, or to wax-hunting parties coming to Sierra from elsewhere in Yucatán. The batab of Teabo, Pedro Couoh, alluded to this practice in 1678 when he told Bishop Escalante that "those who lack [wax] have to pay [for it] between the caciques, magistrates, and commissioners."[46]

There were undoubtedly other configurations and participants not well captured in the archives. There is, for example, trace evidence of Spaniards becoming involved. Juan Chan and his four companions reportedly sold wax to multiple Spaniards, including Chan's former employer, a Spanish agent for the royal treasury named Antón Julián. Another record from the Camino Real region describes a Spaniard named Francisco de Magaña entering the montaña to trade directly with fugitives.[47] Some Afro-Yucatecans may also have become involved in the transfrontier wax trade. Matthew Restall has shown very clearly that enslaved and free members of Yucatán's "black middle" served ubiquitously as commercial agents and managers for Spaniards in the collection of goods, including wax, from outlying Maya towns.[48] (A mulatto exservant ran wax collection for repartimientos in Calkiní during the 1660s, for example.)[49] These positions would have placed many Afro-Yucatecans in closer proximity to the frontier than the mostly urban-dwelling Spanish population was, but besides a chance encounter between a mulatto ranch foreman in Hopelchén and six merchants from La Pimienta in 1622 (in which no transaction took place), the archive is completely silent on the subject.[50]

The extent of participation by non-Yucatec Mayas is also unclear. The documentary record in Yucatán generally does not discriminate between Maya-speaking ethnic groups in the borderlands, settling instead for generic pejoratives like *indios montaraces, infieles,* or even *caribes.* In all cases wherein witnesses or prisoners were explicitly asked about their origins, they claimed to have come from Yucatec Maya towns within the province. The two independent groups most likely to have traded in wax were Chontales in the Acalan region and Kejaches farther to the east, whose territory brought them into frequent (and often violent) contact with both colonial and refugee Yucatec Mayas.[51] While the Acalan Chontales are thought to have been displaced or assimilated by Yucatec refugees by the early seventeenth century, there is evidence of Kejach communities having access to iron tools, which they traded on to the Itzá on occasion.[52] However, I have yet to find any specific examples of these or other nearby groups such as the Lacandón, Chol, or Itzá Mayas directly participating in the contraband wax trade.[53] We cannot presume that they never did, but most of the information other scholars have unearthed on commerce in the southern lowlands points to cacao, annatto, and vanilla as the articles of choice in that region.[54] Given the balance of evidence and the region's political and territorial configuration at the time, I strongly suspect that provincial and refugee Yucatec Mayas were responsible for the overwhelming majority of contraband wax trade, while independent groups farther to the south used them as intermediaries.

A scant few sources speak to the quantities of wax involved. In 1669 the Franciscan guardian of Sahcabchén—discussed in greater detail later—complained that during five months of tumult, more than a hundred fanegas (ca. 5,000 kg) of salt were spirited into the forest in exchange for wax and little else.[55] It is unclear how much wax a hundred fanegas of salt could fetch (and the friar might well have been exaggerating), but the notion of the transfrontier economy of a single small district absorbing several tons of salt in just a few months speaks volumes to the trade's potential scale in Sahcab-chén and elsewhere. Furthermore, to cull a few anecdotes from Francisco de Mirones's journal that Jones also highlighted, a Yucatec Maya man from Ticul told Mirones in 1623 that he was offered "all the wax he wanted" by two mer-chants from La Pimienta whom he had encountered near Hopelchén. In addi-tion, the batab of Hopelchén told Mirones that he had seen three men go to Ixpimienta with loads of salt and blue yarn and each came back with what appeared to be "four *arrobas* [of wax] melted into molds," or about three hun-dred pounds total.[56] They were offered more but were limited by what they could carry. Thus, without horses or mules, these three men had crossed the frontier and returned from La Pimienta with enough wax for a small town's annual repartimiento.[57] La Pimienta's capacity and reputation for wax com-merce was apparently undimmed forty years later; the merchant from Oxkutzcab who led his mules into La Pimienta in 1663 and several times prior would not have repeatedly made such a long journey (some two hundred kilo-meters as the crow flies) without anticipating a well-laden return trip.[58]

The amount and value of the wax flowing into Yucatán caused no small measure of conflict among some of its participants. This commerce was not a free-for-all, and reports of violence surrounding the gathering of wax were not unusual.[59] Although Yucatec Mayas throughout the province and in the borderlands were united by language and custom, there was little political unity beyond the frail *pax hispanica* imposed by conquest (and whatever sway this had did not extend into the montaña). Communities, and especially Maya elites, were fiercely protective of their territory and the economic activity therein. On one occasion, for instance, the council of a Yucatec Maya town along the camino real sought to protect its hinterland from encroachment by a Spaniard by denouncing him to the governor for purchasing wax in the montaña. The council's action and their assumption that the governor would take action shows how, in Matthew Restall's words, "not only were Spaniards worried about the black market, but Maya *cabildos* were well aware of that concern and tried to exploit it in their own interests."[60]

Spaniards were not the only ones being shut out of the business. There are several cases of indigenous elites using their political power to keep other Yucatec Mayas out as well. When Juan Chan and his fellow merchants were arrested near Campeche in 1602, it was not a Spaniard but rather Pablo Coy, the batab of Chiná, who promptly brought them before the nearest magistrate and specifically accused them of contraband trade.[61] Moreover, in 1663, when the merchant dispatched from Oxkutzcab by batab Diego de la Cámara came upon a group of refugees from the same town living in the montaña, the batab's response was to dispatch a raiding party that hunted them down, arrested them, and returned them in chains to Oxkutzcab, where they were jailed and their property (which included balls of beeswax) seized.[62] While their motives remain unstated, in both cases the batab's action had the effect of protecting his own interests as they pertained to wax. As explained earlier, elites like Pablo Coy and Diego de la Cámara had their own ways of profiting from the wax business, chiefly by collecting stockpiles that they could sell to their townspeople for repartimiento payments or to wax expeditions from farther afield. Interlopers like Juan Chan, who peddled wax to anyone with a spare machete or handful of salt (or to cash-bearing Spaniards), were a threat in this sense. For Diego de la Cámara, meanwhile, his objection was likely that the fugitives were from his own town; by both fleeing *and* selling their own wax, they were undercutting his authority over town and country, not to mention depriving him of customers.

From Sahcabchén to Chancenote, there were refugees entering the colony to sell wax, provincial Yucatec Mayas leaving the colony to buy it or to become merchants in their own right, Spaniards entering the borderlands to trade for it directly, and batabo'ob dispatching middlemen to secure it. Jones's impression was that this illicit trade gave Yucatec refugees and independent groups in the southeastern Yucatán Peninsula a means to access the global economy, but the additional sources and geospatial data explored in this chapter indicate that its historical significance in the northern lowlands was greater still. The broadened reach to the south and east afforded by trade dramatically increased the amount of wax that flowed through Yucatán's frontier areas. The impact can be seen not only in the general spatial distribution of repartimientos, which heavily favored the south and east, but also in the different ways in which many Yucatec Mayas on either side of the frontier took advantage of the trade and protected their own interests within it. Spaniards, who did little more than pocket and export the wax, stood at the extreme end of a complex system of ecology, politics, and trade largely built and controlled by Maya hands.

BEESWAX AND THE SAHCABCHÉN UPRISING, 1668–1671

Beeswax emerged as the foremost concern during an uprising in Sahcabchén from 1668 to 1671, when some twelve thousand Yucatec Mayas deserted the region between Champotón and Laguna de Terminos and fled east into the montaña. To be sure, there were a multitude of direct and indirect causes for the uprising: the 1640s and 1650s had been terrible years for most of Yucatán, bringing with them a catastrophic yellow fever epidemic, a smallpox outbreak, a two-year famine, a multiyear drought, and two hurricanes.[63] To make matters worse, the colony's governor in the late 1660s, Rodrigo Flores de Aldana, dramatically increased repartimiento requirements when he came to power, placing recovering Yucatec Maya communities throughout the province under further strain.[64] Additionally, with rising tensions along the frontier and repeatedly unanswered pirate raids along the west coast came generalized anti-Spanish sentiment, particularly in Sahcabchén where refugee groups to the east used a combination of recruitment, prophecy, and threats to encourage provincial Yucatec Mayas to flee into the montaña.[65]

There is sufficient evidence to support all of the above as possible causes, but in much of the documentation, beeswax stands out as first among equals. A flurry of communications crisscrossed Sahcabchén's frontier as both secular and religious authorities sought to return the absconded Yucatec Mayas, among which were several letters from the batabo'ob and leadership of newly independent towns. The communiqués contained reasons for their flight, petitions for better terms in exchange for their resettlement, or even outright refusals to reenter Spanish jurisdiction. They tended to blame some combination of repartimientos, limosnas, violence, and forced labor for the uprising, but requirements for supplying wax figured most prominently. In a 1670 letter to the governor, for example, the batabo'ob of three newly independent towns blamed a combination of violence, forced labor, and wax repartimientos (specifically) for their flight:

> Many are the reasons that we left our pueblos. The first was for the entrance of the enemy into it twice and for [their] having taken and destroyed our livelihoods, and with this the outrages and collections put upon us, because the wax that each one [of us] accommodated was fifteen pounds and the total of it all was forty-eight arrobas [1,200 lbs/545 kg]. And this quantity they paid us in repartimiento every two months without ever charging us less. And this was three times per year, which caused us to bargain away our clothes and as much as we had, because the judges forced us [to do] it with whippings and jail . . . they also took us and our wives to the dyewood ranchos to serve the Spaniards, where we did much labor.[66]

A similar letter from the town of Sayab blamed repartimientos, limosnas, and tributes, but the annual repartimiento of twelve pounds of wax per person and various wax limosnas totaling four-and-a-half pounds per year were singled out firstly and in the most detail:

> Sir, it has been a long time since we left our town because of the harm we received from the judges of your repartimientos, who gave us money for wax and it came to twelve pounds of wax for each man paid at a real per pound . . . to pay for it we bought it at two reales per pound. And a pound of cochineal to each man and [for] he who did not have it at the time of payment it cost twelve reales per pound to pay that which was demanded, or four pounds of wax for it. . . .
>
> . . . And to this we add the limosna of the friars. In the festival of our pueblo each married man gives two pounds of wax and on All Saints Day another two pounds of wax and a real of candles, and half a pound of wax for the *monumento* [memorial].
>
> . . . Sir, the judges, encomenderos, and guardians are doing us great harm . . . it has been twenty-five years that we have been in this montaña and for others twelve years since they arrived . . . and we are happy to be in our pueblo. And this is the truth . . . here, sir, we write that which we wish to do, and we do it willingly. About this we shall say no more.[67]

Other letters follow a similar pattern of singling out wax amidst lists of burdensome repartimientos, limosnas, tributes, and forced labor.[68] No written communication, however, delivered this sentiment as effectively as one of the opening events of the Sahcabchén revolt. In 1668, before they fled into the forests to the east, the population of Dzacabuchén—the district's most important town and only Spanish outpost—destroyed the house of the official in charge of repartimientos and the chandlery where wax was processed. The Franciscan who reported the uprising made no other mention of property destruction in his letter, suggesting that every other edifice in the town was spared.[69] This targeted action and the continued emphasis on wax during the revolt was hardly surprising considering the amount of it being extracted from Sahcabchén in the 1660s compared to other parts of Yucatán. The highest recorded wax repartimiento in the Cifuentes visita—which covered the same time period as the Sahcabchén uprising—was twelve pounds per tributary, reported by the town of Tituc.[70] Unlike Tituc, which was exempt from all other repartimientos, Sahcabchén's denizens still faced additional requirements for small amounts of textiles and cochineal.[71] Meanwhile, the batabo'ob of Ychtok, Tanlum, and Kukuitz in Sahcabchén stated that their annual wax repartimiento was fifteen pounds per tributary, and in Sayab it was twelve. One 1670 letter from the town of Titub set forth the shockingly high figure of one arroba (25 lbs/11.3 kg) per tributary, the highest such figure I have ever come across.[72]

Just how much of Sahcabchén's wax repartimientos and limosnas were being supplied by transfrontier commerce is unclear, but it was probably a substantial amount. There is evidence of significant commerce between encomienda towns and independent regions south and east of Campeche as early as 1602, when Juan Chan and his fellow merchants were captured. Wax traders and wax hunters were apparently so common that, in 1604, a Franciscan relied on them to serve as letter couriers between the Franciscan order and independent Yucatec and Kejach settlements in the montaña.[73] During the Sahcabchén revolt proper, one of the first actions by refugees living in the forests to the east was to begin smuggling wax back into the province, dispatching people and horses loaded with wax into the *cabecera* (administrative center) of Dzacabuchén and other encomienda towns beyond to trade with Mayas who had elected to stay behind.[74] According to the previously mentioned 1669 letter from Sahcabchén's Franciscan guardian, the volume of trade was immense. He wrote that in just five months "more than a hundred fanegas [about 5,000 kg] of salt have left from here into the forest, not including that which [already] leaves the towns of this district: soap, axes, and other things without number."[75]

The Sahcabchén case highlights the complex relationship between Spanish demands for wax (extracted through repartimientos and limosnas), Maya resistance and flight, and the push-pull dynamic the commodity created along the frontier. The region was clearly rich in beeswax compared to nearly every other part of the province, and Spaniards, both secular and religious, sought to capitalize on the commodity's abundance along Yucatán's southwestern frontier. Like elsewhere in the northern lowlands, however, that demand fostered an active clandestine trade in beeswax between the provincial towns and their independent neighbors, whether Yucatec Mayas or other groups. Then, in 1668, a rebellion sparked at least in part by large repartimientos and limosnas for beeswax saw thousands of Mayas from Sahcabchén flee into the forest. To sustain connections with the Mesoamerican economy that provided both metal tools (which were immensely useful) and salt (which was necessary) many of them turned to an activity they knew firsthand to be profitable— the smuggling of beeswax back into the very region they had just fled.

In this case, even some Spaniards apparently came to realize the contradiction. When the dust began to settle after the Sahcabchén revolt and some fugitive Mayas began negotiating for peaceful relationships with the Crown, one of the conditions for peace proposed by Francisco de Escobedo (the new governor) in 1671 was that "you must open a road so that commerce can be had with [Mayas who want to remain in the forest] and so that the indios can go from all of this province to cut wax and so that they are not impeded, and that [those who remain in the forest] can come down to sell their wax without impediment. And, as well, they must trade and communicate like *indios poblados*."[76] In other words, the governor understood that the Spanish province could not have it both ways and—to his mind, at least—that the smuggling of wax was a necessary evil. Spanish judges, priests, and friars could not squeeze borderland districts like Sahcabchén for large amounts of wax while simultaneously trying to stamp out the independent enclaves that supplied a substantial amount of it. Demanding more wax risked driving even more Mayas out of the province to pursue better opportunities and autonomy, and invading the montaña was not only a waste of time and resources (an attempted invasion of Sahcabchén's hinterland to round up fugitives in 1668–69 was a fiasco), but it would also jeopardize a key supply line for the most lucrative industry in Sahcabchén. Escobedo thus offered a compromise in the hope that if there had to be trade it could at least be on open and familiar terms: conducted over roads, available to Mayas from elsewhere in the province, and done in the manner of "indios poblados," whatever that entailed.

Several batabo'ob accepted Escobedo's offer to resettle in exchange for a reduction and delay in tribute, but other towns (like Tzuctok and Sayab) remained in the montaña.[77] While the Franciscans gained access to some of these settlements, there is no indication of roads being built or of formal trade opening in the years immediately after 1671. Yucatec Mayas who lived along the province's margins were keenly aware that, in this matter at least, they held the advantage. Some of Sahcabchén's independent towns made this commanding position clear during negotiations with the governor and the Franciscan order in 1670–71, including six batabo'ob who wrote quite unambiguously that "if they introduce to us labor or repartimientos of wax or cochineal or other [goods], we will have to totally depopulate and will go back again."[78]

Pedro Bracamonte y Sosa mused in 2001 that "there were many different ways for the [Mayas] of the montaña to exercise great influence in the province of Yucatán, especially at the end of the sixteenth century and throughout the seventeenth."[79] A large clandestine or semi-clandestine wax economy that funneled the melted-down nests of wild honeybees from unconquered borderland and independent regions into Yucatán could have been chief among them. There were thousands of Yucatec Maya refugees living in the Yucatán Peninsula's wax-rich borderlands along with independent Maya groups such as the Kejach, Chontal, Lacandón, and Itzá during the seventeenth century, all of whom desired metal tools and required salt. As a result, numerous provincial and refugee Yucatec Mayas entered the profitable business of wax commerce, whether as buyers, sellers, smugglers, or gatherers. The spatial distribution of seventeenth-century wax repartimientos, the presence of wax in acts of resistance along the frontier, the geographic spread of the documentary evidence on transfrontier trade, and the broad socioeconomic cross section of people involved in it behoove us to consider the significance of wax, both to the that industry proper and to the wider history of the northern Maya lowlands.

For Spaniards, the transfrontier wax trade was a double-edged sword, though they usually did not acknowledge it as such. On one hand, it greatly increased the total area from which Spaniards could obtain wax, however indirectly. Towns in outlying districts such as Sierra, Beneficios Altos, Sahcabchén, and Tizimín could rely on trade to sustain higher repartimientos and limosnas than would have been possible had they relied only on their own territory. On the other hand, the very existence of a lucrative trade in wax made flight across the frontier a much more viable option for Mayas in the same districts. Thus, the Spaniards were placed (or, rather, placed themselves) in the bizarre position of relying on and buttressing the position of fugitive Mayas, a disliked and worrisome entity that one chronicler called a "multitude of barbarian indios, infidels, idolators, and apostates—flesh-eating wolves in human form."[80]

For Yucatec Mayas, meanwhile, the wax trade they had created often offered significant opportunities. In addition to making flight a more viable option, the transfrontier wax trade was a boon for provincial batabo'ob who could afford to hire their own merchants. Using their access to cash and labor to their advantage, they could secure personal stashes of wax to resell to their own townspeople or to Mayas traveling from farther afield in search of wax they could not find at home. For other communities the wax trade afforded significant political leverage. Governor Escobedo admitted exactly that in 1671 when he passively agreed to allow several of Sahcabchén's newly independent communities to remain in the forest, offering to more or less leave them alone so long as they continued to trade in wax and allowed Mayas from elsewhere to enter their territory to harvest or buy it. With that being said, we should not be fooled into thinking that beeswax was universally useful and lucrative to all Yucatec Mayas everywhere. The potential it afforded for commercial gain and autonomy was precisely what led many communities and elites to act decisively—at times violently—to protect their markets and territory from Spaniards and rival Mayas alike. It is also worth bearing in mind that no matter what was happening to the south, the task of trekking to Sierra and beyond for wax remained a burden for Yucatec Mayas in northwest Yucatán.

With regard to indigenous borderlands in the colonial Americas, beeswax offers a case study of natural product extraction in spaces that were beyond European control but still subject to the ripple effects of contact, conquest, colonization, and rise of capitalist economies in Latin America. Beeswax extraction in Yucatán was a complex chain of gathering, commerce, and export in which the Spaniards controlled only the latter. The rest was an entirely Maya affair, wrapped up in local politics and economics and stretching far into the unconquered south, where it was integrated into indigenous landscapes and trade patterns. The long reach of Maya trade certainly benefited the bottom lines of repartimiento contract holders and the priests collecting a pound of wax for each baptism. However, wax was also mobilized to serve indigenous interests as a source of salt, tools, income, or political leverage. To continue the theme of contradiction that has run through this chapter, the history of wax in the seventeenth-century northern Maya lowlands shows on one hand just how far the ramifications of colonization could extend, but on the other how in certain contexts of indigenous resistance and innovation the tendrils of empire could be blunted or twisted into opportunities.

NOTES

1. For further information on Sánchez Cerdán and his attempts to conquer the independent regions east of Campeche in the late sixteenth and early seventeenth centuries, see: Chuchiak, "'Fide, Non Armis'"; Bracamonte y Sosa, *La conquista inconclusa*.

2. Archivo General de Indias (AGI), México 130, ff. 84r–91v. This document has also been transcribed and published in Solís Robleda and Peniche, *Documentos*, 12–18.

3. It was common for Yucatec Maya orphans (defined in the Spanish sense as any child who had lost both parents) to be sent to Spanish households in the cities to be "cared for." According to Farriss this care was, in reality, a form of servitude, explaining why Juan Chan would have described his vocation in Mérida after being orphaned as "servant." Farriss, *Maya Society*, 171.

4. AGI, México 130, f. 84v.

5. AGI, México 130, f. 85r.

6. Robert Patch, for example, went to great lengths in *Maya and Spaniard* to calculate the outsized role of beeswax in Yucatán's economy as an export commodity and a source of wealth for individual Spaniards through the repartimiento system in the late seventeenth and early eighteenth centuries. See Patch, *Maya and Spaniard*, 81–89; Patch, "(Almost) Forgotten Plants of Yucatán," 565. Mentions of wax and meliponiculture are also found here and there in works by Nancy Farriss, Manuela Cristina García-Bernal, and Matthew Restall.

7. Jones, *Maya Resistance to Spanish Rule*, 244.

8. Dean, *With Broadax and Firebrand*, 45–50; Richards, *Unending Frontier*, 482–86; Kates, "Persistence of Maya Autonomy."

9. For information on the wax industry's decline, see Patch, *Maya and Spaniard*, 159.

10. Prior to the early twentieth century, beeswax was required for papal and episcopal processions, Candlemas, paschal candles, and baptisms. *Missale Romanum* (1570); Brand, "Honey Bee in New Spain and Mexico"; Crane, *World History of Beekeeping*; Newson, "Piety, Beeswax," 6. Newson points out that Yucatecan wax made it at least as far south as Peru. While it is possible that some beeswax candles were used in New Spain's mining industry, I have not come across any evidence to that effect. An expensive material, beeswax was unlikely to have been used in place of tallow in such a context.

11. Żrałka et al., "Discovery of a Beehive"; Wallace, "Strange Case of the Panucho Plugs."

12. These are the *sak xik'* (*Trigona nigra nigra*), *kantsac* (*Scaptotrigona pectoralis*), *e'ho'ol/taj ka'ab* (*Cephalotrigona zexmeniae*), *tzetz* (*Melipona yucatanica*, exceedingly rare), *kuris ka'ab* (*Trigona fuscipennis*), and *niit kib* (*Lestrimelitta niitkib*); González-Acereto, "La importancia de la meliponicultura," 38; Terán and Rasmussen, *La milpa de los mayas*, 12; Quezada Euán, *Biología y uso de las abejas*, 25–43.

13. Quezada Euán, *Biología y uso de las abejas*, 15–20; Yurrita, Ortega-Huerta, and Ayala, "Distributional Analysis of Melipona," 248; Ayala, "Revisión de las abejas.".

14. See Wallace, "History and Geography of Beeswax Extraction."

15. García Bernal, "El gobernador de Yucatán," 163; Baskes, *Indians, Merchants, and Markets*, 35, 37; Patch, *Maya and Spaniard*, 85–86; Patch, *Indians and the Political Economy*, 82–83, 111–12.

16. These figures were calculated using documentary records of repartimientos in which both a town's approximate population and annual wax quota could be determined. The most thorough example is a Franciscan report on repartimientos from 1700 in the AGI that was normalized using a census from the same year: AGI, México 1035, ff. 6–11, 676–731. Another data run was derived from wax quotas between 1665 and 1669 that were recorded in a 1669 visita, normalized with an incomplete census from 1666; AGI, Escribanía 318A, cuad. 13; García Bernal, "El gobernador de Yucatán," 240–60; García Bernal, *Población y encomienda*, 102–6.

17. AGI, México 369, ramo 5, ff. 1039r–73r; Quezada, "Tributos, limosnas, y mantas"; Quezada, *Maya Lords and Lordship*, 51; Farriss, *Maya Society*, 325.

18. This is a rough average; some parts of Yucatán, especially the far northwest, were entirely exempt from wax repartimientos by 1700. Households in the southwestern and southeastern corners of the colony, meanwhile, had to collect upwards of ten pounds per year. The five- to eight-pound figure is representative of almost everywhere else, however, including the regions of Valladolid, Sierra, Tizimín, Chancenote, and Camino Real.

19. According to tribute records from 1549, Spanish encomenderos and the Crown could apparently expect an annual rendition of 60,950 pounds (27,646 kg) of wax from Maya towns; Paso y Troncoso, *Epistolario*, 5:103–81. Between 1664 and 1669 Rodrigo Flores de Aldana, the governor of Yucatán, purchased 196,655 pounds (89,201 kg)—almost 40,000 pounds per year—from Mayas in just three of the colony's eight districts, most of which was shipped to Central Mexico; AGI, México 369. See also García Bernal, "Visita de fray Luis de Cifuentes," 247. Another governor, Antonio de Cortaire, collected 39,825 pounds (18,064 kg) every six months, and the export of wax to Central Mexico that he oversaw in 1720–21 totaled 163,125 pounds (73,992 kg); Patch, *Maya and Spaniard*, 89. Given that these all represent mere portions of the provincial total and do not include wax collected through ecclesiastical fees and limosnas, a general estimate of more than 100,000 pounds per annum appears appropriate.

20. Patch, *Maya and Spaniard*, 27; Farriss, *Maya Society*, 39; Clendinnen, "Yucatec Maya Women," 432, 437.

21. The practice of long-distance wax expeditions emerged in the 1560s and continued to grow into the seventeenth century. Scholes and Adams, *Don Diego Quijada*, 2:124–25; Landa, *Relación*, 125–26; AGI, Indiferente 1530, no. 17.

22. No thorough surveys of wild stingless bee nesting characteristics have been conducted in the northern Maya lowlands, but according to surveys of species done in Panama and Costa Rica of species common to both those countries and the Yucatán Peninsula, a trunk DBH (diameter at breast height) of twenty centimeters is the bare minimum for most tree-dwelling species. Van Veen and Arce, "Nest and Colony Characteristics"; May-Itzá et al., "Morphometric and Genetic Differentiation"; Roubik, "Nest and Colony Characteristics."

23. Hunt, "Processes of the Development of Yucatan," 51, 55–59; Patch, *Maya and Spaniard*, 107–22; García Bernal, "Desarrollos indígena y ganadero en Yucatán," 377–81.

24. AGI, México 1035, ff. 676–731.

25. This is judged by the increased incidence of transfrontier trade and the emergence of long-distance wax-gathering expeditions, as well as passing remarks in the archives attesting to the poor availability of wax in the north compared to the south and east. See, for example, AGI, Indiferente 2987, articles 14 and 17; AGI, Indiferente 1530, exp. 17; Scholes and Adams, *Don Diego Quijada*, 1:124–25; Landa, *Relación*, 125–26.

26. AGI, Escribanía 318 passim, especially 318A, cuad. 13; AGI, México 369B, ramo 4, ff. 709r–712v. See also García Bernal, "El gobernador de Yucatán," 240–60.

27. These regions, and those delineated in map 3.2, are based on the *partidos* [districts] into which the province of Yucatán was divided in the eighteenth century.

They also correspond to major population groupings and regional trends of politics, environment, and production. See Wallace, "History and Geography of Beeswax Extraction."

28. Gerhard, *Southeast Frontier*, 62.

29. AGI, Contaduría 920, exps. 1 and 2; García Bernal, "El gobernador de Yucatán," 168.

30. AGI, Escribanía 326A, ramo 3, pieza 2, ff. 6v–66r.

31. AGI, Escribanía 326A, ramo 3, pieza 2, f. 5v.

32. AGI, Escribanía 326A, ramo 3, pieza 2, f. 68v. All translations by Geoffrey Wallace.

33. For details on the conversion of wax to cash, see Patch, *Maya and Spaniard*, 88.

34. AGI, Escribanía 326A, ramo 3, pieza 2, ff. 57v, 51v. *Batab* (*batabo'ob* plural) is a Yucatec Maya term denoting a head of town government, synonymous with the Spanish terms *cacique* or *cacique gobernador* as they were used in colonial Yucatán.

35. The Spanish invasion and conquest of Tah-Itzá in 1697 dramatically altered the structure and volume of regional commerce by effectively destroying one of its largest participants and increasing the Spanish presence throughout the lowland border areas.

36. A by no means exhaustive list of historical and archaeological research detailing or touching on transfrontier trade in the northern lowlands includes Roys, *Political Geography*; Scholes and Roys, *Maya Chontal Indians*; Oland, "Long-Term Indigenous History"; Morandi, "Xibun Maya"; Awe and Helmke, "Sword and the Olive Jar"; Pugh, "Maya Sacred Landscapes at Contact"; Oland and Palka, "Perduring Maya"; Farriss, *Maya Society*; Jones, *Maya Resistance to Spanish Rule*; Bracamonte y Sosa, *La conquista inconclusa*.

37. López de Cogolludo, *Historia de Yucatán*, book 8, chap. 9, 444.

38. AGI, México 130, ff. 84r–91v.

39. Scholes and Roys, *Maya Chontal Indians*, 316–17; Chase and Chase, "Postclassic Temporal and Spatial Frames"; Freidel, "Terminal Classic Lowland Maya"; McKillop, "Development of Coastal Maya Trade"; Patch, *Maya and Spaniard*, 18–20; Kepecs, "Native Yucatán and Spanish Influence"; McKillop, *Salt*; Kepecs, "Mayas, Spaniards, and Salt"; Ardren et al., "Connections beyond Chunchucmil."

40. Jones, "Agriculture and Trade"; Farriss, *Maya Society*, 18; Jones, *Maya Resistance to Spanish Rule*, 157; Bracamonte y Sosa, *La conquista inconclusa*, 347.

41. Jones, *Maya Resistance to Spanish Rule*, 164–70. See also "Diary of Captain Francisco de Mirones" in Scholes and Adams, *Documents Relating to the Mirones Expedition*.

42. Jones, *Maya Resistance to Spanish Rule*, 186. See also "Comisión al capitán Guillen Peraza de Ayala," AGI, México 925.

43. Scholes and Adams, *Documents Relating to the Mirones Expedition*, 20.

44. AGI, México 369, f. 537v.

45. AGI, México 909, ff. 1486v–1537r; also described in Jones, *Maya Resistance to Spanish Rule*, 242–45.

46. AGI, Escribanía 326A, ramo 2, pieza 1, f. 56v.

47. AGN, Civil 2013, cuad. 1, ff. 4r–5v; see also Restall, *Maya Conquistador*, 175; Restall, *Maya World*, 186.

48. Restall, *Black Middle*, 67, 114, 129, 139.

49. Restall, *Black Middle*, 129.

50. Scholes and Adams, *Documents Relating to the Mirones Expedition*, 21–22.

51. Bracamonte y Sosa, *La conquista inconclusa*, 30–31; Scholes and Roys, *Maya Chontal Indians*.

52. Scholes and Roys, *Maya Chontal Indians*, 69–70; Bracamonte y Sosa, *La conquista inconclusa*, 74.

53. Scholes and Roys, *Maya Chontal Indians*, 69–70.

54. Jones, "Agriculture and Trade"; Caso Barrera and Aliphat Fernández, "Cacao, Vanilla, and Annatto."

55. AGI, México 307, ff. 6r–6v; reproduced in Solís Robleda and Peniche, *Documentos*, 1:82.

56. Scholes and Adams, *Documents Relating to the Mirones Expedition*, 19, 21.

57. About a third of the towns included in the Cifuentes visita, for instance, owed three hundred pounds or less in any given year between 1665 and 1669.

58. Scholes and Adams, *Documents Relating to the Mirones Expedition*, 21.

59. Scholes and Roys uncovered frequent references to wax-gathering parties from the north being attacked or waylaid when they entered the montaña, for instance; see Scholes and Roys, *Maya Chontal Indians*, 228, 234, 404. In Beneficios Altos, one Franciscan in Peto reported having served as a priest to a man who "was hanged because he killed two others to rob them of their wax." AGI, Escribanía 326A, ramo 3, pieza 2, f. 51v.

60. Restall, *Maya World*, 186. See also AGN, Civil 2013, ramo 1, ff. 4–5; Restall, *Maya Conquistador*, 175.

61. AGI, México 130, ff. 84r–91v.

62. AGI, México 909, ff. 1486v–1537r.

63. Campos Goenaga, "Sobre Tempestades"; Patch, *Maya and Spaniard*; Whitmore, "Population Geography of Calamity"; Solís, *La vida en Yucatán*; Mendoza et al., "Frequency and Duration of Historical Droughts"; Cook and Borah, *Essays in Population History*.

64. See García Bernal, "El gobernador de Yucatán"; Alexander, "Isla Cilvituk."

65. Alexander, "Isla Cilvituk," 176; Bracamonte y Sosa, *La conquista inconclusa*, 253–61.

66. AGI, México 307, ff. 75v–81v. Also available in Solís Robleda and Peniche, *Documentos*, 128–29. "The entrance of the enemy" probably referred to raids by refugees, free Mayas (perhaps Kejaches), or pirates.

67. AGI, México 307, ff. 34v–35v. The letter uses the term *monumento*, presumably referring to the feast day of the local or parish saint.

68. See, for example, AGI, México 307, ff. 33r–34v; AGI, Escribanía 308A, cuad. 10 ff. 24v–31r; AGI, Escribanía 318A, ff. 420r–420v. See also Solís Robleda and Peniche, *Documentos*, 108–10, 142–44.

69. AGI, Escribanía 318A, cuad. 13, ff. 409r–410v. See also García Bernal, "El gobernador de Yucatán," 184.

70. AGI, Contaduría 920, exps. 1 and 2; García Bernal, *Población y encomienda*, table 4, pp. 102–6; García Bernal, "El gobernador de Yucatán," 168.

71. Wax was overwhelmingly the commodity of choice for repartimientos and limosnas in Sahcabchén. The few sources that bring up the subject of textiles in the region hint at an annual extraction of 1.5 *paties* (a length of thin cotton cloth that was a universal commodity in repartimientos) per married female. There are few comparable data points for this figure, but from the few single-town encomienda population figures available in the 1666 census, it appears that the average textile repartimiento was some 2.4 paties; AGI, Contaduría 920, exps. 1 and 2; AGI, Escribanía 318A; García Bernal, *Población y encomienda*, table 4, pp. 102–6; García Bernal, "El gobernador de Yucatán," 168. In 1700 the average pati repartimiento was closer to 2 per married female; AGI, México 1035, ff. 6–11, 676–731. Thus, while repartimientos for paties were slightly below average in Sahcabchén, those for wax were among the highest in the province, if not the highest.

72. AGI, México 307, ff. 33r–34v.

73. AGI, México 138, ff. 27v–32r. See also Bracamonte y Sosa, *La conquista inconclusa*, 95.

74. AGI, México 307, ff. 6r–6v. Also described in Bracamonte y Sosa, *La conquista inconclusa*, 278–79.

75. AGI, México 307, ff. 6r–6v.

76. AGI, Escribanía 308A, cuad. 10, ff. 28v–31r.

77. García Bernal, "El gobernador de Yucatán"; García Bernal, "Visita de Fray Luis de Cifuentes"; Bracamonte y Sosa, *La conquista inconclusa*, 293, 316, 325.

78. AGI, Escribanía 308A, cuad.10, ff. 28v–31r. See also AGI, México 307, ff. 33r–34v. Some thirty years later, the town of Dzibalchén, south of Hopelchén, successfully rejected repartimientos with a similar ultimatum; see AGI, México 1035, f. 718r; Patch, *Maya and Spaniard*, 92.

79. Bracamonte y Sosa, *La conquista inconclusa*, 15.

80. Villagutierre Sotomayor, *Conquest of the Province of the Itza*, 96–97.

PART II

Indigenous Power and Charismatic Leadership

CHAPTER 4

When Giants Walked the Earth

CHIEF TASCALUSA, HERNANDO DE SOTO, AND THE PRECOLONIAL MISSISSIPPIAN BORDERLANDS OF THE SIXTEENTH-CENTURY US SOUTH

Robbie Ethridge

He was a giant." So wrote Luys Hernández de Biedma, factor on the expedition of Hernando de Soto, describing the sixteenth-century Indian leader Tascalusa.[1] Other Spanish eyewitnesses concurred, one remarking that Tascalusa "was a man, very tall of body, large limbed, lean, and well built."[2] Another compared him to a famously large guard of the Spanish emperor and also remarked that Tascalusa was of "very good proportions, a very well-built and noble man."[3] A fourth account elaborated that Tascalusa "towered over all the others by more than a vara [yard, or roughly a meter] and appeared to be a giant, or was one."[4] Tascalusa was *mico* (principal chief) of the province of Tascalusa, a large Indian polity in present-day central Alabama in the US South.[5] He was not only of great physical stature, but also of great social and political stature, a giant of a man and a giant of a leader. This essay explores what Chief Tascalusa can tell us about Indian leadership of the ancient US South before and right at the time of European contact, and about how Indian leaders, from their initial encounters, manipulated, negotiated, and resisted the European invasion.

Recent scholarship on the Americas has made clear that borderland encounters between natives and Europeans were not straightforward stories of European conquest and consequent domination. Rather, the outcome varied depending on the native polities and people involved, the duration of the encounters, whether the encounters were direct or indirect, and whether they involved military action, trade, alliance building, marriage, slaving, missionizing, colonizing, and so on.[6] In addition, we need remember, as the events at Tascalusa will demonstrate, in many cases, Indian polities and people rather than Europeans were foremost in Indian minds. Furthermore, recent scholarship emphasizes that an event we may think of as a single encounter, such as the de Soto expedition, must be parsed for its variety of encounters.[7]

Although the encounter between Tascalusa and de Soto most likely pre-cipitated the decline of Tascalusa's reign, direct encounters were not always the disruptive forces we have assumed them to be. For example, recent archaeological investigations reveal that the polity of Chicaza, in present-day eastern Mississippi, was not severely unsettled by the presence of de Soto's army, even though the army stayed there for several months and had an inten-sive, albeit brief, military engagement with the warriors of Chicaza.[8] Archae-ological evidence indicates that the polity was still intact after de Soto's departure and remained so for several more decades.[9]

Canvassing the late sixteenth- and early seventeenth-century US South shows that Indian people exercised much discretion and decision in their responses to Europeans; or, put another way, they exercised much agency. Agency can be seen in the varied native responses to Europeans across space and time, which included such disparate strategies and outcomes as accom-modation, manipulation, diaspora, coalescence, fight, isolation, militariza-tion, trade intensification, avoidance, xenophobia, re-emplacement, religious revitalization, and openness, among others. These responses were oftentimes predicated on the intersection of internal and external factors to native life, and any single polity or group exercised a spectrum of responses over time.[10] We can now safely assume that native people were not passive victims who simply reacted to the European invasion, they directed and shaped it, and they made decisions about their lives and their futures. The story of Chief Tascalusa and Hernando de Soto is a case in point.

Before moving into the narrative, I first need to explain how we know what we know about Tascalusa and this place at this distant time. The Hernando de Soto expedition was one of several European expeditions sent to explore and settle colonies on the North American continent in the sixteenth century. De Soto, a seasoned conquistador who had become wealthy through par-ticipating in the expeditions through present-day Nicaragua and Peru, launched this expedition in 1539 from Cuba and soon thereafter landed in present-day Tampa Bay, Florida. Over the next four years, de Soto and his army of more than 650 soldiers, horses, dogs, and a herd of pigs trekked through much of the precolonial indigenous world in the heartland of the present-day US South. The expedition was a failure. Not only did the army not find any precious metals, but they also failed to establish any military outposts or colonies. More than half of the soldiers perished during the expedition, as de Soto himself did, in 1542, on the banks of the Mississippi River. The survivors limped back to New Spain steering makeshift rafts in a desperate attempt to flee the large indigenous naval forces that patrolled the Mississippi River.[11]

In 1540, two years before his death, de Soto encountered Chief Tascalusa, who spent about ten days with the Spanish army in October of that year. The chronicles from the de Soto expedition are some of the only known written descriptions of that time and place and, for us, of Tascalusa, the town where he lived, the events in which he participated that fall, and the power he wielded.[12] There are four reports from the de Soto expedition—one by Biedma, the factor, or royally appointed record-keeper for the expedition; another by Rodrigo Rangel, de Soto's personal secretary; and another by a Portuguese man known only as the Gentleman of Elvas. Finally, the Incan mestizo writer Garcilaso de la Vega, who was not a member of the expedition but interviewed three of the soldiers who returned, penned an account intended as a literary narrative.[13] Scholars have vetted these four accounts, and most conclude that Biedma and Rangel are the most reliable, that Elvas likely fleshed out his memory of events with details lifted from Rangel, and that Garcilaso is the least reliable in terms of chronology, events, and details but provides a compelling and insightful story nonetheless.[14]

In addition, archaeologists working in the US South have long pondered the large earthen mounds that dot the US southern landscape from the Atlantic to the Great Plains, from present-day St. Louis to the Gulf shores.[15] We now understand these earthworks were built between about 900 and 1600 CE, which archaeologists call the Mississippi Period and in which Tascalusa came to power. The story of the Mississippian world begins with the rise of the great indigenous city of Cahokia. Around 1000 CE, people living along the middle Mississippi River near present-day St. Louis underwent a dramatic transformation in life—they built one of the largest cities in the world and adopted a new world order that mandated a restructuring of their political, social, and religious lives. This new way of life lasted for more than seven hundred years and spread throughout the US South and much of the Midwest.

Fig. 4.1.a. Artist's rendering of Moundville, ca. 1200 CE. (Drawing by Steven Patricia, 2004)

During the Mississippi Period native peoples in the region reorganized themselves from independent, egalitarian farming villages into the type of political organization that anthropologists call chiefdoms. Except for Cahokia, most chiefdoms were characterized by a two-tiered social ranking of elites versus commoners, a civic and religious capital where the elite lineages lived, and five to ten affiliated farming towns in close proximity up and down a river valley. The capital towns oftentimes had one or more flat-topped, pyramidal earthen mounds situated around a large, open plaza. Although the capital towns could be quite large, the outlying towns were small, with average populations of 350 to 650 people; and an entire chiefdom might average between 2,800 and 5,400 people. The mico lived atop the largest mound in

Fig. 4.1.b. Photograph of Moundville Archaeological State Park. (Courtesy of the University of Alabama Museums. Photograph by Sean Shore, Strategic Communications, University of Alabama.)

the capital while lesser members of the chiefly lineage lived on the lower mounds. Commoners lived in houses circling the mounds, around the plazas in the capital, and in surrounding farming towns. Again, except for Cahokia, chiefdoms were geographically small, usually encompassing about 25 kilometers (16 mi) along a river valley, and chiefdoms were separated from each other by about 33 kilometers (20 mi) of uninhabited space, what archaeologists call buffer zones.[16]

Some leaders established secondary mound towns a few miles away from the capital and instituted a second tier of control; archaeologists refer to these more elaborate polities as complex chiefdoms (figure 4.1). However, sometimes chiefdoms and complex chiefdoms merged to form larger political units that archaeologists call paramount chiefdoms, which could incorporate small and complex chiefdoms, as well as their affiliated farming communities. Over the seven-hundred-year history of the Mississippian way of life, many simple, complex, and paramount chiefdoms rose and fell. This rising and falling, or cycling, was an internal dynamic common to Mississippian chiefdoms, and the life span of a typical chiefdom, no matter its size, was about two hundred years.[17] Map 4.1, based on archaeological evidence and the de Soto chronicles, presents an estimated composite map of the Mississippian world at the time of the de Soto entrada. As the map shows, at the time of contact in the sixteenth century, dozens of small, complex, and paramount chiefdoms existed in the South, all at varying stages of rise, fluorescence, and decline.

Chiefdoms were largely self-sufficient through a mixed economy of local hunting, gathering, fishing, trading, and agriculture. Although people in the US South had been growing various crops for almost two thousand years when the Mississippian world emerged, corn (maize) provided the basic caloric intake and foodstuff for Mississippian people, and they grew it intensively. Chiefly elites also sponsored traders who maintained far-flung trade networks through which they obtained nonlocal goods such as copper, shell, mica, high-grade stones like flint, and other materials that elite-sponsored artisans fashioned into emblems of power, prestige, and religious authority.

In some ways, one could describe these chiefdoms as theocracies because the elites were closely associated with religious beliefs and their authority was underwritten by divine doctrine. Elites were most likely considered either close affiliates of or actual earthly representations of divine beings; they constituted a class of priests and prophets who were the religious experts and whose duties were to oversee rituals and ceremonies. In addition, they controlled and commissioned the making of religious icons and emblems that represent some of the finest artwork in all indigenous North America. These objects, however, did not necessarily represent a unified religion for the Mississippian world. Rather, they symbolized a set of basic concepts and principles that were shared among various polities. In other words, there probably was not one religion that united the whole of the Mississippian world for seven hundred years but, rather, several religions deriving from a core set of fundamental beliefs and assumptions.[18]

The prestige goods circulated almost exclusively among the elites, who exchanged them to garner allies, who conspicuously displayed and distributed them during various status competitions such as feasting events and who, under sumptuary laws, wore them as insignias of status and office.[19] War iconography is prevalent on Mississippian artwork, indicating that warfare imbued all aspects of daily life.[20] The palisaded towns that typically lay on a chiefdom's borders and the large buffer zones between chiefdoms also suggest that warfare was not just important but probably endemic.

Archaeologists are uncertain about the extent and nature of a mico's authority and power. They generally agree that the chiefly elite constituted an

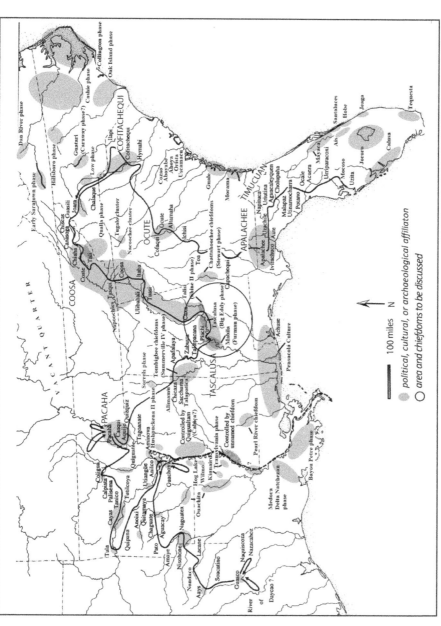

Map 4.1. The US South and the Mississippian World, ca. 1540, showing the route of Hernando de Soto, the area, and chiefdoms discussed in this chapter. (Map by Robbie Ethridge)

important political body and that they held permanent offices of high rank and authority, with the mico holding the highest office. It appears, however, that a mico's consolidation of power varied from one chiefdom to another, spanning a continuum from autocratic power to being simply the first among equals. In some cases, elite lineages were the sole decision-making bodies, could conscript labor, draft armies, command tribute, and so on. They controlled valued resources such as food, labor, and production of prestige items, and they maintained institutional inequality through social management, ideological hegemony, finance, debt, and exchange relationships. The large capitals of complex chiefdoms like Moundville (figure 4.1) most likely represented a strongly ranked, strictly hierarchical society.[21]

On the other hand, some Mississippian polities were decentralized. These polities lack evidence of health disparities between the elites and non-elites, large-scale redistribution of resources, and full-time craft specialization. In these cases, chiefly power was less autocratic and was constrained by councils and kinship groups whom the mico and other elites were obliged to consult. In other words, these Mississippian chiefdoms were heterarchies where power was shared among kin groups, and the mico and his or her elite lineage would have been the first among relative equals.[22] In fact, over the seven-hundred-year history of the Mississippi Period, decentralized, heterarchical chiefdoms stood side-by-side with a spectrum of political structures up to centralized and highly autocratic chiefdoms. Despite their diversity, archaeologists have come to agree that these chiefdoms were bound together in what could be called the "Mississippian world," and that polities of various sizes, complexities, ideological convictions, degrees of centralized governance, and cultural expressions existed within a network of political, economic, cultural, and social relationships.

De Soto depended on local food supplies, which explains why he was very concerned with locating populous towns and polities and why he traveled with a herd of pigs, which he reserved for starvation food. In fact, many of de Soto's movements were guided by his need for food and his search for precious metals.[23] Yet, as map 4.1 illustrates, de Soto appears to have bypassed several large polities altogether. Mississippians, with their mixed economy of hunting, fishing, foraging, and agriculture, grew enough corn and other foodstuffs to provide a surplus for each town and to stock a communal granary in the capital that the chief oversaw. De Soto's large army was restricted in hunting and foraging by the constant fear of Indian attacks, and they usually depleted the surpluses of the towns through which they passed, angering local populations.[24] In fact, one can see in map 4.1 that when the Spaniards reached the edges of the Mississippian world, they were forced to turn back toward the heartland because ahead there were thinly dispersed populations whose local food stores could not feed the army. Only in the Mississippian world did people grow enough surplus at the local level to feed such a large army when it passed through their towns.[25]

The Mississippian world also was a place of great linguistic diversity where inhabitants spoke some twenty known languages from five language families: Algonquian, Muskogean, Iroquoian, Siouan, and Caddoan.[26] Languages within the same family were not necessarily mutually intelligible, but Southeastern Indians were superb linguists and many could speak several languages. Obviously, de Soto, traveling the breadth and width of the Mississippian world, had need of interpreters from the moment his army stepped off their boats in present-day Tampa Bay. In fact, de Soto's first attempt to communicate with local Indians through "signs"—meaning hand gestures—was a dismal failure.[27] However, in an unfathomable stroke of luck, soon after landing de Soto encountered Juan Ortiz. Ortiz was a young man from the 1527–28 Pánfilo de Narváez expedition who had been captured by the local Indians and enslaved for twelve years before de Soto rescued him. During his years in captivity, Ortiz had learned two of the local Timucuan languages, which he could translate into Spanish.[28] As the army progressed in their march, de Soto needed Indian translators who could speak to one another then relay information to Ortiz. Ortiz died at the chiefdom of Utiangüe, in present-day eastern Arkansas, and although several of the young Indian boys and girls captured along the way had learned some Spanish, Ortiz's death severely distressed de Soto and imperiled the expedition.[29]

Let us now return to the story of Tascalusa's encounter with de Soto. Granted, we have documentary accounts of a mere sliver of Tascalusa's reign, less than two weeks really. Still, placing this snapshot of the mico within the larger archaeological and ethnohistorical context of Mississippian life, we can begin to discern the outlines of the political and social structure of the chiefdom of Tascalusa and the nature of Tascalusa's power, all of which shaped his encounter with de Soto. I propose that Tascalusa was in the process of building a paramount chiefdom at the time he met de Soto and that he took advantage of de Soto's presence to communicate his authority across his own polity as well as two, or perhaps three, other polities over which he held influence.[30] Consider the first meeting between de Soto and elites from Tascalusa. Before reaching Tascalusa, de Soto and his army had traveled through much of present-day Florida, South Carolina, North Carolina, and eastern Tennessee, where they entered the paramount chiefdom of Coosa (also spelled Cosa). The paramountcy of Coosa encompassed nine chiefdoms and stretched more than 250 miles from eastern Tennessee to central Alabama.[31] Figure 4.2 is a graphic representation of de Soto's route through central Alabama, as related by Rangel and depicting the various towns and polities though which the army passed. De Soto had forced the mico of Coosa to accompany him through the province in order that Coosa warriors would not attack the Spaniards. When they entered Talisi, the southernmost chiefdom of the paramountcy, Coosa informed de Soto that they had reached the boundary of his province, that they were about to cross into the territory of Tascalusa, and that he, Coosa, had no control once they crossed the border. At that point, de Soto released Coosa, who left angrily because de Soto refused to free his sister as well.[32]

De Soto stayed at Talisi about three weeks. Apparently, while at Talisi, if not before, he had heard Tascalusa described as "a powerful lord and very feared."[33] De Soto then could not have been surprised when emissaries from Tascalusa came to Talisi to deliver a message from their mico. These emissaries were "principal Indians," meaning that they were elites from the chiefdom.[34] Tascalusa's nephew, who was nearly as large as his uncle, headed the contingent.[35] The message from Tascalusa was one of peace and servitude: that Tascalusa "desires as he does life to see and serve your Lordship."[36] The messenger continued that Tascalusa offered his land and his vassals to de Soto so that as the expedition traveled through his polity, they would be received in peace and love and be served and obeyed. De Soto, in what was undoubtedly a show of power, ordered the trumpets to be sounded and his mounted soldiers to display their horsemanship.[37] The Indians, as de Soto was quite aware, were unfamiliar with horses and terrified of them. Afterwards, de Soto reciprocated Tascalusa's goodwill by giving his nephew some beads and cloth to give to the mico.[38]

Although Tascalusa himself is absent from this encounter, we learn several things about him. For one, Tascalusa had heard of de Soto, most likely long before the latter's arrival in Talisi, indicating that the mico's communication networks reached deep into Coosa. Also, like many Mississippian leaders that de Soto met, Tascalusa obviously found it beneath himself to come to de Soto—all visiting leaders traveled to a mico of high standing, not the other way around. As protocol required, Tascalusa sent a select group of

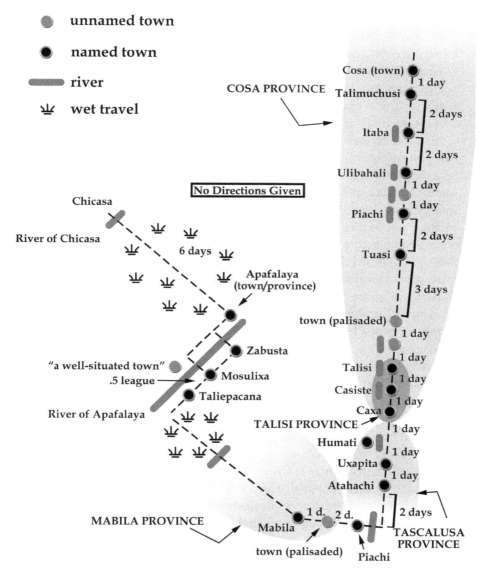

Legend:
- ⬤ unnamed town
- ⬤ named town
- ▬ river
- ☩ wet travel

Cosa (town) · 1 day
COSA PROVINCE
Talimuchusi · 2 days
Itaba · 2 days
Ulibahali · 1 day
Piachi · 1 day
Tuasi · 2 days
3 days

No Directions Given

Chicasa
River of Chicasa
☩ ☩ 6 days ☩
☩ ☩ ☩
☩ ☩
Apafalaya (town/province)

Zabusta
"a well-situated town"
.5 league
Mosulixa
Taliepacana
River of Apafalaya
☩ ☩
☩ ☩
☩ ☩

town (palisaded) · 1 day
· 1 day
Talisi · 1 day
Casiste · 1 day
Caxa
TALISI PROVINCE
Humati · 1 day
Uxapita · 1 day
Atahachi · 1 day

MABILA PROVINCE
Mabila · 1 d. · 2 d. · 2 days
town (palisaded) · Piachi
TASCALUSA PROVINCE

Fig. 4.2. Graphic reconstruction of de Soto's route through central Alabama, showing chiefdoms of Coosa (Cosa), Talisi, Tascalusa, Piachi, and Mabila, according to Rangel. (Courtesy of University of Alabama Press. Drawing by Jeremy Davis.)

dignitaries, headed by his nephew, to parlay with de Soto and most likely to gather intelligence about the Spaniards, the size of their army, and so forth.[39] We should not construe Tascalusa's greeting of peace and servitude as a capitulation to de Soto. Rather, across the South such language was part and parcel of the diplomatic etiquette between powerful leaders.[40] In other words, this first encounter indicates that Tascalusa was acting much like other powerful chiefs in the Mississippian world.

That emissaries from Tascalusa were allowed into Talisi is another important piece of information. We know that Mississippian polities were in perpetual conflict, that warfare played an important role in the Mississippian world, and that men's status and chiefly authority were derived from exploits in war.[41] We also know that in some cases, ambitious chiefs and their elites built complex and paramount chiefdoms, such as Coosa, through allegiances with other polities across a region using force, persuasion, or both.[42] Remember that de Soto heard the people of Talisi feared Tascalusa, indicating that the mico was a threatening neighbor. Remember also that Talisi, according to Chief Coosa, was the southernmost chiefdom in his province (see figure 4.2), so Tascalusa's threat to Talisi was also a challenge to Coosa. Yet the people of Talisi allowed Tascalusa's emissaries to enter their province without confrontation. This fact could indicate that Talisi's mico was considering, or was being forced into, an alliance with Tascalusa, and hence, breaking away from Coosa. De Soto's presence in Talisi, then, presented an opportunity for Tascalusa to assert his authority over Talisi and present a challenge to Coosa.

Another assertion of Tascalusa's chiefly authority can be read in the greeting rituals between him and de Soto when the two finally met. Soon after de Soto left Talisi, he entered the province of Tascalusa. Once across the border, the army traveled for three to five days, passing several towns before arriving at the capital, called Atahachi, which is where Tascalusa and his family lived (see figure 4.2).[43] Atahachi is most likely the Charlotte Thompson archaeological site, which places the town on the upper Alabama River, near its confluence with the Tallapoosa and Coosa Rivers.[44]

As de Soto usually did when approaching a capital town, he and his vanguard paused about one league from Atahachi, and he sent his *maestre de campo* (field marshal), Luis de Moscoso, with fifteen mounted soldiers to announce his arrival. Moscoso returned with the good news that Tascalusa welcomed de Soto in peace, "whenever he wished to come."[45] When de Soto arrived, Tascalusa was awaiting him on the balcony of his summer house, on top of a mound. The floor of the balcony was covered with woven cane mats, on which were placed two cushions, upon which Tascalusa sat. Around forty years old, Tascalusa struck a regal figure. He was dressed in an elaborate turban, which, Rangel stated, "gave him an appearance of authority," and draped over his shoulders was a full-length feather cape, or matchcoat.[46] The mound fronted a large plaza, around which many noblemen were arranged, with the most important ones closest to the mound. Always standing to one side of the chief was a "very graceful Indian" holding a staff topped by a large, round frame the size of a shield, covered with a deerskin on which was painted a white sun circle against a black background.[47] According to Elvas, the colors were so perfect that the ensign looked like it was made of finely woven taffeta.[48] On the other side a second attendant held aloft a large, feather-covered fan with which he shaded his mico from the sun (figure 4.3).[49]

Fig. 4.3. Late Mississippian Timucuan chief and his wife. (Engraving by Theodore de Bry from Jacques Le Moyne, 1591. Plate XXXIX, "Chief Satouriona and his wife go for a walk," Florida Center for Instructional Technology, University of South Florida.)

Let us analyze this scene within the larger context of what we know about Mississippian political orders. Later ethnohistoric evidence suggests that Mississippians were matrilineal, meaning that they traced descent through the female line. Each matriline was part of a larger kinship grouping known as a clan, and both the clans and the matrilines were ranked.[50] Later documentary evidence from Spanish Florida indicates that within a chiefdom the towns were also ranked. Therefore, a chiefdom drew its mico, or principal chief, from the highest-ranking member of the highest-ranking lineage in the highest-ranking clan of the highest-ranking community within the cluster of five to ten towns that constituted it. The other lineages and towns were integrated into the political system through a ranked council over which the mico presided. The council consisted of *oratas* (also *holatas*) from all the towns, a Muskogean word that the Spanish translated as "magistrates" but that modern scholars translate as "headmen." Occupying the highest seats in the mico's council, the oratas also had their noble counselors, known in Muskogean as *inihas* or *henihas* (advisor or assistant). The henihas occupied the lower seats in the mico's council. There appears to have been a category of language specialists knowns as *yatika* in Muskogean, who served as interpreters and spokespersons.[51] Thus, the highest-ranking orata held the title of mico and lived atop, and was oftentimes buried in, the mound. All the oratas were drawn from the highest-ranking lineage in the highest-ranking clan within their respective towns. Since clans crosscut towns, the highest-ranking clan in each town was most likely the mico's clan. Hence all or most leadership posts probably came from the mico's clan and one's relationship to the mico determined one's status.[52] The native word for the leader of a paramount chiefdom, if there was one, goes unrecorded, except that Spanish conquistadors in the US South recognized such a position and called the man or woman holding it *cacique grande* (grand chief).[53]

Returning to Atahachi, that Tascalusa, alone, was seated on the mound indicates that he was indisputably the highest-ranking person in the chiefdom. The noblemen with Tascalusa probably represented the oratas who composed the chiefdom council, arrayed by rank around the plaza, with the higher ranked men standing closer to the mound and Tascalusa. The relationships between the oratas and the mico likely varied from chiefdom to chiefdom. In some cases, the oratas and their communities may have maintained autonomy from the mico, and the mico's authority came from maintaining good ties with the various constituents of his chiefdom by providing feasts, gifts, safe storage for foodstuffs, and so on. In other cases, the mico may have had more control over the oratas, even delegating oratas to each community.[54] We know, for example, that the principal chief, known as the Great Sun, of the early eighteenth-century Natchez chiefdom appointed several of his male kin to preside over the towns in the chiefdom. We also know that some of these kinsmen eventually began to conspire against the Great Sun.[55] In fact, archaeologists agree that intra-polity political jockeying must have been chronic, making the Mississippian political structure particularly unstable.[56]

In the case of Tascalusa, there are indications that he held considerable power over other oratas. For one, all the de Soto accounts describe him as a powerful, much respected, and feared lord who ruled over many lands with many vassals, or subordinate towns and polities, and who held considerable influence in at least three or four polities (Tascalusa, Talisi, Piachi, and Mabila).[57] Then there was his general demeanor and countenance. When de Soto entered the plaza at Atahachi, he dismounted and climbed the ramp of the mound to greet Tascalusa. Tascalusa did not rise, but rather sat "quiet and composed, as if he were a king, and with much gravity."[58] De Soto, in his usual display of power, ordered his horsemen to gallop their horses through the plaza, "turning them from one side to the other, and at times toward the cacique [Tascalusa]."[59] Biedma insisted that running the horses, along with jousting matches and horse races, were performed to entertain Tascalusa.[60] Whether the display was intended as intimidation or festivity, de Soto clearly hoped to impress Tascalusa. But if he were impressed, Tascalusa certainly did not show it. Biedma reported that Tascalusa "appeared to think little of all this," and Elvas elaborated, "He with great gravity and unconcern from time to time raised his eyes and looked as if in disdain."[61] Tascalusa then invited de Soto to sit with him and, according to Elvas, pronounced that he received de Soto with pleasure and happiness as if the Spaniard were one of his brothers, which would have been a great compliment. Tascalusa continued that he wanted only to serve de Soto and that his motives were pure.[62] The last statement was all subterfuge since there is every indication that Tascalusa was already planning a surprise attack against the Spanish when they reached the province of Mabila. De Soto later asked that Tascalusa give him burden bearers and women, a habitual request of de Soto's that inevitably created ill will with local Indians. Tascalusa refused, replying that "he was not accustomed to serving anyone, rather . . . all served him."[63]

By these accounts, Tascalusa carried himself with much dignity, gravity, and authority, and he understood himself as not answering to anyone. De Soto had seen similar behavior before when chiefs of even small chiefdoms displayed an elite demeanor and separated themselves symbolically and materially from the hoi polloi by such means as having noblemen carry them on litters, having a retinue of attendants, bestowing prestigious gifts on visiting dignitaries, and adorning themselves with finely crafted accessories. Still, de Soto had encountered the type of imperial authority Tascalusa displayed on only a few occasions—at Cofitachequi, Coosa, and Quigualtam— all of which were large paramount chiefdoms with micos that apparently wielded much power or influence over their constituents and over much territory.[64] Although he ultimately would challenge de Soto in battle, at this first meeting, Tascalusa performed authority and power as Mississippian protocol warranted, sending a message of his stature to not only de Soto but also his constituents and public officials. Some scholars have questioned whether the Spaniards might have exaggerated the behavior of Tascalusa and other chiefs, or perhaps, through ethnocentric eyes, read into the behaviors their own Spanish norms of court and monarchy.[65] I would counter that the chroniclers did not describe all chiefs as "kings," and furthermore, that they were seasoned conquistadors who had traveled widely and had much experience with political systems different from those of Europe. I am not convinced that the chroniclers habitually misconstrued what they saw, though I do agree that we must be careful in our modern interpretations of what they saw.

Tascalusa's carriage certainly appears to have been that of a man of considerable weight and status in the chiefdom, but that is not necessarily a measure of his power to compel others. For that, we must continue peering into this window onto his leadership for other clues. Examining the events leading up to the battle of Mabila reveals additional patterns in Tascalusa's leadership role. When Tascalusa rebuffed de Soto's request for burden bearers and women, it may have been because he was not accustomed to serving others, as he said, but he also took this opportunity to lure de Soto into the trap he was setting at Mabila. According to Biedma, Tascalusa promised that he would give de Soto both burden bearers and women at "another town of his, which was called Mavila."[66] De Soto, who was used to getting what he wanted when he wanted it, grew enraged at this and ordered his men to detain Tascalusa. Tascalusa scoffed at de Soto's attempt to restrain him, but then turned to confer with his principal men before abruptly agreeing to sleep under the eyes of Spanish guards.[67]

The next day, Tascalusa accompanied the army to Mabila. Since we know that Tascalusa was planning a surprise attack, he probably went with de Soto voluntarily, or at least without resistance, since it appears he had always intended to lead the Spaniards to Mabila. Further evidence of his willingness to go with de Soto is that two attendants accompanied Tascalusa, as did several of the oratas. After leaving Atahachi, the army, along with Tascalusa and his entourage, traveled about two days before entering the adjacent town or perhaps province of Piachi, which was probably on the Alabama River.[68]

The main event at Piachi was a river crossing. De Soto was traveling with an army of about six hundred men, plus all their horses and pigs, and by this time, the army had captured about one hundred Indian slaves who traveled with them. The sheer size of the expedition meant that crossing deep rivers such as the Alabama was an arduous and time-consuming affair.[69] The one at Piachi proved especially problematic and took several days. For one, the mico of Piachi was hostile. He refused to assist the Spaniards and, even though Piachi was a river town, insisted that he had no canoes or watercraft to lend. Consequently, the Spaniards spent two or more days making rafts. The whole time, Piachi warriors waited in ambush to pick off any stray soldiers, creating much tension and killing at least one who had gone in search of an escaped Indian female slave. De Soto, angered by such defiance, declared to Tascalusa that he would burn him alive if he did not hand over those responsible for the killing. Tascalusa calmly replied that he would comply once they got to Mabila. In terms of the actual crossing once the rafts were built, the chroniclers tell different stories. Biedma does not even mention it; Rangel relates that the mico of Piachi staged some sort of resistance; and Elvas writes that the Indians of Piachi were cooperative and rowed the Spaniards across in safety.[70]

Despite the discrepant descriptions of the actual crossing, we can examine the events at Piachi for what they tell us about the relationship between Tascalusa and Piachi. Piachi was a small town situated about two days' travel from Atahachi through uninhabited lands (see figure 4.2). Since Mississippian chiefdoms were typically separated by a buffer zone of about thirty-three kilometers (roughly twenty miles) of uninhabited territory, a two-day march through uninhabited land suggests that Piachi was most likely a separate chiefdom rather than a distant frontier town of Tascalusa's chiefdom.[71] However, one clue that Tascalusa held some influence here is that de Soto demanded that Tascalusa, rather than the chief of Piachi, turn over the culprits involved in slaying the Spaniard. Another is that neither Tascalusa nor any of his entourage was molested while at Piachi. Occasionally, de Soto would force a chief out of his or her chiefdom to accompany him into a neighboring polity. In many such cases, local Indians would kill the foreign chief upon the trespass, which is perhaps why the chief of Coosa did not want to venture any farther than Talisi.[72] In this case, Tascalusa and his men were left unharmed.

Yet, if Tascalusa held sway or power in Piachi, why would the mico of Piachi show such hostility to de Soto, given that Tascalusa was with the army? After all, when de Soto forced the chief of Coosa to accompany him through that paramount chiefdom, the chief quickly quashed any hostilities that warriors in his territory displayed toward the Spanish.[73] There are a few possible answers in the Piachi case. One may be that Piachi was an autonomous polity, that Tascalusa, in fact, held no authority there, and that the local chief was acting on his own accord. Another may be that Tascalusa and Piachi were uneasy allies because Tascalusa, in his bid for a paramountcy, had violently subdued the smaller chiefdom. In this case, perhaps Piachi wanted to take advantage of the situation to wrest independence from Tascalusa by attacking the Spaniards without regard to Tascalusa's safety. De Soto witnessed similar machinations elsewhere in the South.[74] And finally, perhaps Tascalusa and Piachi were in alliance or at least collusion, and Piachi staged and prolonged the river crossing to delay de Soto long enough to allow Tascalusa's war chiefs to finish the war preparations at Mabila. My guess would be the last.

Corroborating evidence that Tascalusa had or was building a paramount chiefdom comes from the events at Mabila. After crossing the river at Piachi, Tascalusa sent some of his entourage ahead to Mabila, ostensibly to command the Mabila chief to prepare and provision for their arrival, and de Soto insisted that a few of his soldiers accompany them.[75] In hindsight, it is clear that Tascalusa sent them ahead to check on the war preparations and to alert the assembling warriors of their arrival in a few days. Tascalusa told de Soto several times that Mabila was one of his vassals, indicating that it was a subordinate chiefdom. Tascalusa's ability to conspire with the people of Mabila and perhaps with those at Piachi, both of which lay some distance from Tascalusa, certainly lends credence to the inference that he headed or was building a paramount chiefdom and that both Piachi and Mabila had come under his sway.

De Soto and Tascalusa marched for three days through uninhabited territory before reaching the first towns of Mabila. This buffer zone between Piachi and Mabila indicates that Mabila was a distinct chiefdom. Once they crossed into the territory of Mabila, the chroniclers stated that the province was fertile and well populated, and that they traveled for another day before reaching the town of Mabila.[76] Archaeologists have yet to locate this town, although recent investigations place it somewhere on the upper Alabama

River.[77] The de Soto narratives describe it as a relatively small settlement, heavily fortified with a palisade that encircled the entire town. The chroniclers do not mention a mound at Mabila, meaning that it likely was not the capital of the province. De Soto and Tascalusa arrived at Mabila in the vanguard, while the rest of the army pillaged the countryside for food and supplies.[78]

As the vanguard approached the town, the mico of Mabila came out to welcome them with a full retinue of "many Indians playing music and singing." Mabila's mico, as was the custom, offered his services and a gift of blankets to de Soto.[79] He offered de Soto the option of encamping either outside the palisade wall or in the town. Before de Soto entered through the palisade gate, however, one of the soldiers he had sent ahead alerted him that something was amiss. The soldier informed de Soto that over the past few days he had seen many well-armed warriors entering the town and the townspeople strengthening the palisade. Indian men had also been busy dismantling the houses outside the palisade walls, clearing the environs as if in preparation for battle. Never one to back down, de Soto opted to stay in the town despite the warning, and he entered it with Tascalusa and only the forty other Spaniards in the vanguard.[80]

At this point, tensions must have been taut. The Indian forces at Mabila were ready to attack. De Soto and his men, knowing that the rest of the army lagged a good half day behind them, must have been seriously concerned about walking into an ambush. But de Soto proceeded into the town, "walking with the Indians, chatting, as if we had them in peace," and seated himself under a balcony with Tascalusa.[81] The Mabila mico assured de Soto that all was well and, to distract the Spaniards and soothe tensions, he ordered twenty women dancers, accompanied by singers, to perform for the visitors.[82]

De Soto's men, who were keeping close watch in spite of the lithe dancers, noticed that all the houses in the town were "filled high and low with concealed people."[83] The number of warriors concealed at Mabila is unknown— Biedma claimed there were five thousand, Rangel and Elvas only noted there were many.[84] Rangel stated that de Soto, upon seeing the armed warriors in the town, abruptly slammed on his helmet and ordered the vanguard to mount their horses and leave the town immediately to warn the rest of the army that Mabila was armed to the teeth and ready for battle. The warriors at Mabila then took command of the gates at the palisade, trapping de Soto and a few of his soldiers inside and shutting the rest of the army outside.[85]

Tascalusa at one point asked de Soto's permission to stay at Mabila, rather than continuing with the march. De Soto, obviously now aware that not all was as it seemed, refused, and Tascalusa, retorting that he wished to confer with his oratas, suddenly rose from the balcony and entered a nearby house. De Soto ordered Tascalusa out of the house; Tascalusa refused and warned de Soto that if the latter "wished to go in peace he should go immediately and should not insist on trying to take him out of his lands and dominion by force."[86] Elvas remarked that de Soto, hearing the fury in Tascalusa's voice, "endeavored to soothe him with pleasant words," but Tascalusa made no reply and, "on the contrary, he withdrew very haughtily and disdainfully to a place where the governor [de Soto] could not see or talk with him."[87] De Soto then commanded the captain of his guard to extract the mico by force. The guard went to the door of the house, saw dozens of Indian warriors with bows drawn, and retreated. De Soto then commanded one of Tascalusa's principal men, who was nearby, to carry a message to Tascalusa, but the man "with much hautiness [sic]" refused to do so. One of the Spaniards, Baltasar de Gallegos, who was next to the Indian man, seized him by the arm to force him to obey, at which point the Indian and the Spaniard tussled. Gallegos drew his sword and either cut off the Indian man's arm or severely slashed open his back.[88] With this incident the warriors hidden in the houses of Mabila poured out in a ferocious onslaught of bows and arrows, war clubs, and hand-to-hand combat.

At this point in the narrative, the chroniclers lost sight of Tascalusa. But what can we deduce about Tascalusa as a leader during the time he is in our line of sight at Mabila? For one, it is obvious that Tascalusa and the Mabila mico were co-conspirators who had planned this attack for some time. Furthermore, Tascalusa persuaded de Soto that he wielded power not only in his own chiefdom, but also in Piachi and Mabila, and he then manipulated the Spaniards into going to Mabila. Although the exact number of Indian forces is unknown, at least several thousand appear to have been mustered for this attack. Since chiefdoms did not have standing armies, notifying and gathering this many men would have taken days. Recall that chiefdoms were fairly small, with populations averaging around 3,500, of which only about 875 would have been fighting men.[89] Therefore, Tascalusa would have had to gather Indian troops from across several polities to amass such a large army. We can surmise that at least three, maybe four, polities—Tascalusa, Talisi, Piachi, and Mabila—were involved in the conspiracy and provided warriors.[90] Finally, although the attack was planned, the battle began spontaneously when Tascalusa finally faced off against de Soto and Gallegos consequently injured one of Tascalusa's principal men. I do not want to make too much of the last point, but we could speculate that the person in charge at Mabila was indeed Tascalusa, that all the warriors had sworn to protect him, and hence that Mabila and all the warriors gathered there were part of Tascalusa's paramount chiefdom and had some allegiance to him.

There are also clues from the events at Mabila as to the western boundary of Tascalusa's paramountcy. One is Tascalusa's retort that he would not allow de Soto to take him out of his "dominion"; this remark would indicate that Mabila was the westernmost boundary of it. In addition, after the battle, when de Soto departed Mabila, the army marched west for five days through uninhabited lands, indicating a buffer zone separating Mabila, and perhaps Tascalusa's paramount chiefdom, from the surrounding polities. These polities were small and independent, and there is no indication that they participated in the battle.[91]

I will not go into the details of the battle here. Suffice it to say that after a hard day of fighting, Tascalusa and his warriors dealt a severe blow to de Soto, killing about two dozen Spaniards and a dozen horses, injuring virtually everyone in the army, and burning the town and all of the Spaniards' supplies. Afterwards, de Soto encamped near Mabila for a month, nursing the wounded, fashioning more weapons since they had lost most of theirs in the battle, and ransacking food and supplies from the surrounding countryside. Tascalusa's forces did not attack again.[92]

Why did Tascalusa not press his advantage and attack de Soto's forces in their weakened state? The absence of a second attack can be understood in terms of the rules of war during the Mississippi Period. Warfare was often conducted as a punishment, not necessarily to annihilate an enemy. Typically, Mississippian chiefs would lead their warriors into a single battle then retreat. This is most likely why Tascalusa's army did not strike again—the mico had punished the haughty Spaniards and taught them a lesson.[93] Although Tascalusa and his allies did not destroy the Spanish army, they did do them much harm and destroy many of their supplies and horses. In addition, they succeeded in pushing the Spaniards out of their provinces.

The Indian forces, too, were severely weakened. We do not have a good reckoning of the Indian dead and injured. We are unsure whether Tascalusa survived the battle but do know that his nephew perished. The chroniclers estimate about three thousand Indian men were killed, but scholars believe this number to be exaggerated.[94] Still, the large estimates tell us that the battle was costly and that every town in every chiefdom that participated undoubtedly lost scores of their fighting men. We do not know whether Tascalusa and his warriors saw the outcome as a victory. Given the number of Indians slain, I would venture to guess that they did not. In addition, recall that de Soto's army plundered the countryside for weeks, both before and after the battle. In revenge, de Soto also gave orders to raze all homes and towns in the vicinity. Between de Soto's scorched-earth tactics and the losses they suffered in the battle, many Indians fled from the area soon after the battle.[95]

If Tascalusa did survive the battle, his power base and his bid for a paramountcy appear to have been considerably diminished. The hints we have as to Tascalusa's fate come from the Charlotte Thompson archaeological site (Atahachi) and the brief mention of the province when a contingent from the Tristán de Luna y Arellano expedition passed through about fifteen years later, in 1560. The large mound at Charlotte Thompson was still in use in 1560, as evidenced by the Spanish goods recovered from it, meaning it was still the capital town of a chiefdom.[96] However, the de Luna chronicles do not tell tales of a formidable giant ruling over vast lands and many polities. In fact, Tascalusa barely garners notice in the de Luna reports.[97] Moreover, the archaeology shows that several of the surrounding mound sites and small farming communities were abandoned at that time. All this evidence suggests that by 1560 Tascalusa was no longer the noteworthy paramountcy that de Soto had encountered twenty years earlier, and that the fortunes of Tascalusa and his heirs had indeed taken a turn for the worse.[98] The archaeology suggests that the paramountcy, and perhaps the chiefdom of Tascalusa, disintegrated around fifteen years after the de Luna visit, by 1575, if not earlier.[99]

Why would the encounter with de Soto have precipitated a decline in Tascalusa's chiefdom given that other violent encounters, such as that at Chicaza (mentioned early in the chapter) did not cause the polity to fail? Most scholars agree that military encounters resulting in heavy losses at the hands of de Soto's army often destabilized the chiefdoms involved. This was probably the case at Napituca in northern Florida and Anilco in Arkansas.[100] Unlike in the battle at Chicaza, the Indian deaths and casualties at Mabila were severe. Demographically and militarily, a chiefdom could not sustain heavy losses of fighting-age men, and the chief who led his or her warriors into such a battle would suffer a significant loss of respect and authority. In addition, de Soto's prolonged stay in and ransacking of the region around Mabila would have seriously depleted local food stores. Although Mississippian people knew much about utilizing wild plant and animal foods, a shortage of stored cultivated crops would have meant hardship for all and starvation for some. Chiefs derived their authority partly from being able to procure and secure stores of food for just such emergencies, and if a leader failed on this count, then political unrest would have erupted in that polity.[101] In addition, it is reasonable to presume that leaders' religious authority would have been undermined by such failures, which would have called into question their possession of divine favor. Such strains on a leader could easily erupt into full-scale rebellions. Mississippian polities were no strangers to internal political stresses, and factions often developed within and between ruling lineages, resulting in a continuous jockeying for power within the political order.[102]

It is likely that de Soto's presence upset the Mississippian balance of power in other ways as well. Records from the expedition across the South describe several instances when micos of subordinate chiefdoms challenged and defied the authority of the chief under whose power they had fallen—this happened at Chicaza, Cofitachequi, Coosa, and Casqui.[103] In these political struggles, the more powerful mico often enlisted de Soto's influence and military aid to extinguish the rebellion. In some cases, a savvy lesser mico used de Soto to bolster his or her authority in challenging an overarching mico, as happened at Casqui. Tascalusa, on the other hand, used de Soto's presence to further his own ambitions, although ultimately he seems to have miscalculated the outcome. In any case, given the fragile nature of the ties binding complex and paramount chiefdoms, the presence of a new and powerful ally or foe could easily upset the balance of geopolitical power, resulting in a reshuffling of authority. The military losses at Mabila combined with de Soto's depletion of local food supplies could have created civil and religious unrest throughout Tascalusa's chiefdom along with undermining his standing at Mabila, Talisi, and Piachi, thereby threatening his paramountcy.

De Soto and his army were one of the first and last European expeditions to witness the Mississippian world of the native US South. The next Europeans to penetrate the interior South arrived more than one hundred years later, and what they saw was a world in the process of collapsing and restructuring—of transforming itself. De Soto's march did not precipitate the fall of the Mississippian world. Although virtually all the chiefdoms through which de Soto passed were gone by the early eighteenth century, we now understand that this decline was mostly a process of piecemeal disintegration and reorganization as chiefdoms fell and people regrouped, sometimes more than once, over the span of almost two hundred years. The reasons for this transformation and restructuring are multifaceted and include not only the instabilities wrought by the de Soto entrada, but also a combination of elements that created what I have called the "Mississippian shatter zone," a large region of instability. Among these elements was the inherent structural instability of the Mississippian world and the inability of chiefdoms to withstand the full force of colonialism: the introduction of Old World pathogens and the subsequent serial disease episodes and loss of life; the Europeans' inauguration of a nascent capitalist economic system through a commercial trade in Indian slaves, animal skins, and guns; and the intensification and spread of violence and warfare through the Indian slave trade, and especially through the emergence of militaristic native slaving societies who sought larger shares of the European trade.[104]

Native people did not disappear, however. Rather, they lived in and through the Mississippian shatter zone, devising strategies not only to survive but at times to take advantage of the upheavals of early European colonization. In the process they were transformed from the precontact Mississippian political and social entities such as Tascalusa, Coosa, Mabila, Chicaza, and Quigualtam, to post-contact, globally situated political and social entities known as the Chickasaws, Creeks, Choctaws, Catawbas, Yamasees, and so on. Thirty-five years after de Soto's trek through Tascalusa, the survivors of the fallen polity migrated slightly upstream to the confluence of the Coosa and Tallapoosa Rivers. Here, they would survive the shattering of their political, religious, and social orders due to the sustained European colonial invasions of the seventeenth century, not as Tascalusa Indians but, along with refugees from present-day Tennessee and Georgia, as the core of the Alabama Indians.[105] The people who became the Alabamas by the mid-seventeenth century would form part of the Muscogee (Creek) Confederacy in the eighteenth century.

Tascalusa's encounter with de Soto occurred deep in the heart of Indian country, in what we are calling the borderlands, where deeply rooted social, political, and cultural norms shaped indigenous responses to the Spanish presence. Contrary to the usual trope of Spaniards facing Indian polities weakened by disease, de Soto encountered Tascalusa at a high point in the career of the chief and of his polity. In this encounter, Tascalusa's political ambitions dictated that he must demonstrate not only a growing network of influence throughout the region, but also decisiveness, strength, good inter-polity diplomatic skills, military prowess, and courage. Tascalusa was not bewildered or stymied by de Soto's arrival. He may not have fully understood the Spaniards or their motives for the expedition, and he does not seem to have been interested in either, but he knew how to act, behave, and resist in the face of an unwelcomed and belligerent foe.

NOTES

I thank Joaquín Rivaya-Martínez and Gerardo Lara Cisneros for inviting me to contribute a chapter to this volume. I appreciate their patience, kind guidance, and insightful critiques. It has been a pleasure working with them. I delivered a version of this essay at the University of North Carolina, Michael Green Lecture Series in 2014, and I thank Theda Perdue, the Departments of Anthropology and History, and the UNC American Indian Center for the invitation. I dedicate this chapter to the memory of Mike Green.

1. Biedma, "Relation," 232.

2. Elvas, "True Relation," 96.

3. Rangel, "Account," 291.

4. Garcilaso, "La Florida," 328.

5. "Mico" is a Muskogean word that in the sixteenth century most likely designated the highest political office of a polity. Scholars have translated it as "principal chief" or "chief"; Hudson, *Knights of Spain*, 127. Additionally, Spanish explorers often called a polity by the name of its mico, or vice versa, which means that Tascalusa may or may not have been the name by which the local people knew the mico or their polity.

6. Barr, "There's No Such Thing"; Blanton, "Tracking an Entrada"; Ethridge, "Differential Responses"; Legg et al. "Appraisal of the Indigenous Acquisition"; Mathers, "War and Peace."

7. Blanton, "Tracking an Entrada"; Boudreaux, Meyers, and Johnson, introduction to *Contact, Colonialism, and Native Communities*; Ethridge, "Differential Responses."

8. Biedma, "Relation," 236–37; Boudreaux et al., "Early Contact Period"; Elvas, "True Relation," 105–9; Legg et al., "Appraisal of the Indian Acquisition"; Rangel, "Account," 297–98.

9. Atkinson, "Historic Contact Indian Settlement"; Atkinson, "de Soto Expedition," 63–68; Boudreaux et al., "Archaeological Investigations in the Chickasaw Homeland," 33; Boudreaux et al., "Early Contact Period"; Clarke, "Analysis of the Contact-Era Settlements," 34–59; Cobb et al., "Beyond Yaneka," 59, 63–72, 120, app. B; Legg et al., "Appraisal of the Indigenous Acquisition"; Smith, "Sherds with Style," 81.

10. Ethridge, "Differential Responses."

11. The most thorough account of the de Soto expedition through the native South is Hudson, *Knights of Spain*.

12. In addition to the chronicles mentioned here, there are documents relating to the organization and launch of the expedition and to the lawsuits de Soto's wife filed after the expedition. However, only two brief manuscript fragments and one unsigned and undated manuscript map contain information on the activities of the

expedition in North America; Braund, "De Soto Map," 45–53; Clayton, Knight, and Moore, *de Soto Chronicles*; Lankford, "How Historical?"

13. Biedma, "Relation"; Elvas, "True Relation"; Garcilaso, "La Florida"; Rangel, "Account."

14. Hoffman, "Introduction," 13–16; Galloway, "Incestuous de Soto Narratives"; see also the essays in Galloway, *Hernando de Soto Expedition*; and Lankford, "How Historical?"

15. For summaries of this work, see Anderson and Sassaman, *Recent Developments*, 152–90; Blitz, "New Perspectives"; see also Bowne, *Mound Sites*.

16. Anderson, "Stability and Change"; Anderson, *Savannah River Chiefdoms*, 4–9; Hally, "Territorial Size"; Hally and Chamblee, "Temporal Distribution," 424; Livingood, "Many Dimensions"; Steponaitis, "Contrasting Patterns"; Steponaitis, "Location Theory." Cahokia is the exception to these patterns. It was an expansive polity whose capital city was one of the largest in the world at the time. The distinctions of Cahokia are such that many archaeologists categorize it as a state-level society rather than a chiefdom; for an introduction to these debates see Pauketat, *Chiefdoms*, and Anderson and Ethridge, "Book Forum."

17. Anderson, "Stability and Change"; Anderson, *Savannah River Chiefdoms*, 4–9; Hally, "Nature of Mississippian Regional Systems"; Hally, "Platform Mound Construction"; Hally, Smith, and Langford, "Archaeological Reality"; Steponaitis, "Location Theory."

18. Brown, "Sequencing the Braden Style"; Knight, "Farewell"; Lankford, Reilly, and Garber, *Visualizing the Sacred*; Reilly and Garber, introduction to *Ancient Objects and Sacred Realms*, 4–5.

19. Ethridge, *From Chicaza*, 18–24.

20. Dye, "Art, Ritual, and Chiefly Warfare"; Lankford "Some Cosmological Motifs," 14–15, 21–27; Reilly, "People of Earth," 127–29.

21. Blitz, "New Perspectives," 4.

22. Blitz, "New Perspectives," 5.

23. Hudson, Smith, and DePratter, "de Soto Expedition," 19.

24. Elvas, "True Relation," 77.

25. Ethridge, "Navigating," 65; Hudson, *Knights of Spain*, 14.

26. Hudson, *Southeastern Indians*, 22–25.

27. Rangel, "Account," 255.

28. Biedma, "Relation," 225; Elvas, "True Relation," 59–61; Hudson, *Knights of Spain*, 83; Rangel, "Account," 255.

29. Elvas, "True Relation," 130, 154; Ethridge, "Navigating," 82–83.

30. With slight variations, my ethnohistorical analysis agrees with Hudson in *Knights of Spain*, 230–31, as well as with archaeologists' observations; see, especially, Regnier, *Reconstructing Tascalusa's Chiefdom*,129–40; Jenkins and Sheldon, "Late Mississippian/Protohistoric Ceramic Chronology," 70, 85, 95–104.

31. For the history of this polity see Smith, *Coosa*.

32. Biedma, "Relation," 232; Elvas, "True Relation," 93–95; Rangel, "Account," 285–88.

33. Ethridge et al., "Comparative Analysis," 167; Rangel, "Account," 288 (quotation).

34. Elvas, "True Relation," 95; Rangel, "Account," 288.

35. Rangel, "Account," 288, 291.

36. Elvas, "True Relation," 95.

37. Elvas, "True Relation," 95; Rangel, "Account," 288.

38. Elvas, "True Relation," 95.

39. Lankford, *Looking for Lost Lore*, 98–114; Smith and Hally, "Chiefly Behavior."

40. Lankford, *Looking for Lost Lore*, 111–12; Smith and Hally, "Chiefly Behavior," 100.

41. Dye, *War Paths, Peace Paths*, 145–52.

42. Beck, "Consolidation and Hierarchy"; Blitz, "Mississippian Chiefdoms"; Hally, Smith, and Langford, "Archaeological Reality"; Smith, *Coosa*.

43. Biedma, "Relation," 232; Elvas, "True Relation," 95–96; Ethridge et al., "Comparative Analysis," 167; Rangel, "Account," 288, 290.

44. Hudson, *Knights of Spain*, 230–31; Jenkins, "Tracing the Origins," 214–16, 221, 223; Regnier, *Reconstructing Tascalusa's Chiefdom*, 81; Sheldon, "Present State," 120; Waselkov, Derry, and Jenkins, "Archaeology of Mabila's Cultural Landscape," 230–31. However, Regnier, in *Reconstructing Tascalusa's Chiefdom*, 44, suggests the Big Eddy and Thirty Acre Field sites may also be contenders.

45. Rangel, "Account," 288.

46. Rangel, "Account," 290.

47. Biedma, "Relation," 232; Elvas, "True Relation," 95–96; Rangel, "Account," 290–91, quotation on 291.

48. Elvas, "True Relation," 96.

49. Biedma, "Relation," 233.

50. Hudson, *Southeastern Indians*, 184–96.

51. Hudson, *Juan Pardo Expeditions*," 64–67.

52. Ethridge, *From Chicaza*, 47–48; Hudson, *Juan Pardo Expeditions*, 61–62, 65; Knight, "Moundville"; Knight, *Mound Excavations at Moundville*, 364–65; Knight, "Puzzles of Creek Social Organization."

53. The term "cacique" comes from Taino, a Caribbean language, and translates as "chief" or "leader." Spanish explorers and colonists adopted the term and later applied it to native leaders across the Americas; Hudson, *Juan Pardo Expeditions*, 63.

54. Ethridge, *From Chicaza*, 48.

55. Barnett, *Natchez Indians*, 44–45, 64, 86–87; Lorenz, "Natchez," 158–59; Milne, *Natchez Country*, 120–48.

56. Anderson and Sassaman, *Recent Developments*, 167; Blitz, "Mississippian Chiefdoms"; Hally, "Platform Mound Construction"; Jenkins, "Tracing the Origins," 191–95; see also Curet, "Chief Who Is Dead."

57. Biedma, "Relation," 232–33; Elvas, "True Relation," 96–99; Ethridge et al., "Comparative Analysis," 168–69; Hudson, *Knights of Spain*, 231; Rangel, "Account," 291–94.

58. Rangel, "Account," 291.

59. Biedma, "Relation," 232; Elvas, "True Relation," 96 (quotation).

60. Biedma, "Relation," 232.

61. Biedma, "Relation," 232; Elvas, "True Relation," 96.

62. Elvas, "True Relation," 96.

63. Biedma, "Relation," 232 (quotation); Rangel, "Account," 291.

64. Biedma, "Relation," 230, 232; Elvas, "True Relation," 82–83, 92, 133, 155, 157; Hudson, *Knights of Spain*, 172–75, 214–15, 340–41, 390–94.

65. Blitz, "Mississippian Chiefdoms," 15–16; Galloway, *Choctaw Genesis*, 110–11.

66. Biedma, "Relation," 232.

67. Biedma, "Relation," 232; Elvas, "True Relation," 96; Rangel, "Account," 291.

68. Biedma, "Relation," 232–33; DePratter, Hudson, and Smith, "Hernando de Soto Expedition"; Elvas, "True Relation," 96; Ethridge et al., "Comparative Analysis," 169–71; Hudson, *Knights of Spain*, 233–34; Rangel, "Account," 291.

69. Ethridge, "Navigating," 70–72.

70. Biedma, "Relation," 232–33; Elvas, "True Relation," 96–98; Ethridge et al., "Comparative Analysis," 170–71; Hudson, *Knights of Spain*, 234–35; Rangel, "Account," 291–92.

71. Ethridge et al., "Comparative Analysis," 170–71; Hally, "Territorial Size"; Hally and Chamblee, "Temporal Distribution," 424.

72. Elvas, "True Relation," 95, 105; Hudson, *Knights of Spain*, 228, 259; Rangel, "Account," 288, 296.

73. Biedma, "Relation," 232; Elvas, "True Relation," 94–95; Hudson, *Knights of Spain*, 218; Rangel, "Account," 284–85.

74. Biedma, "Relation," 238–40; Elvas, "True Relation," 106, 117–20; Hudson, *Knights of Spain*, 298–303; Rangel, "Account," 297, 300–4.

75. Elvas, "True Relation," 98; Rangel, "Account," 292.

76. Biedma, "Relation," 233; Elvas, "True Relation," 98; Ethridge et al., "Comparative Analysis," 171–72; Rangel, "Account," 292.

77. Regnier, *Reconstructing Tascalusa's Chiefdom*, 42–43; Waselkov, Derry, and Jenkins, "Archaeology of Mabila's Cultural Landscape," 232. Archaeologist Ashley Dumas organized a session at the 2021 Southeastern Archaeological Conference in Durham, NC, titled "The Marengo Archaeological Complex," in which her team presented much evidence for locating the polity of Mabila in Marengo County, Alabama. The site of the battle, however, still eludes us.

78. Biedma, "Relation," 233; Elvas, "True Relation," 98–99; Ethridge et al., "Comparative Analysis," 172–73; Rangel, "Account," 292.

79. Biedma, "Relation," 233; Elvas, "True Relation," 98 (quotation); Rangel, "Account," 292. These would not have been like the cloth or wool blankets found in the Old World but rather were likely well-worked, luxurious animal skins used as blankets and wraps.

80. Biedma, "Relation," 233; Elvas, "True Relation," 98; Ethridge et al., "Comparative Analysis," 172–73; Rangel, "Account," 292.

81. Biedma, "Relation," 233.

82. Biedma, "Relation," 233; Elvas, "True Relation," 98–99; Rangel, "Account," 292.

83. Rangel, "Account," 292.

84. Biedma, "Relation," 233; Elvas, "True Relation," 98; Ethridge et al., "Comparative Analysis," 174; Rangel, "Account," 292.

85. Rangel, "Account," 292–93.

86. Biedma, "Relation," 233; Elvas, "True Relation," 99 (quotation); Ethridge et al., "Comparative Analysis," 172–73; Rangel, "Account," 292.

87. Elvas, "True Relation," 99.

88. Biedma, "Relation," 233; Elvas, "True Relation," 99 (quotation); Rangel, "Account," 292.

89. Hally, "Territorial Size."

90. There are some indications that warriors from Coosa may have joined the Indian forces; see Hally, *King*, 490–91; Hudson, *Knights of Spain*, 245–46. Perhaps Tascalusa persuaded Coosa to join his forces, which would have added considerably to the ranks.

91. Biedma, "Relation," 236; Elvas, "True Relation," 104–5; Ethridge et al., "Comparative Analysis," 175–78; Rangel, "Account," 294–97.

92. The accounts of the battle are quite exciting; see Biedma, "Relation," 233–36; Elvas, "True Relation," 99–104; Ethridge et al., "Comparative Analysis," 173–74; Hudson, *Knights of Spain*, 238–49; Rangel, "Account," 292–94.

93. Ethridge, *From Chicaza*, 51–52.

94. Ethridge et al., "Comparative Analysis," 174.

95. Regnier, *Reconstructing Tascalusa's Chiefdom*, 135–36.

96. Regnier, *Reconstructing Tascalusa's Chiefdom*, 76–82.

97. Priestly, *Luna Papers*, 291.

98. Jenkins, "Tracing the Origins," 223–36; Regnier, *Reconstructing Tascalusa's Chiefdom*, 135–37.

99. Ethridge, *From Chicaza*, 66–69; Galloway, *Choctaw Genesis*, 161; Hudson et al., "Tristán de Luna Expedition," 36–39; Jenkins, "Tracing the Origins," 224–27; Priestly, *Luna Papers*, 291; Regnier, *Reconstructing Tascalusa's Chiefdom*, 135–37.

100. Ethridge, *From Chicaza*, 60–61; Hudson, *Knights of Spain*, 110–15, 238–49, 266–74, 336–38.

101. Blitz, *Ancient Chiefdoms*, 69–97, 123–25, 176–78, 180–81; Ethridge, *From Chicaza*, 61; Wesson, "Chiefly Power and Food Storage," 157–58.

102. Ethridge, *From Chicaza*, 60–88; Hally and Chamblee, "Temporal Distribution," 429.

103. Hudson, *Knights of Spain*, 179–80, 228–29.

104. Ethridge, "Creating the Shatter Zone"; Ethridge, *From Chicaza*, 3–5; Ethridge, introduction to *Mapping the Mississippian Shatter Zone*, ed. Ethridge and Shuck-Hall, 2; Hudson, introduction to *Transformation of the Southeastern Indians*, xii–xxxvi.

105. Ethridge, *From Chicaza*, 67–73.

CHAPTER 5

Picax-andé Ins-tisle and the Llaneros

APACHE POWER IN THE INDIGENOUS BORDERLANDS OF THE LATE-EIGHTEENTH-CENTURY SOUTHERN PLAINS

Cuauhtémoc Velasco Ávila and Antonio Cruz Zárate

On July 10, 1787, Colonel Juan de Ugalde, military commander of the Provincias Internas de Oriente (modern-day Texas and northeastern Mexico), was campaigning against the Mescalero Apaches in the Pecos River region when Picax-andé Ins-tinsle, high chief of the Lipiyan, or Llanero, Apaches, appeared before him to negotiate a peace agreement. The Spanish knew virtually nothing about the Llaneros, whose territory lay far beyond their own frontier outposts. The Apache leader told the colonel, "There are only three captains: the Great One up above, you, and me. The first one is watching us, listening to what we say, so we will see who does not speak the truth." Ugalde was surprised to hear such words come "from a gentile," given that "someone of Catholic instruction could not have said more." The resulting agreement committed the Lipiyans to assisting the Spanish against other Apache bands. In exchange, the Spanish were to supply the Lipiyans with gifts and military support against the Comanches.[1]

The Lipiyans have received little attention in the existing historiography, which generally holds that the only Apaches active in northeastern New Spain in the 1780s were the already defeated Mescaleros and Lipans, both of whom desperately sought Spanish protection. Gary Anderson argued that in the eighteenth century the Apaches were ceding territory to their enemies, fragmenting into small bands, and losing access to bison hunting grounds, and that by the 1780s, they could no longer resist the Spanish.[2] According to Pekka Hämäläinen, the Comanches had taken complete control of the southern Great Plains by then, thus consolidating an impenetrable "empire" and forcing the Apaches to take refuge in the hills along the Rio Grande or in missions and presidios.[3] Our sources however paint a different, and exceptionally rich, portrait of the Lipiyans, who successfully competed for the resources of the southern Great Plains in the face of Comanche power. In the process, they extended the indigenous borderlands that the Spanish termed "Apachería" considerably farther north than is generally believed. Those sources also reveal the critical role of the charismatic Picax-andé— recognized by various Apache groups as a political and spiritual leader—in the interethnic relations and geopolitical balance of the region.[4]

The Apache nation consisted of a combination of peoples and rancherías (bands) who recognized one another through their language and cultural features, even if that recognition at times failed to evoke empathy.[5] Since the early eighteenth century, Comanches and other indigenous groups had been pushing the plains, or eastern, Apaches to the margins of the Great Plains. The Jicarillas had fallen back to northwestern New Mexico, the Faraones and Mescaleros to the region between the Pecos River and the Rio Grande, and the Lipans to the banks of the Nueces River and Rio Grande. In the southwestern plains, Natages and Lipiyans, also known as Llaneros, lived between the Pecos and Colorado Rivers. Despite a certain confusion in the sources regarding these three ethnonyms, which at times appear to refer to different groups, the generic term *llaneros* usually applied to the Lipiyans and at times to the Natages as well, while some sources considered both to be part of the Mescaleros.[6] The Lipiyans possibly originated from the Apaches called "Carlanas," some of whom relocated to the area of Pecos Pueblo, New Mexico, where they traded while also serving as explorers and intermediaries in a multiethnic alliance promoted by the interim governor of New Mexico, Tomás Vélez Cachupín, between 1749 and 1754.[7]

In November 1786, an expedition of 226 men commanded by Captain José Menchaca of Aguaverde Presidio reached a region Spaniards called Los Arenales. Sherry Robinson locates Los Arenales, a Spanish toponym that alludes to sandy terrain, in Monahan Sandhills, Texas. Menchaca ordered the destruction of a "fort" that Mescalero Apaches were rumored to maintain, seemingly at the same place to which inspector Hugo O'Conor had relocated some Natages several years earlier. Mechaca's discovery confirmed that Apaches had taken refuge in Los Arenales. The sand dunes in the area allowed them to defend themselves and survey the surrounding country, where "various water wells" enabled their subsistence in this arid region.[8]

In the same month the governor of New Mexico, Juan Bautista de Anza, reported a visit from two "Lipan" captains who requested a resumption of the trade that they had carried on in Pecos Pueblo "thirty-five or forty years" earlier, a fact suggesting that the emissaries were really Carlanas/Lipiyans. Anza accepted on the condition that they not disturb the peace that had been in effect with the Comanches for the preceding two years, to which the chiefs agreed.[9]

At the beginning of 1787, a firm alliance existed among Natages, Lipiyans, and Mescaleros. In February of that year, Comandante General Jacobo de Ugarte y Loyola learned that the Mescaleros wanted to make peace at the Presidio del Norte (located at Junta de los Ríos, today Ojinaga; hereafter, "El Norte"); consequently, he sent Captain Domingo Díaz to negotiate the terms. By the end of March, eight chiefs had gathered at the presidio—Alegre, Ligero, Patule, Zapato Tuerto, El Quemado, Montera Blanca, Cuero Verde, and Bigotes el Bermejo—each one representing his respective ranchería. Each promised to release captive Spaniards, cease hostilities, and settle down to a life of farming in the area, all in exchange for being allowed to trade with the presidio, to hunt, and to "make" their *mescales* (that is, to harvest the mescal agave on which their subsistence depended) when they so requested. The Mescaleros had sent messengers to the chiefs Natagé and El Calvo ("the bald man," the name given to Picax-andé in Nueva Vizcaya), based, respectively, in the Sierra de Guadalupe and in "the sand dunes . . . getting ready for a bison hunt," to have the chiefs join them near the presidio.[10]

The resulting peace would soon face a severe threat, however. In April, troops from Coahuila under the command of Colonel Ugalde attacked the people of Zapato Tuerto in the Sierra del Carmen, killing three Indians and capturing aa handful of prisoners along with their small herd of horses. On hearing the news, Captain Juan Bautista Elguezábal sent an emissary to remind Ugalde that the Apaches he had attacked were at peace and had been authorized to collect mescal in the sierra, and he should therefore return both the animals and the prisoners.[11] But Ugalde disdainfully ignored the warning and pushed forward with his campaign by attacking the ranchería of Cuerno Verde.[12]

As he was concluding his expedition, Ugalde learned that many bison were present in the *arenales* near the Colorado River, some eighty leagues from the Pecos River. Moreover, there was "a great captain named Pica-gandé [*sic*], which means Strong Arm . . . whose nation was called *llaneros lipiyanes*." This chief led many Indians "well armed with rifles, arrows, bows, spears, shields and *cueras* [leather jackets]." These Apaches had proved their bravery and bellicosity in repeated skirmishes with the warlike Comanches. The Lipiyans had never considered abandoning the territory they still controlled, despite the proximity of those enemies, nor had they sought peace with the Spanish presidios.[13]

Ugalde decided to go north of the Pecos River with a detachment of more than two hundred men to attack the Lipiyans and supply his troops with meat. After nine days of suffering much hardship and a shortage of water while crossing open plains, he reached the vicinity of the Colorado, where he was able to supply his troops with water and a wealth of meat, skins, tallow, and lard. Ugalde could thus verify the bountiful resources of Lipiyan territory: endless grasslands, groves of mesquite trees, natural wells, watering holes, rivers, wild dates and figs, deer, rabbits, mustangs, and enormous herds of bison. "It can be called a promised land!" the colonel wrote, "since it has all that is needed for human life . . . the Lipiyans said truthfully that they had no reason to steal in order to eat!"[14] Three unarmed Lipiyans then presented themselves before Ugalde, insisting that their nation consisted of "a significant number of warriors" and that they were sworn enemies of the Comanches but never of the Spaniards, not having had dealings with nor received gifts from the latter. Their leader, Captain Picax-andé, whom they respected and obeyed for his age, bravery, and integrity, wished to meet Ugalde in person to request that he receive them under his "protection and friendship," a request that Ugalde accepted.[15]

On July 10 Ugalde crossed the Pecos on his way back toward Coahuila. Seeing that Picax-andé and six Lipiyans were approaching, he stopped near the river, ordered that a rustic dais be erected, and sent a Mescalero and some Lipans who were part of his expedition to receive the visitors. The Lipiyan captain crossed the river and advanced to "within about six steps" of Ugalde, who came out to receive him since, as he wrote, "this practice ought to be observed even among barbarians . . . and extending a hand, I led him to the aforementioned dais, where I sat down, placing him on my right, with the officers and *padre capellán* [chaplain] in a circle seated on skins, the Lipiyans, Mescaleros, and Lipans behind me, and the other people forming another circle around us." Ugalde served them "meat, *pinole* [ground corn], biscuits, and cigars," but before eating, the Indian chief, a man of some fifty years of age, "with the face and presence of a soldier," issued the declaration with which we began this chapter. Ugalde began to enumerate his own military merits as "a lash to everyone wicked and . . . a protection for the good," omitting to mention that his determination to make war on the Indians had resulted in subjugating many of them. Three Lipiyan captains then reflected on the character and authority of Picax-andé as the implacable enemy of the Comanches, and as someone who had never had to threaten the Spanish in order to eat nor had stolen their horses. Picax-andé himself acknowledged that he had heard of the colonel's actions and stated his desire for peace even though he had never been disposed to accept the proposals of the soldiers at El Norte. He thanked Ugalde for the reception and declared that he sought only the latter's friendship. The colonel took pride in having the Lipiyan chief come willingly to surrender peacefully to him and answered that it was "for his own good," since being with him, "he had nothing to desire, nor anyone to fear."[16]

On July 11 the entourage set out with Ugalde at the head of his soldiers, and the Lipan, Mescalero, and Lipiyan captains leading their respective men. Now reunited with the entire Spanish force, they resumed their dialogue. Ugalde emphasized that from that moment on he expected the Lipiyans to be enemies of the Mescaleros who threatened Spanish settlements and haciendas, to avoid creating Apache rancherías between Spanish-held territory and the San Pedro River, to provide information when they learned of some encampment in the mountains north of the Bolsón de Mapimí, and to support the Spanish troops in their campaign. In return, he promised, the King of Spain would furnish Picax-andé with abundant gifts and would support him in his war against the Comanches. The Lipiyan chief accepted and asked to be given a copy of the agreement, but with Ugalde's own signature on it. After eating, Ugalde presented and dressed Picax-andé with "a scarlet cloak . . . a red sash, a silk cap, and a painted handkerchief," requesting that he show it off all over the camp. The following morning Ugalde gave Picax-andé knives, supplies, and a horse for himself, as well as pinole, biscuits, *piloncillo* (hard brown sugar), and tobacco for his followers. After this the Lipiyans left, apparently satisfied and pleased with the kind treatment and the gifts.[17]

In early November, Governor Fernando de la Concha in Santa Fe received a visit from some Lipiyans led by "Captain Brazo Fuerte" ("Strong Arm"; that is, Picax-andé himself), who carried with him a letter of safe conduct signed by Ugalde at the Milpitas arroyo. Requesting to be admitted in peace, they soon withdrew, declaring themselves pleased with the treatment and the gifts they received.[18]

When Ugarte learned of these events, he sarcastically expressed his delight that Ugalde had obtained an agreement with the "great captain" of the Lipiyans. Far from seeing them as a separate band of Apaches, he believed that the Lipiyan nation was "as old, well known, and inimical to us" as the Mescaleros, and that, considering the Lipiyans' "negligible numbers, and their proximity, union, and kinship" with the Mescaleros, they did not deserve to be considered "a separate body." Ugarte also played down the importance of the pact, since, if the Lipiyans were not hostile to the Spanish, there was no advantage in making them stop their incursions, unless they provided strong support to subdue rebellious Apaches.[19]

But Viceroy Manuel Antonio Flórez, an advocate of using the iron fist against the Mescalero Apaches, played up Ugalde's every deed. Despite Ugarte's lengthy argument for reprimanding Ugalde's cruel campaign and his doubts about the colonel's supposed achievements, the viceroy elected to give Ugalde all the resources he might need to keep the Mescaleros under his control, and to furnish the Lipiyans and Lipans with gifts. In addition, he authorized a formal title for Picax-andé as captain and leader-in-chief of the Lipiyans, Mescaleros, and Lipans, and following Ugalde's insistence on a free hand in warring against the Apaches, Flórez proposed dividing the Provincias Internas into two separate commands.[20] The Comandancia del Poniente, which included the Californias, Sonora, Nueva Vizcaya, and New Mexico, were to remain under Jacobo de Ugarte, while Juan de Ugalde was to command the Oriente, including Texas, Coahuila, Santander, Nuevo León, and the districts of Saltillo and Parras, originally part of Nueva Vizcaya.[21]

In early 1788 Ugarte and the captains of Nueva Vizcaya tried to maintain peace with the Mescaleros in the face of provocations from the Coahuila troops. The captain of El Norte, Domingo Díaz, dispatched two Mescaleros to invite the Lipiyans to join the peace accords, sending Picax-andé "two of my own best horses as a gift, since this leader is the god of the others and all obey him, and many of them consider him their general."[22] A few days later the messengers returned to report that the Lipiyan chief, obeying Ugalde's summons, had left to confer with the latter in Coahuila, but he would return via El Norte.[23]

In response to Picax-andé's complaint that he lacked horses, Ugalde sent Lieutenant José Menchaca to the Lipiyan camp with forty steeds as well as cattle, corn biscuits, pinole, and cigars. Menchaca sent an advance unit of two soldiers to announce their arrival, but they soon returned with an Indian who informed the lieutenant that "the great captain Picax-andé Yns-tinle had been attending a religious ceremony since daybreak [that] should conclude when the sun goes down"; during the ceremony no one could interrupt him, nor could people from outside approach him. Menchaca took up a position on a hill from which he could see the camp and observed that all the adults and children in the encampment, naked from the waist up, barefoot, and with their hair loose, waited in complete silence in front of the best tent, which they entered in turns, four at a time. The ceremony went on until sunset without anyone speaking, eating, drinking, or smoking.[24]

After the ritual concluded, Menchaca was allowed to enter the camp, where he received a warm embrace from Picax-andé himself, who accepted with much satisfaction "the gifts that I had prepared for him, ordering that they be distributed among the families of that huge village, with the equality and proportion that a father observes with his sons." Menchaca tried to return immediately, but Picax-andé refused to let him leave, stating that he would hold a dance in his honor, then he returned to his tent. That night "a great number of Indians, both male and female," gathered in a broad semicircle that they illuminated "with kindling placed at regular intervals," and began a *mitote* (dance) that lasted until dawn, and which involved "extraordinary ceremonies, powerful shrieks, and songs that had the sole object of wishing destruction on their worst enemies, the Comanche Indians."[25]

When his people at last retired, Picax-andé went to his tent, explaining to Menchaca that he was going to carry out a ceremony like the one held the day before and requesting that Menchaca begin his return at midday, as dictated by the ritual he was to perform. As a result, Menchaca managed to observe the complex ceremony more closely and determined that it involved only Lipans "who were to enter to offer their submission or tribute inside the tent of the great captain," even though everyone came to watch. Menchaca also noted that none of the leading captains of the Lipans, Lipiyans, or Mescaleros dared to look Picax-andé directly in the face and that everyone rendered him homage.

It is difficult to find ethnographic descriptions of a ceremony like the one Menchaca witnessed. In June 1789, Second Lieutenant Casimiro Valdés asked the Lipiyan captain Xatti-es-cha about the nature of Picax-andé's god and how they communicated; Xatti-es-cha replied that he did not know because, even though Picax-andé held him in high regard, when the chief was speaking with this god only his wife could be in the tent. When both entered, all the others had to remain kneeling at a certain distance, without lifting their heads and with their eyes shut, since anyone who opened their eyes would die instantly. From the interior of the tent were heard songs, a bell, and much speaking, followed by a loud sound resembling a thunderbolt. Afterwards, Picax-andé would emerge, ask everyone to rise, and tell them that he had spoken with his god.[26] The ceremony of giving gifts to Picax-andé may have been a form of Lipan ritual submission, which apparently the Mescalero chiefs living near San Fernando also performed when they asked Ugalde for permission to honor the Lipiyan chief sometime later.[27]

On March 5, 1788, in Santa Rosa, Picax-andé appeared with "six captains and fourteen prominent Indians of different and populous groups who recognize his leadership," having left a large encampment at the source of the San Rodrigo River, some thirty leagues away. According to Ugalde, the power of Picax-andé became evident "more and more each day, owing to the excessive number of high-ranking captains among the Apaches who accept him as their superior, pay him obedience as if he were a natural prince, and worship him as an oracle through whose voice, they believe, the idols speak."[28]

Picax-andé entered Santa Rosa with his retinue, all covered with skins and feathers, the horses decked out in protective covering, and the men shooting their rifles into the air. Ugalde saw them from the door of his house and, in reply, shot off three rounds of artillery as they approached. A round of hugs followed, a show of mutual respect prior to negotiations. Ugalde led by the hand the Lipiyan chief who, "full of satisfaction and assisted by all of his people," sat down beside the comandante. Ugalde gave one of his usual speeches that concluded by recognizing that he was inclined to ratify the peace accord, since the Apaches had a captain who was "incapable of betraying his word."

For his part, Picax-andé stated that "he was captain because he had inherited the position from his ancestors" as "captain of many captains," that "he had never used his power against the Spanish," but that neither had he wanted to seek peace, because many times he had seen Indians and Spaniards fail to live up to their agreements. He assured the Spaniard that "it being far from his way of thinking to break agreements, he had always declined to make them, so that he did not want to see them violated and thereby involve himself in a completely unnecessary war."[29]

When it came time to eat, tables were arranged in the same meeting room, and Ugalde conducted Picax-andé to his reserved seat, where he had prepared a special plate. However, the four captains who composed Picax-andé's escort did not want to be separated from him, and therefore, it was necessary to provide a special table to accommodate this "group of bodyguards."

After the dinner, Ugalde explained that the viceroy had ordered that Picax-andé be recognized as captain and main *caudillo* (leader) of the Lipiyan, Lipan, Mescalero, Sende, Nit-ajende, and Cachu-ende nations and given the name Manuel Picax-andé Ins-tinsle de Ugalde. The caudillo was presented with a staff of office and a parchment title, written on "a bordered parchment, with the royal coat of arms" and the portraits of the commander general and the Lipiyan captain. That afternoon, following a nap, Picax-andé asked that his title be shown to his captains and to the Indian women, an opportunity that Ugalde used to emphasize the distinction of the favor that the viceroy had granted.[30]

During the visit, it became clear that Picax-andé was intent on countering the Comanches' might, whereas Ugalde's goal was waging war on the Mescaleros. The day after his arrival, Picax-andé expressed his desire to destroy the Comanches and asked that Ugalde not treat them like friends when he was in Texas, arguing that he could defeat the Comanches in short order were it not for the Spanish assistance. Ugalde then interrupted the chief to emphasize that he himself had never been a friend of the Comanches but was obligated to maintain peace in Texas if "they did not give him cause for war." In this way Ugalde avoided making a commitment that he could not keep, since the Comanches had made peace with the Spaniards in 1785 in Texas and in 1786 in New Mexico.

Friday, March 7, was a feast day, and as Ugalde was getting ready to hear mass, Picax-andé appeared with his interpreters, saying that he wanted to accompany the commander to the church. "It being impossible to dissuade him from that idea . . . he entered and maintained a reflective attention worthy of the most scrupulously observant Catholic." As they were exiting the building, the chief remarked that the "performance had come off quite well and had greatly pleased him." At noon on Saturday, Ugalde distributed among the peaceful Mescaleros the rations that he normally gave out on Sunday, in this instance doing so personally and substantially increasing the quantity to impress his guest.[31]

At nine in the morning, immediately after a Sunday mass that Picax-andé once more attended, the Lipiyan chiefs, Spanish officers, prominent settlers, and peaceful Mescaleros met at Ugalde's residence, where the Spaniard conferred the staff and parchment title on Picax-andé to the latter's immense satisfaction and the delight of all those present. The Lipiyan chief then hugged the commander and all the Spaniards but not the other Indian captains. When Ugalde insisted he do so, Picax-andé explained that the only

Indians who were allowed to touch him were his guards, but he would allow it for Ugalde's sake on such a momentous occasion. It was evident, however, that he embraced the captains with great care, and they showed him the highest respect. A crowd waited in front of the house and, when they saw the Lipiyan captain and his attendants come out, they fired their rifles in the air, set off three cannon shots, and cheered their great leader with "loud shouting." After the meeting, wrote Ugalde, "food was served for all Indians, regardless of age and sex," including more than two hundred peaceful Mescaleros and the Lipiyan captain's retinue.[32]

A week later Ugalde visited the Lipiyan ranchería, halfway between Santa Rosa and the San Rodrigo River, with the intention of making a speech to as many Lipiyans as possible. As Ugalde approached the meeting place, a large party of Indians appeared, using "the whistle customarily used by Comanches" and gesturing and shooting their rifles to honor the visitor. At the center of this party was Picax-andé "dressed like a Spaniard in his red uniform, trimmed with silver, carrying the staff" he had received. Upon reaching the camp, Ugalde distributed among the Indians "a number of cattle," along with four bundles containing sweet bread, tobacco, and various trinkets.

Picax-andé visited Ugalde once again on the afternoon of March 16 to hand over three captives. He explained that the Lipiyans had bought them from the Mescaleros and Sendes, who in turn had obtained them from the Gileños, but that he considered it unjust to keep them as prisoners given the peace accord. In exchange, he asked for horses that he could use to pay the former owners of two of the captives. Ugalde approved the deal, adding that while he had never paid ransom for recovered prisoners, he was nevertheless disposed to supply the horses not as a payment for the "items he was handing over," but rather as a "personal gift" in favor of those who "truly desire friendship with the Spanish."[33]

Lastly, Ugalde summoned most of the people to inform them of the agreement and what they had to do if they wished to act in their own best interests, explaining to them the strength of the Spanish and the "northern Indians" (that is, the Comanches and their allies), which they could "surely" and "shortly verify." Now that he had reached an understanding with the Lipiyan captain, the lesser-ranking Lipan and Mescalero captains promised to comply faithfully with what he proposed, "all for the desired and suitable end of harmony in the provinces." At eight in the evening, after Picax-andé had withdrawn to his tent, the Indians began a dance like the one described earlier, which lasted until two in the morning.

The following day, before Ugalde departed, Picax-andé asked him to prohibit the supplying of shotguns and munitions to his Comanche enemies in
San Antonio de Béxar and New Mexico. Ugalde considered this request "fair
and reasonable," replying that he could do as requested in Béxar, which lay
within his jurisdiction.[34] Ugalde tried unsuccessfully to find out more concerning the rituals that Menchaca had witnessed. Despite having "broached
many times the matter," both Picax-andé and the Mescalero captains simply
avoided the topic.[35]

On March 30, 1788, Ugalde received a message from Aguaverde, reporting
that some Indians had provoked a horse stampede in which six animals disappeared. Second Lieutenant Casimiro Valdés rode out with sixteen men to
follow their tracks, and although he failed to locate the culprits, after considerable exploration he deduced that they were Lipans.[36] The next day Ugalde
ordered Valdés and an interpreter to go to Picax-andé and request "with deep-
est friendship" that he "conduct a search" for the guilty parties and, upon
capturing them, send along the thieves and the stolen animals, assuring Picax-
andé that he would not kill the men but only punish them.[37]

Valdés left San Fernando with twenty men. Upon reaching the San Diego
River he found that the Lipiyan ranchería had abruptly fled the day before,
and based on their tracks, had separated into two groups. He cautiously followed the tracks and, when he reached the Rio Grande, he encountered the
Lipan captains José Antonio, Moreno, and Casimiro, together with several
armed men. They told him they had heard that the Spanish were going to
attack both them and the Lipiyans, who were camped nearby and who
were ready to escape to their own lands at a moment's notice. Valdés urged
them not to believe this "nonsense" and explained that he bore a letter from
Ugalde to Picax-andé. Toward midnight Picax-andé himself arrived. Embrac-
ing the second lieutenant, he asked, "Sir, what is happening here? Why do
the Spanish want to kill me and all my people?" Once Valdés cleared up the
misunderstanding, Picax-andé referred to Ugalde as "my father, the Great
Captain" and assured the Spanish that "he would not believe false reports,"
since "he was a true friend to the Spanish, as would be seen in time."[38] Picax-
andé then dictated to the interpreter a letter for Ugalde, reporting that he
had discovered two horses from Villa de San Fernando and had sent for the
two guilty parties to be punished.[39]

On April 12, the Mescaleros who had been camped at Santa Rosa since
March 6 failed to show up for their Sunday rations; moreover, there had been
several murders (a soldier, his brother, a slave, and a settler), along with

robberies and other crimes. Ugalde blamed everything on the Mescaleros, calling them prisoners to "the corrupting vices of murder and theft, which are inherent in their inhuman condition." He immediately sent Valdés to inform Picax-andé that the Mescaleros had been "violating their word" and that Ugalde counted on him to wage war against them and not to receive them ever again in his rancherías.[40] On April 16 Ugalde received a reply from Picax-andé stating that it was necessary "to pursue them until they are no more."[41] That month, Ugalde sent orders—in reality a hodgepodge of apologies, suggestions, invitations, and veiled threats—to the Lipiyan chief.[42] There is no proof that this document ever reached Picax-andé, who appears not to have come to Santa Rosa until December.

Meanwhile, on May 2, Ugalde informed Ugarte, who had now become commander of the Poniente (Western) Provinces, of Picax-andé's visit to Santa Rosa and of his own "faithful" compliance with the accords, asking him to "observe the peace" with the Lipiyans in the provinces under his authority.[43] Ugarte expressed surprise that Ugalde had attacked the peaceful Mescaleros at El Norte in March 1787, and answered laconically and in a somewhat ironic tone that he could not issue any such orders, since they ran counter to the viceroy's own April 15 instructions that "in the subsequent peace [there was to be] no group of Apaches either in this province or in New Mexico . . . and for the Lipiyans, Lipans, and Mescaleros to enjoy peace under the exclusive authority of our government, they are to relocate to Coahuila or its surrounding territory."[44] Ugarte similarly expressed skepticism about the trustworthiness of Picax-Andé, whom the Mescaleros claimed had participated in various thefts in Coahuila, in cooperation with the Natages and certain Lipans, though he acknowledged individuals beyond the chief's control may have committed the acts.[45] Shortly thereafter Ugalde persuaded the viceroy to leave "to his judgment peace with the Lipiyans and Lipans, along with war with the Mescaleros," even though the viceroy had previously ordered Ugalde to coordinate his campaign against the Mescaleros with Ugarte.[46]

An incident in early August gives some of idea of Picax-andé's prowess as a warrior. He was camped with all the Lipiyans and three Lipan rancherías near the old San Sabás Presidio and the Colorado River when Comanches attacked them at daybreak. The Lipiyan chief ordered his people to keep their families in their tents and "mounted his horse in the face of great difficulty, for the Comanches were pouncing on him" but he managed to defeat them, killing thirteen Comanches, including two "handsome" captains.[47]

Picax-andé sent the Lipan captain Daunica-Jate to inform "his father" Ugalde that he had fought the Comanches "with the title hanging from his shoulder," and that he had not visited Santa Rosa because he was extremely busy. Daunica-Jate stated that "he had never seen a man like the Lipiyan captain," who in full view of everyone "had killed four men with his lance," including one who was wearing "the uniform they give at San Antonio de Béxar." He had also taken from the Comanches many mules and saddled horses.

On December 31, Picax-andé appeared at the Valle de Santa Rosa accompanied by a Lipiyan man, two Lipan captains, and nine prominent Lipan men, along with Valdés and other soldiers. The comandante received him "warmly and with manifestations of joy," for he was eager to settle on the terms of the campaign against the Mescaleros. Picax-andé opened by saying that he had come only to please Ugalde, but that he had to return to his own territory directly, since he was meeting the Lipans and the captains of his own people for a *carneada* (bison hunt) along the Pecos River. Ugalde agreed to let him leave, requesting that he return in two months to arrange the terms of the campaign, to which the Lipiyan chief agreed. Ugalde urged Picax-andé to turn against the Mescaleros, emphasizing their treachery and cruelty and underscoring his desire for revenge. Expressing his own anger, the Lipiyan chief insisted that the next time he came across the Mescaleros, "he would bind them and send them as prisoners," and that "if they resisted, he would kill them" and send Ugalde their heads. On the basis of this conversation, Ugalde reported to the viceroy that every day his friendship with Picax-andé was becoming "tighter, stronger, and more lasting."[48] Yet in his heart Ugalde nursed doubts about the Lipiyan's true relationship with the Mescaleros, given the chief's evident lack of interest in a campaign against them. For that reason, he ordered Valdés to escort the chief back to his ranchería and secretly spy on him.[49]

They departed on January 3, 1789, and after stopping in two Lipan rancherías, reached Las Vacas Pass on the sixth, where they sent up a smoke signal for the Lipiyans to come out and receive them. Once in the ranchería they smoked the ceremonial pipe three times while Picax-andé, in a lengthy speech, extolled the fine treatment he had received from the "great captain of the Spaniards, the great esteem with which he had been treated," the gifts he had received, and how satisfied he was—but he said nothing about the Mescaleros. Finally, he announced that everyone should treat Valdés like a Lipiyan captain owing to the latter's great concern for them, a statement that the people received with an enormous "din of enthusiasm," pledging to obey

Valdés while the captains came forward to embrace him. They then took Valdés to a tent that was "well arranged and embellished with hides," where he received a stream of visits from the captains and chiefs, until Picax-andé ordered them to let the Spaniard rest.[50]

The following day Valdés went with an interpreter to the tent of the main chief, where he was warmly received. He learned that two Mescalero captains had arrived during the night and had been welcomed, for they were not renegades and one of them was the brother of Picax-andé's wife. They had come to ask Picax-andé to intercede with Ugalde to make peace with them. Valdés replied that neither he nor the "great captain" were surprised that Picax-andé had contact with the Mescaleros at El Norte. Further, they knew all the Indians living with or related to Picax-andé "were subject to his authority" and that the chief would not allow them to harm Spaniards. Picax-andé then ordered his men to bring forward the Mescalero captains, Alegre and Zaragate, both of whom embraced Valdés. Once again "a huge number of Indians [gathered] before the tent of the great captain," and Picax-andé now spoke of Ugalde's anger "with the Mescaleros who had broken the peace," and he vowed not to rest until he had rigorously punished them.[51] Valdés next received visits from the Lipiyan captains, their women, and "many other Indians, both men and women"; around three in the afternoon the Mescalero chiefs joined the group. They announced their desire to meet Ugalde, for just as he had so tenaciously warred against them, they knew that he treated with utmost kindness those with whom he was at peace. Moreover, they offered to pursue those Mescaleros who had once lived in peace at Santa Rosa (Quijegusya, Patule, and El-lite) to ensure that they would neither cause harm nor break away from Picax-andé's authority.[52] Later that day, in Picax-andé's tent, the chief informed Valdés that while waiting for the Lipans to embark on their carneada, his people would be hungry and therefore he requested that Valdés personally provide him with "some cattle, sufficient corn, and a *tercio* [bark-wrapped bale] of tobacco," along with long knives and other "trifles," all to be brought to the San Diego River, where he would distribute the gifts among his people. Valdés agreed to this request.[53]

The following morning Picax-andé reiterated to Valdés, and in front of his own people, his thanks to Ugalde and his vow to capture as many Mescalero renegades as he came across. As he was traveling back to Santa Rosa, Valdés questioned the interpreter, a man who had been held captive among the Mescaleros for many years. The interpreter replied that he had seen several Mescaleros in the tents of the more remote rancherías, that he had been told of eighteen Mescalero tents, and that he presumed that the other captain, the aforementioned El-lite (also known as Quemado) was there, for he had seen his children and various Indians of his ranchería. El-lite, he went on to speculate, had not presented himself before Valdés because he was one of the renegades of Santa Rosa. The interpreter added that he knew from experience that the Mescaleros were brothers and relatives of the Lipiyans, and that it was impossible for the two to be "separated or turned against one another." Picax-andé was married to Alegre's sister and Alegre in turn to Picax-andé's sister, and thus were "all bound together." Consequently, when the Mescaleros committed a theft, they went to Picax-andé and shared the spoils with him, in exchange for which he took them in and defended them.[54]

On his return to Santa Rosa on January 14, Valdés shared this information with Ugalde confirming the latter's suspicions regarding Picax-andé. Instead of taking revenge immediately, Ugalde decided to have Valdés return once more to the Lipiyans with the promised gifts, instructing him "to understand more fully the thinking of the main chief of the eastern Apachería" by questioning the Lipan captain Dabegsil-sete (known to the Spanish as Casimiro), who had been raised from childhood alongside Valdés and had maintained a longstanding friendship with him.[55]

On January 18, Valdés met with Picax-andé, Zaragate, and some Lipiyans at the San Rodrigo River, where he handed over the gifts. On Picax-andé's orders, "the Indians held a celebration by killing several" cattle. Later, the chief called Valdés aside and asked whether it had angered Ugalde to learn that he had Mescaleros with him. Valdés responded in the negative, stating that the commander trusted Picax-andé and knew that whoever was in his company was also under his authority. The chief then summoned Alegre and Zaragate, who received the news with satisfaction.[56]

Throughout that afternoon and evening Valdés and Picax-andé held long conversations, the latter insisting that when he encountered the Mescalero captains Juan, Patule, and El-lite, he would have the opportunity to show himself true to his word by handing over "either the person or the head of any of them." Dabegsil-sete was present during the lengthy conversation. Later, when he was alone with Dabegsil-sete, Valdés asked him his opinion regarding the peace accords with the Lipiyan, assuring the Lipan that if he "comported himself faithfully," Ugalde would place him above the other Apache chiefs. The Lipan was silent in fear that word of the conversation would reach Picax-andé, and only responded after Valdés again promised to say nothing to anyone besides Ugalde. Valdés recorded Dabegsil-sete's answer as follows: "Picax-andé himself never stole from or harmed the Spanish, but his people ran with the Mescaleros, the Sendes, and with other Indians, staging attacks and killings, and he had seen them return with shod horses and mules, and with many valuables." Moreover, when the Indians returned with their spoils, each one gave Picax-andé a horse, a mule, a bit, or some other item. He suggested that Valdés observe the horses to confirm he was telling the truth, for some wore identifiable horseshoes, and further, during the dance he should pay attention to the jewelry the women wore. In addition, he informed the Spaniard that their ranchería included some seventy-eight Mescalero tents, and the captain El-lite was hiding in one. Dabegsil-sete concluded that the Lipiyans could not quarrel with their Mescalero brothers and relatives.[57]

At sunrise Picax-andé summoned his people yet again. This time Valdés began the conversation by discrediting the power of the Mescalero chief Juan and his followers, assuring the audience that Ugalde could easily subdue them, since he commanded a larger number of troops, horses, and supplies, all of which he would use to punish "those who have done wrong." Picax-andé then declared that the Mescaleros in question "merited nothing else than to be killed, and with them and their families out of the way, never to be remembered again." He continued that the Lipiyans would be the friends of the Spanish "until death," and that if even one of the Indians were to misbehave, he would be killed, "since the rest should not have to suffer for the mistakes of one, for it was understood that those who had been born there should also die there." Picax-andé's wife spoke next, asking the crowd in a loud voice to recall "the kindness and care with which the Spaniards treated them." She begged them not to put her husband in a bad light, and even less the "Capitán Grande" (that is, Ugalde). Everyone promised to comply. This unusual intervention of an Apache woman in a public event shows that her views influenced the community, particularly since there were other Mescaleros in the audience.

Dabegsil-sete had told Valdés that a Lipan man had enslaved a Spanish youth whom the Sendes had taken prisoner along the frontier. With Picax-andé's assistance, Valdés was able to ransom the youth in exchange for a horse, a sarape, a bit, a long knife, and two shoemaker's needles. Subsequently, Picax-andé summoned Zaragate and Alegre, and ceremoniously instructed the interpreters to explain to them as best as possible that after eating he had fallen asleep, and in his dream, he had spoken with "the Great Captain up above [God], who had commanded him not to fail in anything that he had offered the Spanish." Picax-andé had promised as much to God, and therefore "he would rather die than fail to keep his word." The "Great Captain up above" had also told him that when Valdés died, "all those of his nation would die," for which reason Picax-andé asked Valdés not to take any risks when he went out on his campaigns. According to Valdés, the chief communicated this "news" to all the captains "so that they knew what God had revealed to him." It was obvious that the Lipiyan chief's followers believed he had divine connections.

After concluding this statement, Picax-andé announced that "he had decided to invite all of his people to a dance." After evening prayers, wrote Valdés, "everyone came out with their drums, flutes, and other instruments, and they went about singing until they came to my tent and that of the captain Picax-andé, where they formed a circle in order to celebrate a mitote" that lasted until dawn. During the dance, Valdés did indeed confirm that many Apaches wore Spanish clothes and the women wore "on their arms fine fabrics of crimson and blue, well made and quite expensive." He tried to buy one to show to Ugalde, but the Indians refused to sell.[58]

On the last day of his visit, Valdés went to the Lipiyan chief's tent. Picax-andé's wife received him with great kindness and "words of endearment," stating that she considered him her "son," that Picax-andé was his "father," and that he had nothing to fear from either of them. Valdés took this opportunity to look over the chief's horses, and he recognized several stolen animals, including twelve or fourteen mules that had been stolen from a Francisco de Yermo in Coahuila the preceding August. He said farewell to Picax-andé and Dabegsil-sete, both of whom "repeated all the reassurances" they had given him earlier. Dabegsil-sete managed to take Valdés aside to ask that the lieutenant trust him and that Ugalde likewise trust him and keep his secret.[59]

When Valdés returned on January 22, he confirmed to Ugalde the "illegal doings" of Picax-andé. Indeed, Ugalde had been seeking evidence of violations of the peace accord to determine the proper course of action.[60] Two Mescalero prisoners also testified that Picax-andé himself had taken part in the Mescalero uprising and had conspired with other chiefs to steal the horses of the Aguaverde company, a plot that was never carried out.[61]

To justify his radical change of mind and gain permission to launch a campaign against the eastern Apaches—excluding for the moment the Lipans—Ugalde wrote to the viceroy that Picax-andé had acted with "perfidy" and he was a man "whose heart is as corrupt as it is false." For that reason, peace with the Lipiyans had ended, and it was now essential to act "with arms in hand" in order to "punish similar conduct." The "ferocious and inhuman war" that the Apaches waged necessarily gave the king the right "not only to subdue but also to destroy them."[62] Ugalde considered it to be "of utmost importance to remove this powerful and respected head of the eastern Apaches, owing to his long tenure of leadership among them, his well-proven valor (for the Indians consider no one to be his equal), and above all, a superstitious power that leads them to obey him unquestioningly."[63]

On February 15, a messenger reached Santa Rosa with news that the Mescalero chiefs Zapato Tuerto and Patule had asked to be received in peace, something denied them days earlier at El Norte on the viceroy's orders. Ugalde told the messenger that they would be well received. Various Mescalero chiefs from the surrounding rancherías also began to arrive. Ugalde strung them along with lies, assuring them that he was fully inclined to reach a peace accord. Zapato Tuerto and Patule expressed remorse for the uprising of the previous year. El-lite was more cautious; he did not bring his people until March 23. When El-lite finally arrived, Ugalde summoned all the Mescaleros, men, women, and children, to a general meeting the following morning. The commander kept his own men hidden, with instructions to respond only to certain prearranged signals. With all the chiefs gathered in Ugalde's house, the commander launched into a fiery speech, saying that he had warned them of what would happen if they violated the peace. In an uninterruptible harangue, he asked about the motives of the rebellion and, without waiting for a response, continued that "the blood that they had spilled with such impunity would be avenged in that instant," and they were to choose between prison or death. Immediately, he signaled his troops to enter; Ugalde seized Zapato Tuerto and Patule by the arms and handcuffed them, and had the soldiers take prisoner all who were present. Only two warriors resisted arrest, and both were killed. Ugalde thus carried out what he called "the most formidable blow to the Mescalero Apaches," imprisoning forty-two men, including five captains, and thirty-six women.[64] Viceroy Flórez applauded the capture of the Mescaleros and ordered that they be sent to Mexico to be deported to some place across the sea (see chapter 7), but he warned Ugalde about a possible response from the Lipans, who idolized Picax-andé.[65]

Ugalde's capture of the Mescaleros had enormous repercussions for the region. In April 1789 Valdés reported having heard from two Lipans that Picax-andé had relocated his rancherías, blustering and threatening the colonel for having captured the Mescaleros in such a treacherous fashion.[66] Ugalde sent Valdés to the Lipan rancherías to confirm the rumor, instructing him that if the report should prove false and the caudillo were to be found "at peace" Valdés should "treat him and pamper him with the utmost concern and friendship," offering him "cattle, corn, beans, or tobacco" if necessary. When Valdés reached the ranchería of the Lipan leader Dabegsil-sete, he learned that Picax-andé had sent an Indian named Nataehé to Santa Rosa to investigate what had happened, and Nataehé had seen the Mescalero prisoners. Enraged, Picax-andé went into his tent to consult with his deity. At a religious ceremony the next day he declared that he could no longer trust the great captain of Santa Rosa, since everyone could end up being captured, like the Mescalero chiefs; that Ugalde was the Indians' worst enemy because he was perpetually campaigning against them, and that this was why Ugalde "did not have a wife." He announced they all should relocate to Los Arenales. Early the next day "he ordered the tents to be taken down . . . mounted his horse, armed as if for war, and cried out . . . that if the Great Captain of the Spanish was daring, so was he, and they would see each other man-to-man someday . . . that he feared neither the Spanish nor the Comanches," and that he would avenge the Apache prisoners. Valdés reportedly scoffed at this report, assuring the Lipans that Picax-andé "had gone mad," and that "they would see what would happen if the Lipiyan provoked the Great Captain."[67]

In May, Ugalde sent Valdés once more to the Lipan rancherías to "form a clear and conclusive judgment" concerning Picax-andé's behavior, further requesting that he dispatch the captains Chul-ul and Caballada with the objective of persuading Picax-andé to return to the place where he had been camping or some other location close to Santa Rosa. The messengers were to explain to Picax-andé that Ugalde "greatly regretted [his] departure, because he greatly loved him and valued his friendship"; that Ugalde wished to know why he had departed so that Ugalde could "punish any Spaniard who had lied to him or somehow hurt his feelings." But if the Indian chief rejected Ugalde's friendship, the messengers were to ask that he return the "staff and title of captain" and to inform him that Ugalde was about to launch a campaign against all Mescaleros, which "would last until he had killed [Picax-andé] and had verified his nation's complete extermination."[68]

Valdés himself was almost attacked by a group of Mescaleros under Alegre's leadership. Thanks to the intervention of his friend Dabegsil-sete and other Lipans, he was able to escape certain death and managed to open a conversation with Alegre himself, with other Mescalero chiefs, and even with certain Lipiyans. Every day, however he felt enormous tension among the Apaches, many of whom wanted to kill him because he had directly taken part in the treachery against the Mescaleros. Valdés announced that Ugalde would soon take the offensive against his enemies, but at the same time he wanted to maintain his friendship with Picax-andé, to whom he sent two stout horses and two mules. He requested that the Lipiyan return the staff and parchment title if he did not wish to continue the peace accord with the Spanish. The messengers immediately left for Picax-andé's ranchería, but Alegre remarked that the Lipiyan chief "was greatly afraid, because he was able to divine what would happen." His god had appeared to him, warning him not to trust Ugalde, because regardless of what the latter professed, his real intention was to kill all the Indians as he "thought of nothing else but exterminating" the Apaches. The Mescaleros had repeatedly urged Picax-andé to come to Santa Rosa and negotiate for the prisoners' release, but he refused because he did not trust Ugalde. Valdés agreed to mediate in persuading his commander to avoid war against the Lipans and to release the Mescaleros. Upon returning to Santa Rosa, he declared that all his soldiers would have died were it not for the Lipans, who proved the "love and respect" they held for Ugalde.[69]

Meanwhile, Ugalde himself was busy proving Apache treachery to Viceroy Flórez and speeding up preparations for his campaign. Jacobo de Ugarte also sent a letter to the viceroy, essentially advocating for his different approach to Indian pacification. In the letter he praised the governor of New Mexico for persuading the Yutas, Jicarillas, Navajos, and Comanches to act with "good faith and loyal behavior," a "fortunate achievement . . . previously . . . considered impossible." As he reflected, "the same thing will always happen with any Indians if one knows how to treat them and understands their peculiar character."[70] This had been Ugarte's goal when he had originally made peace with the Mescaleros in El Norte, and for the preceding two years he had assiduously sought the viceroy's approval for this course of action. His differences with Ugalde regarding their approach to the Apaches had caused the viceroy to issue an ultimatum to Ugarte in May 1789: reject all treaties with the Apaches and force them to remove themselves from El Norte, thereby creating the state of semi-war to which Ugarte would have to respond.[71]

Before departing, Ugalde informed Flórez that he was prepared for a campaign of two hundred days, with the objective of making a frontal assault on the Lipiyans and Mescaleros, who "with cruelty, persistence, treachery, and ingratitude" had menaced the eastern provinces and Nueva Vizcaya.[72] Before beginning his march in August 1789, he sent Valdés ahead to make false offers of peace in order not to alert the various Mescalero rancherías that lay along the Rio Grande. On the twentieth, Ugalde attacked the ranchería of Zaragate, inflicting great loss of life, taking numerous prisoners and "whatever the attacked Indians possessed," including 180 animals.[73] A flesh-colored loin-cloth worn by one of the dead identified him as Captain Xat-ys-an, a personal friend and companion of Picax-andé's.[74] The Spanish suffered only one death and one man wounded. Following his normal practice, Ugalde talked up his "substantial, difficult, and praiseworthy blow" and tried to use it to secure recognition for two of his subordinates and a promotion for himself.[75]

But Viceroy Flórez, who was Ugalde's chief supporter, had been relieved of his post in February 1789; in his place the king had appointed Juan Vicente de Güemes, the second Count of Revillagigedo, who took office in October.[76] The new viceroy's enlightened approach influenced the colony's frontier governance. In May, Ugarte sent the king a lengthy manifesto in which he laid out his differences with Ugalde and the serious unrest caused by the latter's mistakes. He would later communicate directly with Revillagigedo to inform him of the situation in the Provincias Internas.[77]

On being informed of Ugalde's initial actions in October, the new viceroy rebuked the bellicose commander for treacherously violating the guidelines of José de Gálvez's "Instrucción," which stipulated that "following sustained warfare, peace will always be granted to Indians who seek it. . . . There can be no justification for acting with perfidy or bad faith when dealing with our enemies, nor will such means ever be acceptable for the king's armed forces."[78] However, this communication did not reach Ugalde immediately, for he avoided any official communications that might limit his actions in the field. In April, Revillagigedo wrote to Ugalde once more, demanding a reply to his letters and complaining that his operations were generating "enormous hostilities" in Coahuila and Nuevo León, given the fact that most of the troops Ugalde commanded came from these two provinces. The viceroy ordered Ugalde to call off the campaign immediately and report to him on the situation. Some days later Revillagigedo drew up a list of formal charges against Ugalde and ordered him to appear in Mexico City as soon as possible to answer for his conduct.[79] Ugalde remained on campaign until August 2, however, and did not reply to the viceroy until October.[80]

In January 1790, Ugalde reported having led an attack by some 210 Spanish troops and 140 Comanches on two Apache rancherías "of different nations . . . the strong right arm of the Apachería" (probably an allusion to the meaning of Picax-andé's name) on his way to Los Arenales. He had inflicted numerous casualties and taken both prisoners and horses, thereby "humbling the pride of the greater part" of the Apachería.[81] In the end, though, the person whose pride was most humbled was Ugalde himself. Eventually, he was forced to return to the viceregal capital where he was stripped of his commands and had to undergo a lengthy investigation in response to Revillagigedo's accusations.

Picax-andé tried to approach Ugarte in the months that followed. In June 1790, an Apache chief named Pedro Barrio arrived in El Paso to report that the Lipiyan chief, acting as main leader of the Llaneros and Natages, wanted to make peace. Ugarte ordered that Picax-andé come with his people to El Norte, to the rancherías of his friends Alegre, Volante, and José, where he would be received by "a good Spanish captain whom the Mescaleros know," under orders to welcome him and grant him peace, so long as the Lipiyan chief should agree "to harm no part of the king's dominions."[82] That December, Captain Domingo Díaz awaited Picax-andé as main leader of the Apachería, having consulted with the Mescalero rancherías that recognized his authority.[83] The outcome of this event remains unknown, but in the following years the Lipiyans continued trying to establish peace and trade agreements.

In April 1791, the governor of New Mexico, Fernando de la Concha, received word that a great ranchería of Llanero Apaches, under their captain Brazo de Hierro (Picax-andé), had requested peace, with their Jicarilla relatives acting as intermediaries. The Lipiyans came to Pecos, where the governor himself met them, along with Ecueracapa, the main "Comanche general." As a precondition to peace, de la Concha stipulated that they hand over the eleven Comanche and eight Spanish prisoners currently in their possession, each prisoner to be exchanged for a horse. After considerable reluctance the Apaches accepted the arrangement. After staying in Pecos for twenty-three days, the Llanero Apaches left on a bison hunt, but they offered to return there in June with well-tanned hides to hold a fair.[84] Picax-andé's contacts with New Mexico and El Norte would continue for some time.[85]

In sum, the historiography has dedicated scant attention to the Lipiyans, who are usually considered a subgroup of the Mescaleros or Lipans. Our sources reveal however that numerous bands of Mescaleros, Lipiyans, and Lipans retained their distinct identity and autonomy in the 1780s by using their abilities as warriors and diplomats. In the indigenous borderlands of the Apachería, the various rancherías and their respective chiefs constantly interacted to hunt, trade, wage war, and engage in diplomacy. The Lipiyans remained on the plains, retaining their direct access to bison, with no assistance from (and little contact with) the Spanish, a point on which Lipiyans prided themselves. Their military strength allowed them to organize bison hunts and lend protection to other Apaches who faced the threat of Comanches.

Chief Picax-andé functioned as spiritual guide, oracle, and high military leader of Lipiyans, Natages, Lipans, and Mescaleros. His seemingly direct contact with the supernatural, together with his ability to predict future events, allowed him to collect tribute in the form of ceremonial gifts that he later redistributed among his followers. His political and spiritual leadership, his strong kinship ties to the Mescaleros, and the fealty and devotion that Lipans professed to him allowed him to unify a good part of the eastern Apachería against their common enemies (Comanches and, later, Spaniards). He thus wove together a complex pan-Apache alliance strengthened through marriages between various leaders' families. The public intervention of his Mescalero wife during a general assembly in front of visitors suggests that Apache women were not as subordinate as is often believed, and that their opinions mattered to the community.

The Apaches reaffirmed their identity through deeds of war and through dialectical exchanges laden with cultural values. In the indigenous border-lands of the Apachería, Europeans had to adapt to native practices and expectations. Thus, diplomatic encounters between Apaches and Spaniards involved an intensely symbolic give-and-take that included overblown receptions, ostentatious clothing, military displays, rifle shots, cannon blasts, embraces, generous meals, gifts, and use of kinship terms. Nevertheless, it was a person's word that mattered most in the Apachería. Ugalde himself explicitly acknowledged that he had used lies, treachery, and betrayal, thus responding to the prophetic words that Picax-andé had directed to him at their first meeting: "We will see who does not speak the truth."

NOTES

1. Juan de Ugalde, "Extracto y sumario de la primera campaña [. . .]," Valle de Santa Rosa, August 15, 1787, AGN, Provincias Internas (hereafter PI), v. 112, ff. 413r–413v.

2. Anderson, *Indian Southwest*, 136–40.

3. Hämäläinen, *El imperio comanche*, 97–103.

4. Few discussions of the Llaneros/Lipiyans and Picax-andé are available in print; see Nelson, "Juan de Ugalde," 438–64; Gunnerson, *Jicarilla Apaches*, esp. 263–82; Robinson, *I Fought a Good Fight*, 133–66; Velasco Ávila, *Pacificar o negociar*, 36–37, 41–42, 46, 56–59, 134. Published in 1940, Nelson's article is more narrative than interpretive; focuses on the Spaniards, particularly Juan de Ugalde; contains some disputable translations; and ends somewhat abruptly upon the last meeting between Ugalde and Picax-andé. Gunnerson's and Robinson's discussions rely extensively on Nelson.

5. By "ranchería" we refer to a nomadic band of hunter-gatherers, which was the meaning of the term at the time. Spicer called them "agricultural bands"; see Spicer, *Cycles of Conquest*, 12–15; also Martínez, *Troublesome Border*, 48.

6. Moorhead, *Apache Frontier*, 200–3.

7. Gunnerson and Gunnerson, *Ethnohistory of the High Plains*, 6–7; Tomás Vélez Cachupín to Francisco Martín del Valle, Santa Fe, August 12, 1754, AGN, PI, v. 102, ff. 447–48; John, *Storms Brewed in Other Men's Worlds*, 328–29.

8. José Menchaca, "Extracto en que [. . .] compendia el diario de la expedición [. . .]," Cuartel de la Villa de San Fernando, November 31, 1786, AGN, PI, v. 112, ff. 366–68; O'Conor, *Informe*, 78; Robinson, *I Fought a Good Fight*, 134.

9. Juan Bautista de Anza to Jacobo de Ugarte y Loyola, Santa Fe, November 18, 1786, AGN, PI, v. 65, f. 320v. Concerning the treaties with the Comanches, see Rivaya-Martínez, "Diplomacia interétnica"; and Velasco Ávila, *Pacificar o negociar*, 40–81.

10. Jacobo de Ugarte y Loyola to Domingo Díaz, Chihuahua, February 12, 1787; Díaz to Ugarte y Loyola, Presido del Norte, March 29, 1787; and Díaz to Ugarte y Loyola, Guajoquilla, April 13, 1787, Biblioteca Pública del Estado de Jalisco (hereafter BPEJ), Audiencia de Guadalajara, Ramo Civil, 199-1-2431, ff. 4–7, 14–15.

11. Domingo Díaz to Jacobo de Ugarte y Loyola, April 13, 1787, BPEJ, Audiencia de Guadalajara, Ramo Civil, 199-1-2431, ff. 13–14.

12. Elguezábal to Jacobo de Ugarte y Loyola, El Norte, April 27, 1787, BPEJ, Audiencia de Guadalajara, Ramo Civil, ff. 52–53; Velasco Ávila, *Pacificar o negociar*, 111–15.

13. Juan de Ugalde, "Extracto y sumario de la primera campaña [. . .]," Valle de Santa Rosa, August 15, 1787, AGN, PI, v. 112, f. 412; Nelson, "Juan de Ugalde," 438–39.

14. Ugalde, "Extracto y sumario," AGN, PI, v. 112, ff. 412r, 413v; Morris, *El llano estacado*, 262.

15. Ugalde, "Extracto y sumario," AGN, PI, v. 112, ff. 412v–413v; Nelson, "Juan de Ugalde," 438–42; Wade, *Native Americans*, 209–13; Domingo Díaz to Jacobo de Ugarte y Loyola, January 20, 1788, AGN, PI, v. 112, ff. 190–91.

16. Nelson, "Juan de Ugalde," 442–44.

17. Ugalde "Extracto y sumario," ff. 415r–v.

18. Fernando de la Concha to Jacobo de Ugarte y Loyola, Santa Fe, November 10, 1787, AGN, PI, v. 65, ff. 55–56.

19. Jacobo de Ugarte y Loyola to Viceroy Manuel Antonio Flórez, Arizpe, November 12, 1787, AGN, PI, v. 112, ff. 112v–113r.

20. Gálvez, "Instrucción formada en virtud de Real Orden de S. M., que se dirige al señor Comandante General de Provincias Internas don Jacobo Ugarte y Loyola para gobierno y puntual observancia de este superior jefe y de sus inmediatos subalternos," México, August 26, 1786, reprinted in Velázquez, *La frontera norte*, articles 8–10.

21. Draft of a letter from Manuel Antonio Flórez to Juan de Ugalde, México, November 21, 1787, AGN, PI, v. 112, ff. 299r–303r; Velasco Ávila, *Pacificar o negociar*, 127–30.

22. Domingo Díaz to Jacobo de Ugarte y Loyola, Real Presidio del Norte, January 20, 1788, AGN, PI, v. 112, ff. 190r–91r.

23. Díaz to Ugarte y Loyola, Real Presidio del Norte, January 31, 1788, AGN, PI, v. 76, f. 265v.

24. Nelson, "Juan de Ugalde," 454; Juan de Ugalde, "Diario [. . .]," Presidio de San Antonio de Béxar, May 2, 1788, AGN, PI, v. 111, ff. 205r–6r.

25. Juan de Ugalde, "Diario," ff. 206v–8r. Nelson, "Juan de Ugalde," 455–56, contains a translation of Menchaca's description of the ceremony.

26. Casimiro Valdés, Villa de San Francisco, May 18, 1789, AGN, Indiferente Virreinal, box 645, exp. 5, ff. 11r–11v; Casimiro Valdés, Villa de San Francisco, June 7, 1789, AGN, Indiferente Virreinal, box 645, exp. 5, f. 28v. According to Crawford and Kelley ("Ceremony and Ritual," 111–17), certain Apache ceremonies were conducted by ritual specialists who by means of dreams and visions had acquired a supernatural power known as *diye*.

27. Juan de Ugalde, "Diario," Presidio de San Antonio de Béxar, May 2, 1788, AGN, PI, v. 111, f. 215v.

28. Juan de Ugalde to Manuel Antonio Flórez, Valle de Santa Rosa, March 10, 1788, AGN, PI, v. 111, ff. 164r–65r. Carlisle (*Spanish Relations*, 27) mentions that Apache shamans were able to predict the results of a battle.

29. Juan de Ugalde, "Diario," May 2, 1788, f. 209v–210r; Nelson, "Juan de Ugalde," 456–57; Moorhead, *Apache Frontier*, 241.

30. Ugalde, "Diario," ff. 210v–11r; Nelson, "Juan de Ugalde," 457–58. Ugalde himself proposed Picax-andé's name, choosing Manuel in honor of Viceroy Manuel Antonio Flórez, even though he claimed that the Indian chief had requested the name; see Juan de Ugalde to Manuel Antonio Flórez, Valle de Santa Rosa, October 22, 1787, AGN, PI, v. 76, f. 90r. Concerning the names of the Apache bands, Moorhead (*Apache Frontier*, 248–49) follows Antonio Cordero in arguing that the Sende appear to correspond to the *sejen-ne*, or Mescaleros; the Nit-ajende to the *ytangen-ne*, or Faraones; and the Cachu-ende probably to the *cuelcajen-ne*, or Llaneros.

31. Ugalde, "Diario," ff. 212r–13v; Nelson, "Juan de Ugalde," 460–61.

32. Ugalde, "Diario," f. 215; Nelson, "Juan de Ugalde," 461.

33. Ugalde, "Diario," f. 217.

34. Ugalde, "Diario," f. 218. Nelson ("Juan de Ugalde," 462–64) offers additional details on Ugalde's visit to the Lipiyan camp.

35. Ugalde, "Diario," f. 215v.

36. Leandro Martínez Pacheco to Juan de Ugalde, San Fernando, March 30, 1788, AGN, PI, v. 111, f. 242r–v.

37. Juan de Ugalde to Leandro Martínez Pacheco, Presidio de Río Grande, March 31, 1788, AGN, PI, v. 111, ff. 242v–44r.

38. Leandro Martínez Pacheco to Juan de Ugalde, Villa de San Francisco, April 12, 1788, AGN, PI, v. 111, ff. 250r–53v.

39. Manuel Picax-andé Ins-tisle de Ugalde to Juan de Ugalde, Cabecera del Río San Diego, April 5, 1788, AGN, PI, v. 111, ff. 244r–45v. According to Minor (*Light Gray People*, 84–85), Picax-andé wanted to avoid using Casimiro Valdés as an intermediary and therefore wrote directly to Ugalde, whom he recognized as his "father."

40. Juan de Ugalde to Leandro Martínez Pacheco, Campo de Río Frío, April 12, 1788, AGN, PI, v. 111, ff. 245v–49r; Juan de Ugalde to Manuel Antonio Flórez, September 24, 1788, AGN, PI, v. 111, ff. 258v–59r.

41. Picax-andé to Juan de Ugalde, Paraje del Río Grande y juntas de las Vacas, April 16, 1788, AGN, PI, v. 111, ff. 254r–v.

42. Juan de Ugalde to Leandro Martínez Pacheco, presidio de San Antonio de Béxar, April 28, 1788, AGN, PI, v. 111, ff. 255r–v; Ugalde, "Instrucción contenida en el anterior oficio," presidio de San Antonio de Béxar, April 28, 1788, AGN, PI, v. 111, ff. 255v–56v.

43. Juan de Ugalde to Jacobo de Ugarte y Loyola, San Antonio de Béxar, May 2, 1788, AGN, PI, v. 112, ff. 264–264v.

44. Jacobo de Ugarte y Loyola to Juan de Ugalde, Chihuahua, June 12, 1788, AGN, PI, v. 112, ff. 265r–v.

45. On the same date Ugarte explained to Viceroy Flórez that Picax-andé was known in New Mexico as El Calvo and was the same chief upon whom they had waited in order to reach a peace accord with the Mescaleros in El Norte, when Ugalde's intervention forced him to "change his plans." Jacobo de Ugarte y Loyola to Manuel Antonio Flórez, Chihuahua, June 12, 1788, AGN, PI, v. 76, ff. 333r–39v.

46. Juan de Ugalde to Manuel Antonio Flórez, Monterrey, September 24, 1788, PI, v. 111, f. 264; Flórez to Ugalde, México, December 29, 1788, AGN, PI, v. 112, ff. 358r–59r.

47. The account of this incident is in Juan de Ugalde to Manuel Antonio Flórez, Punta de Lampazos, November 21, 1788, AGN, PI, v. 111, f. 265r–68r.

48. Juan de Ugalde to Manuel Antonio Flórez, Valle de Santa Rosa, April 1, 1789, PI, v. 159, ff. 237r–38v.

49. Moorhead, *Apache Frontier*, 252–53; Casimiro Valdés, "Diario [. . .]," Villa de San Francisco, January 11, 1789, AGN, PI, v. 159, f. 279; Juan de Ugalde to Manuel Antonio Flórez, Valle de Santa Rosa, April 20, 1789, AGN, PI, v. 159, ff. 266r–69r.

50. Casimiro Valdés, "Diario," AGN, PI, v. 159, f. 278v.

51. Valdés, "Diario," ff. 279r–v.

52. Valdés, "Diario," ff. 300r–v.

53. Valdés, "Diario," f. 301r.

54. Valdés, "Diario," ff. 300, 301v–2r. According to Minor (*Turning Adversity into Advantage*, 12), matrimonial ties among the Apaches amounted to political alliances among the rancherías, although there is no evidence that Picax-andé directed or sent incursions against the Spanish.

55. Valdés, "Diario," ff. 269r–79r.

56. Casimiro Valdés, "Diario de [. . .] la segunda visita [. . .]," Villa de San Francisco, January 23, 1789, AGN, PI, v. 159, ff. 303r–4v.

57. Valdés, "Diario de [. . .] la segunda visita," ff. 305r–7v. Unless otherwise noted, all quotations are from this source.

58. Valdés, "Diario de [. . .] la segunda visita," ff. 314r–15r.

59. Valdés, "Diario de [. . .] la segunda visita," ff. 315v–16v.

60. Juan de Ugalde to Manuel Antonio Flórez, Valle de Santa Rosa, April 20, 1789, AGN, PI, v. 159, ff. 270v–71v.

61. Ugalde to Flórez, f. 271v.

62. Ugalde to Flórez, ff. 273v–74v.

63. Ugalde to Flórez, f. 274v.

64. Juan de Ugalde to Manuel Antonio Flórez, Valle de Santa Rosa, April 1, 1789, AGN, PI, v. 159, ff. 237–61; Moorhead, *Apache Frontier*, 253–54; Velasco Ávila, *Pacificar o negociar*, 143–45.

65. Manuel Antonio Flórez to Juan de Ugalde, México, April 29, 1789, AGN, PI, v. 159, ff. 263r–65v.

66. Casimiro Valdés to Juan de Ugalde, Villa de San Fernando, April 28, 1789, AGN, Indiferente Virreinal, box 645, exp. 5, f. 2v.

67. Casimiro Valdés, "Diario," Villa de San Fernando, May 18, 1789, AGN, Indiferente Virreinal, box 645, exp. 5, ff. 11r–12r.

68. Juan de Ugalde to Casimiro Valdés, Villa de Santa Rosa, May 22, 1789, AGN, Indiferente Virreinal, box 645, exp. 5, ff. 15r–16v.

69. Casimiro Valdés, "Diario," Villa de Santa Rosa, June 7, 1789, AGN, Indiferente Virreinal, box 645, exp. 5, ff. 18r–29v.

70. Jacobo de Ugarte y Loyola to Manuel Antonio Flórez, Chihuahua, July 31, 1789, AGN, PI, 193, ff. 197r–98v; Fernando de la Concha to Jacobo de Ugarte y Loyola, Santa Fe, July 3, 1789, AGN, PI, 193, ff. 199r–200r; and Ugarte y Loyola to de la Concha, July 21, 1789, AGN, PI, 193, ff. 200r–v.

71. Velasco Ávila, *Pacificar o negociar*, 139–49.

72. Juan de Ugalde to Manuel Antonio Flórez, Paso del Astillero, August 14, 1789, AGN, PI, v. 159, ff. 329r–32v.

73. Juan de Ugalde to Manuel Antonio Flórez, campsite at the Paso del Astillero, September 12, 1789, AGN, Indiferente Virreinal, box 645, exp. 5, ff. 36r–42v.

74. Ugalde to Flórez, 43v.

75. Ugalde to Flórez, ff. 43v–47v.

76. Navarro García, *Don José de Gálvez*, 472.

77. Jacobo de Ugarte y Loyola to the king, Chihuahua, May 8, 1789, AGN, PI, v. 77, exp. 1, ff. 2r–55r; Ugarte y Loyola to the Conde de Revillagigedo, Chihuahua, November 20, 1789, AGN, PI, v. 193, f. 466.

78. Viceroy Revillagigedo to Juan de Ugalde, México, October 27, 1789, AGN, Indiferente Virreinal, box 645, exp. 5, ff. 65r–67r. Concerning the situation in the Provincias Internas upon Revillagigedo's appointment to the viceroyalty and the consequences of Colonel Juan de Ugalde's policies, see the report that Jacobo de Ugarte y Loyola presented in November 1789: Ugarte y Loyola to Viceroy Revillagigedo, Chihuahua, November 20, 1789, AGN, PI, v. 159, ff. 466r–77r.

79. Viceroy Revillagigedo to Juan de Ugalde, April 27, 1790, Archivo General de Simancas, Secretaría de Guerra, 7043, 1, images 137–43.

80. Juan de Ugalde to Viceroy Revillagigedo, Valle de Santa Rosa, October 7, 1790, AGN, Indiferente Virreinal, box 645, exp. 5, ff. 76r–77r.

81. Juan de Ugalde to the comandante de la Compañía y Presidio de Monclova, Campo del Río de Medina, January 19, 1790, Archivo General de Simancas, Secretaría de Guerra, 7043, 1, images 95–100; Moorhead, *Apache Frontier*, 255.

82. [Francisco] Xavier de Uranga to Jacobo de Ugarte y Loyola, El Paso, June 13, 1790; and Ugarte y Loyola to Uranga, Chihuahua, June 19, 1790, AGN, PI, v. 191, ff. 261r–65r.

83. Moorhead, *Apache Frontier*, 267–68; Pedro de Nava to Domingo Díaz, Valle de Santa Rosa, January 11, 1791, AGN, PI, v. 224, ff. 13r–14v.

84. Fernando de la Concha to Viceroy Conde de Revillagigedo, Santa Fe de Nuevo México, April 20, 1791, AGN, Indiferente Virreinal, box 645, exp. 1, ff. 8v–13v. In 1792 New Mexico governor Fernando de la Concha reported that in that province the Lip-iyan chief was known by the name of Tiediltheeilde (Arm of Iron); see de la Concha to Viceroy Revillagigedo, Chihuahua, January 12, 1792, AGN, PI, v. 171, f. 421v.

85. Flagler, "La política española," 231–32; Robinson, *I Fought a Good Fight*, 156–57.

PART III

Imagined Borderlands

Colonial Discourses and Indigenous Realities

CHAPTER 6

The Hows and Whys of Naming Indios

THE CASE OF THE BOLSÓN DE MAPIMÍ

Chantal Cramaussel

In this essay I analyze a series of terms used in the documents of New Spain to refer to various indigenous groups that inhabited the Bolsón de Mapimí, a region covering parts of the current Mexican states of Coahuila, Chihuahua, and Durango. When seen from a multidisciplinary perspective, the cultural and historical context of these terms suggests that while the naming criteria the Spanish employed were hardly random, in most cases they followed neither ethnonyms (terms referring to a specific ethnic-political identity) nor gentilics (terms alluding to a human group within a specific geographical space).

Geographers refer to the southernmost region of the Chihuahuan Desert as the Bolsón de Mapimí. It is an arid land that takes its name from the eponymous village in the state of Durango, established as a real de minas (mining center) at the end of the sixteenth century. With an average annual rainfall of 264 millimeters (10.4 inches), it is one of the driest regions in all of Mexico. The region that was historically termed Bolsón de Mapimí is larger, bounded on the north by the Conchos River and the Rio Grande, on the west by the Sierra Madre Occidental, on the east by the Sierra Madre Oriental, and on the south by the Nazas River basin (see map 6.1).

The Bolsón remained out of Spanish control during the days of the viceroyalty. Hispanic presence in the region was sporadic because it lacked the arable land or mineral wealth necessary to attract settlement. Nevertheless,

141

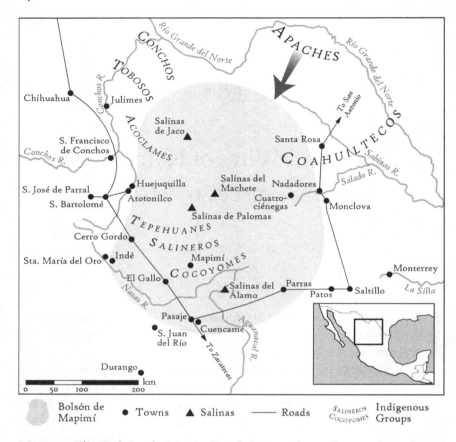

Map 6.1. The Bolsón de Mapimí and its periphery during the colonial period. (Map © G. Wallace Cartography & GIS after original by Chantal Cramaussel)

the mountain ranges of the Bolsón, which provided springs of fresh water and a more tolerable climate, were inhabited by itinerant Indian groups who dominated the territory, and who frequently raided surrounding Hispanic settlements.[1] The only Spanish presence within the Bolsón was the real de minas (later a presidio, or military outpost) of Mapimí, founded in 1599 but abandoned at various points thereafter.[2] The Bolsón also served as a refuge for all sorts of recalcitrants, including fugitive Indians, Indians who had avoided Spanish domination altogether, and criminals from the fringes of colonial society. Ongoing thefts of cattle and especially of horses at their hands plagued the reales de minas, presidios, missions, ranchos, and haciendas lying to the east, south, and west of the Bolsón; and assaults were a common problem on surrounding roads.[3] In this way the Bolsón became an "interior" borderland, and remained so even as Mexicans and US nationals began to populate the region north of the Rio Grande in the early nineteenth century.

Spaniards identified numerous indigenous groups in this region, as borne out by lists with more than two hundred names applied to various peoples.[4] In some cases one term might encompass a wide variety of indigenous groups speaking the same language, while other terms might serve to distinguish between those groups.[5] The multiplicity of names reflected in part the fact that Indians had to separate into small groups for purposes of hunting and gathering in the Bolsón, due to its meager supply of water and arable land. Moreover, wars and alliances, together with the processes of evangelization and exploitation, generated a need to identify and name a near infinity of subgroups. The same Indians were not always designated with the same terminology, a point William Griffen documented by comparing two sources from 1693.[6] Orthography of names varied considerably, and the denominations themselves occasionally changed over time. Criteria for the selection of names also differed geographically on occasion, for example, between Nueva Vizcaya, located to the west, and Coahuila, located to the east of the Bolsón. Certain generic labels such as *conchos, tepehuanes del desierto,* and *coahuiltecas* declined in usage throughout the eighteenth century.[7] All these facts have bequeathed to us an immense terminological confusion that, given the absence of documents generated by the Indians themselves, greatly hampers our ability to chart processes of ethnogenesis.

In the Bolsón and surrounding regions, use of certain indigenous languages extended over truly vast spaces. But it would be a mistake to equate linguistic communities with political or territorial entities, given that conflicts raged among groups speaking the same language throughout the entire colonial period. As Griffen noted, certain autochthonous tongues of the Bolsón were related and many natives were polyglots, facts that make it all the more difficult to pin speakers of a certain language to a particular zone. Subsistence practices of groups resident in different zones varied according to the ecological characteristics of their territories. There were hunter-gatherers who planted only small plots in riparian areas of the Bolsón, as well as more sedentary farmers in the valleys of the Sierra Madre Occidental, but they all dispersed seasonally over large distances to hunt and gather, at times mixing among themselves.[8] Moreover, indigenous societies in this region lacked centralized authority and recombined based on armed conflict and ties of kinship. The testimony of a certain Diego, of the Acoclame people, confirmed this fact when he was interrogated regarding certain Indians who rebelled against the Spanish in February 1706: "They are not Chizos, who are at peace in the presidio of San Francisco de Conchos, and they are of the Zizimble nation, who are those who at present are prisoners, up to five indios of said nation, and they call them Chizos because they travel into the north. And when the opportunity presents itself, they go out to rob and murder, and said Zizimbles join with the Acoclames, who are their relatives and always live with them."[9]

Nevertheless, the Spanish did distinguish three large linguistic groups in the Bolsón: Conchos, Tepehuanes, and Coahuiltecans. The Conchos called themselves *yolli* (undiscovered). "Concho" appears as a gentilic as early as the sixteenth century along the Conchos River, so named because of the large mollusk shells found in its bed. But the Conchería (that is, the territory inhabited by Concho speakers) stretches as far as the foothills of the Sierra Madre, from the area of modern-day Chihuahua City to Namiquipa and Casas Grandes, more than three hundred kilometers (186 miles) from the Conchos River.[10] Of the 126 different groups Griffen distinguished, he identified 50 as Conchos. As we shall see, this proliferation was due to the fact that the encomienda system artificially fragmented the Conchos into subgroups.

The so-called *tobosos* were also Conchos.[11] As Salvador Álvarez has explained, "toboso" initially referred to an encomienda assigned to a conquistador in 1600 for his hacienda, Atotonilco, on the western edge of the Bolsón.[12] During the Tepehuan uprising of 1616–20, when encomienda Indians fled from that estate to the Salinas del Machete (today the Salinas del Rey in Coahuila), in the heart of the Bolsón, they were identified as "Conchos Tobosos." On various occasions the Tobosos fled from the San Buenaventura mission in Atotonilco, the place where the Spanish had congregated them, and for that reason the governor of Nueva Vizcaya declared a war of "fuego y sangre" (fire and blood) against them, a phrase implying death to Indian combatants and slavery for the rest.[13] On other occasions, however, the Tobosos fought alongside the Spanish against other rebellious Indians and labored on behalf of the European invaders. They promised to collect salt at "Santa María de los Tobosos" (likely the place later known as the Salinas de Jaco), discovered by the Spanish in 1639 (salt was a critical input in silver production at San José de Parral).[14]

In 1644 the Tobosos joined with other Conchos in a general uprising. During the revolt, which began at the San Francisco de Conchos mission, the

Conchos of all the adjacent rancherías (Indian encampments) connected with the haciendas of San Bartolomé in Santa Bárbara Province, along with Julime and Mamite laborers (both Concho groups) who worked in the mines at Parral, fled in fear of reprisals in the event that the Spanish considered them spies or accused them of collusion with the rebels.[15] In the second half of the seventeenth century, Spaniards began to distinguish the Tobosos from the other Conchos and to identify hostile Indians as "tobosos." In 1652 the Tobosos took refuge on a hill called Nonolat, near the Jaco salt flat, where they were defeated by Governor Diego Guajardo Fajardo. Sources state that most of the Indians perished in combat, preferring to commit suicide by throwing themselves from the summit rather than surrender, while others fled to remote parts of the Bolsón.[16] Henceforth, the Tobosos largely disappear from the documentation of the area east of Parral; the final references to them appeared in Chinarras (near San Felipe de Real de Chihuahua) in 1725, and in San Francisco de Conchos in 1728.[17]

Elsewhere, the term "Toboso" also appears in a 1667 letter from Governor Antonio de Oca y Sarmiento. In writing to the king to request the construction of military forts along the *camino real de tierra adentro* (the royal road leading into northern New Spain), he initially labeled the rebel Indians as "Cabezas, Salineros and their allies, the Toboso and Acoclame nation, and the Chizos, the Cíbolos, and their allied nations." Later in the letter, however, he seemed to lump them all together as "Tobosos," a group apparently not included in his successful campaign against the "Conchos." The map accompanying this document identified only two hostile groups in the Bolsón: "Tobosos" in the north and "Salineros" in the south.[18] As Governor Lope de Sierra Osorio explained in 1678: "on the right side of the camino real there are hills and mountain ranges frequented by eleven nations of hostile Indians, the fiercest of whom are the tobosos, as they are commonly called."[19] It was also thought that the Tobosos were "the only ones who, owing to the small size of their bows, could fight on horseback.[20]

Allusions to the Tobosos gradually disappeared from the documentary record of Nueva Vizcaya over the course of the eighteenth century. Reports of their extinction benefited the Spanish governors, who could claim credit for exterminating their enemies; but the same reports also aided the Tobosos themselves, who could then escape death or slavery by reason of supposedly having ceased to exist. In this way the Tobosos of Nueva Vizcaya blended into the other Conchos, who were considered to have been reduced to obedience to the Spanish Crown.

In the eighteenth-century official correspondence from the northeastern provinces, by contrast, "tobosos" seems to refer to no group in particular. Acknowledging their existence hardly threatened the interests of colonial authorities, and doubtless for this reason Tobosos are often mentioned throughout the century.[21] In 1735, for example, certain Tobosos took up arms in the *marquesado* (lands originally assigned to the marquis) of Aguayo, and in Agualeguas and Sabinas, both settlements in Nuevo León.[22] In Nuevo Santander and Texas the Tobosos appear into the late colonial period, although it is not clear whether these Indians were really Conchos/Tobosos displaced from the Bolsón or were simply referred to in this fashion because they were warlike.[23]

In the second half of the seventeenth century, the Salineros/Cabezas, together with those Tobosos who had survived the Nonolat massacre, became the Spaniards' main enemies. In 1660 *licenciado* Diego Medrano, curate of Durango, informed the archbishop that the Salinero nation was "made up of different lineages that use that name," and that it included some of the most warlike of peoples. Suspecting that the Salineros of the Jesuit mission of Tizonazo operated as spies for both rebellious Indians and those who staged attacks along the camino real, he proposed closing that mission and resettling the Salineros far from the highway.[24] In 1667, when some Salineros rose up, the Spanish suspected they were allied with others of that nation, including Indians who had been living in peace for a long time in the colonial settlements. The Salineros of Tizonazo consequently had their throats cut.[25] Others were condemned without trial to slow death in the mills of the *haciendas de beneficio* (that is, haciendas where minerals were processed), where their labor required them to inhale potentially fatal mercury fumes.[26]

Like the Tobosos, the "salineros" disappeared from the eighteenth-century documentation of central Nueva Vizcaya, although they continued to show up in Coahuila after 1750. In this context though, the term may refer generically to Indians who exploited the salt flats that lay on both sides of Salado River, in the eastern Bolsón.[27]

From the eighteenth century onward, there are recurrent mentions of the Cocoyomes, rather than the Salineros, in the southern Bolsón. The Spanish tried to exterminate them as they had the Acoclames to the north, for they considered both peoples to be major obstacles to the colonial enterprise.[28]

Following the supposed annihilation of the Tobosos, enemy Conchos became the so-called Acoclames in eighteenth-century Nueva Vizcaya. The Acoclames appeared in the documents as early as the 1620s, when they reportedly were mixed with the Tobosos and the Nonojes.[29] Beginning in 1698 Spanish correspondence classified them not as peaceful Indians, but rather as *apóstatas* (apostates), when they fled from the Atotonilco mission, which was the original settlement of the Tobosos.[30] The Spanish defeated the Acoclames in clashes at Las Cañas in 1703 and in the Sierra Mojada two years later. The same epithet appears, nevertheless, in the 1770 map by Nicolás de Lafora.[31]

In reality the Conchos/Acoclames consisted of numerous subgroups. A captured Indian interrogated in 1704 regarding rebellious Acoclames specifically mentioned Gavilanes, Chizos, and Sisimbles, further stating that the last two were included among those "bearing the name of Conchos" and were located near the juncture of the Conchos River and the Rio Grande, bordering on the territories of the Apaches and Cíbolos of New Mexico. In fact, Pedro de Rivera's 1729 map classified the Cíbolos as "Conchos."[32] In Nueva Vizcaya, references to pacified Chizos in missions like San Francisco de Conchos became increasingly common, although the same documents also refer to Chizos involved in rebellions.[33]

The first natives the Spanish came to know in both the Mapimí region and the province of Santa Bárbara were the Tepehuanes, a name that appears in northern New Spain from 1590 on. The term retains its etymological meaning from Nahuatl; namely, a reference to inhabitants of the sierra.[34] But the documents also mention "Tepehuanes del desierto," perhaps so called because of their proclivity for establishing rancherías in the Bolsón. They were also called Salineros because it fell to them to gather salt in Salinas de Palomas and Salinas del Machete for the miners of Parral.[35] Some of these were known as Cabezas, the name of an encomienda granted to the hacendado of Cerro Gordo in 1646.[36] A half century later, in 1693, Juan Fernández de Retana, captain of the Conchos Presidio, distinguished between two of these Indian groups: the "Cabezas de huacal" in Nueva Vizcaya and the "Cabezas" who ranged between Texas and New Mexico.[37]

Allusions to Tepehuanes in Nuevo León and Coahuila appeared in the first decades of the seventeenth century and were recurrent later.[38] In 1626 the governor assigned the Tepehuan cacique Malaquí to the Hacienda El Muerto, "along with his people, women, and children . . . given the absence of workers and native residents." We also find references to Tepehuan inhabitants within the jurisdiction of Monterrey, living under the command of a Captain Ventura, in the nearby haciendas of Santa Catalina and Los Nogales. As late as 1653, two Tepehuanes of an old encomienda grant lived on the latter estate.[39] Tepehuanes also appeared in the parish registries of Parras throughout the entire seventeenth century, but under the self-assigned name of *ódame* or *odahame* (meaning "people," a term that Tepehuanes in Chihuahua still use today).[40] As is true in the case of the Tobosos, it is often difficult to know whether these groups were native to the region or had been displaced from somewhere else (as seems to have happened to the cacique Malaquí). Like the other principal ethnic groups of northern New Spain, the Tepehuanes lacked central authority and often warred among themselves. Those of the sierra clashed with those of the desert in 1652, when Guajardo Fajardo enlisted more than one hundred Indian allies to attack the Tobosos of the Bolsón.[41]

The Coahuiltecans, meanwhile, concentrated in the eastern Bolsón, in the area near Monclova, where the presidio of Coahuila ("inner territory" in the local language) was established six years before the creation of the eponymous province in 1687. Carlos Valdés has determined that all Coahuiltecans spoke the same language, and that the Spanish artificially divided them, along with the Conchos and Tepehuanes, into a multitude of different groups.[42] Perhaps the most convincing evidence for the existence of a common language was Fray Juan Larios's attempt to compile a Coahuiltecan vocabulary in 1675. Although a similar work created in 1732 is no longer extant, we do possess Bartholomé García's 1760 Coahuiltecan dictionary. In this work García provided the longest list of named native groups, but excluded peoples living in areas to the west or south of the Bolsón, a fact that would appear to contradict Griffen's hypothesis that the Cocoyomes and Cabezas were Coahuiltecans.[43] At least some of the Cabezas came from the valleys west of the camino real and lived alongside the so-called Tepehuanes de la Sierra, with whom they probably shared the same language.[44]

In works dealing with colonial Coahuila there is a tendency to treat as native to the region Indians who had clearly been displaced from the west and north of the Bolsón. The Cocoyomes, Chizos, Cabezas, and Tobosos who feature in Saltillo's municipal archives all came from somewhere else.[45] Nevertheless, the Coahuiltecans appear neither in the Conchos mission nor in the long list of *naciones* mentioned in connection with Mission Santa Rosa de Viterbo de los Nadadores.[46]

Intergroup alliances complicated the scenario even further. At the beginning of the eighteenth century, an alliance of Acoclames, Cocoyomes, Tobosos, and Coahuiltecans attacked various settlements in Coahuila. Similarly, Julimes (the name of a mission on the Conchos) and Gavilanes (a splinter group of the Acoclames) joined with Coahuiltecans in raids along the Rio Grande in 1708; they purportedly set out from Coahuila to attack Parras to the southeast and Parral to the west.[47] Ten years later they claimed additional victims in Nadadores and San Buenaventura. However, the most serious attack took place in 1721, when Cocoyomes (Salineros), Tobosos, Acoclames, Sisimbles (Conchos), and Tripas Blancas laid siege to Monclova, seat of the provincial government and where numerous settlers had taken refuge. Few survived, with even the lieutenant governor perishing in the fray. From there the attackers headed to Parras, where several inhabitants, among them some Tlaxcalans, also met their end.[48] On July 28, 1722, "the entire coahuileña nation" was trapped in the Sierra de Corrales, southeast of Santa Bárbara Province; Acoclames and Cocoyomes found themselves forced to surrender. The Coahuiltecans vanished from the documentary record following that symbolic defeat, much as the Tobosos did after the Nonolat massacre and the Salineros did after the killings at Tizonazo.

Following the bloody raids on Monclova and Parras, in which more than two hundred people perished, the Spanish unleashed a merciless war that ended in the near total extinction of the Bolsón groups. The Coahuiltecans turn up in Parral between 1701 and 1725, the latter being the date of their final defeat.[49] In 1727 Spanish authorities confirmed that only select Cocoyomes (Tepehuanes), Acoclames, and Chizos (Conchos) remained in rebellion. By 1746 Viceroy Marqués de Altamira believed that the various peoples—the Acoclames, Tripas Blancas, Tobosos, Tosimoras, Gavilanes, and Cíbolos—had disappeared altogether. Twenty-four years later, Fray Agustín de Morfi confirmed that José Berroterán, captain of the Conchos Presidio, had eradicated the Cocoyomes and Tobosos (probably using that latter term somewhat generically).[50]

Throughout the eighteenth century, the wars of fire and blood, together with the enslavement of native peoples, gave way to systematic, legal deportations to Central Mexico and the Caribbean islands in 1771, 1723, 1725, and 1726.[51] Article 187 of the regulations issued by Pedro de Rivera stipulated, "The captains of the presidios that exist from El Pasaje to Conchos are to pay the utmost attention to eradicating those Indian nations known as Cocoyomes, Acoclames, Tripas Blancas, Terocodames, Zizimbres, Chizos, and Gavilanes, all of which threaten [Nueva] Vizcaya, and to do away with them, it is necessary to capture them using cunning, flattery, or force—without killing them—and send them as prisoners to the area around Mexico."[52] All the aforementioned groups lived in the Bolsón. Bishop Pedro de Tamarón y Romeral issued a similar edict in 1765: "for rebels it would be best to remove them from their native land and transport them across the sea . . . so that they do not return." To buttress his argument, he cited the example of certain Seris who, after escaping from prison, had incited others to rebel.[53]

Spaniards classified the Indians into broad groups: by language and according to whether they were hostile. But they also used an immense multitude of terminologies that reflected the nature of their own relations to the group in question. Many names identified encomienda Indians handed over to the settlers of northern New Spain.[54] From the sixteenth century onward, the Spanish had launched incursions to enslave "Conchos," mainly along the banks of the river by the same name. The founding of the real de minas of San José de Parral in July 1631 marks a time of peace and a break in the slave raids. Pacified Indians pledged to obey God and king and had to pay tribute to the Crown, for which reason settlers established systems of obligatory labor known as encomienda and repartimiento.

A similar fate befell the Indians of the Bolsón who came into contact with Santa Bárbara Province following the Spanish arrival. The Indians assigned to encomienda among the *estancieros* (rural property owners) of the valley continued to be called Conchos, but with a variety of added qualifiers: Conchos de la Chorrera (close to modern-day Chihuahua City), Conchos Hobomes, Conchos Olbayaguames, Conchos Chizos, and so forth.[55] Some of these names derived from indigenous etymology but were nevertheless applied haphazardly, at times referring to terms of self-designation used prior to contact or to a place that some particular group happened to frequent (as was probably the case with the "Chizos," the namesake of a mountain range in today's Big Bend National Park, in Texas) or to some characteristic of the group.

Where settled populations were absent, what historians refer to as the "war encomiendas" of northern New Spain authorized the Spanish to congregate Indians living sometimes as far as hundreds of kilometers away.[56] As late as 1668 in the province of Santa Bárbara, for example, encomienda Indians seem to have come from as far away as the junction of the Conchos River and the Rio Grande and even beyond the Rio Grande itself. A list of Santa Bárbara encomenderos from 1715 mentioned Cacalotes, Mezquites, Posalmes, Oposmes, Cíbolos, Poclames, Julimes, and Tapacolmes.[57] Some "Cacalotes" were also placed under the encomienda of the Valle del Pilón, in Nuevo León.[58]

When an hacendado managed to settle Indians next to his hacienda, he was rewarded with a title of encomienda. In those titles we usually find the appointment of a cacique, someone supposedly linked to his subjects by kinship. After naming a cacique, the encomendero could look for other Indians in the same area. The governor of Nueva Vizcaya handed out encomienda

Indians regardless of their traditional mode of subsistence. It is altogether probable that many of the Tobosos and other Indians distributed in the Saltillo region combined farming with hunting and gathering.[59]

In northern New Spain even peaceful Indians not assigned to encomiendas had to pay tribute to the Crown and were subject to repartimientos that furnished the Spanish colonists with forced labor.[60] The governor or alcalde mayor assigned them to hacendados who needed laborers; the arrangement typically lasted only a few months, although at times might continue for longer.[61] Following the consolidation of the mission system in the seventeenth century, the Spanish began to identify Indians by the name of the mission to which they had been assigned, as in the cases of the Julimes and Tapacolmes. However, the missions proved transitory institutions that were secularized when the Indians, now Christianized, had been integrated into colonial society.[62] At the same time, many Indians who remained for long periods on estancias and haciendas were called *indios laboríos* or simply indios, even though they had originally been placed in a mission.[63]

Rather than taking advantage of the potential labor of nearby missions, many Spaniards preferred to organize a large-scale labor market, forcing Indians to travel over immense distances. In this way, the natives of Sinaloa and Sonora, supposedly residents of missions, came to be the majority presence in the mines of San José del Parral.[64] Unlike their encomienda counterparts, these Indians received the name of their province as part of the repartimiento process. The names mentioned in San Bartolomé are not duplicated at San Francisco de Conchos, confirming that each colonial settlement drew Indian laborers from a different area.

The Conchos who lived close to settlements, who were easy to identify and had been given out in encomienda, usually kept their name of origin. In the parish registers of San Francisco de Conchos, there are only two cursory references to Conchos between 1694 and 1743, the other Indians being (in descending order of frequency) Tarahumaras, Chizos, Tobosos, Cuicatomes, and Auchanes. The last two groups were settled in Santa Cruz de los Auchanes, in the area immediately adjoining the Julimes mission, on the banks of the Conchos River. There are also scattered references to Nonojes, Sisimbles, Acoclames, Julimes, Apaches, Cholomes, Jocomes, Borrados, Cíbolos, Tapacolmes, and Chichitames. All these peoples originated along the banks of the Conchos or the Rio Grande, with the possible exception of the Borrados, who came from Coahuila, and the Jocomes, possibly native to the Janos region.[65]

In Santa Bárbara Province, Indians of the Bolsón were distributed via encomienda or repartimiento to a single property owner. In San Bartolomé, just as in San Francisco de Conchos, we can link each group with a particular hacendado who, in the burial registries and also at times in baptism and marriage registries, is listed as the owner of the property where the people in question worked. This is the context of a 1657 statement in which an Indian described the Concho nation as being spread out, and "the particular names that are given to that nation come from the declaration of the governors of said nations, men who enter into their lands to fetch them in the time of the [wheat] harvest."[66]

Later encomiendas awarded to the settlers of Coahuila, founded in 1687, were perhaps even more coercive than those of central Nueva Vizcaya: instead of being allowing to return to their native lands, the Indians had to remain congregated at the encomendero's hacienda. Hence the term *congrega* that emerged in northeast New Spain, where missions like Santa Rosa de Viterbo de los Nadadores also lent their names to the list of Indian classifications.[67] Each group of reduced Indians received its own name, thus giving rise to an infinity of designations that did not necessarily reflect any pre-Hispanic social divisions. Although certain terms persisted for a long time, as Cecilia Sheridan argues, it is not clear that they actually referred to the same groups or that they reflected some process of identity linked a new sense of territory.[68]

As in the case of the so-called Tobosos who disappeared west of the Bolsón while persisting for decades farther to the east, the assigning of appellations varied from one region to the other. The Cíbolos, who appear as "Cíbolos-Conchos" in the 1727 Barreiro map, received frequent mention in documents from Parral, but seemed to be unknown as a group in Coahuila in 1729. That year the viceroy recognized the Cíbolos as allies and ordered the captain of the Monclova Presidio and Governor José Antonio de Ecay y Múzquiz to treat them with respect. The latter replied that "in all the years that I have served in these lands . . . I have not heard of such a nation of Indians, nor of any regions or places that might be their place of habitation." Rather, he identified the Indians of the Bolsón and the north side of the Rio Grande as Apaches, Jumanos, and Pelones."[69] Somewhat later, however, cartographer Nicolás de Lafora did indeed identify the presence of Cíbolos in the Coahuila mission.[70]

When the Acoclames (that is, the Conchos/Tobosos) and Cocoyomes (Tepehuanes/Salineros) were defeated, "Apaches" of northern origin took their place. Over the course of the eighteenth century, these people either displaced or integrated into their own society the autochthonous inhabitants of the Bolsón.[71] A report from 1851 stated that Cholomes, Cocoyomes, and others had all been absorbed into Apache society.[72] As had already happened with "Toboso," "Salinero," "Acoclame," and "Cocoyome," the appellation "Apache" became a generic term used to indicate hostile nomads regardless of ethnic origin, and by the nineteenth century it had even come to include the Apaches' ancestral rivals, the Comanches.[73] By that point encomienda had ended, the colonial population had grown, and there was no longer any need for repartimiento, so Indians were only identified by their nation when they entered into some sort of peace agreement.

In conclusion, the attempt to identify the ethnicities of indigenous peoples of the Bolsón de Mapimí using colonial documents confronts us with all the same problems that faced those documents' authors. In contrast to common assumptions, most of the terms that the Spanish used were neither gentilics linked to a specific territory nor names used for a specific ethnic group. Bolsón natives were organized into itinerant bands that underwent constant realignment and whose territorial limits changed according to the circumstances of the moment. The Spanish tried to label all of these peoples, at times using indigenous words, but the Spaniards' main interest was to situate the groups in question into colonial society in some way (as either friends or enemies, or as belonging to missions, encomiendas, haciendas, and so forth).

Some groups ended up integrating into New Spain's society; others, probably those at a demographic disadvantage, opposed the colonial regime and were practically exterminated over the course of the eighteenth century. Alternating periods of peace and war influenced the appearance and disappearance of certain appellatives. Governors and captains stopped using the names of groups whom they had supposedly exterminated. Meanwhile, those Indians who did not join their ethnic group in rebellion had a clear motive for changing their self-identification to dissociate themselves from hostilities and thereby escape the repression that was certain to follow. For these reasons, a number of appellatives changed as a result of indigenous rebellions and the retributive campaigns in which those rebels were allegedly annihilated. These changes did not necessarily reflect one Indian group displacing another. In this way, hostile "Conchos" came to be called "Tobosos," then the "Tobosos" were in turn replaced by the "Acoclames," and the "Coahuiltecas" vanished altogether in favor of the "Apaches."

NOTES

1. Cramaussel, "El Bolsón de Mapimí."

2. Cramaussel and Carrillo Valdez, "El difícil poblamiento de Mapimí," 63–93.

3. Ortelli, *Trama de una guerra.*

4. Griffen, *Culture Change*, 159–69; Churruca Peláez et al., *El sur de Coahuila en el siglo XVII*, 108–14; Valdés, *La gente del mezquite*, 105–6; Sheridan Prieto, *Fronterización*, 233–93.

5. Griffen differentiates separate peoples, although at times the same groups appear more than once in his lists. See *Culture Change*, 159–69.

6. Griffen, *Culture Change*, app. 4, 176–77; Valdés, *La gente del mezquite*, 105.

7. It is believed that the Tepehuanes of central and northern Durango, where colonial settlement occurred at a relatively early date, assimilated into mestizo society during the nineteenth century. This left only the Tepehuanes of the Sierra Madre Occidental, who were divided into two groups: those of Chihuahua (speakers of Odami), neighbors of the Tarahumara; and those of Durango, who in linguistic terms were subdivided into speakers of O'odham and Audam, and who were neighbors of the Huichols and Coras. See Cramaussel, "La región de San Francisco de Lajas," 19 (map).

8. Griffen, *Culture Change*, 133–37.

9. "Autos contra los acoclames, cocoyomes y otras naciones aliadas por rebeldes a la real corona," December 3, 1705, Milicia y Guerra, Sediciones, Real de San José del Parral, AHMP.FC.C11.013.138.

10. Griffen, *Indian Assimilation*, 1 (map), 2 (original gentilic); Griffen (*Culture Change*, 42) mentioned that the Conchos were considered separate from the Jumanos.

11. Griffen (*Culture Change*, 42) is the only scholar who has suggested that Toboso and Concho were different languages, something that seems improbable for the reasons outlined in this essay.

12. Álvarez, "Agricultores de paz."

13. Porras Muñoz, *La frontera con los indios*, 169.

14. Álvarez, "Agricultores de paz," 321.

15. Cramaussel and Rosales Villa, *San Francisco de Conchos*, 42–48.

16. Cramaussel, "Indios de paz contra indios de guerra."

17. Griffen, *Culture Change*, 101; Cramaussel and Rosales Villa, *San Francisco de Conchas.*

18. "Carta de Antonio de Oca Sarmiento, gobernador de Durango, fechada en Parral el 9 de marzo de 1667," AGI, Guadalajara 29, ramo 4, no. 37. "Toboso" comes from *toba*, the name of a volcanic rock found in the area. It is the toponym of a Spanish village in La Mancha, whence hails Dulcinea, a prominent character in Miguel de Cervantes's *Don Quijote*. In northern Mexico, "toboso" refers to a type of forage grass whose scientific name is *Peluraphis mutica*. The mythical region of Cíbola was said to lie somewhere north of the Rio Grande. There are indications that the Cíbolos were bison hunters.

19. Álvarez, "Agricultores de paz," 350.

20. Navarro García, *Don José de Gálvez*, 21.

21. Álvarez, "Agricultores de paz," 353.

22. Griffen, *Culture Change*, 72.

23. González Rodríguez assumed that they were the same Indians from the Bolsón; see "Los tobosos, bandoleros y nómadas."

24. Porras Muñoz, *La frontera con los indios*, 167.

25. Juicio del gobernador Antonio de Oca y Sarmiento, 1670, AGI, Escrituras Públicas, 396a; "Información hecha a pedimiento de la república del Parral, de cómo el haber llevado a sangre y fuego el pueblo de Tizonazo ha sido en servicio de ambas majestades y bien común del reino," December 6, 1667, AHMP.FC.C11.007.068, Milicia y Guerra, Sediciones, Real de San José de Parral.

26. Consider the case of an Indian named Nicolás in Parral, in 1667, in Cramaussel, *Poblar la frontera*, 197.

27. Several Seris were also classified as "salineros" for no other reason than that they customarily gathered salt; see Mirafuentes Galván, "Relaciones interétnicas."

28. "Consulta no. 64, sobre si se les debe hacer la guerra a fuego y sangre a los indios enemigos," 1704, AGI, México, 475.

29. "Consulta no. 64," AGI, México, 745; Porras Muñoz, *La frontera con los indios*, 168.

30. "Autos contra los acoclames, cocoyomes y otras naciones aliadas por rebeldes a la real Corona," 1705, AHMP.C11.13.138.

31. Cramaussel, "El exterminio de los chizos."

32. Cramaussel, "La función de la cartografía colonial."

33. "Consulta no. 64," AGI, México, 475.

34. Cramaussel, "De cómo los españoles clasificaban a los indios"; Cramaussel, *Poblar la frontera;* Cramaussel and Carrillo Valdez, "El difícil poblamiento de Mapimí"; Hickerson, *Jumanos*, 47.

35. In 1643 a missionary of San José del Tizonazo stated that he had evangelized "the tepehuana nation, called salinera." See Averiguación de Francisco González cumplido contra D. Luis de Monsalve, 1643, AGI, Escribanía de Cámara, 170c.

36. Cramaussel and Carrillo Valdez, "Don Santiago Alonso."

37. Griffen, *Culture Change*, app. 4, 176–77.

38. Griffen, *Culture Change*, 40, 43–44, 72; Sheridan Prieto, *Fronterización*, 332 (map).

39. "Visita general del gobernador Martín de Zavala de 1626, en el paraje de Los Muertos. Los indos son asignados a la hacienda de Alonso Diez de Zamudia," and "Visita de Juan de Zavala de 1653," Archivo Municipal de Monterrey, Ramo Civil, vol. 7, exp. 9. I thank the late Raúl García Flores for sending me these documents.

40. If we combine references to "tepehuanos" or "tepeguanes" and "ódames" or "odahames" they constitute a fairly populous group. And if we add "salineros," they would outnumber the Laguneros and Coahuiltecans.

41. Cramaussel, "El exterminio de los chizos."

42. Valdés, *Sociedades y culturas;* Valdés, *La gente del mezquite.*

43. Cited in Valdés, *Sociedades y culturas*, 28–30. The prolix title of García's book was *Manual para administrar los santos sacramentos de penitencia, eucharistia,*

extrema-unción y matrimonio a los indios a las naciones pajalates, orejones, pacaos, pacóas, tilijayas, alasapas y otras muchas diferentes, del río San Antonio y Río Grande pertenecientes a el Colegio de Santísima Cruz de Querétaro como son: los pacuáches, mezcales, pamposas, tacames, chayopines, venado, pamaques, y toda la juventud de pihuiques, borradas, sanipaos y manos de perro; see also Griffen, *Culture Change*, 135.

44. See, for example, Cramaussel and Carrillo Valdez, "Don Santiago Alonso." The individual studied in this article was gobernador of the Cabezas and a native of Cerro Gordo (today Hidalgo, Durango).

45. A map in Valdés, *La gente del mezquite*, 114, labels Julimes, Chizos, Tobosos, and Cabezas.

46. Valdés, *Sociedades y culturas*, 28, 74–75.

47. Valdés, *Sociedades y culturas*, 205.

48. Valdés, *Sociedades y culturas*, 207–9. Regarding the context of this attack, see Cramaussel and Carrillo Valdez, *Coahuila o "tierra adentro."*

49. Griffen, *Culture Change*, 159. Somewhat surprisingly, Cecilia Sheridan does not include the Coahuiltecans in her lengthy tabulation of "nativos en propiedad"; see Sheridan Prieto, *Fronterización*, 311–18.

50. Griffen, *Culture Change*, 103.

51. Griffen, *Culture Change*, 63, 68; Venegas Delgado and Valdés Dávila, *La ruta del horror.* The deportations multiplied in the waning years of the colonial era and, in fact, continued after independence; see Cramaussel, "La violencia en Chihuahua"; Cramaussel, "El exterminio de los chizos."

52. The reglamento is reprinted in Pedro de Rivera y Villalón, *"Diario y derrotero*, 251.

53. Tamarón y Romeral, *Viajes pastorales.*

54. The traditional historiographic ignorance about northern encomiendas began to change at the end of the twentieth century; see Cuello, "Persistence of Indian Slavery"; Deeds, "Rural Work in Nueva Vizcaya"; Cramaussel, *Poblar la frontera*, 206–19 (see the list of encomenderos on 363–66).

55. Cramaussel, *Poblar la frontera*, 363–66.

56. This sort of encomienda existed in Nueva Galicia; see Álvarez, *El indio y la sociedad colonial norteña*, 46–65. The same held true for other regions of the Americas, such as Paraguay; see Saeler, "Survival and Abolition."

57. Numerous Julimes and some Posolmes also appear in the parish registers of San Bartolomé; see Cramaussel, *Poblar la frontera*, 214, 363–66. Along with the Posolmes, Poclames (or Polacmes), and Oposmes, the Mezquites feature in a list of Conchos native to the Junta de los Ríos; see Griffen, *Indian Assimilation*, 34–35. Cacalotes, Oposmes, and Tapacolmes apparently came from beyond the Rio Grande; see Griffen, *Culture Change*, 177.

58. Garza Martínez, "Poblamiento y colonización," 437.

59. Cuello, "Persistence of Indian Slavery."

60. Cramaussel, "Forced Transfer of Indians," 184–208.

61. Cramaussel, *Poblar la frontera*, 219–34.

62. The process of secularization began with Archbishop Juan de Palafox y Mendoza in 1641. But the 1641 order to secularize a series of Franciscan missions was

revoked in 1656; see Cramaussel and Rosales Villa, *San Francisco de Conchos*, 41–42; Porras Muñoz, *Iglesia y estado*, 207, 490. Secularization was however carried out in various Franciscan missions in 1754. In 1751, twenty-two Jesuit missions were secularized; see Deeds, "Rendering unto Caesar."

63. This happened throughout the Spanish Empire; see Jackson, "La raza," 116–25.

64. Cramaussel, "Forced Transfer of Indians."

65. In *Indian Assimilation*, Griffen argues that the Julimes were not Conchos but rather Jumanos. Cholome is the name of a ranch near the Julimes.

66. "Litigio entre los capitanes Alonso Montes de Oca, Bernardo Gómez y Francisco Peinado por una encomienda," 1657–58, AHMP.FC.A5.1.10.

67. Hoyo, *Esclavitud y encomiendas*.

68. Sheridan Prieto, "Reflexiones"; Sheridan Prieto, *Fronterización*.

69. "Derrotero de Ecay y Múzquiz," cited in Rodríguez-Sala, *La expedición militar-geográfica*, 56.

70. Griffen, *Culture Change*, 101.

71. Griffen, *Culture Change*, 103. According to Griffen, "Apache" originally referred to any Indian of northern origin.

72. Langberg, "Inspección de las colonias militares." Griffen makes the same point in *Culture Change*, 101.

73. Cramaussel, "La violencia en Chihuahua."

CHAPTER 7

Fearing Apaches into Existence

THE DISCURSIVE BORDERLANDS OF NUEVA VIZCAYA AND CUBA IN THE LATE EIGHTEENTH AND EARLY NINETEENTH CENTURIES

Paul Conrad

"A border is a dividing line, a narrow strip along a steep edge. A borderland is a vague and undetermined place created by the emotional residue of an unnatural boundary. It is in a constant state of transition. The prohibited and forbidden are its inhabitants."

Gloria Anzaldúa, *Borderlands / La Frontera*

As the 2018 election neared in the United States, President Donald J. Trump warned of a looming invasion of the country by migrants traveling north through Mexico from Central America. While a US military assessment deemed the actual security threat posed by this migration to be nominal, Mr. Trump and his associates argued otherwise, suggesting that it might be necessary to deploy as many as fifteen thousand troops to the border to prevent the crossing of alleged gang members, "unknown Middle Easterners," drug traffickers, and other "very tough fighters." Many people countered Trump's rhetoric by pointing out that the migrants consisted largely of families, including women and children, seeking asylum. Yet a significant proportion of the US population indicated that they supported the president's actions and shared his point of view. Hundreds of so-called citizen militia members even headed to the border to help protect it. The specter of dangerous outsiders stoked fear among a portion of the US population that led them to believe their families and property might be under threat and to support those who claimed they would protect them. While the migrant caravan was real, it also took on a discursive significance outsized to the on-the-ground reality of the situation.[1]

This story from a present-day North American borderland provides an entry point to borderlands of prior centuries. Two hundred years ago, as in our present world, the presence or anticipated migration of people deemed dangerous or foreign could be historically influential. In the eighteenth century, however, the outsiders from the perspective of colonial officials and settlers were often indigenous peoples, as natives sought to defend their homelands against invaders and pursue their economic, territorial, and cultural aims. Euro-American fears of native people were sometimes legitimate, as broad swaths of North and South America remained under indigenous control centuries after European colonization began. Expansionary indigenous polities dominated some colonial outposts, taking people and property at will, much to the lament of colonists. Yet even legitimate worries were often manipulated, exaggerated, and filtered through racial, religious, or ethnic stereotypes. Rhetorical frontiers lingered in some places long after colonial rule had in fact consolidated, as a rustled cow or two could be deployed as evidence of an Indian threat that warranted military investments, tax breaks, or other benefits.[2]

Among the groups most often cast as dangerous, as the "very tough fighters" of the eighteenth- and nineteenth-century borderlands of North America, were Apache Indians. They were (and are) known to themselves by variants of the term "Ndé" (the people), as well as by specific band names referencing ties of geography, culture, and kinship. Historically, however, their independence, mobility, and subsistence practices, which included livestock raids, often sparked outsiders to label them otherwise: as enemies—as the word "Apachu" translates from the Zuni language—or as thieves, criminals, barbarians, bloodthirsty beasts, and worse. Apache groups were not united in one large tribal political structure, and the homelands of distinct bands stretched from Arizona to Texas, Kansas to Chihuahua. In part because of imperial forced migration policies that attempted to control Apaches by moving them elsewhere, knowledge and fear of Apaches reached across an even farther flung geography over time. During the eighteenth and nineteenth centuries, Apaches were said at one time or another to be a threat to

Euro-American lives or property in Arizona and Alabama, Santa Fe and Veracruz, Chihuahua and Havana.[3]

This essay examines a historical moment in the second half of the eighteenth century when Apaches were deemed a threat to colonial societies in two distant places: Nueva Vizcaya (the present-day states of Chihuahua, Durango, and parts of Coahuila, Mexico) and Cuba. It might seem obvious at first glance that concerns about Apache groups in the former place were more legitimate. After all, Apache homelands and Spanish land claims overlapped there. Yet a comparison of these two contexts reveals how in both places the Apache presence took on a discursive life of its own. In Nueva Vizcaya, for example, so-called *indios bárbaros*, especially Southern Apache bands, were blamed for all manner of societal troubles, even as investigations into captive-taking, homicides, and livestock rustling suggested that actors of various ethnicities and affiliations were involved. Concerns about the loyalties of Spanish subjects, including mission Indian pueblos, and their potential affinities for Apaches, ultimately played a role in the decision to wage war on Apache groups and deport those taken prisoner out of the region, including to Cuba, to labor.[4]

Familiar concerns about Indians ultimately emerged in Cuba as well, however, after some natives escaped into the countryside from households and military fortification projects. Hacienda owners began complaining about murders, robberies, and house burnings that they believed had been committed by gangs of Indian runaways, perhaps joined by escaped black slaves. Amidst the Haitian Revolution, a slave revolt that began in 1791 on a neighboring island and ultimately upended French colonial rule, the threat posed by Indians banding with slaves was intolerable. It was thus met with significant resources, including hefty bounties on the heads of the alleged leaders and substantial funds expended on tracking parties. Even more so than in the case of Nueva Vizcaya, however, evidence that Indians were actually the primary instigators of unrest in the countryside of Cuba was limited. Sightings of Indians were few and far between, and many observers expressed confusion over the ethnic identity of those runaways they had seen.[5]

These disparate but interconnected contexts both illustrate key characteristics of borderlands, defined here as "zones of plural sovereignty" where the legal, political, or cultural authority of one group overlapped with those of others. Each borderland examined in this chapter, for example, was shaped by racial, religious, and ethnic stereotypes, as well as by fragmentary understandings or misperceptions and creative inventions and manipulations. In sum, they proved as much discursive as material in character, as threats posed by Apaches and other native people to colonial societies did not have to be well grounded to be influential. As a result, even relatively small numbers of people deemed dangerous or foreign could exercise a historical influence outsized to their demographic or military power.[6]

Long before Apaches supposedly troubled the countryside of Cuba, they had interacted with colonial societies on the North American mainland. By the time of the first entrées into the North American West by European-led expeditions in the sixteenth century, Athapaskan-speaking peoples later known to the Spanish as Apaches and Navajos occupied homelands in the mountains and plains that surrounded the agricultural villages of Pueblo Indian peoples. While it is difficult to ascertain with precision the political and cultural divisions that existed at this time, it is clear that Apache groups' loyalties and self-understandings were already differentiated based on kinship and geographical residence, as they would be in later times. They shared an ancestral language, but not all dialects were mutually intelligible. Still, groups sometimes allied in the face of a common threat, particularly those groups that shared geographic proximity and ties of kinship formed by intermarriage as bases for mutual aid. The most influential leaders historically could compel followers from more than their own local group or those that composed their larger band or tribe, but they could never speak for all people outsiders viewed as "Apaches." There was no pan-tribal political structure.[7]

Despite the reality of political fragmentation, outside observers often assumed a larger Apache "nation." On the one hand, the meaning of the Spanish term *nación* during this period generally reflected a basic idea of ethnic or cultural homogeneity among a people more than any unifying political structure. Yet in its application to Apaches and other indigenous peoples, observers sometimes deployed "nación" to suggest coordination and shared motivations in ways that served their own interests. One of the best examples of this is the way that residents of New Mexico and adjacent provinces drew upon the claim that the entire Apache nation was at war with them in the seventeenth century as a means to legitimize the indiscriminate exploitation of native slaves, owing to their status as enemies captured in a supposedly just war. In 1658, New Mexico governor Juan Manso issued a "sentence of death" against the Apache nation for resisting Spanish rule and drew upon it as a basis for exporting native men, women, and children of varied origins and ethnicities into New Spain as laborers. While the Spanish foothold in New Mexico was in fact tenuous—as the famous Pueblo Revolt of 1680 illustrated—the idea that an Apache nation had waged incessant war against either the Spanish or Pueblo Indian peoples was pure fiction. Both before and after the arrival of the Spanish, Apache groups' relations with outsiders were varied and often characterized by mutual aid. Even violence—including raiding for livestock, foodstuffs, and captives—could be assimilated into productive exchange relations, as the ransom of captured kin offered new opportunities for the exchange of needed resources.[8]

The Apache-Spanish borderlands shifted south in the eighteenth century. While historical actors—and some historians—describe Apaches as migrating into or invading New Spain from the north during this period, it was as much the northward movement of Spanish colonial society as Apache migrations that led to new zones of interaction during this period. As Chantal Cramaussel reveals in chapter 6, the Bolsón de Mapimí—a dry basin straddling Nueva Vizcaya and Coahuila—emerged as a key site of such interactions. Offensive wars and deportation campaigns against the allied bands of indigenous groups that had previously inhabited the basin coincided with new mining strikes that led to the establishment of the Real de Minas de San Francisco de Cuella in 1709, which grew into the newly named villa of San Felipe el Real de Chihuahua by 1718. This burgeoning settlement fueled the opening of new ranching and farming lands to supply it.[9]

As Spanish settlements in New Spain spread north and grew in population, Apaches sensed opportunities and greater numbers traveled south on raiding and trading expeditions. Some Apache groups—particularly those whose territories lay in the southern Plains, such as the Lipans and Mescaleros—interacted more with the Spanish during this period as they faced increased competition from indigenous peoples such as the Comanches. Yet the homelands of other Apache groups—including those who came to be known as Chiricahuas centered in what is now southern New Mexico, Arizona, and northern Chihuahua—did not change very much during this period, even if their mobility for raiding, trading, and war expeditions increased to an extent.[10]

As in the past in New Mexico, the Apache presence within Spanish colonial society in northern New Spain in the eighteenth century generated complex reactions as fear and misunderstanding mingled with perceived opportunities. The lack of a uniform reaction or approach to Apache people was in part a reflection of the diverse interests of residents of the region during this period. While some Spanish landowners feared Apache raids, many mission Indian communities saw more benefit than risk in Apache trading partners. Much to the lament of some royal observers, mission Indians along the lower Rio Grande at mid-century might attend mass one day and then "go around on horseback trading with Apaches" the next. The populous Tarahumara (Rarámuri) pueblos of the Sierra Madre also saw opportunities in the exchange of livestock, foodstuffs, and clothing with visiting Apache traders.[11]

Even as relations with actual Apache Indians were often productive, the idea of a looming Apache threat became increasingly influential. After the imposition of a royal sales tax, or *alcalaba*, of 2 percent in Nueva Vizcaya in 1726, opposition to the tax or to any increase in it often centered on the idea that northern New Spain was an "Indian frontier," and its communities already contributed to help provide for their self-defense. While most requests for complete exemption from the tax were unsuccessful, emphasis on the Indian threat undoubtedly played some role in keeping the tax significantly lower in the northern provinces than elsewhere in New Spain.[12] Petitions against taxation on the grounds of being situated on an Indian frontier were ubiquitous. Residents of Saltillo, Coahuila, opposed increases in the alcabala in 1777, 1778, and 1780 by arguing that the city was positioned on a "frontier" and that its citizens had always defended it against enemy Indians. The same was true in Parras, Nueva Vizcaya, where two powerful hacendados protested directly to the king against a tax increase in 1782 by arguing that "Parras was still an Indian frontier." Residents of the mining town of Parral made a similar argument in 1790, arguing that they should be exempt from the alcabala based on living on a frontier "invaded" by Apaches.[13]

The ways in which the threat of enemy Indians was understood and mobilized by one wealthy landowner and presidio commander in the mid-eighteenth century is particularly illustrative. Don Joseph de Berroterán was a military officer who had been involved in campaigns against the mobile indigenous groups of the region in previous decades, but in more recent years both he and his presidio's company at Conchos had largely been engaged in other pursuits, including tending his growing herds of livestock.[14]

As Spanish officials considered reorganizing or disbanded presidios in areas where independent Indians no longer lived, Berroterán drew upon Apache Indians as a pretext to argue for the preservation of his post. In October 1747, he reported to the viceroy of New Spain on the Apache migrations into Nueva Vizcaya and Coahuila that he had observed in recent years. He noted that the forced removal of many of the area's previous indigenous groups in the early 1700s (including to the Caribbean) had left the rugged mountains and deserts abutting Spanish settlements free for the taking. Hundreds of Apaches had now made these lands their own. In referring to the recent past, Berroterán described his relations with these migrants as friendly. The Apache leader Pascual visited Berroterán's presidio at Conchos every three months or so to trade buffalo hides and deerskins for "tobacco, flour, sugar, arms, and clothing." Pascual had even allowed some Apache children to be baptized as a part of these exchanges. When he looked to the future of the Apache presence, however, Berroterán turned apocalyptic. If the Apaches south of the Rio Grande now numbered only four hundred, he believed there to be "countless" more north of the river, and he envisioned that once they migrated south, "once they penetrate and move into [the Bolsón de Mapimí] they will occupy almost all the eastern side of Nueva Vizcaya and the western side of Coahuila, and will easily destroy both these important jurisdictions." Even as he traded with Apaches like Pascual, Berroterán warned that the Apache presence could be a stepping stone toward the loss of entire provinces of northern New Spain.[15]

The supposed Indian threat was a highly malleable rhetorical tool, as Berroterán's interpretation of recent raids on nearby haciendas further illustrated. He explained that the haciendas of El Alamo, Sierra de Albino, San Juan del Río, Rama Zarca, and Cadena had all been raided at the beginning of 1747, "with sixteen to eighteen lives lost" but was unclear about who had perpetrated these raids. Some attributed these actions to the Apaches, but Berroterán was unsure whether those responsible "were [those] who remained of the defeated enemy [the Tobosos], some of those who are scattered from [mission] pueblos, or the more than 400 Apaches who are ensconced in the hill country."[16] In fact, killings and thefts could be invoked to make any number of arguments: mission Indians were backsliding in the faith, civil authorities were failing to prosecute crimes, or military forces were needed to contain the attacks of independent Indian groups. Berroterán's description of the Bolsón de Mapimí as a safe haven for a vague but menacing enemy highlighted this malleability. "The heathen enemies, unconverted *and* apostate," he stated, "come from settlements tucked away there, and their movement will always continue like the waves of the sea." Whether it was backsliding natives in mission pueblos—the apostates—or Apache Indian migrants—the unconverted—Berroterán suggested that the Indian threat was as permanent as the ocean. The subtext, of course, was that his own position should be beyond reproach.[17]

Perhaps because such arguments were so familiar to them by the mid-1700s, royal officials in Mexico City and Spain did not fall for Berroterán's bait, and his presidio was in fact disbanded in 1751. A *fiscal* (crown attorney) in Mexico City argued after reviewing Berroterán's reports that the Apache presence was hardly the threat he made it out to be. In his view, it made no sense to continue spending money on useless presidios to chase "a few Indian bandits who lived only off what they rustled and robbed." After all, "even in this capital of Mexico," he explained, "and all the cities, villas, and major populations of the kingdom, there are thieves and all kinds of evildoers." In population centers, such acts were handled as crimes and punished accordingly, even if they could not be prevented entirely.[18]

If Berroterán lost the debate in this case, the basic questions he raised remained pertinent in the years to come. How many murders and thefts were too many, and how should they be punished? What distinguished a frontier or borderland from a population center or heartland? These questions were more than just theoretical matters, but rather had potential material implications, as Berroterán's story and the broader tradition of communities drawing upon the idea of Indian attacks for tax advantages reveals.[19] Berroterán's claims of a looming Apache "illness" did not immediately materialize. After his visita of the region in 1761, for example, the bishop of Durango noted that while the Apaches took a few animals, "it was not with the excess of past years with the [Tobosos]." Most Apaches remained in the mountains, he explained, traveling at times to "the regions of the north, which have no known end," likely to trade.[20] The governor of Coahuila wrote similarly about Apache trade relations during this period and explained that his jurisdiction was at relative peace, except for an occasional raid. The only solution, in his mind: "more settlements."[21]

The threat of Apache Indians was more complex than just looming destruction in El Paso and other communities along the Rio Grande. In 1762, for example, the captain of Presidio del Norte, Manuel Antonio San Juan, issued an order warning that no residents, whether Spanish, Indian or "de color quebrado" (of broken color) could trade with the Apaches for seeds, firearms, or livestock. San Juan explained his fear that residents, in seeking their own personal gain, would bring danger to themselves by inviting Apaches into their homes to trade. Yet, perhaps in an effort to control the trade, he did not restrict dealing with Apaches altogether, but ordered that trade be carried out "in the light of day" in the town plaza. Military officials elsewhere also reported that Apaches came frequently to sell their wares. In Janos in the late 1750s, for example, they described repeated visits from Chiricahua Apache women, who entered the fort carrying wooden crosses and asked to sell firewood to the soldiers.[22]

At war councils in the 1770s, Spanish military officers would claim that war with Apaches had begun in 1748. Yet much of the contemporary evidence from local communities paints a more complex picture, suggesting that "war" was neither underway nor inevitable in the 1750s or early 1760s in Nueva Vizcaya or Coahuila.[23] The key spark for an eventual war between Spaniards and Apaches was not the occasional mule herd stolen by a few Apache men, but the decision to blame Apaches for a much broader livestock rustling economy in which multiple groups—native and Hispanic alike—had long been involved. Military campaigns in the summer and fall of 1765 reflected signs of a shift in Apache-Spanish relations. Alférez Joseph Luzero was sent in pursuit of Apaches who had allegedly raided ranches near El Paso, even though presidio captains there had long noted that Suma and Cholome Indians were the more frequent perpetrators of such actions.[24] He commanded a party of more than two hundred militiamen, enlisted soldiers, and Indian auxiliaries. In September, the party came across a Chiricahua Apache camp of twenty-three men, women, and children in the Sierra of Sacramento. Outnumbered nearly ten to one, the Apaches had little chance to escape; six were killed and seventeen taken captive. Luzero distributed the spoils of this battle to the militiamen and Indian scouts: buffalo hides, antlers, clothing, saddles, bows and arrows, corn, and other items. The mules and horses they found seemed to confirm that the attack was justified, as they carried various brands: "some from this presidio, others from New Mexico, others from farther into Nueva Vizcaya, and some without a brand." As Luzero explained his logic, he knew Apaches had stolen these animals because "they don't buy them or raise them," a statement that ignored the evidence of Apache trading practices reflected in the spoils of his own campaign.[25]

Similar campaigns in the late 1760s on Apache camps similarly used any branded animals discovered as evidence that raids had been committed by Apaches and as justification for further attacks on them. Yet, as in the case of Lucero's campaign, local residents and officials also sometimes discovered evidence that contradicted their assumption that any theft or killing had been committed by "the enemy," "the infidels," or the "barbarians."[26] The presidio captain of La Bahía (Texas) explained in 1769, for example, that area residents feared Lipan Apaches had been spying on their herds. When one foreman had come upon two Indians stealing corn from his employer's fields, and had fired upon them "thinking they were Apache," he discovered that they were in fact men from the local mission. A 1769 attack on a man driving his cowherd from Texas to Coahuila further elucidated the problem of attributing attacks exclusively to Apaches. Headed south into Coahuila from Presidio La Bahía, Joseph Antonio Carrera had been cornered by a group of "naked" Indians, firing arrows upon him. After "he miraculously escaped unharmed," he meandered from mountain to mountain, fleeing the Indians, until he arrived in Santa Rosa "without even a hat." After officials sent men to investigate, they traced the tracks of the naked raiders not to Apache camps in the mountains, but into the mission of San Francisco de Bizarrón.[27]

Influential military officers and royal officials failed to grapple with the ambiguity or complexity of evidence regarding the perpetrators of livestock rustling, escalating war against Apaches instead. It is striking, however, that some friars, local magistrates, and governors believed that missionized Indians and migrant workers contributed as much if not more to the lack of security in the northern provinces of New Spain. In the 1750s and 1760s, friars, governors, and even presidio captains reported that Sumas, Tarahumaras, and others were raiding as "thieves from inside the house." While they often blamed Apaches for having "perverted" these Christians Indians, they also reported having observed a much larger trading economy along the Rio Grande that illustrated mission Indians needed little persuading to join with Apaches in mutually beneficial enterprises. If some local officials wanted to end the loss of livestock, they found themselves facing legal constraints such as the lack of witnesses and what they described as "the delicate matter" of punishing Indians living in missions and risking their desertion. Whereas some historical actors—such as Berroterán—were unquestionably self-interested and manipulative in their portrayals of Apache Indians as they sought to gain the benefits that casting Nueva Vizcaya as a frontier entailed, others were legitimately concerned and confused by the situation at hand.[28]

This multiplicity of viewpoints has in turn influenced historical understandings of the period, as scholars have weighed and emphasized different perspectives and source material in their writings. On one end of the spectrum, scholarship emphasizing indigenous agency and power has seen in this period evidence of native expansion as Apache and Comanche mobility turned Hispanic heartlands into indigenous territories, or at least has told a story of "both sides having suffered." Certainly, one need not look far to find supporting evidence, as many official reports of the period tally the impressive number of thefts, murders, and captives taken by the "bárbaros" in the Interior Provinces of New Spain in the years after 1750.[29] Advancing a quite different view are historians who have highlighted correspondence and documentation from local archives, particularly economic and demographic data. These scholars, while acknowledging that livestock rustling was occurring, have revealed the "Apache" presence to be as much a discursive or useful rhetorical device. Though provocative—and ultimately in many ways convincing—this type of analysis also risks eliding the very real historical consequences that rhetorical manipulation and exaggeration had on historical actors, including on Ndé men, women, and children.[30]

Considering both types of documentation reveals that the discursive and material characteristics of these borderlands were inextricably linked, and even the most patently false concerns about Apache Indians could prove influential. Illustrative of this historical dynamic is a particularly thorough investigation into alleged collusion between Tarahumara and Apache Indians conducted in the early 1770s, which appeared to confirm not only that Spanish subjects had been involved in raiding and other violence, but that many of the crimes had been carried out by a large interethnic community ensconced in the Sierra Madre. While one scholar has drawn upon these investigations to describe the "cultural creativity" of interethnic raiding bands in colonial Nueva Vizcaya, I argue that the evidence warrants greater skepticism and perhaps better illustrates the ways in which fears of dangerous outsiders—Apaches in this case—operated within colonial societies, and in turn how internal societal concerns shaped and influenced their relations with outsiders.[31]

This investigation began with a perfectly ordinary event: the apprehension of a suspicious vagrant in March 1773. After six lashes, this Tarahumara man confessed to a local magistrate (corregidor) in Chihuahua that he had been involved in homicides that occurred the previous November. In fact, he explained that for the past two years he and five other men had been turning mules and horses over to Apaches. The magistrate, Pedro Queipo de Llano, explained to the governor of Nueva Vizcaya the implications of this revelation. He noted that local residents had long been convinced that the success of Apache raids must be explained by "secret intelligence and collusion" with the Tarahumaras, especially with the many Tarahumaras who deserted their pueblos without approval from their priests or governors. Of course, vagabondage was by no means unique to Tarahumaras, but the governor explained that in this context, desertion (or mobility) had become synonymous with leaving to "kill and rob like bandits committing bloody crimes under the name of the declared public enemy, the Apache."[32]

As Queipo de Llano apprehended accused participants, and they identified more suspects, he placed nearly one hundred men and women in custody within a few weeks of beginning his investigation. Testimony conducted under the threat or application of corporal punishment produced an elaborate portrait of the situation. Corroborating fears that violence was not being perpetrated solely by enemy Indians, witnesses described the central role that a clandestine interethnic community had played in sending out raiding parties from mountain camps. Headed by a man named Calaxtrin—who was identified by one witness as an Apache but by most simply as an Indian—this community was described as varying in size from several hundred to a thousand and as supposedly including individuals from diverse castes and backgrounds: blacks, mulattoes, Indians, mestizos, and even Spaniards. Apaches supported this community's existence by providing both needed trade goods and discursive cover. Raiding for mules and horses supplied the Calaxtrin band with meat and means of transport but also with valuable commodities that Apaches wanted to purchase in exchange for arrows, hides, blankets, and clothing. Because the band used arrows and dressed in clothing obtained from the Apaches, their raids had almost always been attributed to those Indians.[33]

By June 1773, Queipo de Llano had taken fifty-eight confessions and discovered more than two hundred accomplices. He claimed that no fewer than thirty-five Tarahumara pueblos were implicated. He had also uncovered rumors that various Tarahumara towns intended to join to achieve "the end with the Spaniards." The investigations were cast as a startling revelation: the real culprits behind an "infinity of excesses" had been proven to be Tarahumaras, mestizos, and mulattoes, not Apaches. As Governor Fayni summarized the implications: "our forces will make little progress even if we finish off the whole Apachería, because the thief will still be in the house." He claimed that the Apaches had not taken even one horse or mule that had not been turned over to them by Tarahumara-led bandits. In other words, the situation that governors and military officers like Joseph Berroterán had long warned against—Apaches turning Tarahumaras and other native subjects against the Spaniards—now seemed a reality. Almost as quickly as it started, however, the hunt for treasonous Spanish subjects met an abrupt end. A month into the investigation, the city council of Chihuahua met and decided to order a halt to it. Queipo de Llano's apprehension of dozens of suspects had caused "a terrified panic" in Tarahumara villages, and in the interests of "calming them down" the council decided the mass inquiry must be abandoned. Instead, the magistrate was to proceed against only the principal leaders of the raiding bands, because to do otherwise would risk producing logistical challenges and would require a military force that might be difficult to muster.[34]

Even proceeding against the alleged ringleaders proved far from easy, however, as officials ran up against the challenge of proving cases for which they had little evidence other than coerced testimony. Some questioned whether Queipo de Llano had been overzealous, and he actually undermined his own credibility by stating that "the fear of punishment makes [the suspects] say unimaginable things." Of some two hundred individuals apprehended in the spring of 1773 under suspicion of livestock rustling or collusion with Apaches, some died in prison in Chihuahua while others labored in public works projects from which they were able to escape. This would not be the first time that fears of clandestine relations between colonial subjects and enemies proved influential. Another investigation ten years later resulted in the apprehension of nearly one thousand Tarahumara men and women, including some of the same individuals implicated in the earlier episode. This time, witnesses explained how for the past twenty years they had been dealing with Apaches, who had stayed with them in their houses "with the same security as in their own [camps]."[35]

It is impossible to determine definitively how many of the damaging raids Nueva Vizcaya and neighboring provinces experienced during this period were the work of Apaches versus mission Indians or Spanish criminals. Descriptions of Apache camps attacked by Spanish forces do indicate that at least some of the interethnic trade relations described by witnesses in the investigation of the Calaxtrin maroon community were occurring. Moreover, the devastation described in some alleged Apache attacks, including the indiscriminate destruction of property, does fit with Apache practices of warfare, which emphasized retaliatory destruction over the apprehension of enemy property. In fact, by this time sustained campaigns into Apache lands resulting in the capture of a growing number of Chiricahua and Mescalero Apache prisoners destined for Chihuahuan jails gave Apaches plenty of motivation to pursue war in lieu of previous, less destructive attacks on Spanish-affiliated settlements.[36]

What this 1773 investigation illustrates most conclusively is the ways in which the Apache presence in northern New Spain generated confusion, fear, and opportunism that was historically influential independent of any documented danger. It helped conjure rumors of interethnic gangs with one thousand members, limitless Apache warriors flooding across the Rio Grande, and looming pan-Indian rebellions that would spell the end of all Spaniards. Although the supposed discovery that Tarahumaras, mulattos, and perhaps even Spaniards may have committed raids and homicides attributed to Apaches led hundreds of those accused to be incarcerated, it did not change the course of ongoing military campaigns against Apaches in the 1770s and 1780s. The very fact that officials ultimately quashed these inquiries suggests that they feared the investigations might be the spark that ignited Tarahumara rebellions that could prove costlier than war against Apaches.[37]

Maintaining (or consolidating) the Spanish regime in northern New Spain ultimately took precedence over reforming or punishing its subjects. Instead, official reports drew indiscriminately upon histories of raiding to justify further military action against Apaches rather than already reduced Indians. Voluminous and detailed local reports describing raids suffered over time by a vague enemy were compiled in a Chihuahua archive, then simplified into clear-cut statistics attributing all the damage to Apaches. In war councils during the 1770s, military officers contended that war against unpacified Indians had begun in 1748, and that in the years since, Apaches alone had committed more than four thousand murders, stolen thousands of livestock, and caused more than eleven million pesos in losses to the regional economy, statistics that most historians have echoed.[38]

One military officer envisioned a strategy beyond offensive war to bring a close to the hazy and shifting borderlands of northern New Spain, one that ultimately would be embraced: send Apaches elsewhere. As Hugo O'Conor wrote in 1774, "When [other Indians] infested these frontiers, it was necessary for the infamous Don Josef Berroterán . . . to exterminate them, both by killing them in battle and by sending them [away] as prisoners." Through such measures, O'Conor explained, Berroterán had brought peace to the region "for many years."[39] If O'Conor believed that such actions were extreme—he explained "he would not use the same means with the Apaches without permission"—he still advocated that exile was the only hope to achieve a lasting victory. "If fear of death obliges them to settle in towns," he explained, "as soon as the troops withdraw . . . they will return to the mountains and return to their past customs of robbing with even greater animosity." It is striking that he viewed displacement to Mexico City as an inadequate solution. "Even if they are sent to workshops in the capital," he noted, "Apaches are so warlike [that] the men as well as the women can easily return to their homelands." Ultimately O'Conor recommended that "only by transporting them to windward islands in small groups will we ever see these frontiers free of these enemies."[40]

If the viceroy and his advisors initially rejected the idea of sending Apaches to the Caribbean, it was not long before the weight of evidence came to support O'Conor's claims. The idea that even women could break out of jails and return home was manifest by Apache captives' determination to do just that, as groups of women escaped from the jails in Saltillo in 1773 and Chihuahua City in 1776. By the 1780s, soldiers were in fact conducting captives beyond Mexico City to the Gulf Coast and loading them on ships to the Caribbean. Yet the goal of frontiers free of enemies ultimately proved a chimera, as the deportation of Apache prisoners from one borderland helped spark the creation of another.[41]

In the heart of the Caribbean, as in northern New Spain, Spanish officials worried about security. After the English captured Havana during the Seven Years' War and subsequently exchanged it for Florida, the Spanish Crown worked to improve its defenses and guard against the future loss of valuable Caribbean islands. Labor shortages were filled through various means, including hiring available slave labor and importing convict labor from New Spain and elsewhere. By the 1780s, Cuba was a dumping ground for people cast as dangerous or undesirable, owing both to its labor needs and to the perception that islands made natural, secure prisons. The fates of Apache prisoners of war became linked to these broader trends after they proved able to escape from tobacco farms and households within New Spain where they had been destined to labor. Officials ultimately believed it was necessary to put an expanse of ocean between them and their homelands. Apaches were not alone, as the Spanish deported other native people deemed to be rebels or enemies during this period as well, especially Coahuiltecan speakers from northeastern New Spain.[42]

Apache Indians were initially welcomed upon their arrival in Havana. Undoubtedly, this reception was shaped in part by the ignorance of the local populace about the history of native-Spanish relations in northern New Spain or the details of the context in which natives had been captured and forcibly removed from their homelands. When the viceroy of New Spain had asked the governor of Cuba, Diego José Navarro, about shipping natives to his jurisdiction in 1780, Navarro had imagined an Apache neighborhood being set aside in Havana. Once Apaches were taught Spanish and instructed in

Catholicism, he believed they would prove valuable laborers. Even someone with some historical knowledge expressed the view that while Apaches might be "perverse" in their own lands, removal from their homelands would cure such inclinations. Linking geography and behavior, this official explained his belief that Apaches "would not exercise their bloody passions" in the Caribbean.[43]

Many residents of the island apparently agreed, though the fact that the more than four hundred Apaches embarked to Cuba in the 1780s and 1790s were distributed for free to those who petitioned to receive them likely assuaged any concerns that did exist among potential masters. By the time of their arrival in Havana, any specific ethnic descriptors had been erased in official documentation in favor of more generic terms, especially *indio meco*, shorthand for "Chichimeco," a category long applied to allegedly uncivilized, pagan Indians. Mecos were not necessarily understood to be dangerous, however, and in cases where documentation exists, the vast majority of native captives were successfully distributed to Havana households, fortification projects, and institutional settings. Occasionally, some captives did languish in confinement in the recently completed fortress known as La Cabaña, particularly due to age and appearance. In fact, native women as old as ninety are described as arriving in Havana. Just as the value of enslaved Africans declined precipitously after middle age, so too did the perceived value of these *indios de conquista*, as one Havana resident described them.[44]

Elsewhere, I have examined the expectations of Havana residents who requested Apache captives, as well as Apache captives' experiences upon arriving in Havana. Several key points are important to summarize here to assess Cubans' eventual ideas about the danger natives posed. While the lack of specific ethnic descriptors makes it difficult to track Apaches and other natives in the source material after their arrival in the Caribbean, evidence suggests that many labored over a long term. Some, especially those of a young age, were able to informally enter Cuban society, even though there was no official mechanism by which they could shed their legal status as prisoners of war. For others, their experiences of labor depended (as it has for all people who have experienced bondage historically) on the whims of masters and the specific tasks to which they were put, which usually broke down along gendered lines. Women were assigned to domestic work; men to public works projects. Mortality rates also appear to have been significant, if notices of deaths sent from masters to the governor are any indication.[45]

The experiences of the bulk of Apaches and other native captives arriving in Cuba is worth foregrounding at the outset because historians examining this history have tended to highlight the exceptional cases of those who escaped bondage. In part this is because native runaways gained significant attention from officials and generated a substantial volume of documentation, which make their stories more accessible than the mundane experience of forced labor endured by most native prisoners of war in Cuba. Such evidence has drawn attention for other reasons as well, however, especially as an illustration of resistance, of the ways in which the oppressed were able to thwart the designs of their oppressors. As Christon Archer, one of the first historians to consider this history in depth, argued, "Apaches were no less dangerous in Cuba than they had been in their own homelands," a view largely echoed in subsequent scholarship. While provocative, this conclusion warrants a critical reconsideration. It not only has the potential to elide the experience of the majority of Apaches who were not able to escape, but also risks reflecting the racial and ethnic stereotypes of historical actors, who often argued that Apaches were inherently violent, despite plenty of evidence to the contrary. More than anything, however, it risks taking at face value source material that is in fact inconclusive as to whether Apaches—or any Indians, for that matter—were the perpetrators of murders, robberies, and livestock raids that residents and officials of Cuba began complaining about at the end of the eighteenth century.[46]

Just as the idea of an Apache invasion in northern New Spain was shaped by shadowy fears of Apache-led runaway gangs and interethnic collusion, so too was the idea of Indian-led maroon communities in the Caribbean. While the threat posed to Spanish sovereignty by Apache groups had some grounding in reality in northern New Spain, in both places indigenous (or Afro-indigenous) borderlands emerged that reflected the racial and religious ideas, and material and ideological interests, of local residents as much as they did the actions of Apache people. As in Nueva Vizcaya, the threats posed by Apaches and other natives did not have to be tangible to be historically influential. Amidst the Haitian Revolution on the neighboring island of Hispaniola and ongoing concerns about black runaway communities in Cuba itself, rumors of dangerous Indians unsettling slaves and attacking settlements were understandably worrisome.[47]

While reports of Afro-Indian maroon communities (*palenques*) eventually emerged in sites across the island, it was in the countryside west of Havana in the district of Filipinas that the most serious reports, sightings of Indians, and campaigns to kill or capture Indian runaways occurred. By the spring of 1800, for example, a local magistrate in Pinar del Río, Josef de Aguilar, had determined that a gang of Indians was responsible for a string of murders, homicides, and livestock thefts that had been hindering the prosperity and growth of his jurisdiction in recent years. In a later report, Aguilar detailed with precision the damage caused by the Indian runaways: 23 people killed, including a pregnant woman and her three children; 13 people injured; 11 houses burned; livestock rustled from 93 haciendas; and 18 haciendas abandoned entirely since 1796.[48]

Reports like these led the governor of Cuba, the Marques de Someruelos, to lobby beginning in 1799 against the transport of Apaches to the island, "unless they were children." He highlighted the "terrible example for African slaves that such barbarian Indians introduced." While the Spanish Crown did issue a decree approving the education of Apache children arriving in Cuba, they did not formally agree to shut down the transport of native prisoners of war to the island, much to Someruelos's chagrin. He continued to plead his case to the royal authorities, however, especially after he became convinced that one of the "most notorious" palenques on the island was led by two Indian men named "El Chico" and "El Grande."[49]

In the meantime, Someruelos and other local authorities, including the city council (cabildo) of Havana, had worked together to combat the problem they believed that native runaways posed. After a militia captain named José Gavilán successfully recaptured six native runaways who had escaped from fortifications in Havana and killed a black slave while traveling through an area plantation, Someruelos commissioned Gavilán to bring order to the western district and other areas of the island that had complained about Indians. In October 1802, the governor, cabildo, and slave consulate jointly issued a bounty on the heads of the Indians El Chico and El Grande, who were to be brought in dead or alive: 2,000 pesos if dead, 3,000 pesos if alive.[50]

The bounty and commissioning of a military captain were only the latest in a string of efforts to recapture Indian runaways. Gavilán's first task on arriving in the district of Filipinas in western Cuba in October 1802 was to clean up after his predecessors. To supplement local efforts, Someruelos had previously released convicts from Havana-area jails, believing they would be motivated by promises of liberty to kill or apprehend the Indian runaways. From what Gavilán observed, however, they had simply returned to their previous lives of crime, setting fires, stealing, and killing. In fact, he concluded these men were likely responsible for at least some of the murders and robberies local officials had attributed to Indians.[51]

After sending the convicts back to Havana, Gavilán and his men began looking for El Chico, El Grande, and the other members of their group. For weeks, they explored the mountains and coasts of the area without sighting Indians or blacks. Before the new year, Gavilán decided to split his men into two groups in the interests of covering as much ground as possible. A few days later, Gavilán's lieutenant, Eugenio Malvar, finally encountered the Afro-Indian palenque face-to-face. Malvar described the gang as including the two Indians, El Chico and El Grande, and five other men, "two pardos, one negro, and another two like guachinangos" ("red snappers," a term originally from Nahuatl that people in Cuba used to describe natives from New Spain).[52]

It was El Grande whom Malvar and his men approached first, as the other members of the palenque kept their distance. Darting for the hills, Malvar ordered that attack dogs be set loose on him, and one dog latched onto the Indian man and felled him. Malvar then took matters into his own hands, stabbing the Indian to death with his machete before racing to join his men and provide them assistance against El Chico and the rest of the runaways. As Malvar loaded his pistol, arrows rained down on him from the palenque, striking his left arm as he ran out of bullets and powder. Though Malvar believed he had injured El Chico, the Indian and his companions managed to escape.[53]

The skirmish had left multiple members of Malvar's party wounded and one dead, but they had succeeded in killing El Grande and prepared to claim the 2,000-peso bounty. They separated the Indian's head from his body and shipped it to the governor in Havana in a vat of brandy as proof of their success. Malvar also presented the statements of eighteen individuals attesting to the alleged crimes committed by the Indians and their companions in recent days. These witnesses reported that the Indians had attacked farms, stealing clothing and furnishings, killing a number of dogs, and perhaps most shockingly, severing the hand from a statue of the Virgin Mary at a local parish and profaning the chapel's holy water.[54]

As in Nueva Vizcaya, however, other evidence suggests the threat of Indian runaways was not as clear-cut as some reports made it out to be. Other firsthand accounts of encounters with Indian runaways hardly paint them as particularly dangerous. When one party of local men commissioned before

Gavilán had briefly captured three Indians, the men had explained through signs that they needed directions to the coast to "find a way to embark" from the island. By conveying a desire for religious instruction, they succeeded in persuading the men to provide them with food and water before they slipped away again into the hills. While references to seeking some way off the island clearly reflected the unique challenges of forced migration to Cuba, I am also struck by the familiarity of this scene. Runaways may have been employing cultural knowledge rooted in social interactions in North American borderlands—requesting baptism as a means of obtaining temporary asylum—to successfully navigate life in the Caribbean.[55]

In other cases, scant firsthand observation of Indians mixed with racial stereotypes to fuel fears outsized to the real threat Apaches and other natives posed on the island. Noting a strange absence of black runaways during the 1790s, magistrate Aguilar in Pinar del Río had hypothesized to the governor in Havana that Indians' propensity for violence accounted for the change: "Indians had killed them all." One creative scheme Someruelos devised to bring an end to palenques of Indians was similarly shaped by racialized views. He suggested at one point that the Indians might finally be recaptured if they could be lured to abandoned farms by Spanish militiamen painted in blackface and pretending to be slaves. Since the Indians would think the livestock were tended by "simple" (black) slaves, they would surely attack, and the militiamen could pounce and kill or capture these Indian instigators of disorder in the countryside once and for all. While it is unclear whether this fascinating plot was ever carried out, it illustrates the racialized lens through which Someruelos observed the contested lands of his jurisdiction and sought to wrest back control of them: simple black slaves and murderous, thieving, barbarian Indians versus cunning and capable Spaniards.[56]

Ultimately, the efforts of Gavilán and others to track Indian palenques in 1802 and subsequent years illustrate how shadowy much of the evidence mobilized to lobby against the importation of Apache and other native captives was. Despite expending significant resources and spending long periods traveling through the mountains, these tracking parties did not observe anyone. Even when they did come across runaways, their observations were sometimes contradictory. Some people, like Malvar, reported seeing precise numbers of Indians and Africans. But others reported seeing blacks or mulattos, guachinangos, Mexicans, or perhaps even whites (*blancos*). Whether the Indians they did encounter were indeed Apaches is also unclear. After all, Apaches were not the only natives transported to Cuba from northern New Spain or else-where during the eighteenth century. Finally, it should be noted that no spe-cific evidence actually supported the idea that El Chico and El Grande led the palenque that they were a part of—their leadership simply seems to have been assumed. Some observers reported that the Indians traveled and camped sep-arately from the blacks, raising questions about their degree of collaboration with and leadership of the latter.[57]

I do not mean to suggest that runaway communities were merely figments of residents' imaginations. It is possible that El Chico and El Grande were Apaches who had escaped from Havana or its surroundings. Perhaps they had even managed to communicate with runaway African slaves and mastermind raids on plantations and ranches. Apache men may have found in an Afro-Indian palenque a place where they could live out a life somewhat like the lives they had lost in being displaced from home, or in the very least, a life that offered an alternative to arduous forced labor. Perhaps they still hoped to return home, as that tantalizing story of Indians "seeking a way to embark" suggests. Whatever the identities and numbers of runaways during this period, it was as much Spaniards' shadowy fears of cunning, violent Indians leading slaves in revolt as the real dangers they posed that led Governor Someruelos to claim that Apaches were entirely incapable of being kept secure and put to work unless they were children. In fact, there was plenty of evidence to the contrary. In the middle of the frantic hunt for El Chico and El Grande, for instance, Apache Indians continued to labor in Havana households. Others continued to work in shipyards and on public works projects. If some managed to flee into the countryside, others adapted to difficult circumstances, navigat-ing their lives as best they could by forging new social ties, challenging their masters' expectations and demands day after day, or seeking redress through official legal channels.[58]

The escape of Indians gained such attention—and thus provided so much historical documentation—because this scenario fed into racialized fears of a countryside out of control. Concerns about a countryside turned border-land triggered governors and magistrates in Cuba to give Apaches a level of attention far outsized to their actual threat. As in northern New Spain, how-ever, fears of Apache Indians and their collusion with other segments of soci-ety, however imaginary, had material effects. For some non-native convicts it meant a release from incarceration and a return to crime, which could then be blamed on Indians. For at least two residents of Cuba, it meant becoming widows, as their husbands died in the effort to hunt the "wild Indians." One of these women even received three slaves as compensation, entangling the lives of enslaved Africans with events in the Spanish-Indian borderlands of Cuba. In one town, the death of a prominent resident, supposedly at the hands of Indians, even became the source of a folksong that endured into the early twentieth century.[59]

The idea of a countryside out of control also influenced native captives themselves. Six native men who had run away and been accused of killing a black slave were sentenced to new terms of forced labor elsewhere, deemed too dangerous to remain on the island. For many more, the resistance of Havana officials to their transport to the island ultimately meant they languished in jails in Mexico City. Some Apaches remained imprisoned in jails in New Spain as late as 1816. For others, the stereotype of dangerous Apaches may have contributed to officials ignoring their well-reasoned requests for release from bondage. Such was the case for two meco men named Carlos and Manuel, who pleaded that the viceroy "lift their chains" and allow them some rest after years of labor in Havana and Veracruz. Their only crime, as they saw it, was "having been born among heathens." Their petition was read but left unanswered.[60]

The story of Apache Indians and the fears they sparked in two disparate but interconnected places—Nueva Vizcaya and Cuba—speaks to this volume's broad examination of indigenous borderlands. Several decades of scholarship have cast new light on indigenous agency, highlighting patterns of native territoriality and political power in the Americas. In addition to examining native grounds, empires, and other examples of indigenous power, scholars may still fruitfully look within colonial domains to find historically influential indigenous spaces. These stories of interethnic maroon communities in northern New Spain and Cuba, and the reactions they generated, illustrate how zones of overlapping cultural, political, and legal authority were not confined to the edges of European empires or the native-controlled territories beyond them. Yet, they also highlight the ways in which borderlands could be as much discursive as material. Borderlands were sometimes generated by what Gloria Anzaldúa has termed "the emotional residue" of human-created boundaries—fear, manipulation, or misunderstanding— more than by physical contestation or well-grounded threats to a society's security or sovereignty. Even the most imaginary of borderlands could have historically influential effects that led to violence, incarceration, and the death or forced migration of hundreds of people, dynamics that remain evident in our world today.[61]

NOTES

1. Gonzales, "Trump Says"; Miroff and Ryan, "Army Assessment of Migrant Caravans"; Domínguez, "No permitiremos 'invasión'"; Qiu, "Trump's Evidence-Free Claims"; Wagner, "Trump Highlights"; Grant and Miroff, "Citizen Militia Groups"; Birnbaum, "Poll."

2. For a recent overview of borderlands scholarship focusing on North American history see Hämäläinen and Truett, "On Borderlands." For works exploring dynamics of indigenous power, or alternatively, the rhetorical and ideological uses of Indians by colonials see, for example, Hämäläinen, *Comanche Empire*; Barr, "Geographies of Power"; Weber, *Bárbaros*; Ortelli, *Trama de una guerra*.

3. Forbes, *Apache, Navaho, and Spaniard*; Griffen, *Apaches at War and Peace*; Record, *Big Sycamore Stands Alone*; Jacoby, *Shadows at Dawn*; Eiselt, *Becoming White Clay*; Blyth, *Chiricahua and Janos*; Babcock, *Apache Adaptation*; Sweeney, *From Cochise to Geronimo*. The mention of worries about Apache prisoners of war in Alabama draws from chapter 8 of my book *Apache Diaspora*.

4. Deeds, *Defiance and Deference*; Cramaussel, "De cómo los españoles clasificaban a los indios"; Ortelli, *Trama de una guerra*; Babcock, *Apache Adaptation*; Conrad, "Empire through Kinship."

5. For the transport of indigenous people, including Apaches, to the Spanish Caribbean see Yaremko, *Indigenous Passages to Cuba*; Archer, "Deportation of Barbarian Indians"; Conrad, "Indians, Convicts, and Slaves"; Vázquez Cienfuegos and Santamaria García, "Indios foráneos en Cuba"; Venegas Delgado and Valdés Dávila, *La ruta del horror*. See also Pike, "Penal Servitude"; Childs, *1812 Aponte Rebellion*.

6. DeLay, *North American Borderlands*, 3. My approach to discourse and power on colonial borderlands draws from Stoler, "Tense and Tender Ties"; Stoler, *Carnal Knowledge*; Foucault, "Subject and Power"; and Anzaldúa, *Borderlands / La Frontera*.

7. Opler, "Apachean Culture Pattern"; see also works in n. 4.

8. Brooks, *Captives and Cousins*, esp. 1–39; Cramaussel, "De cómo los españoles clasificaban a los indios"; Cramaussel, *Poblar la frontera*; Reséndez, *Other Slavery*, esp. 76–124; Zavala, *Los esclavos indios*.

9. Jones, *Nueva Vizcaya*; Gerhard, *North Frontier of New Spain*; Martin, *Governance and Society*; Radding, *Wandering Peoples*; Frank, *From Settler to Citizen*.

10. The Spanish generally named these people based on the geographic features of their homelands: "Gila" referencing the river that straddled the mountains favored by the Chihene (Warm Springs) band, "Chiricahui" after the favored mountain range of the Chokonens. Babcock, *Apache Adaptation*, esp. 19–60; Anderson, *Indian Southwest*; Deeds, *Defiance and Deference*, esp. 104–30; Ortelli, *Trama de una guerra*; Ortelli "Enemigos internos"; Griffen, *Culture Change*.

11. On broader Spanish descriptions of fluid relations with Apaches and their interactions with missionized natives, see Fray José de Arrangegui to the Viceroy, June 11, 1715, AGN, México, Historia, vol. 20; José Enrique de Cosio to the Viceroy, September 1, 1744, AGN, Historia, vol. 20; "Testimonio de los Autos que se formaron [. . .] los Robos de los Sumas infieles y la liga que tienen con los Apaches Mescaleros, 1751,"

AGI, Seville, Guadalajara, leg. 191; Lorenzo Cancio to Marqués de Cruillas, October 2, 1763, AGN, Provincias Internas, vol. 25; "Diario de la campaña executada por el Governor de Coahuila Don Pedro de Ravago y Terran en el año de 1747 para el reconocimiento de las margenes del Rio Grande del Norte," Rábago y Terán to Güemes y Horcasitas, January 23, 1748, AGN, Historia, vol. 52.

    12. Ortelli, *Trama de una guerra*, 61.

    13. Ortelli, *Trama de una guerra*, 65.

    14. "Captain Berroterán's Report on the Condition of Nueva Vizcaya (1748)" in Hadley, Naylor, and Schuetz-Miller, *Presidio and Militia*, 167–226 (cited hereafter as Berroterán Report). For the manuscript copy of this report, also consulted by the author, see Berroterán to Güemes y Horcasitas, April 22, 1748, AGI, Guadalajara, leg. 191.

    15. Berroterán Report, 194.

    16. Berroterán Report, 200.

    17. Berroterán Report, 191.

    18. Fiscal to the Marqués of Altamira, December 5, 1748, AGI, Guadalajara, leg. 191.

    19. Ortelli, *Trama de una guerra*, 61.

    20. Bishop of Durango to Marqués de Cruillas, September 9, 1760, AGN, Provincias Internas, vol. 69.

    21. Jacinto del Barria to Marqués de Cruillas, November 15, 1760, AGN, Provincias Internas, vol. 25.

    22. "1762 vando proclamado para que sus havitadores no vendan ni cambien semillas, ni armas [. . .] a los apaches," reel 7, Cd. Juárez Municipal Archives part II, microfilm on file at the University of Texas at El Paso. For Janos see "Diario de novedades," January 1757 to November 1758, reel. 6, Janos Microfilm Collection on file at the University of Texas at El Paso.

    23. Ortelli, *Trama de una guerra*, 53–82. For after-the-fact primary-source claims that war began in 1748 see "Junta de Guerra y Hacienda," April 2, 1772, AGN, Provincias Internas, vol. 132; "Sobre la Junta de Guerra celebrada en Chihuahua," June 29, 1778, AGI, Guadalajara, leg. 276.

    24. See "Testimonio de los Autos que se formaron [. . .]," AGI, Guadalajara, leg. 191; "Decreto de Junta, San Phelipe de Real," August 23, 1754, AGI, Guadalajara, leg. 194.

    25. "Carpeta, Año de 1765, Correspondencia con el Teniente Governador, y Capitan del Presidio del Pueblo del Paso del Norte D. Pedro la Fuente," AGN, Provincias Internas, vol. 102.

    26. For an especially rich volume of sources that illustrate the issue of vague attribution described here, see San Felipe Real de Chihuahua, Archivo del Ayuntamiento de Chihuahua, Chihuahua, México, fondo Colonial, sec. Justicia, caja 14, exp. 4 (cited hereafter as AACh). Microfilm copies of this collection are available at the University of Texas at El Paso, though the microfilms have not been professionally organized or indexed. The original materials in Chihuahua are thus much more usable for researchers. See also Barrandegui to González, February 19, 1770, AGN, Provincias Internas, vol. 42; Report of the council of war convened in Mexico City by Viceroy Don Antonio María de Bucareli on April 2, 1772, AGN, Provincias Internas, vol. 132.

For non-Apache livestock rustling, see Ortelli, *Trama de una guerra*, 139–64; Merrill, "Cultural Creativity."

27. V.e Assensio del Raso and Leonardo Ramírez to Joseph de Castilla y Therán, November 12, 13, 14, 1769, AGN, Provincias Internas, vol. 231.

28. Such concerns had a longer history: see Barrutia to Marqués de Casa Fuerte, April 29, 1729, AGN, Provincias Internas, vol. 154. In 1754, the principal citizens of Chihuahua presented a joint statement warning that the Apaches threatened to "completely break the obedience of the Tarahumaras"; see "Decreto de Junta, San Phelipe de Real," August 23, 1754, AGI, Guadalajara, leg. 194. On the "delicate" issue of prosecuting mission Indians, see Alderete to Castilla y Terán, November 15, 1769, AGN, Provincias Internas, vol. 231.

29. On Apache raids as a looming presence in Nueva Vizcayan history, see Deeds, *Defiance and Deference*; Weber, *Spanish Frontier*; Alonso, *Thread of Blood*; Blyth, *Chiricahua and Janos*. For Texas, see Wade, *Native Americans*. Recent studies interpreting indigenous violence in the North American West as political agency include Hämäläinen, *Comanche Empire*; DeLay, *War of a Thousand Deserts*; Barr, "Geographies of Power."

30. Ortelli, *Trama de una guerra*; Cramaussel, "De cómo los españoles clasificaban a los indios"; Martin, *Governance and Society*; Frank, *From Settler to Citizen*. For another account that focuses on material exchanges but highlights the complexity of interethnic interactions during this period, see Anderson, *Indian Southwest*.

31. Merrill, "Cultural Creativity"; Conrad, "Empire through Kinship."

32. Fayni to Bucareli, March 20, 1773, AGN, Provincias Internas, vol. 132. Though this letter is written by Fayni, he is summarizing the reports sent to him by Queipo de Llano, the corregidor of Chihuahua.

33. See "Expediente formado sobre la colusión, y secreta inteligencia de los Tarahumares," AGN, Provincias Internas, vol. 132. For specific descriptions of the Calaxtrin band, see the declarations of José Rodriguez, José del Río, and José Manuel Moreno de los Reyes, Durango, June 21 and 22, 1723, within this file. See also Merrill, "Cultural Creativity."

34. Queipo y Llano to Fayni, March 23, 1773, and Queipo y Llano to Bucareli, April 20, 1773, AGN, Provincias Internas, vol. 42.

35. On fear of punishment, see Queipo y Llano to Joachin Manuel Robles, April 30, 1775, AGN, Provincias Internas, vol. 132. For Apaches staying in Tarahumara camps and the outcomes of 1770s and 1780s investigations into Tarahumara-Apache relations, see Jacobo Ugarte y Loyola to Garrido y Durán, January 4, 1787, AGI, Guadalajara, leg. 287.

36. On Apache ideas of warfare see Opler, *Apache Life-Way*, 370–75.

37. For 1780s military campaigns, see Babcock, *Apache Adaptation*, 105–40; Santiago, *Jar of Severed Hands*.

38. See Cutter, *Defenses of Northern New Spain*. Historians have tended to draw upon Spanish statistics on Apache violence uncritically. See, for example DeLay, *War of a Thousand Deserts*, 12; Babcock, "Rethinking the Establecimientos," 383–84.

39. Hugo O'Conor to the Viceroy, March 8, 1774, AGN, Provincias Internas, vol. 154. O'Conor was not alone in citing such figures, noting that they were proven "by documents" in the archives—presumably those such as the more than 260-page file in the Chihuahua archive cited in n. 27.

40. O'Conor to Viceroy, March 8, 1774, AGN.

41. On women's escapes see Felis Fran.co Pacheco, Saltillo, to Viceroy July 27, 1773, AGN, Provincias Internas, vol. 23; D.n Juan de Ugalde to Viceroy, Santiago de la Monclova, January 25, 1778, AGI, Guadalajara, leg. 275.

42. On the range of native groups transported to Cuba at this time, see Yaremko, *Indigenous Passages to Cuba*; Venegas Delgado and Valdés Dávila, *La ruta del horror*; Conrad, "Indians, Convicts, and Slaves"; Conrad, *Apache Diaspora*, esp. chap 5.

43. Conrad, "Indians, Convicts, and Slaves," 75–76.

44. Conrad, "Indians, Convicts, and Slaves," 76–79. For numbers of Apaches arriving in Cuba, see also Conrad, "Captive Fates," 259–60.

45. Conrad, "Indians, Convicts, and Slaves."

46. Archer, "Deportation of Barbarian Indians," 383; see also n. 4 for works examining Apaches in Cuba.

47. For historical context and influence of Haitian Revolution, see Dubois, *Avengers of the New World*.

48. Francisco Ramos, Pinar del Río, to the Marques de Someruelos, Havana, April 2, 1803, AGI, Cuba, leg. 1720.

49. Archer, "Deportation of Barbarian Indians," 381–83. For El Chico and El Grande, see "Extracto del sumario formado por D. Josef Gavilán comunicado por el S.or Presid.te Governador Capitan General a esta Junta en oficio de 9 de Febrero de 1803," AGI, Cuba, leg. 1720.

50. On the bounties for El Chico and El Grande, see Real Consulado, Havana, to Someruelos, October 14, 1802, AGI, Cuba, leg. 1720.

51. "Extracto formado por D. Josef López Gavilán," López Gavilán, Consolación del Norte, to Someruelos, January 22, 1803, AGI, Cuba, leg. 1720.

52. Conrad, "Indians, Convicts, and Slaves," 84–85.

53. Gavilán, Consolación del Norte, to Someruelos, January 22, 1803, AGI, Cuba, leg. 1720.

54. Gavilán to Someruelos, January 22, 1803, AGI; Conrad, "Indians, Convicts, and Slaves," 85.

55. On the actions of Indian runaways in this district, see Rudesindo de los Olivos, Santa Cruz de los Pinos, to Someruelos, May 16, 1800, AGI, Cuba, leg. 1720: "lo que querían era saber el camino de la buelta de arriba para solicitar modo de embarcarse."

56. Joséf de Aguilar, Pinar del Río, to Someruelos, April 2, 1803, AGI, Cuba, leg. 1720.

57. "Extracto formado por D. Josef López Gavilán," López Gavilán, Consolación del Norte, to Someruelos, January 2, 1803, AGI, Cuba 1720. For Yucatec Mayas transported to Cuba, see, for example, Yaremko, "Colonial Wars and Indigenous Geopolitics," esp. 179.

58. Conrad, "Indians, Convicts, and Slaves," 75–82.

59. For the release of convicts from jails, see Gavilán to Consulado, Havana, November 19, 1802, AGI, Cuba, leg. 1720. For slaves granted to widows, see Doña María Josefa Ortega, Havana, to Consulado del Ayuntamiento, Havana, May 14, 1805, AGI, Cuba, leg. 1720. For folksong, see Venegas and Valdés, *La ruta del horror,* 224.

60. For the case of native men accused of murdering a slave, see "Autos crimin.s seguido de oficio contra los Yndios Rafael, Vitaque, Oste, y Cle s.re la muerte del Negro Pasqual esclabo," AGI, Cuba, leg. 1716. For Apaches remaining imprisoned in Mexico City jails, see Archer, "Deportation of Barbarian Indians," 384–85. For Carlos and Manuel's request for release from bondage, see Mecos to Viceroy José de Iturrigaray, October 14, 1805. Documents contained in this file reveal that their first petition arrived and was brought to the viceroy's attention in March 1805; they petitioned again in October. AGN, Indiferente Virreinal, box 5908, exp. 50. Though the file contains several petitions from these two Indian men and documents investigating their history, it contains no evidence that they were in fact freed.

61. Anzaldúa, *Borderlands / La Frontera,* 25.

CHAPTER 8

Guaraní Territorialization

STATE NARRATIVES AND INDIGENOUS LOGICS
IN SOUTH AMERICA'S EIGHTEENTH-CENTURY
BORDERLANDS

Guillermo Wilde

B eginning in the late eighteenth century, the Spanish Crown renewed
its territorial colonization of South America and, in so doing, sought
ways to control peoples in borderlands that previously had not been
completely subjugated to colonial authority. At that time broad regions within
the jurisdictions of Paraguay and Río de la Plata that remained vulnerable to
attacks by European enemies of the Spanish Crown contained peoples whom
the Spanish referred to as *naciones infieles* (unconverted nations). During the
first two centuries of conquest and colonization, the Spanish Crown had
maintained a policy of segregating and "protecting" the indigenous populations, a policy that favored the persistence of ethnic diversity and heteroge-
neity. Beginning in the last decades of the 1700s, however, it began to promote,
in both discourse and practice, the assimilation and homogenization of these
peoples into colonial society. Early on, a considerable portion of the indigenous population had been subordinated to the colonial regime via such institutions as encomienda (forced tribute or labor) and *pueblos de reducción*
(forced settlement of natives into Spanish-supervised communities). Some
groups had however managed to avoid full incorporation into these institutions, either by opposing them directly or by maintaining an ambivalent
relationship with them. Official typologies and policies of the colonial

administration clearly distinguished between these two groups. The former, particularly members of the indigenous elite, received rights and privileges derived from integration into the colonial regime; the latter were met with tactics ranging from persuasion to punitive expeditions.

The various Guaraní-speaking groups that inhabited the region had a long history of ties to colonial activity, and for the most part they had adopted the colony's economic, political, and social patterns (urbanization, cabildos, Catholicism, and so forth). Yet a large diversity of warring, nomadic bands controlled broad riverine and mountain areas of the Chaco. They were referred to generically as Guaycurúes: people who did not speak Guaraní and who consistently opposed both the colonizers and other indigenous peoples.[1]

The different labels and ethnic classifications formed part of a broader process of territorialization in which identities were delimitated and territorially mapped as ethnic objects. This process, which some authors have characterized as ethnification or ethnogenesis, was superimposed upon logics that escaped straightforward ethnic categorization and that operated at micro-sociological and political levels involving indigenous actors as much as colonial agents.[2] This chapter aims to recover the complexity of these dynamics in Paraguay and the Río de la Plata region. The process of Guaraní territorialization extended over four centuries of history. In it we can identify at least three discrete periods. First was the colonial era, marked by specific policies toward native populations, in particular encomienda and pueblos de reducción, decreed by the Spanish monarchs. Second came the national era, beginning with the conclusion of Paraguay's War of the Triple Alliance (1865–70) and the consolidation of the nation-states of Argentina, Paraguay, and Brazil. The modern classifications of ethnic groups date from this period. Finally, the contemporary (or perhaps postcolonial) era has been characterized by the emergence of pan-indigenous discourse and global legislation regarding the environment, patrimony, and human rights. Only the colonial era falls within the scope of this chapter.

This analysis presents key features of Guaraní territorialization. While official discourse increasingly circumscribed indigenous territory into a contiguous area, one that was discretely and homogeneously divided among different indigenous "nations" or imperial jurisdictions, indigenous territorial logic revealed the porosity of those limits, whether ethnic or imperial, based on strategies far removed from (or at times close to) normative and typological definitions. These indigenous logics were woven into dynamic social patterns that endured over long periods and outlived both the fall of the Iberian empires and the dissolution of the reducciones.

ETHNIFICATION AND TERRITORY

The first period of territorialization began early in the colonial era, with the creation of such institutions as encomienda and pueblos de indios under the supervision of Franciscan or Jesuit priests. At the beginning of the sixteenth century, the Spanish who founded and settled in the city of Asunción (1537) encountered diverse indigenous groups with whom they formed alliances for trade and social interchange. Backed by the support of allied indigenous leaders, the conquistadors explored new regions in the coming decades, founding the towns and villas of Ciudad Real (1556), Villa Rica del Espíritu Santo (1570), and Santiago de Jerez (1580). This period was marked by the conquistadors' search for precious metals, something that required indigenous collaboration.[3] It soon became clear that no valuable mineral deposits existed and that the region was destined to remain marginal to colonial power. These facts led the conquistadors to value Indian labor as a basic economic resource and to increase pressure on their old allies. Under such circumstances the repartimiento, or encomienda, became a key economic and political institution. It consisted of granting Spanish encomenderos the right to administer indigenous labor in exchange for providing them with religious instruction and seeing to their defense and well-being.[4]

Two types of encomienda existed in the Paraguay region: *militaria* and *originaria*, also known as *yanacona*. The first type obligated Indian men aged eighteen to forty-nine to pay tribute to an encomendero through stints of labor (or *mitas*) totaling sixty days per year, during which time they were required to move to the jurisdiction where their services were required. The second type of encomienda involved the tributary and his family living permanently within the encomendero's jurisdiction, in order to provide "personal services." Although encomienda, *mitazgo*, and *yanaconazgo* were different institutions from a legal perspective, they were frequently confused in the Paraguayan context. Raids, known as *sacas* or *rancheadas*, conducted with the object of enslaving hostile Indian groups, were extremely common in this early period, and naturally resulted in a radical fragmentation of communities.[5] The exploitation to which the Indians were subjected, together with the series of epidemics that swept through the region, caused drastic demographic declines in the early years of colonization. This circumstance led colonial authorities to

issue a series of ordinances beginning in the mid-1500s aimed unsuccessfully at curbing the encomenderos' abuses. Yet, successive ordinances aimed
at regulating the encomiendas or repartimientos de indios failed to end the
problem. It would not be until the 1611 inspection of the *oidor* of the Audiencia de Charcas, Francisco de Alfaro, that a new administration managed to
reduce considerably the power of the encomenderos.

As Louis Necker has shown, indigenous resistance remained constant during the entire period of conquest and colonization. The years between 1537
and 1570 witnessed scores of revolts and rebellions, several of which assumed
prophetic tones. More than anything it was the arrival of encomienda (1556)
that spiked tensions and triggered a large-scale demographic collapse. The
old ties of reciprocity between indigenous leaders, ties that had been woven
into the encomienda process, now suffered due to growing economic coercion.
As the Jesuit Maciel de Lorenzana reported, "When the Indians saw that the
Spanish treated them not as relatives and in-laws, but rather as servants, they
began to withdraw and no longer wanted to serve the Spaniard."[6]

Franciscan friars held authority over the first villages of *mitayos* (mita
workers), integrated into the encomienda system somewhere around 1579.[7] A
few decades after their arrival in Paraguay in 1580, the Jesuits launched a program of reductions in the areas farthest from Spanish influence. Like their
Franciscan predecessors, the first Jesuit reductions were part of the encomienda system; but they were soon withdrawn from that structure and
placed in direct service to the Spanish Crown, which permitted them to enjoy
a greater degree of political autonomy and economic self-sufficiency, in sharp
contrast with the earlier pueblos de indios.[8]

Additional changes soon followed. The new regulations established in 1611
by Governor Hernando Arias de Saavedra (known as Hernandarias) and the
oidor Francisco de Alfaro, together with the policies of the first Jesuit provincial, Diego de Torres Bollo, allowed evangelization to advance to border
areas of the Paraná and Uruguay Rivers. The Jesuits explored the widely separated regions of Guairá, Ilatín, and Tape and established seventy reducciones in these places, many of which proved ephemeral. Most of the missions
that the Jesuits founded in the first half of the seventeenth century were
destroyed by *bandeirantes* (adventurers and slave hunters from São Paulo). The
bandeirantes captured thousands of Indians and transported them back to
that city as slaves.[9] Other critical developments in this early period of the Jesuit
missions were the epidemics and the invasions by indigenous groups broadly
referred to as *infieles*.

The 1610s witnessed the establishment of various reductions: Encarnación de Itapúa (1615), Corpus Cristi (1622), Nuestra Señora de la Natividad del Acaray (1619), and Santa María de Iguazú (1626), all along the banks of the Paraná River. Corpus Cristi and Encarnación de Itapúa were reclaimed by settlers who claimed to hold encomienda rights to them. Somewhat later, encomenderos also reclaimed two reducciones founded in the Itatín region (San Ignacio de Caaguazú and Nuestra Señora de Fe).[10] Cumulatively, these events—the corrosive pressures of slave raiding, together with eventual migrations and relocation of the region's entire population because of bandeirante attacks—rendered encomendero claims irrelevant and set the stage for a new Jesuit model based on territorial segregation of the reduced population.

Beginning in the 1620s the Jesuits transferred most of their early reductions southward, to the region of the Paraná and Uruguay Rivers, where they hoped to keep the mission Indians safe from bandeirante attacks. These migrations forced the breakup of earlier social structures as the Indians had to forge relationships in their new region. It is revealing that by the end of the sixteenth century, the greater part of the settled mission population came from distant locations.[11]

The Jesuit missionary model was based on the design of a uniform social, economic, political, linguistic, and urban layout that was gradually consolidated throughout the seventeenth and eighteenth centuries. Although the Jesuit chronicles and correspondence recognize a diversity of groups sometimes speaking different languages, the reduction process tended to homogenize the population and, at least in theory, impose a standardized language, the so-called *lengua general*.[12]

The priests referred to the groups of people with whom they came into contact as "nations." Although this concept was generally applied to speakers of the same language, its usage tended to be lax. Early Jesuit documents from the Guayrá region, for example, identify many denominations, which often superimposed one people over another. The groupings they identified at times spoke languages altogether different from Tupí-Guaraní, such as one belonging to the Gê language family. Over time such diversity either disappeared or else simply became invisible in the mission narrative due to priests' attempts to promote the image of the missions as homogenous spaces. At the same time, there was a tendency to identify ethnonyms with geographical spaces that were more or less defined and circumscribed.[13]

Seen thus, ethnic classification, or "ethnification," seems to have been more an organizing instrument of colonial texts than an actual means of identification among the Indians themselves. That is, it was favored insofar as it proved useful to colonial administrators. In the concrete process of creating the first mission towns, it was not particular ethnic groups that formed the basis of socioeconomic, political, and territorial organization, but rather the so-called cacicazgos, basic sociopolitical units made up of a cacique (in Guaraní, *mburubicha* or *rubicha*) and his followers. In the strictest sense, a cacique was the highest authority in an extended family (in Guaraní, *teyÿ*) that resided in a single *maloca* (longhouse). These family groups were the bricks with which the Jesuits erected their mission towns.

INDIGENOUS SOCIAL ORGANIZATION AND SPATIAL TRANSFORMATIONS OF THE MISSION TOWNS

Sociopolitical organization prior to the Jesuits' arrival remains poorly understood. Early research, based on information provided by Jesuits such as Antonio Ruiz de Montoya, has tended to portray a hierarchical arrangement that does not mesh with information found in other sources of the period. Following Ruiz de Montoya, anthropologist Branislava Sušnik suggested there were four hierarchical levels of sociopolitical and territorial ties. Above the basic unit of the *teyÿ* came the *tekoha* and the *amunda* (both a form of village) and the *guara* (region or province). As Pablo Barbosa and Fabio Mura have observed, Sušnik's structure omits several terms Ruiz de Montoya mentions in his works, terms that might be useful for understanding indigenous sociopolitical organization. These include *terã* or *retã* ("town" or "city")[14] and *tába* (village),[15] a term that in all likelihood would have described many of the encomienda villages of Paraguay from the seventeenth century onward.[16]

Of particular interest here is the 1685 report of the Jesuit Díaz Taño, a defense of the Guaraní caciques against demands by Asunción encomenderos. The document contains various testimonies from priests and functionaries active in the region, and their statements clarify aspects of sociopolitical organization and indigenous territoriality at the moment of contact. In one of these testimonies, a priest named Juan de Salas explains that the region's inhabitants built houses where many families could live. They were so large that each one was called a pueblo. In other regions, there were villages containing multiple houses, "and each one held a cacique who was called *abarubichaí*, whom everyone recognized as their lord, and whom as such they served and obeyed." The priest goes on to say that normally each house had a cacique, and that the villages with several houses had *caciques juntas*.[17] This testimony clearly points to situations in which a cacique or abarubicha (literally, "great man" or "head man") oversaw one or more houses. Although the abarubicha typically governed only one house, in some cases several houses joined together or, as happened when missions were formed, were divided. This and other testimonies in the same document suggest the existence of extended families, each enjoying sufficient autonomy to move to new locations, a decision that fell to the abarubichas. Strictly speaking, those individuals were heads of extended families and were recognized as such by the younger generations that lived with them.

Scant information exists concerning the structure of these houses. One exception is the intriguing 1620 testimony of an anonymous Jesuit concerning Guaranís who lived near Asunción. He reported that Indian houses were of different sizes, had thatched roofs supported by forked posts, and lacked internal divisions. The families lived separated by the supporting posts and shared a common fireplace. His description continues, "They sleep in certain nets that the Spanish call *hamacas* [hammocks], which they tie to the posts intentionally placed there when they construct the house, and the hamacas are so close and strung together that at night no one is able to pass through the house."[18]

Although the document contains few specifics, it is reasonable to suppose that these houses were what Ruiz de Montoya identified as the basic pre-Hispanic sociopolitical units (teyÿ), whose dimensions, although not known with any exactitude, might have accommodated between 150 and 300 persons, and possibly more. Such units were incorporated into the reducciones, an approach that immediately brought about a high degree of internal fragmentation. Heads of families were listed in the mission towns as caciques, while the members of their cacicazgos appear as *mboyas* (that is, *vasallos*, or "vassals," according to dictionaries of the era). Census lists reveal that the number of vasallos, as they were normally called, rarely exceeded seventy persons and averaged between thirty to fifty. The number of cacicazgos seems to have stabilized after the census of 1735, thus allowing the consolidation of a stable urban layout.[19]

We lack clear understanding of the internal logic for the divisions of the teyÿ at the time they were incorporated into the reducciones, but we can suppose that certain members of the extended families, particularly the youngest adults, would have split off from these groups to form autonomous communities. Although the priests made concerted efforts to persuade caciques with large numbers of vasallos to enter the missions, we also know from the order's chronicles that it was precisely those caciques who most stubbornly resisted evangelization. At the same time, the lack of uniform dimensions among cacicazgos incorporated into the different reducciones indicates that the previous social organization held together at least partially. That is, the Jesuits' homogenizing impulse was limited by the preexisting indigenous sociopolitical organization, and that fact helped the Indians to maintain a certain degree of autonomy.

The formation of reducciones thus required the consent of the caciques, who negotiated directly with the priests regarding their people's removal to designated new locations, where they were to live with other relocated groups that, at times, were their bitter enemies. The caciques were key figures in the daily operations of the reducciones. Writing in the opening decades of the eighteenth century, the Jesuit Antonio Sepp reports that at harvest time it was the caciques who received oxen and bulls and distributed them among their vasallos to help carry out the work.[20] Decades later, a colonial official named Francisco Bruno de Zavala explained the way in which lands were distributed. He reported that "the indios hold no lands as individual private property." Rather, each cacique ruled the lands around the village where he and his cacicazgo tilled their fields.[21]

Some testimonies suggest that, at least initially, the structure of indigenous houses retained its integrity but gradually changed with the passage of time. The *Carta Anua* of 1626–27 reports that in two months sixty houses were built in the reducción of Nuestra Señora de la Concepción. In each one lived a cacique with his *parcialidad* [following], or vassals, who typically amount to twenty, thirty, forty, and at times more than a hundred families, depending on the cacique's abilities. The document goes on to state that the houses had no other division that "some posts that run through the middle of the building in places, and serve to hold up the roof, and they mark the living space of each family, which is the distance between one post and the other, one space being for this group, the other for the next."[22] Although the description lacks detail, it does indicate a distinction between parcialidades, which in this case appear synonymous with cacicazgos and families; it also underscores the fact that spatial divisions between families was important from the early period onward.

In time spatial distributions in the reducciones were formalized based strictly on the organization of the cacicazgos, which were carefully tabulated in the village census rolls. The cacicazgos served as the basis for distribution of everything from living accommodations to fields and community chores.

A 1760 testimony from the Jesuit Juan Escandón offers details in this regard. He reported that each village had between twenty and thirty caciques, each of whom distributed to his people fields for planting around the village; the expanse of those fields depended on the size of his parcialidad or cacicazgo. According to Escandón these fields, like everything else, did not belong to individuals but rather to the mission town itself. The same applied to "the houses in which the people live; in them there is also a form of division among cacicazgos, and in one or two sections lives the cacique with his [parcialidad]; and in the other section lives another cacique with his; but the people work collectively to make all these houses, and when necessary they repair them in the same fashion."[23] Some years later, the aforementioned official Zavala provided evidence that these practices outlived the expulsion of the Jesuits. He explained that at the end of the eighteenth century, the cacicazgos resided in "*galpones* or rows of houses of equal size and proportion, covered with thatch, with openings that allowed transit."[24] The number of mboyas in each cacicazgo determined the distribution of rows of houses.

Some Jesuit chronicles do provide details about the distribution of cacicazgos and the so-called parcialidades, the latter apparently a larger unit than the former, in autonomous barrios. The practice probably amounted to an effective tactic of Jesuit social engineering used to avoid conflicts and maintain a certain degree of autonomy for the incorporated groups.[25] Each parcialidad (made up of one or two cacicazgos) occupied a section, or barrio, of the village. Kazuhiza Takeda has recently noted that the barrios conformed to a certain hierarchy, a fact reflected in the census rolls the Jesuits periodically produced. Those that appeared first on the list were the oldest and original inhabitants of the region and had the largest populations. They almost certainly lived near the village's central plaza, while the last on the list were those most recently incorporated and included Indians who had yet to convert to Christianity. This logic of spatial organization also applied to cacicazgos that for reasons of population growth had separated from their village of origin to create a new colony or else join a preexisting village.[26] Thus was born a sense of territoriality that initially drew from cacicazgo ties; in time, however, it became centered on the mission towns, their municipal organization, urban layout, and surrounding fields, all of which were in turn distributed according to a cacique organization that maintained its internal networks over a long period.

The Jesuits also sought ways to mitigate long-standing hostilities that persisted among different groups incorporated in the same mission town. Most commonly this meant promoting joint participation in the mission's liturgical life, together with creating social sectors and categories based on the religious activity and secular administration of the mission. The latter process, which facilitated the governing of the reducciones, depended on cabildo offices, artisanal roles, and positions provided by the church, the militias, and the lay organizations known variously as *cofradías* or *congregaciones*. Many of the Indians involved were in fact literate.[27]

Assumption of these elite roles required strict preparation, and its members naturally enjoyed privileges derived from close association and direct collaboration with the priests. While initially it was the caciques who occupied these roles, the various positions of village governance gradually came to include noncaciques as well.[28]

DETERRITORIALIZATION

Much of this organization began to disintegrate when the Jesuits were expelled from Spanish territories in 1767–68. Although the structure of reducciones remained nearly intact, certain changes did occur regarding their administration. Priests from different orders (Franciscans, Mercedarians, and Dominicans) were sent to the reducciones with orders to take charge of spiritual affairs while leaving economic and political matters to specially appointed Spanish administrators. This new approach immediately stirred much conflict among the different sectors, including members of the indigenous elite.[29] In the era following the Jesuit expulsion, colonial officials emphasized the need to end the practice of segregating indigenous peoples and to fully incorporate them into Hispanic society. Policies aimed at integration prohibited the use of indigenous languages, required the teaching of Spanish, and progressively eliminated community-oriented production in favor of individual farms and businesses. The instructions dictated by the governor of Buenos Aires, Francisco de Paula Bucareli, followed this approach and took their inspiration from measures introduced in Brazil a decade earlier by Governor Mendonca Furtado with the help of his brother, the Marquis de Pombal.[30]

During this period, the reducciones were affected by a series of liberal administrative and economic reforms aimed at promoting both individual initiative and commercial activity. The system of economic distribution based on collective labor had provided a certain equilibrium during the Jesuit era, but that system began to crumble immediately following the expulsion (map 8.1).[31] Pressure increased on those doing collective labor, while epidemics

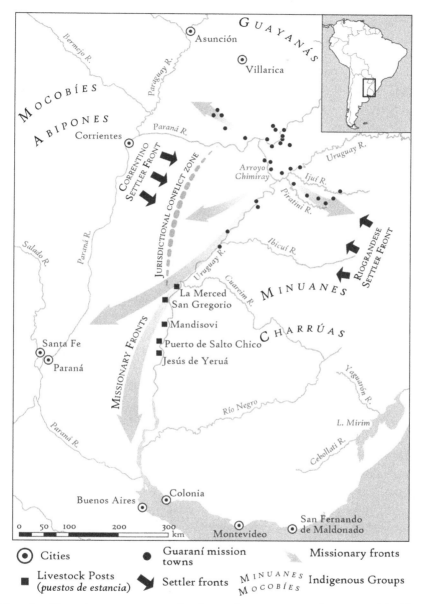

Map 8.1. Frontier outposts and ethnic dispersion in the second half of the eighteenth century. From Wilde, *Religión y Poder*. (Map © G. Wallace Cartography & GIS after original by Guillermo Wilde)

decimated several mission towns.[32] The crisis forced a substantial number of reduced Indians to leave their mission towns either temporarily or permanently. Some fled to the surrounding countryside, but just as many went to other cities and towns where they could find work, either ongoing or temporary, as *concha-bos* [day laborers]. Some took to stealing cattle, at times collaborating with fugitives in the countryside, such as Spanish or Portuguese deserters, descendants of African slaves, and unconverted Indians of diverse origins.[33] These out-migrations produced intense interactions and mixings of peoples, although Guaraní remained the primary language of communication.

In 1800 Viceroy Gabriel de Avilés abolished the system of community labor in the Guaraní reducciones. His objective was to break once and for all the model of economic, social, and cultural segregation that had hitherto governed the villages and instead to promote individual activities linked to commerce, industry, and agriculture. The decree initially affected a list of 323 Guaraní families considered "capable" of earning a living "by themselves." By May 1801, however, 6,212 people had been declared free from work in their communities. The decree was only partially carried out, and it is difficult to determine what criteria were used to select the families worthy of receiving this privilege. Whatever the case, Guaranís seem to have responded quite positively to the decree, and a number of them wrote to thank the authorities or to request the same exemption for themselves.[34]

The decree was applied to the former Jesuit reducciones, to villages once under the control of either Franciscans or the secular orders, and to villages formerly held in encomienda (known in Guaraní as *tava*). By this time, these types of communities no longer differed greatly in terms of their internal workings. In fact, the expulsion tended to move the mission and encomienda models closer to one another, at least from an economic perspective.[35] Between 1768 and the 1790s the former Jesuit reducciones suffered from secular administrative abuses, criollo land invasions, arrival of merchants, and squabbles within the indigenous elite. Partial application of the liberation decree of Viceroy Avilés diminished the well-being of certain mission communities. Many Indians who had not been deemed capable of receiving labor exemptions chose to complain openly or else to flee, thereby accelerating the process of mission disintegration. As Sušnik has pointed out, reduced peoples had long since ceased to comply with collective labor expectations, disobeying the missions' indigenous authorities and often taking refuge among criollo settlers.[36]

In the first decades of the nineteenth century, the former mission district was engulfed in a series of wars unleashed as the Iberian monarchs lost their

American colonies. Although we still know relatively little about the ways in which former mission Indians participated in these conflicts, some evidence points to their direct involvement. At this time we begin to see divisiveness in the different mission towns caught up in the region's geopolitical strife. The Portuguese invaded the mission district in 1801, and seven mission towns remained under their control thereafter. Similarly, Paraguay's government in Asunción opposed the revolutionary junta in Buenos Aires in 1810, which effectively divided the mission district between the two factions. Shortly thereafter the emergence of José Gervasio Artigas and his plan for a confederation in 1812–18 marked a watershed moment when numerous Guaraní leaders emerged to champion the idea of recovering the territorial integrity and autonomy of the mission district, which had all but disappeared during the regional conflicts. Indians took part in crafting laws and proclamations in both Guaraní and Spanish, and they widely circulated these documents throughout the mission towns. These documents reflected new concepts in the era's political language, particularly regarding ideas of sovereignty, citizenship, and representation, all of which burst onto the scene in the context of revolution.[37] With the defeat of Artigas and his followers in the Guaraní missions, the project of recovering territorial integrity was abandoned once and for all, and most of the mission populations dispersed in different directions.

The phenomenon of the blending of peoples of different origins continued to grow throughout the countryside, and an intriguing demographic trend emerged in the first half of the nineteenth century: the disappearance of the term "indio" from the census rolls of Paraguayan jurisdictions. Table 8.1 traces the evolution of this phenomenon over roughly eighty years.

In all probability these figures reflect less the physical disappearance of the indigenous population than its being rendered invisible in administrative documents. Indeed, the "indigenous" population recorded in the 1761 census appears to have become part of the considerably enlarged "nonindigenous" category by the 1846 count. Moreover, the progress of this trend becomes more apparent when traced by percentages across the four censuses. Although linguistic research into this period has only just begun, a few recent studies indicate that a growing Hispanicization of the Guaraní language accompanied the process.[38] Such Hispanicization also takes the form of incorporation of objects from the Spanish world, objects hitherto excluded from the reductions.[39] At the same time, religious practices tended to adopt secular and even heterodox elements that had been kept separate from Guaraní liturgical life.[40]

Table 8.1. Census enumerations of indigenous and nonindigenous people between 1761 and 1846

	1761		1782		1799		1846	
Indigenous population	51,921	61.0%	30,171	31.3%	29,570	27.4%	1,200	0.5%
Nonindigenous population	33,217	39.0%	66,355	68.7%	78,500	72.6%	237,664	99.5%
TOTAL	85,138		96,526		108,070		238,864	

Source: Telesca and Wilde, "Antiguos actores."

It is worth pointing out, however, that if the majority of congregated Indians were progressively absorbed into either the rural population or the region's cities, there were also groups that either rejected the reduction life or else fled their mission towns to return to the forest. The case of the indios infieles called *cainguá* (literally, "inhabitants of the wilderness") proves particularly interesting in this regard. Certain episodes refer to their incorporation into the missions, where they remained for several years. The Cainguás might have included groups of non-Guaraní speakers, peoples who had mostly avoided contact with Spanish settlers. Colonial documents mention repeated attempts to reduce them, especially after the first decades of the eighteenth century, because Spaniards considered them enormously adept at exploring the Paraguayan wilderness, opening paths, and extracting yerba maté.

Thus far we lack systematic evidence concerning when these Indians were incorporated into the established missions. The best known missionary efforts among them were the so-called reductions of the Tarumá region, which lay north of Asunción and south of the Jejuí River, far removed from the original nucleus of thirty Guaraní villages. According to the Jesuit Martin Dobrizhoffer, in 1697 certain Indians known as "Tobatines" were reduced into the village of Nuestra Señora de Santa Fe, but this village collapsed when the Indians fled to the forest.[41] New attempts to reduce the same people came in 1720–21. But under threat of attacks by Indians from the Chaco, they were led once more to the reducción of Nuestra Señora de Santa Fe, where they remained between 1723 and 1733. But this settlement likewise fell apart owing to the challenges of adapting to an existing village, discord with the previously reduced Guaranís, and the demographic crisis that struck villages along the Paraná River from 1732 onward. In 1745 two new reducciones were founded in the Tarumá region, San Joaquín (1747) and San Estanislao (1750), congregating Guaraní groups from different regions.[42] The Tarumá reducciones apparently remained somewhat stable demographically until their dissolution in 1848, when a decree from President Carlos Antonio López abolished the pueblos de indios and retitled all their inhabitants as Paraguayan citizens.

The wilderness to the northeast of the Tarumá jurisdiction was a place where wild yerba forests abounded, and it remained on the margins from the beginning of the independence period. That fact afforded its unreduced indigenous (Cainguá) inhabitants a high degree of autonomy. After the 1840s the state tried to assert firm control over the region, establishing nine Spanish villages, including Concepción, and systematically persecuting the Cainguás who opposed colonization.[43] The Cainguás ultimately managed to escape these attacks, along with the devastating effects of the area's frequent epidemics; they subsequently developed strategies that oscillated between hiding in the wilderness and making sporadic contact with reduction Indians to whom they were distantly related.[44] In this way, ironically, the Cainguás survived the process of missionization, selectively adapting from those spaces elements that seemed useful while maintaining their own fundamental forms of social organization. It would not be until the end of the nineteenth century, in the period following the War of the Triple Alliance, that these Indians began to be identified by new ethnic labels drawn from the frameworks of the emerging nation-state narrative and the new science of anthropology. That history is best analyzed as part of a second period of territorialization beyond the scope of this chapter. But for the moment I return to the forms of indigenous participation that marked the first period.

NATIVE LOGICS

Indigenous peoples participated in the territorialization process by employing negotiation strategies on different levels. Through the agency of their leaders, they bargained with the priests concerning their own initial incorporation into the reducciones, influenced the selection of appropriate locations for the mission towns, and participated actively in community self-government by adopting and exercising various forms of office. The cacicazgos served as the basic organizational unit of missionized peoples. As we have seen, they formed the basis for distribution of the houses, the *chacras* (fields), and the daily chores. The cacicazgo was thus instrumental in organizing both the urban mission layout and territories that surrounded the reductions.

Indian-generated maps often accompanied legal proceedings, providing detailed coverage of the broad area in which Indians moved. One noteworthy example is an attractive map created by the authorities of Santo Tomé village in 1784. In contrast to other cartographic works of the period, this map does not render a visually realistic representation: it pays no attention to degrees of latitude or longitude, its depiction of waterways is clearly distorted, and its orientation is unusual. Presumably, the map emphasizes a pragmatic dimension quite probably linked to daily uses of transportation (whether by land or water) and to networks of circulation among villages and their surrounding environs; that is, the map points to a dynamic concept of space and visually emphasizes lines of communication, especially rivers and roads. Within this network, the reducciones did not constitute closed spaces, but rather nodes within a wider network of regional connections. The map contains the following legend: "We the Corregidor, Cabildo, and Administrator send this map of the lands contained within our jurisdiction, and it faithfully follows the original that is kept in our cabildo house. It includes all the names and distances, according to the document mentioned, and without additional documents beyond that which we are sending. And to testify that it is true we sign it on September 9, 1784."[45]

Judging from this testimony, the Indians kept their papers in an archive in the cabildo house, that archive evidently held information relating to the territorial rights of their villages, and its papers contained information from far in the past that served to defend community rights. That is to say, the map did more than simply reflect an indigenous view of the uses of their territory, it also spatialized the memory of these uses. This dimension was also reflected in another map, created a few years earlier.

In 1773 the Indians of Loreto village initiated legal proceedings against a Spaniard over the use of the yerba fields that lay under their jurisdiction. The lawsuit contains, among other papers, some letters written in Guaraní by village authorities, complaining about the situation, and an eye-catching map in color that lays out the different locations. In the upper lefthand corner of the map is a brief text stating that thirteen caciques claimed use of those yerba fields from long in the past. Their names were Melchor Yaguarendí, Pedro Guaca, Francisco Papa, Nicolás Patagui, Lorenzo Nandabú, Claudio Pirapepó, Martín Sayobí, Esteban Guasé, Miguel Ayucú, Antonio Guarapy, Cristóbal Bié, Ignacio Mboacati, and Pedro Sumey. The map indicates the places where those caciques and their vassals lived, and where the people of the Loreto district extracted yerba. Later in the text is a somewhat curious statement: "It must be known that these caciques were not from Loreto but rather live in Corpus and are of the village Acaray that was founded with Corpus, and together with Itapúa."[46] Although brief and confusing, the text basically references fundamental aspects of the long process of Guaraní territorialization. The first is the already analyzed link between cacicazgos and productive spaces. The second is the history of indigenous migrations beginning in the late seventeenth century. The "village Caray" had been founded in the early 1600s and its peoples were later divided between Corpus and Itapúa owing to the bandeirante invasions.

It remains unclear whether this map, so markedly different from the one described previously, was actually rendered by Indians, but there is no doubt that they informed its creator regarding the exact location of the houses and lands of the caciques in question. Moreover, those Indians clearly told the cartographer the history of their geographic origins and their migrations.[47] Beyond their known use of writing and cartography, then, we must also recognize the Guaranís' ability to store and deploy information concerning the territorial history of the mission towns and their surroundings.

These examples reveal two essential aspects of indigenous territoriality. The first translates to the visual modality what in all likelihood were indigenous sociopolitical networks that linked different spaces. These spaces lay separate from one another and beyond the territorial confines of reduction, empire, or ethnic group. If indeed the Indians were conscious of such (simultaneous and superimposed) confines and could make use of them in certain contexts, the concrete dynamic of their movements consisted precisely in going beyond those limits when necessary. The second aspect underscores the configuration of a political economy of space, one crystalized over more than a century of mission activity in which the Indians, by means of their cacicazgos, came to know and claim territory and pass it from one generation to the next. The eminently practical nature of representations linked to specific circumstances of production reveal the Indians' ability to make use of colonial power while giving it their own stamp.

CONCLUSION

Policies of both the late colonial and early republican era had the effect of gradually homogenizing the population, whether under the category of "subject of the crown" or "citizen of the fatherland." The register of official discourse also depended heavily on the use of ethnic denominations to refer to populations that had been reduced or were soon to be so. If said categories, together with the homogenizing impulse itself, functioned efficiently at the level of colonial administration, in concrete practice the territorial logic of indigenous actors was less guided by essentialized ethnic qualities than by the configuration of social networks and political dynamics that lay outside of (or were concealed within) ethnic categories.

The territorialization process analyzed here began in the sixteenth century with the creation of the first encomiendas and was consolidated with the creation of the Jesuit-supervised pueblos de indios, better known as mission towns or reducciones. Many of the basic features of this specific social, political, and territorial structure outlived the Jesuit expulsion, only to fragment in the second half of the nineteenth century.

Along with the collapse of the mission towns, two elements of this first stage of Guaraní territorialization fell into crisis. One was the Guaraní language, which would cease to be written and spoken as it had been in the missions for almost two centuries. Instead, it would blur into regional expressions of Guaraní that linguists call "post-reductional," bearing the strong imprint of Spanish. The other casualty was the cacicazgos, which survived in some villages until the early nineteenth century, when the last residents of the reducciones underwent their final diaspora.

The twentieth and twenty-first centuries paint scenes of a Guaraní reemergence, one that initiates a new stage in their territorialization process. The groups that had managed to avoid contact with the colonizers will now be rediscovered by agents of the nation-state (officials, travelers, and scientists), and the process of capitalist expansion, well underway since 1870, will place new tensions on Guaraní habitat and social organization.

NOTES

1. Sušnik, *El indio colonial de Paraguay*, I; Saeger, "Warfare, Reorganization, and Readaptation."

2. Pacheco de Oliveira, "¿Una etnología?"; Hill, *History, Power, and Identity*; Boccara, "Mundos nuevos"; Giudicelli, *Fronteras movedizas*.

3. Julien, "Alejo García"; Candela, "Corpus indígenas."

4. Service, "Encomienda"; Roulet, *La resistencia de los guaraní*; Garavaglia, *Mercado interno*; Austin, "Guaraní Kinship"; Kleinpenning, *Paraguay*.

5. Garavaglia, *Mercado interno*.

6. Necker, "La réaction des Indiens."

7. Necker, *Indios guaraníes*; Gandía, *Cultura y folklore*; Molina, "La obra franciscana"; Durán Estragó, *Presencia franciscana*.

8. Maeder, "Las encomiendas."

9. There are no reliable statistics regarding the number of Indians captured during the period when the Paulista bandeirantes were active. Different studies provide numbers ranging from 30,000 to 190,000 persons. See Monteiro, *Negros da terra*; Hemming, *Red Gold*.

10. The peoples of Itatín were gathered near the city of Santiago de Jerez in 1631–32. After a series of divisions, regroupings, and attacks from both bandeirantes and Indians of the Chaco, the Jesuits decided to move these peoples to the area of San Ignacio del Paraná, where they founded two villages: Nuestra Señora de Fe and Santiago. This move came in 1668–69. Concerning the Itatín missions, see Gadelha, *As missões jesuíticas de Itatim*; Combès, *De la una y otra banda*.

11. Maeder, "La población de las misiones."

12. Melià, *La lengua guaraní*; Thun, "La hispanización"; Wilde and Vega, "De la diferencia."

13. Wilde, "De las crónicas jesuíticas." Concerning the problematic nature of Spanish terms for indigenous groups, see chapter 6 in this volume.

14. Ruiz de Montoya, *Arte y bocabulario*, iii, 383.

15. Ruiz de Montoya, *Arte y bocabulario*, 156.

16. Barbosa and Mura, "Construindo e reconstruindo."

17. "Información en favor de los caciques de la nación guaraní en que suplica haber habido siempre caciques," March 22, 1678, AGN (Buenos Aires, Argentina), sala IX.6.9.3, ff. 626r–v.

18. Cortesão, *Manuscritos*, 166–67.

19. Takeda, "Cambio y continuidad"; Takeda, "Los padrones de indios."

20. Furlong, *Antonio Sepp*, 116.

21. González, "Un informe," 162.

22. Leonhardt, *Cartas anuas*.

23. Furlong, *Juan Escandón*, 108.

24. González, "Un informe," 162.

25. Maeder, "La población de las misiones," 89.

26. Takeda, "Los padrones de indios."

27. Neumann, "A escrita dos guaranis"; Neumann, "Razón gráfica"; Neumann, *Letra de indio*; Neumann and Wilde, "Escritura, poder y memoria."

28. Owing to limitations of space it is impossible here to delve into the way that power was exercised in the reducciones or how different indigenous authorities related to each other and with the Jesuits. For recent studies of this topic, see Ganson, *Guaraní under Spanish Rule*, 20; Maeder, *Misiones del Paraguay*; Wilde, *Religión y poder*; Wilde, "Entre las tipologías." For a rigorous analysis of the census rolls, see Takeda, "Cambio y continuidad"; Sarreal, "Caciques as Placeholders."

29. For a detailed exploration of the post-Jesuit changes, see Maeder, *Misiones del Paraguay*; Telesca, *Tras los expulsos*; Wilde, *Religión y poder*; Mariluz Urquijo, "Los guaraníes"; Sušnik, *El indio colonial*.

30. Wilde, "Orden y ambigüedad"; Pinto de Medeiros, "Política indigenista"; and Maeder, "El modelo portugués."

31. Garavaglia, *Mercado interno*; Sarreal, *Guaraní and Their Missions.*

32. For detailed accounts of the effects of epidemics before and after the Jesuit expulsion, see Maeder and Bolsi, "Evolución y características"; Maeder and Bolsi, "La población guaraní"; Livi-Bacci and Maeder, "Missions of Paraguay"; Jackson, "Una mirada a los patrones"; Jackson, "Population and Vital Rates."

33. Concerning similar interethnic alliances along the margins of Nueva Vizcaya and Cuba, see chapter 7 in this volume.

34. Lastarria, *Colonias orientales*, 374–75.

35. Sušnik notes however that despite the imposition of uniform measures for all Indian villages in the region, the former Jesuit reducciones and the *tavas* scorned one another, and having experienced "two different systems of acculturation" remained different. See Sušnik, *Una visión socio-antropológica*, 124; see also Whigham, "Paraguay's *Pueblos de Indios.*"

36. Sušnik, *Una visión socio-antropológica.*

37. Wilde, *Religión y poder*; Telesca and Wilde, "Antiguos actores"; Couchonnal and Wilde, "De la política de la lengua"; Boidin, "Textos de la modernidad."

38. Thun, "La hispanización."

39. Sarreal, *Guaraní and Their Missions.*

40. Sušnik and Chase-Sardi, *Los indios del Paraguay.*

41. The Jesuit Sánchez Labrador offers details concerning the reduction of the Tobatines; see Barcelos, *O Mergulho no Seculum*. Several studies explore the demography of these villages over the entire colonial period; see Maeder, "La población de las misiones"; Maeder and Bolsi, "Evolución y características"; Sušnik, *Etnohistoria de los guaraníes.*

42. Cadogan, "Las reducciones del Tarumá"; Mura and Thomaz de Almeida, "Historia y territorio"; Melià, Grünberg, and Grünberg, *Los Paî-Tavyterã*. See also the recent work by Isabelle Combès, "Etnohistoria, etnocidio y etnogénesis."

43. Sušnik, *Una visión socio-antropológica*; Areces, "Los guaraní-monteses."

44. Sarreal, "Caciques as Placeholders."

45. Furlong, *Cartografía jesuítica.*

46. "El administrador general de los pueblos de misiones don Juan Ángel Lazcano contra don Josef de Velasco por haber beneficiado porción de hierba en los hierbales del pueblo de Loreto," AGN (Buenos Aires, Argentina), sala IX.40.2.5, Tribunales, leg. 12, exp. 33.

47. For a panoramic view of the problems with mission maps, see Furlong's classic *Cartografía jesuitica*; see also the recent studies by Barcelos, "El saber cartográfico indígena," and Levinton, "La micro-región."

PART IV

Indigenous Sovereignty in Unexpected Places

CHAPTER 9

The Chaco de Jujuy

AN INDIGENOUS BORDERLAND IN SIXTEENTH- AND SEVENTEENTH-CENTURY COLONIAL TUCUMÁN

Enrique Normando Cruz

T he colonial period saw the emergence of an indigenous borderland in Tucumán province, in what is now northwestern Argentina: the so-called Chaco de Jujuy, which made up the portion of the Gran Chaco under the colonial jurisdiction of the city of San Salvador de Jujuy (Xuxui). The Spanish founded Jujuy in 1593 as a communication and supply node on the road linking San Miguel de Tucumán with the Potosí mining center of modern-day Bolivia. Despite the early Spanish presence and the economic development in this dynamic region enabled by the mining endeavors in the mountains of Peru, it retained its borderland character until the early decades of the nineteenth century, owing to stubborn native resistance to the system of colonial domination. This chapter presents the first interpretive synthesis of the region's indigenous history over the entire colonial period. It explores the cultural practices, adaptations, and strategies that allowed the natives to resist the conquest and to exert their own influence on a space that was first an outlier of the Inca Empire, then later an internal borderland of war and colonization emanating from the Spanish government in Tucumán.[1]

The scarcity of indigenous sources relating to this topic requires an inter-disciplinary approach. Archaeology, modern ethnography, and ethnohistory allow us to analyze critically the at times distorted documentary sources that typically detail an indigenous "other" characterized by an atavistic savagery, concealing ingenious adaptations of resistance and integration. In addition, I analyze the documentation through the prism of available literature regarding the Chaco's Tucumán frontier, archaeological and ethnohistorical studies of the settlement patterns, and the local and regional ethnicity of the natives in relation to the Inca Empire and Jujuy uplands during the fifteenth and sixteenth centuries. Finally, I explore historical studies concerning the creation of the Spanish colonial regime, as well as indigenous strategies of resistance to this regime during the seventeenth and eighteenth centuries.[2]

Formerly strategically incorporated into the Inca Empire, the nomadic and seminomadic indigenous societies of the Gran Chaco resisted the Spanish tenaciously, giving rise to a peculiar indigenous borderland. The Gran Chaco is a plain covering nearly one million square kilometers in parts of what is now Bolivia, Paraguay, Brazil, and Argentina. By historic and ethnographic convention, its boundaries are usually considered to be the Santa Cruz de la Sierra range and the Chiquitano territory to the north, the vast Andean range to the west, the Salado River to the south, and the Paraná and Paraguay Rivers to the east.[3] Three broad ecological zones parallel one another: the humid to subhumid Chaco Oriental, the transitional Chaco Central, and the semiarid Chaco Occidental, which is where the Jujuy frontier is located.[4] The last zone enjoys a warm, temperate continental climate, with rainfall mainly in summer and dry spells in winter.[5]

Many of the dynamics of the Spanish conquest, which began here in the sixteenth century, resulted from the Chaco's situation as a multiethnic borderland in the pre-Hispanic era. In the mid-fifteenth century, the Incas invaded the mountains and forests east of the Andes, incorporating the region as a Tawantinsuyu frontier containing various ethnic identities as the "Indians of Chiriuana, Tucumán y Parauay" had their own languages.[6] Ethnohistorical studies agree that the Guarani-speaking peoples confronted the Incas successfully and developed diverse processes of ethnogenesis with other Chacoan natives.[7]

The Inca advance to the east from Charcas continued as far as the Chaco de Jujuy.[8] Thus, in Tucumán, the region received a Quechua name derived from the Inca imperial strategy of *chacu*, which supplemented the provisioning of goods with trade relationships and bartering and the hunting of animals.[9] The Inca presence in the mountain spurs of the Jujuy area dates from the period of 1430–1536 CE.[10] The Incas' main interest was the region's natural resources: timber, fish, feathers, honey, minerals, metals, and hallucinogens. They accessed these resources by transplanting groups of conquered peoples (Ocloyas, Churumatas, Tomatas, Yapanatas, Azamatas, Gaypetes, Yalas, Osas, and Paypayas) into the Chaco from the mountains and valleys of Jujuy, to the north of the Zenta and Tarija Valleys.[11] The chronicler Pedro Lozano reported that the people whom the Inca settled in the Chaco were *mit-imaes* (roughly, "transplanted peoples") from Cuzco, and that they gradually cut their ties with their places of origin once the Inca Empire of Tawantin-suyu fell. When the Spanish founded the city of Jujuy in 1593, they divided up its people in order to assign them encomienda duty.[12]

The Inca conquest and colonization of the Chaco triggered a massive displacement of peoples, both native and foreign, which compounded the chaos brought about by the initial Spanish conquest of Tucumán and Jujuy. For this reason, the Chaco's indigenous borderland—bounded by Tucumán, Charcas, Río de la Plata, Paraguay, and Santa Cruz de la Sierra—was inhabited by thousands of Chiriguanos, Tobas, Mocovíes (Mocobíes), Mbayás, and Matacos (or Mataguayos).[13] In addition to Quechua-speaking settlers now cut off from Tawantinsuyu, there were also Guamalcas, Gueleleas, Hurumatas, and "Inga Indians from Cuzco, the Inga captains" (apparently a reference to the Inca military nobles who governed the colonies of the empire's frontier).[14] Given these circumstances, it is hardly surprising that eighteenth-century missionary chronicles emphasized the Chaco's "multitude of nations."[15]

During the sixteenth and seventeenth centuries the Spanish conquered the space formerly integrated into the Inca Antisuyo. Spaniards founded a series of cities along the edge of the Chaco; these cities were placed under the Gobernación de Tucumán, Juríes y Diaguitas, a jurisdiction created by the real cédula of August 1563 and referring to the main autochthonous ethnicities. The gobernación, which included the cities of Jujuy, Salta, Tucumán, Santiago del Estero, Catamarca, and Córdoba, continued until the creation of the Viceroyalty of Río de la Plata in the 1780s. At that point, it was divided into two intendencies: Córdoba del Tucumán, which included the cities of Córdoba, La Rioja, and Cuyo (the last being the capital of a province of the same name); and Salta de Tucumán, governed out of Salta and with authority over Jujuy, San Miguel de Tucumán, Santiago del Estero, and Catamarca.[16]

The Spanish settled in the Chaco de Jujuy, founding towns and establishing new jurisdictions in order to establish more fluid communications between Tucumán, Potosí, and La Plata; to reduce the native population to slave labor; and to overcome the resistance of the "chiriguanaes" (Chiriguanos) of the frontier separating Tomina and the Chaco de Tarija.[17] Based out of the urban centers of Jujuy, Salta, Tucumán, and Santiago del Estero, Spanish settlers raided the Chaco on campaigns of reconnaissance, punishment, or slave raiding. They established their frontier line on the plains of Jujuy (see map 9.1), complete with military outposts, supply points, and a mission of Ocloya Indians.[18] They typically legitimized the enslavement of the natives through accusations of cannibalism. For instance, in a letter written in late 1586, the cabildo of Santiago del Estero asked the king to "license and order incursions against the warlike Indians called "chiriguanas," for they are devil worshippers who eat human flesh."[19] These types of arguments, along with the notion of a "just war," brought about the legalization of the enslavement of Calchaquí Indians in the seventeenth century, and of Tobas and Mocovíes in the Chaco near the end of that century and, especially, during the following one.[20]

Chacoan natives responded to Spanish conquest and enslavement by resisting evangelization and the founding of cities, which hindered Spaniards' penetration into the Chaco de Jujuy's interior until well into the eighteenth century, converting the region into an internal borderland.[21] Ojotaes, Taños, Chiriguanos, Tobas, Mocovíes, and Mataguayos resisted militarily through malones (raids) against the cities, in which they often kidnapped Spanish women and children.[22] Indian tenacity prevented the Jujuy and Salta settlements from consolidating the city of Santiago de Guadalcázar, founded between 1624 and 1628 along the Bermejo River, a few leagues from the mouth of the San Francisco River (map 9.1). The troubled city endured less than a decade and was ultimately abandoned in 1635.[23] Attempts to settle Indians in reducciones bore fruit only in Jujuy, where the Ojotaes and Paypayas moved to villages and Spanish haciendas located near the Río Blanco.[24]

Chacoan natives also resisted culturally, opposing evangelization and maintaining their dedication to traditional beliefs and practices. Campaigns of evangelization—like the one that Pedro Ortiz de Zárate, a priest, settler, and encomendero of Jujuy, waged in the lands of his mercedes de tierra (land grant) on the Ledesma pampas in 1685—failed repeatedly.[25] The diary of a missionary who survived that campaign records that, after killing the friars and their companions, the Indians, who wore paint and were adorned with feathers, "celebrated with drinking, as was the custom of those . . . nations," and from their porongos (large vessels) they consumed vast amounts of guarapo (a drink made from fermented and pressed sugarcane) and chicha (fermented corn beer)."[26]

The founding of the Jujuy customshouse between 1690 and 1703 demonstrated the importance of that city in the robust trade between Tucumán and Potosí, a commerce that extended all the way to Asunción de Paraguay,

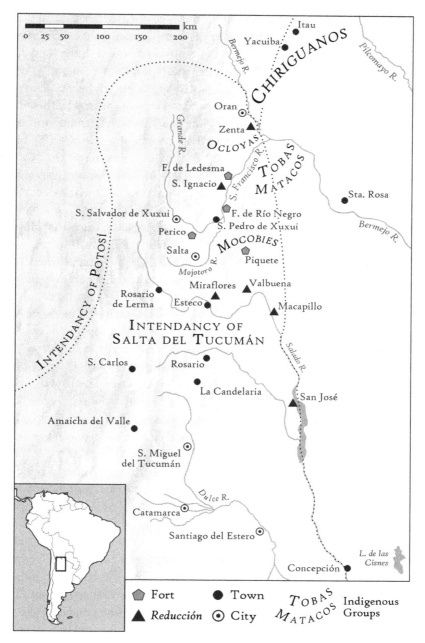

Map 9.1. Major settlements in Jujuy and the surrounding region, ca. 1781.
(Map © G. Wallace Cartography & GIS after original by Carlos Pallán Gayol)

Corrientes (in the modern-day Argentine province of that name), and Cuiabá (in the modern Brazilian state of Mato Grosso) to the east.[27] From that moment onward, the importance of natural resources in the Jujuy hinterlands increased; haciendas and cattle estates multiplied, and with them came heightened demand for indigenous labor, supplied mostly by the Mocovíes, Matacos, and Tobas.[28] Regional economic development spurred by the Potosí mines led to territorial colonization by means of forts, haciendas, and missions, all accompanied by frequent military campaigns. Growing Spanish interest in frontier colonization revealed itself in a new term, the "Chaco Gualamba," which referred to a cultural and historical space intersected by rivers and peopled by rival Indian groups, an unmistakable marker of indigenous resistance to colonization.[29]

During this era new terms for Indians gained currency, labels that alluded more to certain attributes than to a particular ethnic identity. It was said, for example, that some natives were "so swift that the nearby Indians called them by the name *juríes*, which is to say 'ostriches,' and that they are so bold and daring in combat that one of them could take on ten men on horseback."[30] Similarly, the term *frentones* alluded mainly to Guaycurú tribes like the Abipones, Mocovíes, and Tobas.[31] Historical chronicles and ethnographic descriptions reveal other indigenous identities in the region. For example, we find references to Chiriguanos in the upper Bermejo River and at its juncture with the San Francisco River.[32] The Matacos (Wichí) were spread out throughout the region; to the northwest, in the Alto Pilcomayo, there were the Noctenes; the Mataguayos inhabited the western central Chaco, between the Itaú and San Francisco Rivers; and the Vejoz made their home between the Pilcomayo and Bermejo Rivers.[33]

Many Indians reacted against the occasionally violent economic coercion of the Spanish, either intensifying their attacks on cities and haciendas, where they seized both cattle and captives (especially women), or else migrating seasonally, even while others served as soldiers in the forts. The Tobas and Matacos depended on the schools of fish found in the Pilcomayo, Bermejo, and San Francisco Rivers, and that dependency led to a strategy of "moving to produce" that combined defensive war with active raids on haciendas.[34] Small, highly specialized groups of men went out hunting or raiding cattle (both free ranging and penned on haciendas), but environmental changes also generated huge movements of tent communities, or camps, and in some cases of entire tribes. All these movements tended to follow *rastrilladas* (open, commonly used paths) that ran parallel to the waterways, although the Indians at times took advantage of higher ground and denser vegetation to conceal their tracks.[35]

The growth of indigenous incursions along the frontier brought a corresponding increase in military campaigns by Tucumán settlers, aimed at punishing the raiders, rescuing captives, and above all, enslaving Tobas and Mocovíes. In May 1736, for example, Tucumán Governor Matías de Anglés y Gortari informed the Jujuy cabildo that he had returned from a successful frontier campaign against a "host of enemies who had decapitated three people and thrown living infant children into fires, where they perished, and had carried off five Spanish captives and two children."[36] Tucumán Governor Martínez de Tineo complained to the king in 1752: "I realize that taking the men from their houses and sending them across the Chaco is a bothersome task that involves the damages of leaving the families, haciendas, and businesses suspended" with little or no profit.[37] For that reason, some of the captured Indians, mostly women and children, were distributed among the troops of soldiers-settlers who had taken part in the campaigns; the rest were consigned or sold as "pieces" in the markets of Peruvian cities.[38]

The violence of the Spanish conquest persuaded some Chacoan indigenous groups to integrate themselves into the colonial system. In so doing, they secured favorable conditions in exchange for their services to the Crown. For example, Ojotaes and Oclayas (reputedly the descendants of Quechua settlers) served as presidio soldiers in the frontier forts.[39] Governor Esteban de Urízar y Arespacochaga exempted them from paying "taxes or tribute . . . nor shall they provide mita Indians for the cities, by reason of being presidio soldiers . . . with the responsibility of defending the frontier and taking part in campaigns."[40]

The process of institutionalizing colonial rule in the Chaco de Jujuy began in 1773. In exchange for providing labor, the Indians negotiated with hacendados, mayordomos, soldiers, and missionaries for a more favorable integration into Hispanic institutions, one that guaranteed the survival of many of their traditional cultural practices. That year also saw the foundation of a curate that had its seat in Nuestra Señora de los Dolores del Río Negro, in the vicinity of the hacienda Río Negro and its eponymous fort. The idea was to have nine parish priests aid the friars in the San Ignacio de Indios Tobas reducción, founded by the Jesuits in 1756 but administered by Franciscans after the Jesuit expulsion in 1767; their work involved attending the parish soldiers, mestizos, Indian neophytes, and the other inhabitants of the presidios and haciendas.[41]

The parish was founded after a failed uprising by Indians and poor rural residents against the authorities, soldiers, missionaries, mayordomos, and hacendados in 1781–82.[42] Although they had negotiated peace in 1774, the Tobas and Matacos of San Ignacio reducción actually led the rebellion.[43] The revolt's failure, together with the solidification of the church presence there, facilitated the colonization of the frontier by means of the Río Negro curate; the San Ignacio reduction; the presidios of Ledesma, Río Negro, Santa Bárbara, and San Bernardo; the settlements of Río Negro and Pueblo de San Ignacio de los Tobas; the estancia of San Lucas; the outpost of San Borja; the haciendas Río Negro, Sora–Campo Colorado, San Lorenzo–Río Seco, and Ledesma; and finally, the city of San Ramón Nonato de la Nueva Orán, established in 1794 (map 9.1).[44]

A number of forts that were originally established for military purposes ended up as settlements populated by Indians—some neophytes, others soldiers, and some even unconverted—a fact that made these places important nuclei of colonization, as happened at Ledesma.[45] The year 1800 also saw the founding of a settlement based around the fort of Río Negro, made up of its captain, a lieutenant, a second lieutenant, four corporals, a gunsmith, and thirty soldiers, together with the families that homesteaded within and outside of its walls, people from surrounding haciendas, the reduced Indians of San Ignacio, and those who were not part of the reductions.[46] This process gave birth to rancherías, a colloquial term for mestizo dwellings on the frontier.[47]

Haciendas, which mostly grew from royal land grants, successfully established themselves as productive estates in the late colonial period.[48] According to the inventories of the estates of deceased hacendados, these properties included living accommodations, chapels, and storage infrastructure, along with African slaves, hundreds of head of cattle, horses, and mules; plantations of sugarcane, cotton, wheat, coffee, indigo, and rice; and *trapiches* (mills), tools, and machines used for producing sugar and aguardiente.[49]

The workers on these haciendas were either unreduced Indians or ones who had been sent from the San Ignacio reduction, and they managed to impose two principles of their culture: social organization by clan name (*chusma*), and the consumption of gathered resources (*algarroba*) used to resolve inter-ethnic rivalries in a festival context.[50] When the Tobas of San Ignacio fled the mission to gather honey or the fruit of the native algarrobo tree (*Prosopis alba*), they worked alongside the Matacos of San Ignacio from the presidio at Ledesma, gathering in the tents of other unreduced Matacos in order to celebrate traditional beverages made with these two ingredients.[51] In January 1793 the captain of Ledesma presidio informed the frontier's commander-general that he should not be surprised that Indians fled from the haciendas in "trying times of heat wave" without consent, given the fact that it was the time of "their drinking sprees," and with "the algarroba [having past], they go in search of work."[52] The indigenous festive habit of intoxication was strategically embedded in Hispanic society. Large estate owners destined part of the "cane fallen by the wind" to make guarapo, an aboriginal beverage that Spaniards had now learned to make from sugarcane.[53]

Along with haciendas and farms, another space where the Gran Chaco Gualamba natives disputed colonial domination was at the missions. At San Ignacio a pair of missionaries, the soldiers, and an officer of the guard gathered hundreds of Indians to create the Pueblo de Nuestra Señora del Rosario de Indios Tobas in 1756.[54] The founding of this settlement was critical in the system of coerced labor that transformed the Indians into hacienda workers.[55] It also allowed the formation of a mestizo community that the authorities favored as a way of allowing the soldiers of the presidios around the reduction to unwind by means of "trading, entering into illicit relations, gaming, or drinking."[56]

At the same time, Indians found ways to take advantage of the resources of the frontier missions. Within the mission confines they hunted and gathered, obtained well water, and secured food via the cattle they raised there.[57] During a visita of the Cochabamba intendency, next to Tucumán, on January 15, 1788, the newly appointed Governor Francisco de Viedma, noticing the Indians' preference for beef and other cattle-derived products, ordered "the customary trade in salted meat and cheese" banned to prevent the Indians from being cheated.[58]

Indigenous resistance in the Chaco Gualamba forced colonial Spanish mission policy to attend to the Indians' welfare. For example, in August 1806 Juan José Ortiz, friar of the San Ignacio reduction, wrote to the authorities of the Intendency of Salta del Tucumán and to the king himself, warning them that any cutbacks in the provisioning of cattle, biscuits, yerba, and tobacco would provoke "hunger, disobedience, disorder, apostasy, theft, war, blood, and all sorts of evils" among the Indians. His words echoed those of the natives themselves, who "with one voice said that if there are no rations, there will be no conchabos [servants]," threatened to abandon their occasional rural labor, and demanded that the friar write to the king "that we have nothing to eat, and for that reason it is better for us to abandon the Chaco."[59] Similarly, in 1808 the Tobas and Matacos demanded better treatment from the friars and demanded to be provided with meat, biscuits, and tobacco in exchange for remaining in the San Ignacio reduction and working on its haciendas; the alternative, they threatened, was for them to return to the Chaco.[60]

The end of the indigenous borderland of Chaco de Jujuy came slowly. Between the late eighteenth century and 1821 the lands of the Toba Indian reduction were sold to frontier hacendados and military authorities.[61] The forts of Ledesma, Río Negro, Santa Bárbara, and San Bernardo gave way to haciendas of the same names.

In sum, from the sixteenth to the nineteenth centuries, the natives of Chaco de Jujuy showed a tremendous capacity not only for maintaining their independence, but also for integrating themselves into the colonial system on their own terms. During the entirety of this period various indigenous groups destroyed Spanish settlements, resisted evangelization, and raided haciendas to oppose Spanish efforts to reduce them into missions or enslave them. Others served as soldiers in the forts, thereby gaining exemptions from other duties owed to the Crown. To accomplish the population and economic development of the frontier, the Spanish found themselves obliged to adapt to the indigenous context, allowing rancherías that fostered extensive mestizaje and that continued such Indian cultural traditions as the *borracheras* at the algarrobas and the consumption of guarapo. The agency, autonomy, and initiative of the Chaco natives of the Tucumán jurisdiction forced the Spanish to adapt constantly, a fact that certainly justifies referring to the Chaco de Jujuy as an indigenous borderland.

NOTES

1. Garavaglia, "La guerra en el Tucumán colonial"; Cruz, "La nueva sociedad de frontera."

2. In addition to the published writings of missionaries and officials of the seventeenth and eighteenth centuries, I consulted numerous unpublished documentary sources: the correspondence of hacendados and presidio commanders, judicial proceedings (*expedientes*) concerning frontier rebellions, Indian complaints about missionaries, hacienda inventories, criminal trials, records of soldiers' pay, and reports from the governors of Tucumán and the Jujuy cabildo concerning military campaigns against the Indians. These sources are in the archives of Tribunales, Obispado, and Histórico of Jujuy; in the AGN Argentina (since Jujuy and its frontier belonged to the jurisdiction of the Audiencia of Buenos Aires during the late colonial period); and in the AGI. Critical secondary works include Santamaría and Lagos, "Historia y

etnografía de las tierras bajas"; Teruel, "Las tierras bajas"; Ortiz and Ventura, *La mitad verde*; Teruel and Jerez, *Pasado y presente*; Salas, *El Antigal de Ciénaga Grande*; Lorandi, "Pleito de Juan Ochoa de Zárate"; Sánchez and Sica, "La frontera oriental de Humahuaca"; Vitar, *Tucumán y el Chaco*; Gullón Abao, *La frontera del Chaco*; Cruz, "Propiedad, producción y mano de obra"; Santamaría, "Población y economía interna"; Santamaría, "Paz y asistencialismo vs. guerra."

3. Jolís, *Ensayo sobre la historia natural*, 329.

4. The Chaco de Jujuy contains at least three ecosystems. The highest of these lies between 680 and 1,300 meters (2,231 and 4,265 feet) above sea level and is formed by the valleys of the sub-Andean ranges, valleys characterized by extensive riverine lowlands and a temperate subtropical mountain climate with a dry season. Lower down are the humid piedmonts, with an elevation of 350–800 meters (1,148–2,625 feet) above sea level. The local term *pedemontes* refers to a long strip running north-south along the foot of the highest sub-Andean mountain ranges southeast of Jujuy. It is characterized by a summer rainy season and rare freezes in winter. Finally, the zone of contact between the sub-Andean Chaco, or "threshold of the Chaco," forms the transition between the humid piedmonts and the Chaco high plains, the latter at an elevation of 300 to 550 meters (984 to 1,804 feet) above sea level. It is characterized by a warm, tropical climate year-round, its temperatures mitigated by cloud cover. See Braun Wilke et al., *Carta de aptitud ambiental*, 156–57.

5. Castro, "Aportes en torno a la discusión"; Torkel Karlin, Catalán, and Coirini, *La naturaleza y el hombre*.

6. Guamán Poma de Ayala, *Nueva Crónica y Buen Gobierno*, 325–27.

7. Meyers, *Fuerte de Samaipata*.

8. Lorandi, "La frontera oriental"; Lorandi, "Pleito de Juan Ochoa de Zárate"; Oliveto and Ventura, "Dinámicas poblacionales"; Cruz, "Monte adentro."

9. Aguilar Meza, "Las trampas para cazar camélidos."

10. Nielsen, *Celebrando con los antepasados*; Raffino, Nielsen and Alvis, "El dominio Inka"; Albeck, "Producción y lógica de la red vial."

11. Sánchez and Sica, "La frontera oriental de Humahuaca"; Cruz and Jara, "Por encima de las nubes"; Ventura and Scamboto, "La metalurgia de los valles orientales"; Sánchez, "Un viaje entre la historia"; Salas, *El Antigal de Ciénaga Grande*; Espinoza Soriano, "Los churumatas y los mitmas"; Doucet, "Acerca de los churumatas"; Oliveto and Ventura, "Dinámicas poblacionales"; Presta, "La población de los valles"; Presta and del Río, "Reflexiones sobre los churumatas"; and Ferreiro, "El Chaco en los Andes."

12. Lozano, *Descripción cartográfico*, 18. Mitimaes were people transported by imperial design from Cuzco and relocated to this and other regions in order to control local populations and to exploit the resources of target regions via tribute. They received land taken from the original inhabitants, and many never returned to their homelands following the collapse of Tawantinsuyu; see Lorandi, "Las rebeliones indígenas," 290.

13. Fernández, *Relación historial de las misiones*; Matorras, "Diario de la expedición"; Jolís, *Ensayo sobre la historia natural*.

14. Oliveto and Ventura, "Final de la jornada al Chaco."

15. Guevara, *Historia del Paraguay*; Lozano, *Descripción corográfica*. Modern investigators do not always distinguish between the Inca settlers and the autochthonous groups of this part of the Chaco, most of whom spoke Guaraní, Guaycurú, or Wichí.

16. Moutoukias, "Gobierno y sociedad en el Tucumán."

17. Doucet, "La jornada pobladora."

18. Tommasini, *La civilización cristiana del Chaco*; Tommasini, *Los indios oclayas*.

19. Levillier, *Gobernación del Tucumán*, 258.

20. Doucet, "Sobre cautivos de guerra y esclavos indios," 79–96.

21. Oliveto and Ventura, "Final de la jornada al Chaco," 273; Bussu, *Mártires sin altar*; Tommasini, *La civilización cristiana del Chaco*.

22. "Entrada militar, campaña de rescate de cautivas y represión de indios del Chaco, Salta-Jujuy, 13 de mayo de 1736," Archivo Histórico de Jujuy, Archivo Ricardo Rojas (hereafter AHJ-ARR), caja 33, 3, 1736, mayo, ff. 7r–v.

23. Demitropulos, *Apuntes históricas de Ledesma*; Bidondo, "Una discusión"; Doucet, "La jornada pobladora."

24. Sánchez and Sica, "Por ser gente de otra ley"; Sica, "Maíz y trigo."

25. Vergara, *Don Pedro Ortiz de Zárate*. A *mercedes de tierra* was a land grant awarded by the Crown in exchange for services rendered.

26. "Carta-diario del padre Ruiz escrita al provincial padre Tomás Baeza." This document was reconstructed by the chronicler Pedro Lozano, based on Jesuit documentation; see *Descripción corográfica*, 235–41. Consumption of guarapo, chicha, and *aloja* (fermented juice of the *algarrobo* tree with honey or other vegetable ingredients added) was common among the Indians of Chaco; see Arenas, *Etnografía y alimentación*, 350–51.

27. Various studies have traced the mercantile network from the Chaco to the cities of the Tucumán, Corrientes, and Cuiabá and to Mato Grosso in Brazil. See, for example, Santamaría, *Chaco Gualamba*, 21–36; Viñuales, "El territorio y la ilustración." Authorities would later recognize these trade routes; see "Descripción topográfica del terreno que ocupan las fuertes de las fronteras de Salta y Jujuy [. . .] se verá por los Autos donde este mapa va por cabeza, Salta, 27 de agosto de 1759," AGI, Mapas, Buenos Aires, 64.

28. Doucet, "Sobre cautivos de guerra y esclavos indios."

29. Demitropulos, *Apuntes históricos de Ledesma*; Tissera, *Chaco Gualamba*; Santamaría, *Chaco Gualamba*.

30. Kersten, *Las tribus indígenas*, 46.

31. Kersten, *Las tribus indígenas*, 47.

32. Morillo, "Diario del viaje al río Bermejo."

33. Rossi, *Los Wichí*; Sušnik, "Dimensiones migratorias y pautas culturales."

34. Arancibia, *Vida y mitos del mundo mataco*, 5.

35. Santamaría, "Población y economía interna," 181.

36. "Entrada militar, campaña de rescate de cautivas," May 1736, AHJ-ARR, box 33, 3, ff. 7r–v.

37. Doucet, "Sobre cautivos de guerra y esclavos indios," 108.

38. "Recibo de 15 piezas entregadas por Diego Tomás Martínez de Iriarte, Jujuy, 22 de diciembre de 1745," Archivo de Tribunales de Jujuy (hereafter ATJ), carpeta 38, leg. 1264.

39. Testimonio de los autos originales que se remitieron al gobernador sobre la nación Ojotay [. . .], April 14, 1711, ATJ, carpeta 27, leg. 838; Tommasini, *Los indios ocloyas y sus doctrineros*, 148–50.

40. Lozano, *Descripción corográfica*, 384.

41. "Carta de erección del curato del Río Negro, Río Negro, 22 de septiembre de 1773," Archivo del Obispado de Jujuy (hereafter AOJ), carpeta 13, leg. 27, 6 folios; "Información sobre pedimento de matrimonio, Río Negro, 1808," AOJ, carpeta 16, leg. 3; "Pedimento de matrimonio de Félix Martínez, Río Negro, 1810," AOJ, carpeta 11, leg. 54; Page, "Las reducciones-fuertes de los jesuitas."

42. "Testimonio de los autos originales seguidos de oficio contra los reos que se sublevaron en la jurisdicción de esta ciudad, Jujuy, 28 de marzo al 11 de abril de 1781," AGI, Audiencia de Buenos Aires, 143, ff. 1–80.

43. Paz and Sica, "La frontera oriental del Tucumán," 311–22.

44. Sánchez Bramdam, "Se hace camino al andar"; Cruz, "Notas para el estudio"; Poderti, *San Ramón de la Nueva Orán*. In the Chaco frontier "estancia" referred to the raising of animals, usually cattle, in an area that was not under private ownership.

45. "Testimonio de pagamento de la tropa partidaria de la frontera del Río Negro por dos años de sueldo, Río Negro, 1785–1786," AHJ-ARR, caja XC, leg. 2, legajillo 6, 1786; AHJ, ARR, caja XCIII, legajillo 2 (1790); "Reclamo de Lorenzo Revuelta, Ledesma, 1787," ATJ, carpeta 58, leg. 1885. See also "Tadeo Dávila al cabildo de Jujuy, Jujuy, octubre de 1789," AHJ-ARR, caja CXIV, leg. 1, ff. 13, 42, 54.

46. "Testimonio de pagamento de la tropa partidaria del Río Negro, Río Negro, 1785–1786," AHJ-ARR, caja XL, leg. 2, legajillo 6; "Toma de testimonio del fraile jubilado Miguel Lazo de la Bega, Río Negro, 1756," AOJ, caja 11, leg. 29, f. 1.

47. "Solicitud de regreso inmediato de los soldados que se prestan a todo tipo de bajezas en las rancherías de indios, 20 de marzo de 1792," in Correspondencia entre Carlos Sevilla y Gregorio de Zegada, Jujuy, 1780–1800, AHJ-ARR, caja 45, correspondencia 452.

48. "Títulos de merced de tierra de Pedro López de Velasco, Salta, 1764," ATJ, carpeta 42, leg. 1411; "Inventario de bienes de la sucesión de Gregorio de Zegada en el curato del Río Negro, haciendas de Ceibales, Coransulí, Sianso, El Pongo y Rodero, Río Negro–Ceibales–Coransulí–Sianso, 29 de julio de 1794," AOJ, caja 12, leg. 7, 10 folios. Some historians argue that the haciendas were feudalistic establishments associated with precapitalist patterns of patrimonial, or family-based, accumulation; see Cruz, "Propiedad, producción y mano de obra"; Peirotti, *Familia, haciendas y negocios*. Others maintain that it is possible to find haciendas that were more modern and innovative; see Soler Lizarazo and Cruz, "Un proyecto innovador en una hacienda."

49. "Testamento de José de Acuña, Jujuy, 1782," ATJ, carpeta, leg. 1779; Paleari, *Jujuy: Diccionario General*, 4719; "Correspondencia entre Miguel Antonio (de Iturbe)

y Gregorio de Zegada, Jujuy, 1791–1794," AOJ, caja 18, leg. 1 (carpeta 8, docs. 173–97), letters 170–92.

50. Teruel, "Zenta y San Ignacio de los Tobas"; Tommasini, *El Convento de San Francisco.*

51. "Informe sobre fuga y regreso de indios, 11 de marzo de 1793," in Correspondencia entre Carlos Sevilla y Gregorio de Zegada, Jujuy, 1780–1800, AHJ-ARR, caja 45, correspondencia 442.

52. "Informe sobre castigo a los indios trabajadores y deslinde de responsabilidad del mayordomo, 4 de enero de 1793," in Correspondencia entre Carlos Sevilla y Gregorio de Zegada, Jujuy, 1780–1800, AHJ-ARR, caja 45, correspondencia 437.

53. "Carta de Zegada a Iturbe, 24 de mayo de 1794," AOJ, caja 18, Leg, 1, carpeta 8, docs. 173–97, 23 folios; Armatto de Welti, *Diccionario guaraní de usos.*

54. "Recibos de los papeles pertenecientes al secuestro de la residencia de la ciudad de Jujuy y reducción del pueblo de indios tobas entregados a la junta municipal de dicha ciudad de Jujuy," AGN, Sala XI, División Colonia, Temporalidades de Jujuy, 1767–1807 (22.6.1).

55. Teruel, "Zenta y San Ignacio de los Tobas"; Tommasini, *El Convento de San Francisco.*

56. "Informe del envío de los soldados para auxiliar al padre de la reducción de San Ignacio, 11 de marzo de 1792," in "Correspondencia entre Carlos Sevilla y Gregorio de Zegada, Jujuy, 1780–1800," AHJ-ARR, caja 45, correspondencia 438.

57. In 1781 the reduction of San Ignacio had a cattle estancia managed by a black foreman. See "Declaración del Negro Justo," ff. 7–11v. In "Testimonio de los autos originales seguidos de oficio contra los reos que se sublevaron en la jurisdicción de esta ciudad, del 28 de marzo al 11 de abril de 1781," AGI, Audiencia de Buenos Aires, no. 143, ff. 1–80.

58. Viedma, "Descripción geográfica y estadística," 182.

59. "Pedido de fray Juan José Ortiz doctrinero de San Ignacio de los tobas," AGN, Sala IX, Interior, leg. 60, exp. 1 (30.7.9).

60. "Expediente acerca de la fuga de indios de la reducción," in Reducción de San Ignacio de los Tobas, Jujuy, 1808, AGN, Sala IX, Interior, leg. 63, exp. 2–4 (30.8.2); "Testimonio del comandante de fronteras en el fuerte de Ledesma José Suárez del Valle sobre huida en masa de los indios por maltrato de su doctrinero, Ledesma, 29 de marzo de 1808," in Proceso contra el cura de la Reducción de San Ignacio de los Tobas, AGN, Sala IX, Criminales, leg. 55, exp. 4 (32.7).

61. Paz, "La liquidación de las instituciones corporativas."

CHAPTER 10

Pueblo and Genízaro Agency in the Preservation of Indigenous Land

NEW MEXICO, 1815–1825

Gary Van Valen

In this chapter, I examine a period in late Spanish and early Mexican New Mexico that was crucial for the preservation of the land base of indigenous people. Between 1815 and 1825, New Mexico experienced something akin to a land rush in which communally used indigenous and public lands became the target of privatization by New Mexico's Hispano elite.[1] This elite had always been interested in land acquisition, but they found new impetus in reinterpretations of colonial law and then in new Spanish liberal theories of private landownership. The land rush reached its height under the administration of locally born Jefe Político (Governor) Bartolomé Baca (1823–25), when a small group of the elite acquired extensive lands on New Mexico's eastern frontier and sought further land by contesting the rights of existing Native American communities to their own land. Indigenous people resorted to available legal mechanisms and managed to maintain their most important lands. The immediate threat ended along with Baca's term of office, but the events of 1815–25 had a lasting effect on New Mexican land tenure. The agency exercised by indigenous people in preserving their land allowed them to retain land into the period of US rule, when they ultimately would be successful in defending their rights in court.

New Mexico was an overwhelmingly rural and relatively poor province on the farthest frontier of New Spain, and most of its inhabitants needed access to land to make a living from agriculture or livestock. The arid environment restricted access to water, the most important resource for both of these activities. Although parts of New Mexico's mountain ranges receive relatively high amounts of rainfall, agriculture there is difficult due to the cold climate and lack of good soil. The Rio Grande, Pecos, and smaller rivers provide sufficient water for irrigation, and their narrow alluvial plains offer the best opportunities for agriculture. Consequently, the most valuable lands lay along the rivers. Severe droughts had forced Ancestral Puebloan people to move from the Colorado Plateau and relocate along these rivers. As the Spanish built their empire on top of preexisting sedentary indigenous societies, they created the province of New Mexico on a bedrock of indigenous settlements, and so the Spanish also remained close to the rivers, stimulating competition for the control of land in the alluvial valleys. Beyond these rivers, the people of Spanish New Mexico adapted to the scarcity of water by raising livestock, principally sheep. Here too, control of the few sources of permanent water provoked competition over the control of land. A true frontier province, New Mexico was completely surrounded by nomadic Apaches, Comanches, Navajos, and Utes. These indigenous peoples not only competed for land, but their resistance to Spanish expansion restricted the territory under actual Spanish control and resulted in further competition for land resources among the growing New Mexican population.

New Mexico's population was made up of many interconnected identities. The Spanish colonists were generally called vecinos (residents) or *paisanos* (countrymen) in contemporary documents. Recent scholars often refer to them and their descendants as Hispanos. Several groups of indigenous peoples also lived in New Mexico. The name Pueblo Indians, or Pueblos, is a cultural umbrella term for the various town-dwelling indigenous peoples, derived from the Spanish name for their permanent towns, "pueblos." Genízaros were largely Plains or Pueblo Indians separated from their original communities, and many arrived in New Mexico in the Spanish frontier slave trade. Their name stems from the Janissaries, the slave-soldiers of the Ottoman Empire, but it came to mean an intermediate socio-racial group. Genízaros could be indigenous or multiethnic in origin, but as with other socio-racial groups, the Spanish authorities determined how the label was applied. Nevertheless, Genízaros were so important in defending New Mexico from its nomadic enemies that the government created several new frontier pueblos for their settlement.[2] The people known as *criados* had similar origins but never gained a separate ethnic identity. They were household servants raised by wealthy families almost as their own children, but with the expectation of subservience and domestic service; they could be orphans, unwanted children, or, especially on this frontier, captured children from independent indigenous groups.

Until recently, scholars considered "Indian" and "vecino" to be mutually exclusive terms. However, some newer research sheds light on the complexity of Pueblo-Spanish relations. James Brooks and Tracy Brown have emphasized that ethnic identities were not unchanging and that not all Pueblos were conservatives fighting to maintain tradition. Many Pueblos became at least partially Hispanized and joined settlements of either Genízaros or Hispanos. Some *ladinos* (Indians fluent in Spanish) left their pueblos permanently, others moved away but maintained ties, and still others continued to reside in pueblos. Brown has even delineated a category of "Indian vecinos," meaning Indians who left their pueblos, adopted private landholding, the Spanish language, and Christianity, and gained legal recognition as vecinos.[3]

The Spanish government of colonial New Mexico recognized landownership through grants made to Pueblo Indians, Spanish vecinos, and Genízaros. Many of the land grants were issued to communities rather than individuals, although these grant recipients used much of their land in common for grazing, gathering firewood, and other purposes. Until the last years of colonial rule, these grants were concentrated along the Rio Grande and a few tributaries, leaving most of the land beyond as ungranted Crown, or public, land, known in Spanish law variously as *realengo, tierras realangas, tierras baldías,* or *baldíos.*[4] Along with the Spanish vecinos, indigenous people (including Pueblos, Genízaros, and nomadic Comanches, Apaches, Navajos, and Utes) made use of the resources of the public lands.

Spanish laws formally protected the land and water rights of incorporated indigenous communities throughout the empire and guaranteed rights to land designated first as *tierras por razón de pueblo* and later as *fundo legal.*[5] The Spanish interpreted these rights differently in different jurisdictions, but in New Mexico, each indigenous pueblo was guaranteed its "league," understood as a square extending one league in each cardinal direction, defining four square leagues of land centered on its church or cemetery cross.[6] After more than two centuries of Spanish rule (1598–1680 and 1693–1821), Pueblos learned something about Spanish legal protections and expected the local authorities to defend their rights. When local Spanish officials failed to dispense justice, Pueblos could appeal to the provincial governor or to even higher authorities in New Spain. Here again, Pueblo activism is a local manifestation of the deep-rooted tradition of often-successful litigation by indigenous communities throughout the viceroyalty of New Spain, especially in Central Mexico, to defend their land rights.[7]

In the second decade of the nineteenth century, a number of conditions changed, allowing Spanish vecinos (who became Mexican citizens after 1821) to engage in a decade-long land rush. By comparing land grant statistics from two periods of New Mexican history, we can arrive at a rough estimate of the dimensions of this land rush. In the period from 1693 to 1814, the Spanish government made sixty-five grants totaling 1,933,557 acres (7,824.83 sq km), with an average size of 29,747 acres (120.38 sq km). In contrast, the Spanish and Mexican governments made nineteen grants in the land rush decade between 1815 and 1825. These grants totaled 2,741,142 acres (11,093.02 sq km), with an average size of 144,271 acres (583.84 sq km). These statistics should be regarded as imperfect, for they exclude several grants whose date or size are uncertain and rely on later US government determinations of their acreage, which often were less than the grant heirs claimed.[8] Nevertheless, in 1815–25 there is a clear trend of larger grants, and of a larger total area of land granted, than in the previous 121 years. In addition, none of the nineteen grants made between 1815 and 1825 were made to people who identified as Pueblo or Genízaro.

Elite Hispano New Mexicans found inspiration in the liberalism expressed in the actions of the Spanish Cortes of Cádiz (1810–14), the revolutionary congress that assembled during the Napoleonic occupation of Spain and the absence of its Bourbon monarchs. Article 18 of the 1812 Constitution of Cádiz declared that all those with ancestry on both sides from the Spanish dominions, and residing in those dominions, would be Spanish citizens. Europeans born in Spain or the Spanish colonies, Indians, and mestizos thus became equal citizens under the law, with the consequence that none could claim special legal privileges.[9] Since liberal reformers argued that individuals motivated by self-interest would make more efficient use of land than was possible under communal or public tenure, the Cortes began debating the status of these lands. Its law of November 9, 1812, reflected a compromise solution. It ordered the division of the uncultivated lands of Indian pueblos throughout Spanish America, allowing that up to one-half of community lands be divided and put under individual ownership, but only if the community lands were large and the population small. Other community lands and private lands would not be affected. A further law of January 4, 1813, encouraged the privatization of "vacant" public land and "surplus" communal lands (*tierras sobrantes*), and empowered provincial governors to transfer such to private owners. However, community lands deemed "necessary" for a pueblo were not to be divided.[10]

In New Mexico, the Constitution of Cádiz was in effect in 1813–15 and again in 1820–22; independent Mexico replaced it in 1822, but Mexican laws continued to promote liberal ideas of private landholding. Elite Hispano New Mexicans attempted to expand their individual holdings by arguing for the privatization of both community grants and public lands in these years. In fact, regardless of the new justification for acquiring more land, members of the Hispano elite had already begun challenging indigenous landownership several years earlier. Disputes over land began in a fairly standard colonial fashion (over the exact boundaries of Pueblo leagues and over lands outside their leagues), but evolved to incorporate new ideas, sometimes in unexpected ways. As I shall show, different governors took vastly different positions toward protecting Indian land or supporting vecino acquisition of land. Governor Joaquín del Real Alencaster (1804–7), for example, took a number of actions favoring vecinos over Indians, including compelling the sale of Pueblo land, moving Pueblo league boundary markers, and attempting to prohibit the trade between Genízaros and Comanches.[11] Certain of these actions led to an especially acrimonious dispute between Cochiti Pueblo and the vecinos who encroached on its lands. This dispute formed the prelude to the land rush per se, and Cochiti's legal reclamations ironically resulted in the vecinos' discovery of new tactics to contest Indian land claims, and in New Mexican governors' willingness to implement laws restricting Indian land rights. In response, indigenous people also learned new tactics to defend their lands. The next section of this essay will revisit the fairly well-studied legal case surrounding Cochiti Pueblo with an eye to finding the origins of the Hispano elite's land rush in both their actions and those of the Pueblo Indians.[12]

THE LATE COLONIAL CASE OF COCHITI

The origin of the Cochiti land dispute lay in two transfers of land from Cochiti Pueblo to Spanish vecinos that occurred in 1804 and 1806. On February 14, 1804, the *común* (commonwealth) and *naturales* (natives) of Cochiti, through the vecino don Joaquín Pérez Gavilán, sold the tract called Peña Blanca (south of the pueblo league) to the vecino Luis María Cabeza de Baca in exchange for sixteen cattle and horses. According to later testimony by members of

Cochiti Pueblo, they sold the land under compulsion and unwillingly, under an order of Governor Alencaster enacted by *alcalde ordinario* and *capitán de la guerra* Anacleto de Miera y Pacheco (son of the cartographer and alcalde mayor of Pecos, Bernardo de Miera y Pacheco). The tenor of the order was for Miera y Pacheco to go to the Indians and order them to sell the land to Cabeza de Baca without protest, then for Miera y Pacheco to draw up a legal document of the sale. The order also directed Miera y Pacheco immediately to bind and bring to the jail any Pueblo leader (*cabezilla*) who opposed this action. Cabeza de Baca, who had the protection of Alencaster, also took possession of Ogito de Agua (also referred to as Ojo de Santa Cruz), a tract to the east of Cochiti's league, which had been purchased by Cochiti in 1744.[13] The Pueblo of Santo Domingo (Kewa), located to the south of Cochiti, claimed a portion of Peña Blanca and a common boundary with Cochiti lands. Governor Fernando de la Concha (1788–94) had commissioned the Santa Fe vecino don Antonio José Ortiz to mark the Santo Domingo boundary with Cochiti, and these markers remained in place until Governor Alencaster had them moved more than one thousand varas (yards, or roughly meters) to the south to facilitate the transfer of Peña Blanca.[14] The second transfer of land from Cochiti to Spanish vecinos occurred on August 19, 1806, when Pedro Bautista Pino, alcalde ordinario of Santa Fe, brought notice (*hizo comparecer*) to Cochiti governor (*gobernadorcillo*) Santiago Coris; *apoderado* Juan Roque Yurena; Francisco Caiso; Antonio, alias el Chino; and Juan Domingo Carnero about the sale of another nearby tract, the rancho of Sile to the southwest of Cochiti, to Antonio José Ortiz.[15] The dispute arose because in the middle of the rancho of Sile were 540 varas of land sold to "the Indians who were from there, and now are vecinos," whose names were José Archibeque, Felipe Santiago, [Juan] José Quintana, Antonio Jaulesgua, and Domingo.[16] These individuals are examples of the Indian vecinos studied by Tracy Brown. Juan José Quintana, who became the most important representative of Cochiti, is also identified as Indian in some documents and as vecino in others.[17]

In 1810, Juan José Quintana discovered that Spanish law provided for a *protector partidario de indios* to help Indians bring legal proceedings against Spaniards (the post was authorized for New Mexico but had been vacant since 1716). Quintana then helped choose New Mexico's protector partidario by writing to Comandante General Nemesio Salcedo of the Provincias Internas (Interior Provinces) in the name of all of the Pueblos, to request that don Felipe Sandoval be named protector partidario. Sandoval, a vecino of the largely Genízaro pueblo of San Miguel del Bado on the Pecos River, had earned the respect of indigenous people by opposing Governor Alencaster's attempt to prohibit the Comanche trade. Quintana misunderstood the colonial bureaucracy: the protector partidario was subject to and appointed by the Audiencia (high court) of Guadalajara rather than the comandante general in Chihuahua, who was the New Mexican governor's superior. Nevertheless, the comandante general forwarded Quintana's letter to the audiencia, which concurred with the Pueblos' choice and named Sandoval protector.[18]

Having been chosen at least partially because of Quintana's activism, Felipe Sandoval filed a complaint on behalf of Cochiti on June 26, 1812, stating that the sale of Peña Blanca to Luis María Cabeza de Baca was coerced. Soon thereafter, in mid-1812, Governor José Manrique (1808–14) ordered Cabeza de Baca to evacuate the land without compensation. The Spanish hacendado promptly appealed this decision to Manrique's superior, but on October 1, 1812, the comandante general ruled against Cabeza de Baca.[19] Nevertheless, Cabeza de Baca continued unmolested at Peña Blanca until March 1815.

On March 14, 1815, Luis María's son Juan Antonio Cabeza de Baca wrote from Peña Blanca to New Mexico governor Alberto Maynez (1814–16) that he had received an order from "el justicia deste partido" (the local government official, or alcalde) that he and his father should not touch the land beyond Cochiti's boundary marker, which the alcalde Juan José Gutiérrez had built at the direction of Governor Manrique a few years earlier. Juan Antonio Cabeza de Baca claimed that Manrique later ordered the boundary moved back to where an earlier alcalde, José de Miera, had located it. As the Cabeza de Bacas possessed houses and farmland in the disputed land, Juan Antonio stated that they would demand four thousand pesos in compensation if they were forced to move. He also claimed to have the support of the Cochiti governor and most of its people and asserted that the only troublemakers were Juan José Quintana and his partisans.[20] Elsewhere, I have argued that this Cochiti governor was Juan Antonio Ignacio Baca (an ally and a possible relative of the Cabeza de Bacas), and that the land dispute was accompanied by a factional dispute within Cochiti.[21]

Because Santo Domingo claimed part of Peña Blanca, the people of this pueblo also took action to assert their rights. In March 1815, the *hijos del pueblo* of Santo Domingo wrote to Protector Sandoval requesting the measurement of the northern limits of their league with the help of Interim Governor Maynez. The signatories on behalf of Santo Domingo—Governor Juan José Martínez, Teniente (Lieutenant Governor) Baltazar Domínguez, Antonio Alonso, and Juan Ignacio Montoya—gave a brief history of their boundary disputes. They recounted how despite repeatedly asking Governor Manrique to measure the limits of their league, they had only been able to get don Mariano de la Peña to mark them, and only on the pueblo (east) side of the Rio Grande. They mentioned that Antonio José Ortiz had marked the Santo Domingo boundary with Cochiti in the time of Governor Concha and that Governor Alencaster had moved the markers more than one thousand varas.[22] On April 13, the people of Santo Domingo again requested the measurement of their league, as well as the one hundred varas of land they had purchased, and asked permission to appeal to another tribunal if refused.[23] When Alcalde Juan José Gutiérrez measured the league on April 19, he found that most of Ortiz's Sile property (now inherited by his son, Santa Fe vecino Antonio Ortiz) lay within Santo Domingo land. Ortiz later appealed this finding to Coman- dante General Bernardo Bonavía in September.[24]

On April 26, 1815, after meeting with the Cochiti *justicias* and princi- pales, the protector, and the alcalde of the partido of Alameda in his house, Governor Maynez ordered Luis María Cabeza de Baca to move off of the contested property. Cabeza de Baca agreed to leave his houses and other improvements to the Indians after harvesting the current year's crops.[25] Maynez added that the hacendado could recuperate the sixteen animals he had paid Cochiti for the forced sale.[26] On May 23, 1815, Cabeza de Baca peti- tioned the governor for a grant of land at Ojo del Espíritu Santo west of Jemez Pueblo on "being compelled to withdraw my animals to avoid difficulties with the Quintarsas [i.e., Quintanas] Indians." On May 24, Maynez granted Cabeza de Baca's request, no doubt hoping he would leave Peña Blanca to the Pueblos. Previously, in 1766, Ojo del Espíritu Santo had been granted to Jemez, Zia, and Santa Ana Pueblos for their joint use, so Cabeza de Baca not only acquired this former Pueblo land, he also reneged on his promise to leave Peña Blanca.[27] Nevertheless, it appears that Quintana's faction man- aged to expel Juan Antonio Ignacio Baca as governor of Cochiti, for the latter traveled to Durango to present a complaint to Comandante General Bonavía in October 1815.[28]

In 1816, the legal process took an unexpected turn for the Pueblos when the vecinos began to question the validity of the interpretation of the pueblo league as four square leagues. There are at least two reasons for this. One is that Pedro Bautista Pino, while serving as New Mexico's delegate to the Span- ish Cortes, had learned from its Overseas Committee in April 1813 that no law required a pueblo to be given four square leagues.[29] The other is that when

Luis María Cabeza de Baca appealed his case against the Pueblos in Durango in March 1816, lawyers from other parts of the audiencia district of Guadalajara became involved, and they knew that in other parts of that district, Indian towns were guaranteed only one square league.[30] Thus, when on March 18, 1816, Luis María Cabeza de Baca protested Cochiti's claims though his lawyer, Rafael Bracho, the latter defended Cabeza de Baca's claim by stating that "the league conceded to the pueblos for community land should not be one [league] in each cardinal direction [*viento*], *but rather one-half*, in conformity with the Laws of the Indies." Another Spanish official clearly took note of Bracho's argument, for *ojo* (attention) is written in the margin.[31] Bracho later reiterated that "all the pueblos of Indians of these provinces enjoy and must enjoy one league of land divided *in half in each cardinal direction* [viento]."[32]

The Cochiti Indians did not remain idle in the face of this new development, which threatened to undermine their legal arguments for lands outside the pueblo league and to reduce the area of their league, or fundo legal, itself by three-quarters. On August 16, 1816, Juan José Quintana, Antonio Quintana (with the military title of general), Santiago Coris (also with the title of general), Cacique José Antonio Saya, and "various other hijos" visited the Indian protector of Durango, José Joaquín Reyes, who wrote in favor of their claims and doubtless informed them of the existence of the Audiencia of Mexico's General Indian Court (Juzgado General de Indios) as a possible further recourse.[33] Unfortunately for Cochiti, Reyes also opined they had a right only to "a league, divided in half in each direction."[34] On September 26, 1816, four Cochiti representatives traveled to Mexico City to present their case before the General Indian Court; they included Antonio Quintana (recognized as a retired army captain), don Santiago Coris, and others listed simply as Manuel Domingo and Francisco.[35] Despite this extensive travel by the Cochiti representatives in search of judicial recourse, both the General Indian Court (on October 23), and an official named Pinilla in Durango (on October 30) decided that Cochiti's case should be presented to the Audiencia of Guadalajara as part of the normal process to appeal a ruling of the New Mexico governor in his capacity as *subdelegado juez real*.[36]

With the case now before the Audiencia of Guadalajara, its judge, Dr. Francisco Antonio de Landa, on December 31, 1816, ordered Governor Maynez to measure the leagues of both Cochiti and Santo Domingo Pueblos because of litigation over the sites of Sile, Peña Blanca, and Ojo de Santa Cruz. On May 10, 1817, Governor Maynez's successor, Pedro María de Allande (who favored vecinos over Indians), appointed a commission of Spanish vecinos to measure the Cochiti and Santo Domingo leagues, and named Vicente Villanueva to act as protector in place of the deceased Felipe Sandoval.[37]

The Pueblos, fully aware that the vecinos' new interpretation of the fundo legal reduced their land base, now resisted the measurement of their leagues. On May 12, 1817, the Indians of Santo Domingo, showing "blind obedience" to their gobernadorcillo and to their principal Juan Diego Coris, told the commission that they did not want a new measurement of their league.[38] Nevertheless, the commission (accompanied by Gobernadorcillo Coris and other Indians) measured south from the cemetery cross first "the half league that by right belongs to this republic" and marked it with a *mojonera* (cairn), then continued "measuring the other half league that said natives considered theirs," which they marked in the same way.[39] The commission also measured 3,750 varas farther south to the border of the Pueblo of San Felipe, for in between the two pueblos was land Governor Pedro Fermín de Mendinueta (1767–78) had granted jointly to both.[40] On the next day, the commission measured north from Santo Domingo and marked with mojoneras "the half league belonging to said natives" as well as the one-league point. The one-league mark was the boundary of the land of José Miguel de la Peña. They then measured to the east and again marked the half-league and one-league points, the latter at the boundary of "Lo de Basquez" of the heirs of Antonio José Ortiz. Next, measuring to the west across the Rio Grande, they again marked the half-league and one-league points, the latter at the boundary with the land of Nereo Antonio Montoya. From this westernmost point, they then measured another line from the latitude of the cemetery cross to the south to the boundaries of Los Fernández, and to the north to the boundaries of Antonio Ortiz, marking the half-league and one-league points. The commission found that Antonio Ortiz's land was outside the league claimed by the Indians and declared that an earlier measurement of the league by "Don Juan José Gutiérrez, who was alcalde of said pueblo" was mistaken and invalid. The rancho of Ortiz (the Sile property originally sold to the now-deceased Ortiz), was declared outside Santo Domingo's league, and Gutiérrez, who accompanied the commission, admitted his measurement was mistaken "for having made said measurements according to the will of the natives and of their protector."[41]

The next day, on May 14, the commission began work at Cochiti after informing its natives; Luis María Cabeza de Baca was present. The commissioners measured to the north, marked the half-league and one-league points, and ended at the property of the settlement of La Cañada de Cochiti. They measured to the west, ending at the property of Nereo Antonio Montoya. At this point, Interim Protector Villanueva presented a petition to delay the measurements to the east and south. Pedro Bautista Pino, the head of the commission, suspended further measurement until he could examine certain documents. Pino decided that the Indians had been "seduced by their deceased protector" Felipe Sandoval and that they had indeed sold land to Cabeza de Baca as well as to eighteen other families.[42] Villanueva then presented another document, signed by himself and by Juan José Quintana for the "republic" of Cochiti, which stated that the measurements made at Santo Domingo could not be repeated in Cochiti because the latter pueblo only had community lands on the west side of the Rio Grande. The land on the east side, touching Santo Domingo on the south and Santa Cruz on the north, had been sold to Los Fernández for 1,500 pesos and other east-bank land had been sold to Juana Baca. The document stated that Cochiti had insisted on measuring their league because their deceased protector had persuaded them that their league was part of their royal patrimony, which would supersede any subsequent land sales. It went on to say that Cochiti accepted that they had been misled by their deceased protector and they only wanted peace with Luis María Cabeza de Baca.[43]

The Pueblos had clearly recognized the vecinos' intent in marking the half-league points at Santo Domingo and part of Cochiti and, with the help of their protector, were now attempting to save their original leagues. Villanueva and Quintana agreed to blame the deceased Sandoval for inciting the land dispute and to desist from their reclamations against Cabeza de Baca. One vecino however tried to press for the application of the new interpretation of the league. On May 16, Ignacio María Sánchez Vergara wrote that Santo Domingo could not claim more than a half league in each direction, asked Pino to declare the "excess" land part of the realengo, and also claimed that the land Governor Mendinueta had granted to Santo Domingo and San Felipe was uncultivated and therefore should also be declared part of the realengo. He asked that the same be done with Cochiti's land beyond the half league that it was permitted by law. As Ebright, Hendricks, and Hughes have pointed out, Sánchez Vergara was motivated by self-interest, since he desired this "excess" land for himself.[44]

The Audiencia of Guadalajara, which had final say in the case, eventually decided in favor of Cochiti's land claims, but the situation on the ground remained the same. Although Cabeza de Baca was forced to pay the court costs, he remained on the disputed land. On the other hand, nothing came of Sánchez Vergara's opinion, and the pueblos retained their four square leagues.[45] Both sides essentially adhered to the agreement reached on May 14, 1817. The vecinos emerged from the struggle with all of their originally disputed property intact, and their ability to ignore the final decision of the audiencia presaged greater local power yet to come.

MEXICAN INDEPENDENCE AND FURTHER COMPETITION OVER LAND

Mexican independence in 1821 brought little change in policy, as Mexico continued to follow the laws enacted by the Spanish Cortes. Nevertheless, independence allowed local elites greater access to power, as they sat in a provincial (later territorial) legislature called the Diputación Provincial and some served as New Mexican governor. The Hispano elite remained hungry for land, and Genízaros now found their access to land and its resources under threat. The idea that communal land was now divisible and alienable began to be put into practice in at least some Genízaro pueblos. In April 1822, the Genízaro naturales of the Pueblo of Abiquiu informed Jefe Político Facundo Melgares that they had paid their parish priest with a piece of their community land. Melgares brought the matter to the diputación, which decided to annul the land transfer and return the land to the community, while allowing the priest to claim payment by some other means.[46]

The Genízaro people of San Miguel del Bado saw their rights to use common public land for pasture diminished several times, a process that had begun even before Mexican independence. When Antonio Ortiz (the owner of the Sile rancho) petitioned Governor Melgares for a land grant on the Gallinas River in 1818, the governor asked Vicente Villanueva, then serving as alcalde of El Bado, if the land was vacant. Villanueva replied yes, but that the grant would hurt future growth of El Bado's livestock. Notwithstanding, tax assessor Francisco Ignacio de Madariaga declared that the grant would not hurt any third party, and Melgares issued the grant on April 30, 1819. Francisco Ortiz, the new alcalde of El Bado, gave possession to Antonio Ortiz's agent on June 8, 1819.[47] Ortiz's grant was in fact prejudicial to San Miguel del Bado, as the settlement was growing rapidly in the early nineteenth century as it took over Pecos Pueblo's former role as gateway to the Plains. As part of this shift, the priest assigned to Pecos moved his residence to San Miguel del Bado in 1812, and members of Pecos Pueblo moved there as well.[48] Any obstacle between the people of San Miguel and the Plains would be an annoyance as, according to John L. Kessell, "For the average mixed-blood or genízaro who drew a plot of ground at El Vado in 1803, it was not the prospect of a good year for maize or beans that excited him most, but rather the vision of hunting or trading on the plains."[49]

Under the administration of Jefe Político Bartolomé Baca (1823–25), an accelerated land rush took place on New Mexico's eastern frontier. In many ways, Bartolomé Baca's previous life exemplified the career of an hacendado from the Río Abajo region, the rich valley of the middle Rio Grande. A captain of one of the three militia companies created in 1808, he was still serving in that capacity in 1810.[50] He was wealthy, as demonstrated by his being one of the few major contributors to an 1815 wartime loan to the royal government, providing one hundred pesos.[51] Based at San Fernando near Tomé in the *alcaldía* of Belen, he was captain of the Albuquerque militia in 1819, when he petitioned Governor Melgares for land east of the Manzano Mountains. The grant was approved, and Baca was given possession by Alcalde of Tomé José García de la Mora. Baca continued living at his hacienda at San Fernando, but he also built a house on his new grant (at the present Estancia Springs), and his sons José, Juan, and Manuel lived there until Navajo raids made them abandon it in 1833.[52] As the Bartolomé Baca Grant included the salt lakes traditionally used (with much religious ceremony) by several Rio Grande pueblos, a grant of even seemingly unoccupied land could threaten indigenous access to traditional resources.

On December 20, 1823, Governor Baca presented the Diputación Provincial with another request for land on the Gallinas River, this time from Santa Fe vecino and son of Pedro Bautista Pino, Juan Esteban Pino, who incidentally had just joined the diputación as a *vocal* (representative) three days previously. The diputación, with Baca as president, quickly approved Pino's request for the Hacienda de San Juan Bautista del Ojito del Río de las Gallinas (later known as the Preston Beck Grant), extending from the southern limits of Ortiz's grant to the Pecos River. The diputación demonstrated how liberalism could be used to justify the privatization of land by stating that "from the preoccupation with not assigning [private] properties from the common lands, resulted all or the greater part of the backwardness in the agriculture and industry of this province."[53]

Pino was able to defend his claim to this highly desirable land against other petitioners because of the support of the diputación. Only twenty days after the diputación granted the land to Pino, it rejected a petition for the same land from Santiago Ulibarrí, advising him to "solicit and register land that is baldío and does not belong to a specific subject."[54] Then, on February 13, 1824, the diputación received a communication from the alcalde of the *ayuntamiento* (town council) of San Miguel del Bado "making a protest that the inhabitants of El Bado are preferred in that land, and declaring that His Excellency has given that site to the citizen Juan Esteban Pino ignoring the harm it caused to the province and granting land which belongs to the grant of El Bado." The diputación instructed the alcalde to remit the grant of El Bado and other documents to demonstrate their preference to the baldíos.[55] El Bado's response came on April 12 in a letter from the El Bado citizen and vecino Manuel Antonio Baca, who claimed to hold power of attorney for the town, "referring to the general harm that the province, for which he speaks, will receive by giving the site of Gallinas to don Juan Esteban Pino." The diputación dismissed this request, responding that Manuel Antonio Baca was not a member of the El Bado Ayuntamiento and that he had not submitted proof of his power of attorney or any other documents proving El Bado's claim.[56]

The vocales' sarcastic comment that Manuel Antonio Baca spoke for the province reveals something of their derision for this spokesman for lower-class Genízaros who challenged their vision for New Mexico. In many ways, Governor Baca represented the rise of local hacendado interests, and his actions benefited people like himself. On one occasion, he even denied a petition for land between the Rio Grande and the Pecos River, claiming that all of that land was reserved for the use of Plains Indians during their visits. This was patently false, since Baca's own grant of 1819 occupied part of this very area. Obviously, Baca's herds grazed beyond his grant's boundaries, and he acted to prevent competition for grazing. By 1826, however, the excesses of the hacendados had been restrained by Jefe Político y Militar Antonio Narbona (1825–27). In that year, the diputación rejected Juan Esteban Pino's request that his mayordomo be allowed to administer justice on the Hacienda de San Juan Bautista del Ojito del Río de las Gallinas as unconstitutional, suggesting that the *alcalde constitucional* of El Bado could appoint a *comisionado* instead.[57] With Narbona as its president, the diputación was not about to allow hacendados to become feudal lords on their domains.

Pecos Pueblo's lands became a target for land-hungry vecinos who manipulated liberal laws on landownership, creating a struggle that David Weber and Emlen Hall studied in a 1984 *New Mexico Historical Review* article. Specifically, vecinos began using the law of November 9, 1812, to argue that, as the Pecos population was small, half of its communal lands could be divided and granted to individuals. The earliest such petitions in 1821 were not acted on by the government.[58] Then, on February 16, 1824, Bartolomé Baca presented the diputación with a vecino petition for lands "in the land that the few naturales, to which the old and great pueblo of Pecos has today been reduced, do not cultivate." The diputación decided that Baca would hear from the Pecos leaders and inform the diputación about the state of the Pecos church and lands, as well as how much land the petitioning individuals would need. On March 12, Baca reported that the Pecos naturales claimed that they needed all of their farmland for their subsistence, and the diputación decided to deny the non-Indian land petitions.[59] However, by one year later its position had changed, and the legislators decided to use the law of November 9, 1812, to divide the Pecos lands on March 3, 1825.[60] On March 19, the diputación read lists of the individuals who received portions of the Pecos land, which included ten Indian heads of families, eleven vecino heads of families, and seventeen individuals who would receive parts of the sobrantes. The diputación then appointed a commission to verify and mark the division of Pecos land, planning for the Pecos Indians and poor vecinos to pay the commissioners for their work in handing land over to outsiders. So as not to "bother" the Indians and vecinos, the diputación resolved that "their work be paid for with the same excess land that is not included in one or another of the above mentioned."[61] On November 17, 1825, Antonio Narbona, as president of the Diputación Territorial, read a petition from the naturales of Pecos Pueblo asking that their customary land extending one league in the four directions be declared their "immemorial property." The diputación decided to send the petition to the Supreme Government in Mexico City for its interpretation of Article 5 of the law of November 9, 1812, along with an explanation of why the diputación had not treated other pueblos' land in the same fashion. On November 8, Francisco Ignacio de Madariaga clarified the previous day's discussion by adding that "the lands which the Pecos reclaimed are the same ones that this diputación had ordered to be divided among they themselves, giving the remainder to the vecinos that solicited them."[62]

Although the land rush ended for most of New Mexico in 1825, Pecos Pueblo's troubles continued for several years. The pueblo made its own petition in March 1826.[63] Later in 1826, Jefe Político y Militar Narbona and the diputación were still corresponding with the Ministry of Relations about the rights of Pecos Indians and the lands given to non-Indians.[64] Despite several more years of activism by Pecos Pueblo, the actions taken by the Bartolomé Baca government had tipped the scales in favor of vecinos. Pecos filed another petition in 1829, asking that their rights to their property be recognized because they were Mexican citizens. The diputación supported them, but Pecos community member José Cota soon sold part of the league on September 22, 1830, to Juan Esteban Pino.[65]

No other pueblo faced the same fate as Pecos, even though the Baca administration initially advocated for the division of other pueblos' lands based on liberal arguments. On February 16, 1824 (the same day that the diputación first considered petitions for Pecos land), the vocales also read three petitions by eighteen individuals soliciting farmland "in that which is baldío" of the lands of Santo Domingo and San Felipe pueblos. The diputación named José Francisco Ortiz to examine the lands and charged him with "making those naturales understand that His Excellency can dispose of those lands and procure that progress of the decadent agriculture of this vast territory."[66] On March 12, Ortiz reported that he had found three-quarters of a league of "excess lands" at Santo Domingo and San Felipe, but that "those naturales said that said land had been given to them for pasture for their animals." Disregarding the Pueblos' claims, the diputación resolved that Baca, Ortiz, and several other individuals would go to the two pueblos to divide their community lands "in order that each person, recognizing their [private] property, may dispose of it with the same liberty as other citizens, and that in virtue of this division, the excess land that remains will be disposed of on the best terms."[67] These plans were unrealized, however, presumably due to Narbona's taking office in September 1825. Yet even before Narbona's arrival, the vocales had become reluctant to take land from Indian pueblos. On July 19, 1825, when several individuals asked for the "excess" land of Nambé Pueblo, the diputación decided to remit their petition to the Ayuntamiento of La Cañada for information about how the Nambés were using the land of their league.[68] There is no record of any further attempt to divide Nambé lands after this.

Under the Narbona administration, the diputación declined to act when vecinos petitioned for pueblos' sobrantes. Juan Diego Sena petitioned on September 15, 1825, that he and several other individuals be given the "excess" land of the "Ciudadanos Naturales" of San Juan Pueblo. The diputación resolved "to not take this or other petitions of its tenor into consideration, until the Supreme Government of the federation is consulted, asking for a general resolution in a matter of such transcendence."[69] Narbona's administration was the immediate reason that the early nineteenth-century land rush came to an end, yet ten years of indigenous action in defense of their lands was certainly just as important. The agency exercised by indigenous people allowed them to preserve most of their lands during this period.

CONCLUSION

The decade from 1815 to 1825 was an important episode in indigenous-Hispano relations. As I have shown, members of the Hispano elite used three different tactics in their quest for land. In 1816–17, they attempted to reduce the pueblo leagues of Cochiti and Santo Domingo from four square leagues to one by arguing that Spanish law stipulated the smaller figure. In 1821–25, they used the Cortes of Cádiz's law of November 9, 1812, to petition for the division of "excess" communal land at Pecos, Santo Domingo, San Felipe, Nambé, and San Juan. In 1819–25, members of the Hispano elite petitioned for, and were granted, several huge properties on New Mexico's eastern frontier. Pueblo Indians and Genízaros struggled against many of these land acquisitions and attempted usurpations, with Pecos and El Bado arguably losing the most. Vecinos were most successful in their bid to privatize public land on the frontier, but even this land rush came to a halt in 1825. Both the Hispano elite and indigenous people learned from this episode. Bartolomé Baca's policy of granting large parcels of public land to private individuals on the eastern frontier would be revived by another hacendado-turned-governor, Manuel Armijo, from 1837 to 1844. Armijo's preference for this method of transferring land was not an accident: he chose the option that had provoked the least resistance from indigenous people in 1815–25. Despite occasional attempts by Hispanos to acquire Pueblo and Genízaro land after 1825, these indigenous people did not face such a concerted attack on their lands again under Mexican rule. Their lands survived to face other challenges under the US administration, which the indigenous people would eventually win.

NOTES

1. I use the term "land rush" in a broad sense that includes rapid accumulations of land by elites at moments in Latin American history, and do not intend a strict comparison with the openings of Oklahoma land in 1889–95, which are commonly called land rushes or land runs. For the use of "land rush" for elite accumulation of land during the Spanish colonization of Mexico, see Sluyter, "Ecological Origins and Consequences," 173; Sluyter, "From Archive to Map," 513. For use of the term in the Mexican Porfiriato, see Cook and Lindau, *Aboriginal Rights and Self-Government,*

12; and for the Argentine Pampas, see Hamill, *Caudillos*, 81. For a global treatment of Anglophone settler colonies that makes a brief comparison with Argentina, see Weaver, *Great Land Rush*.

2. See Rivaya Martínez, "Reflexión historiográfica."

3. Brooks, *Captives and Cousins*; Brown, "Tradition and Change." Juan Roque Perico of Sandia Pueblo was an example of an Indian vecino; see Spanish Archives of New Mexico (hereafter SANM) II, R. 17, Fr. 846–54 (including "Acta de elección de parroquia of Pueblo of Sandia," January 30, 1814); "Testimony of Juan Roque Perico," April 17, 1819, SANM II, R. 19, Fr. 659–61; Brown, "Tradition and Change," 479.

4. Vassberg, "*Tierras Baldías*."

5. See Wood, "*Fundo Legal* or Lands *Por Razón de Pueblo*."

6. Brayer, *Pueblo Indian Grants*, 8–16; Hall and Weber, "Mexican Liberals," 5–6; Ebright, Hendricks, and Hughes, *Four Square Leagues*, 6–7, 11–12. In Sonora, Indian pueblos were also assigned four square leagues; see Escandón, "La nueva administración misional," 333; Río, "El noroeste novohispano," 277–78.

7. For a historiography of the defense of indigenous land rights in New Spain, see Castro Gutiérrez, "Los ires y devenires," 69–104.

8. Statistics compiled from Williams, *New Mexico in Maps*, 105.

9. Weber, *Mexican Frontier*, 16–17; "Constitución política de la Monarquía Española: promulgada en Cádiz á 19 de Marzo de 1812," accessed August 6, 2020, http://www.cervantesvirtual.com/nd/ark:/59851/bmcx34r3; Ebright, Hendricks, and Hughes, *Four Square Leagues*, 28–29.

10. Royal decree of April 22, 1820 (republication of the Cortes' decree of November 9, 1812), SANM II, R. 20, Fr. 196; Hall and Weber, "Mexican Liberals," 8–10; "Constitución política de la Monarquía Española"; Ebright, Hendricks, and Hughes, *Four Square Leagues*, 29.

11. Kessell, *Kiva, Cross, and Crown*, 434–35; "Los naturales del pueblo de Cochití solicitaron la nulidad de la venta de un rancho situado en su fundo legal; además, presentaron autos sobre la usurpación de otro terreno," Ramo Civil, Año 1816, caja 261, exp. 15, progresivo 3564, Biblioteca Pública del Estado de Jalisco Juan José Arreola (hereafter, cited as "Los naturales . . . de Cochití"). I thank Anne Barnhart of the University of West Georgia Ingram Library for obtaining a copy of this document.

12. Previous treatments of this land case include Twitchell, *Spanish Archives*, 1:360, 372–73, 432–35; Brayer, *Pueblo Indian Grants*, 111, 116–22; Taylor, "Cochití Lands"; Cutter, *Protector de Indios*, 1–2, 88–93; Ebright, Hendricks, and Hughes, *Four Square Leagues*, 169–86; Van Valen, "In Search of Juan."

13. "Los naturales . . . de Cochití." For the Miera y Pacheco family, see Kessell, *Miera y Pacheco*.

14. "Los naturales . . . de Cochití."

15. "Los naturales . . . de Cochití."

16. "Los naturales . . . de Cochití."

17. Nemesio Salcedo to Interim Governor of New Mexico, March 21, 1810, R. 17, fr. 52–53, SANM II; Petition of Juan José Quintana, José Archibeque, Antonio, and Felipe, Indians of Cochiti, February 3, 1812, R. 17, fr. 477, SANM II.

18. In SANM II, R. 17: Nemesio Salcedo to Interim Governor of New Mexico, March 21, 1810, fr. 52–53; letter of Governor of New Mexico, May 31, 1810, fr. 116–17; letter of Vicente Alonzo Andrade, Fiscal and Protector General de Indios of Audiencia of Guadalajara, August 20, 1810, fr. 179–80; Kessell, *Kiva, Cross, and Crown*, 434–35; Frank, review of *The Protector*, 291.

19. Taylor, "Cochití Lands," 52, 57–58.

20. Juan Antonio [Cabeza de] Baca to Governor Alberto Maynez, March 14, 1815, R. 6, SANM I, fr. 1655–56.

21. Van Valen, "In Search of Juan."

22. "Los naturales . . . de Cochití"; Ebright, Hendricks, and Hughes, *Four Square Leagues*, 171.

23. Fray Antonio Caballero to Governor Alberto Maynez, April 13, 1815, R. 18, SANM II, fr. 42.

24. Ebright, Hendricks, and Hughes, *Four Square Leagues*, 21.

25. "Los naturales . . . de Cochití"; Ebright, Hendricks, and Hughes, *Four Square Leagues*, 171.

26. "Los naturales . . . de Cochití."

27. Cutter, *Protector de Indios*, 89; Taylor, "Cochití Lands," 59; US Congress, House, *New Mexico—Private Land Claim of the Heirs of Luis Maria C. de Baca*, 2–5; Bayer, *Santa Ana*.

28. Comandante General Bernardo Bonavía to Interim Governor Pedro María de Allande, October 20, 1815, R. 18, SANM II, fr. 252–53; Van Valen, "In Search of Juan," 74.

29. Hall and Weber, "Mexican Liberals," 10.

30. In territory subject to the Audiencia of Guadalajara, the term *fundo legal* was used for all community lands, the term *ejido* was not used, and towns were to receive a site one league long. Near Guadalajara, this was interpreted as one square league with the town in the center, but in New Mexico, communities received four square leagues centered on the town's church or cemetery cross. See Taylor, "Cochití Lands," 44–45; Radding, *Wandering Peoples*, 358–59.

31. "Los naturales . . . de Cochití"; Ebright, Hendricks, and Hughes, *Four Square Leagues*, 172.

32. "Los naturales . . . de Cochití." Emphasis in original.

33. "Los naturales . . . de Cochití."

34. Ebright, Hendricks, and Hughes, *Four Square Leagues*, 172.

35. "Los naturales . . . de Cochití."

36. "Los naturales . . . de Cochití."

37. Dr. José Blas Abadiano y Jasso to Alberto Maynez, February 8, 1817, R. 6, fr. 1664–66, SANM I; Pedimiento and auto of Rafael Cuentas, January 31, 1817; Cutter, *Protector de Indios*, 91; Taylor, "Cochití Lands," 54, 61; Ebright, Hendricks, and Hughes, *Four Square Leagues*, 173.

38. "Los naturales de los pueblos . . . de Santo Domingo y Cochití en los autos contra don Antonio Ortiz y don Luis María Cabeza de Vaca sobre propiedad de tierras," Ramo Civil, Año 1816, caja 267, exp. 19, progresivo 3658. Biblioteca Pública del Estado

de Jalisco Juan José Arreola (hereafter cited as "Los naturales de los pueblos"); Ebright, Hendricks, and Hughes, *Four Square Leagues*, 173.

39. "Los naturales de los pueblos"; Ebright, Hendricks, and Hughes, *Four Square Leagues*, 173–74, see also 13–14 for a description of how leagues were measured on the ground.

40. "Los naturales de los pueblos"; Ebright, Hendricks, and Hughes, *Four Square Leagues*, 174.

41. "Los naturales de los pueblos."

42. "Los naturales de los pueblos"; Ebright, Hendricks, and Hughes, *Four Square Leagues*, 174.

43. "Los naturales de los pueblos"; Ebright, Hendricks, and Hughes, *Four Square Leagues*, 174.

44. "Los naturales de los pueblos"; Ebright, Hendricks, and Hughes, *Four Square Leagues*, 174–76.

45. Report of Interim Governor Alberto Maynez to Audiencia of Guadalajara, May 31, 1817, R. 6, fr. 1668–69, SANM I; Taylor, "Cochití Lands," 62–65; Van Valen, "In Search of Juan," 78–80; Ebright, Hendricks, and Hughes, *Four Square Leagues*, 176–77.

46. Journal of the Diputación Provincial, April 25, 1822, R. 42, fr. 12, Mexican Archives of New Mexico (hereafter MANM).

47. J. J. Bowden, "Antonio Ortiz Grant," New Mexico History, accessed July 15, 2013, https://newmexicohistory.org/2015/07/17/antonio-ortiz-grant/.

48. Kessell, *Kiva, Cross, and Crown*, 360, 410–20, 424–27; Gonzales, "Genízaro Land Grant," 593.

49. Kessell, *Kiva, Cross, and Crown*, 434.

50. Bloom, "New Mexico," 46.

51. R. 18, fr. 17–18, SANM II.

52. Michael Miller, "Land, Violence and Death: The Bartolome Baca Grant," accessed July 15, 2013, https://newmexicohistory.org/2015/07/21/land-violence-and -death-the-bartolome-baca-grant/.

53. Journal of the Diputación Provincial, December 20, 1823, R. 42, fr. 149–50, MANM. For Juan Esteban Pino's career, see Hall, "Juan Estevan Pino," 27–42; for the Hacienda de San Juan Bautista del Ojito del Río de las Gallinas (renamed as the Preston Beck Grant under US rule), see Hall, "Juan Estevan Pino," 31.

54. Journal of the Diputación Provincial, January 9, 1824, R. 42, fr. 155–56, MANM.

55. Journal of the Diputación Provincial, February 13, 1824, R. 42, fr. 166–67, MANM.

56. Journal of the Diputación Provincial, April 12, 1824, R. 42, fr. 193–94, MANM. Manuel Antonio Baca is probably the Manuel Baca who served the subdistrict of Pecos and El Bado as interim teniente de justicia in 1805 and teniente de justicia in 1809, 1813–14, and 1820; see Kessell, *Kiva, Cross, and Crown*, 424, 506. Manuel Baca was constitutional justice of El Bado in 1822; he was also a second cousin to Luis María Cabeza de Baca; see Twitchell, *Spanish Archives*, 1:268.

57. Journal of the Diputación Provincial, October 19, 1826, R. 42, fr. 435–36, MANM.

58. Hall and Weber, "Mexican Liberals," 12.

59. Journal of the Diputación Territorial, February 16, 1824, and March 12, 1824, R. 42, fr. 170 and fr. 174, respectively, MANM. See also Hall and Weber, "Mexican Liberals," 13–14, 15.

60. Hall and Weber, "Mexican Liberals," 15.

61. Journal of the Diputación Territorial, March 19, 1825, R. 42, fr. 272–73, MANM. See also Hall and Weber, "Mexican Liberals," 16.

62. Journal of the Diputación Territorial, November 17, 1825 and November 18, 1825, R. 42, fr. 313–15, MANM; Ebright, Hendricks, and Hughes, *Four Square Leagues*, 39.

63. Ebright, Hendricks, and Hughes, *Four Square Leagues*, 40.

64. Journal of the Diputación Provincial, October 21, 1826, and October 23, 1826, R. 42, fr. 438–40, MANM.

65. Ebright, Hendricks, and Hughes, *Four Square Leagues*, 42–43.

66. Journal of the Diputación Territorial, February 1824, R. 42, fr. 170–71, MANM. See also Hall and Weber, "Mexican Liberals," 13; Ebright, Hendricks, and Hughes, *Four Square Leagues*, 28, 38–39.

67. Journal of the Diputación Territorial, March 12, 1824, R. 42, fr. 174–75, MANM. See also Hall and Weber, "Mexican Liberals," 13; Ebright, Hendricks, and Hughes, *Four Square Leagues*, 28, 38–39.

68. Journal of the Diputación Territorial, July 19, 1825, R. 42, fr. 284, MANM. See also Hall and Weber, "Mexican Liberals," 16; Ebright, Hendricks, and Hughes, *Four Square Leagues*, 38.

69. Journal of the Diputación Territorial, September 15, 1825, R. 42, fr. 298, MANM. See also Hall and Weber, "Mexican Liberals," 17; Ebright, Hendricks, and Hughes, *Four Square Leagues*, 39.

CHAPTER 11

Do Indians Have Land Rights?

THE CASE OF TIERRAS BALDÍAS AND CHIRIGUANO INTEGRATION IN THE BOLIVIAN LOWLANDS IN THE NINETEENTH AND EARLY TWENTIETH CENTURIES

Erick D. Langer

A ll Latin American governments in the republican era conceived of the lands beyond their frontiers as tierras baldías, empty territories that were bereft of legitimate owners and that the state could grant to whoever would use them most productively. This idea came from the "agricultural argument" in which only relatively intensive agricultural use constituted possession. Yet even those indigenous groups that did cultivate the soil did not have land rights, because they were presumed to live in a prestate society.[1] Thus, as Latin American states invaded indigenous territories they claimed as theirs, they almost never recognized the land rights of the indigenous peoples who resided there. At best, governments permitted religious missions to establish themselves on the Indians' former lands to keep the indigenous peoples in the area and "civilize" them, or they established reservations on some of the worst lands, in recognition that those who had been conquered needed a place to live if they had not been absorbed as dependent labor on the new haciendas.[2]

This is what I assumed also occurred in Bolivia; in fact, my research for many years focused on what appeared to be the only viable option for frontier peoples, which was to choose Catholic missions so as to preserve at least part of their indigenous culture. I concentrated on the Chiriguano Indians, now called Ava-Guaraní, arguably the largest and most important group of indigenous people in the region who had been able to resist encroachment until the late nineteenth century. They were located in what is now the southeast corner of Bolivia, in the eastern foothills of the Andes.[3]

Most members of the Indian communities that did not become missions appeared to have become peons on haciendas, where they suffered under landlord rule, were unable to leave, were tied to estates through debts, and indigenous women and children were pawns to be bought and sold.[4] After decades of working in the archives in Sucre, Santa Cruz, and Tarija, as well as in local ones on the former frontier, I found one exceptional case, that of the community of Caraparirenda in Cantón Ticucha (Azero Province, Chuquisaca Department). In Caraparirenda, the Chiriguano community had received a land grant that preserved their land from the grasp of the neighboring hacendados (large landlords).[5] This seemed to be the only case where an indigenous community on the frontier was able to survive without disappearing into an hacienda or being converted into a mission.

I was wrong. A few years ago, research in the Instituto de Colonización, a little-used depository in the National Archives in Sucre, demonstrated to me another reality. As this essay shows, an unexpected multiplicity of land tenure arrangements existed along the frontier under which Chiriguanos maintained certain land rights. First of all, the community of Caraparirenda was by no means the only community that was able to maintain its lands. At least a dozen other communities registered their land with Bolivian authorities and were able to maintain their rights well into the twentieth century. Access to landlord records showed two other types of relations. Some Chiriguano groups forged largely autonomous villages on landlords' properties. Lastly, settler landlords created domestic ties to the daughters of indigenous chiefs—called *capitanes* or *tubichas*—and thus gained access to indigenous labor without taking over Chiriguano lands.

These patterns are different from the relations that the Spanish, then the republican-era Bolivian states had with the indigenous peoples in the highlands. In the Andean highlands and high valleys, the peasant communities were integrated into the state before the Spanish conquest. The Andean peasant communities, organized into kin-based *ayllus*, had to pay tribute and provide labor to the state, in return for which the state assured the integrity of the communal land base. At the beginning of the republic, the mita, the forced labor requirement for the mines, disappeared though minor labor prestations, such as service to local officials and carrying the mail, remained, as did the tribute requirement. What was different was that, regardless, the Bolivian state guaranteed Andean communities' lands until the end of the nineteenth century. When the legislature abolished the communal lands in 1874, tribute payments on the national level disappeared and the state tried to parcel up the land and give it to individual peasants. This process took many years and remained incomplete. Regardless, the Bolivian state recognized, after some debate, the land rights of highland indigenous peoples to a much greater extent than those of Indians in the eastern lowland frontier, such as the Chiriguanos.[6]

A BRIEF OVERVIEW OF CHIRIGUANO RESISTANCE

Unlike in the highlands, however, the Chiriguanos remained mostly independent during most of the nineteenth century and were not included in the legislation that integrated the Andean peasant communities into the state. To contextualize the land tenure situation, it is first necessary to briefly summarize the bloody history of European-Chiriguano relations. The Chiriguanos had been the fiercest defenders of their territories from the karai, as they called the people of European descent. The term was somewhat derogatory, meaning somebody astute, greedy, and oppressive.[7] Unlike many of the other indigenous groups farther into the Chaco, the Chiriguanos were primarily maize farmers. Indeed, according to some scholars, the Guaraní-speaking Chiriguanos, who had migrated from the Brazilian coast in the sixteenth century, settled in the Andean foothills because the warm, wet, and forest-covered steep hills and north-south valleys were the legendary paradise, where corn and other products grew in abundance and all could live well. They conquered most of the Arawak-speaking native peoples of the region, called Chané, and attacked the Inca Empire.[8] When the Spanish invaded and conquered the Inca Empire from the west, it initiated a centuries-long conflict between the Chiriguanos and the Spanish with their Andean native subjects. Chiriguanos raided almost to the fabulous silver mines of Potosí in the 1560s, forcing Viceroy Francisco de Toledo (1569–81) to personally mount a punitive expedition in 1574. The viceroy's attempt to subdue the Chiriguanos failed and he had to retreat when he fell ill. Instead of attempting another expedition, Toledo set up a series of forts and settlements that largely prevented the Chiriguanos from raiding too deeply into the Andes.[9]

During most of the colonial period an uneasy stalemate existed, during which only slowly were the Spanish able to penetrate farther into Chiriguano territory. As a result of the low-level warfare interspersed with major wars, the Chiriguanos created a society adapted to war. Residence patterns changed to make Spanish raids less lethal and men, including the village chiefs, exalted in their warrior status above all else. The Chiriguanía, as it was called, remained a place of constant conflict. Chiriguano political culture did not permit the unification of the ethnic group into one unit; instead, a number of powerful chiefs, called tubichas, controlled their own villages and other, less powerful chiefs allied with the more populous settlements. These village alliances attacked each other in a never-ending series of skirmishes and at times involved the Spanish in their internecine fights. Attempts by various religious orders, especially the Jesuits, to establish missions among the Indians failed. Only during the very last decades of the eighteenth century, when the Franciscans entered the field from their convent in the frontier town of Tarija, did things change. Altogether, by 1810 the missionaries had succeeded in establishing twenty-one missions with a total population of about twenty-four thousand Indians.[10]

The independence wars that erupted in 1810 and lasted until 1825 wiped out most of the missions. The Franciscans remained royalists and, when the patriot guerrillas entered the territory, were carted off to jail in the main towns then exiled to Spain. Only two small missions, Salinas and Itau, survived as such, each with one elderly missionary who had scant support from the depopulated Tarija convent.[11] Many of the northern missions, in the Santa Cruz Department, remained in the hands of mestizos, but in the south independent Chiriguano villagers regained almost all of the territory they had lost to the Spanish settlers and missionaries in the eighteenth century (see map 11.1).

From independence onward, the Chiriguanos were able to dominate the frontier. Their villages contained the largest number of people and their arms—mainly bows and arrows—were as efficient as the old flintlocks the settlers had. They felt superior to the other indigenous groups, such as the Matacos (now called Weenhayek or Wichí) farther to the south and east. The only group they accorded some respect were the Tobas (who call themselves Qom), who were fierce equestrian warriors and threatened Chiriguano settlements such as those around Caiza.[12] Even so, the Chiriguanos regarded all other indigenous peoples with a certain disdain. The only ones they saw as roughly their equals were the mestizo or European settlers. The Chiriguanía during the early republican period remained a region where different villages, whether they were karai or Guaraní, fought amongst

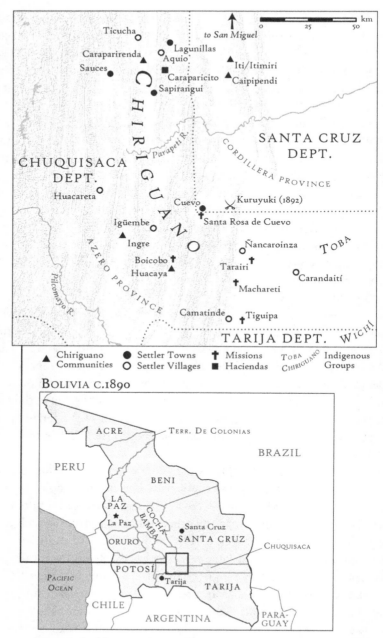

Map 11.1. Tierras baldías in the Andean foothills of southeastern Bolivia in the nineteenth century. (Map © G. Wallace Cartography & GIS)

themselves in ever-changing alliances that maintained a rough military equilibrium where no group could gain the advantage.

It was only in the 1850s and 1860s that the settlers were finally able to gain the upper hand because of the reactivation of the mining industry in the highlands, which led to a thriving cattle trade to supply the mining camps. In addition, the development of new weaponry, such as the revolving pistol and the rifle, meant that the Indians no longer had the military advantage. Settlers moved with their cattle onto Indian land, destroying the cornfields of the Chiriguano villagers. Branislava Sušnik, taking the idea from the early twentieth-century Franciscan chronicler Fr. Angélico Martarelli, posited that the frontier could be seen as a struggle between cattle and maize, in which the invading *cristianos* used cattle to drive out the Chiriguano corn farmers.[13] While there is much truth to Martarelli's exclamation that "instead of colonizing the frontier with men, it has been colonized with cows," the new wealth generated by the Bolivian silver mines and the new weapons made it difficult for the Indians to resist encroachment.

Cattle ranching was by its nature destructive of indigenous communities that depended on maize cultivation. The ranching economy drove settlers into Chiriguano land south of the Parapetí River. Some chiefs requested missions as a means to prevent the destruction of their communities in that region. A number were established on the lands Chuquisaca and Tarija Departments claimed for themselves. The pressure from the ranching economy brought about major conflicts, such as the Huacaya War (1874–77), when Chiriguano allies (most of whom resided on the Franciscan missions) and settler militias were able to defeat a coalition of Chiriguano communities led by the Huacaya chiefs and their Toba Indian allies. As a means of rewarding the settler-combatants and extinguishing forever the resistance of the Huacaya Chiriguanos, in late 1874 the Bolivian Congress passed legislation that granted a half league of land in Huacaya to any white man who could prove that he had contributed to the victory. Ironically, one of the most important Chiriguano communities that had allied with the settlers to fight the Huacaya Indians, that of the Ingre Valley, also lost its lands through this legislation.[14]

In contrast, in the Chiriguanía to the north of the Parapetí River, the settlers engaged in more mixed agricultural activities, including the cultivation of maize and other crops. This meant that landlords were more interested in indigenous labor than land. There, settlers created a more integrative frontier in which the large landlords were willing to keep Chiriguano communities whole as long as they could access the workers. Although landlords in the north also usurped indigenous land, as I will show, some were willing to maintain village autonomy as long as the communities provided the agricultural labor they needed.

The last gasp of indigenous resistance occurred in 1892, when a messianic leader rallied disaffected Chiriguano warriors, including some from the missions, to fight the white usurpers. Although they had some initial success, wiping out several haciendas and killing their inhabitants, the rebels were unable to overrun the missions. Thereafter, a hastily constituted militia consisting mainly of mission Indians along with settlers and a military contingent sent from Santa Cruz defeated the rebellious Indians at Kuruyuki, where the Indians had dug trenches to fight off the invaders.[15] That was the end of overt resistance.

CHIRIGUANO SAVAGERY: THE RHETORIC OF INDIAN AGGRESSORS

The struggle to conquer the Chiriguanos led to many characterizations of their savagery and their otherness. The rhetoric, which did not change over time, created the framework that enabled officials and others to conceive of the Indians as aggressors, without taking into account any right to land. Most official correspondence qualified the Chiriguanos and their close neighbors, the Tobas and Matacos, as invaders. Officials saw settlements as bulwarks against incursions rather than as a defense of land. Thus, in 1833 the corregidor of Sauces claimed that the new settlements of Huacareta and Pirirenda (both places that at the time were populated by independent Chiriguanos) would "present an impressive line against the incursions of the barbarians."[16] In 1897, the same discourse circulated, even though by then many of the places had been turned into mestizo towns: "The towns of Igüembe, Ticucha, Huacaya, Sapirangui, Hucareta [sic], Ñancaroinza, Camatinde, Taringuiti, Ñuapoa, Carandaitihuazu, and others have been established by foreign and national colonizers. It is because of these colonies that the assaults and devastations of the savage hordes have weakened."[17] Examples of this rhetoric exist in many other documents that span the period from independence to the early twentieth century. This attitude, that the Chiriguanos were barbarians and invaders, appears not to have modulated over the nineteenth century.

Even at times when the Bolivian settlers discussed the complexities of Chiriguano indigenous allies and their enemies, such as in the lengthy document related to disputes over the rights of the Chuquisaca and Santa Cruz

Departments over the territory of Cuevo and Ivo, the witnesses characterized the Indians as barbarians and showed they did not consider that the Indians might have land rights nor that their possible land rights had anything to do with the boundary dispute other than when one official from Chuquisaca attacked a community in what Santa Cruz presumed to be its territory.[18]

INDIGENOUS RELATIONS ON SETTLER HACIENDAS

The rhetoric of the savagery and barbarism of the natives in official documents, however, hides the complex interethnic relations that landlords and other settlers had with the Chiriguano population. Two issues stand out that suggest a different reality on the ground. First, Chiriguano access to land that the landlords claimed for themselves changed over time. Second, a significant number of Chiriguano communities used the land grant process designed for colonists to claim rights over their own home territories.

Access to land was one of the most important issues along the frontier. Frontier land legislation from the 1830s suggested a conception of usufruct that was not exclusive to the presumed owner of the land. Thus, Juan Agustín Terán, who received a concession of four square leagues in Sauces and Sapirangui (today Monteagudo and Villa Vaca Guzmán) in Chuquisaca Department, had to permit "labradores or small estancieros" on his property "until they become prejudicial because of their bad conduct or a considerable increase in their herds." These people, also called *piqueros*, were defined as not having more than twenty-five head of cattle and could not remain on the hacienda if their herd increased to more than seventy-five head.[19]

This idea of letting other, relatively autonomous people use and settle on the owner's land grants appears to have been common in the early republican period. The landlord Octavio Padilla, whose base was the latifundio Caraparicito to the north of the Parapetí River, was one of the most important hacendados of the region. He permitted Indians to stay on these lands; for example, when he bought a property in the 1870s he conceded that "some families of Indians [may remain] on the lands of Aquio and other locations due to simple tolerance with the interest of occupying them, paying them an accustomed just salary and to their advantage for their subsistence that they find thanks to the landlords, as occurs in the other farms in private hands."[20]

In other cases, it was clear that Chiriguano chiefs ceded land to karai settlers. Whether this meant that the Chiriguanos remained on their former territories is not clear. For example, one contract stated that "the Indians of these lands [called Yaguapoa and other names] accepted with pleasure that which they finished giving don Manuel P. Durán; the document in which they, the mentioned Indians, ratify their acceptance of March 1867, ceding to said Durán any rights that could be alleged over the lands that they possessed." It is likely that the Indians were expected to work on the ceded lands, though this was not specified in the document.[21] On the other hand, it appears that at some point a teacher [*maestro de escuela*] also lived on the same property "so as to serve as protection and free contract of his work to the Indians of Ibeyeca," which was a section of the landholding.[22] Exactly what the relationship was between the Indians and the schoolteacher must be left to speculation, but if he worked to teach Indian children, this arrangement would have been remarkable for that time and place.

That the landlords valued indigenous labor, even when the chiefs remained relatively autonomous, is evident in a contract with another group of Chiriguanos that lived on Padilla's lands. On his main property, Caraparicito, a Chiriguano village existed whose residents had a relatively independent relationship with him. The capitanes (chiefs) of the village Jaropa and Yacaire declared in 1868:

> We, in our name and that of our warriors [*soldados*] make the following declaration: (1) We know don Octavio Padilla who, as heir to his father don José Padilla, is owner and exclusive proprietor of the hacienda Caraparicito and Itangua . . . whose property we respect and we submit ourselves to live as his true colonists [*colonos*] as we have done for many years, given that neither we nor our soldados are the original settlers but instead, coming from different parts, are consequently without the right to the property other than the shelter and protection that said don Octavio Padilla has given us, with whom we offer to maintain the greatest harmony under the only condition that he leaves us in the possession of the villages [*pueblos*] in which we live and the lands in which we cultivate our crops.[23]

This rather ambiguous passage suggests several possibilities. Octavio Padilla had inherited the property from his father, who had received it in 1825, at a time when the Chiriguanos had retaken much of their lands from landlords and destroyed most of the missions, especially in this sector. It appears that these Indians were refugees from other villages who had settled on the land, probably in return for services to the landlord, though apparently they kept control over their fields.

Almost two decades later, Octavio Padilla requested more land in the aftermath of the 1874–77 Huacaya War. According to legislation passed during the war, all those who had contributed to "the work on the fort and fix[ed] their residence for three years within the limits of the [Huacaya] canyon" had the right to receive half a league of land there. Padilla requested and received a land grant because he claimed that he had provided cattle to the militia during the war and "also has reinforced the column with soldados and Indian archers, allies of the Province of Cordillera, who, armed and mounted at the expense of the said Padilla and maintained for forty days that the garrison lasted at that point."[24] Were the Indians Padilla sent to the front the aforementioned residents on his properties? It is highly likely; if so, Padilla used the Indian residents on his land as troops to expand his own properties.

Another means of gaining access to indigenous labor without conquering the indigenous villages was for large landowners to take as secondary wives some of the daughters of the local caciques. According to one document from 1868, Pastor Durán, a large landowner who lived along the Parapetí River, "for many years was submitted among the Indians of those places and there maintains in concubinage the daughters of the capitanes."[25] Information on these arrangements is scarce, but taking the daughters of the indigenous chiefs as secondary wives would make landlords relatives of the Chiriguano capitanes and thus eligible to access the labor of their villages. Chiriguano women played a key role in the integrative frontier that existed north of the Parapetí River. By providing indigenous women as partners for powerful karai landlords, the Chiriguano communities were able to maintain their autonomy because the landlords became the sons-in-law and brothers-in-law of the chiefs. They then had the right to use indigenous laborers on their estates for farming. Because of these family alliances with the Chiriguano chiefly dynasties, the landlords became defenders of the communities as well, since the autonomous communities became valuable labor reserves for them.

The landlords' alliances with powerful Chiriguano chiefs could help protect farms from raids, especially in the early years of the republic. As I have suggested elsewhere, for the first few decades after independence, conflicts between Chiriguano villages often involved *español-americano* allies on opposing sides. At times, internal conflicts within Bolivian society spilled over into the frontier, where different political factions attempted to mobilize the fierce frontier indigenous warriors for their own purposes, to the detriment of Bolivian frontier stability.[26] The alliances through women bound landlords to certain factions among the Chiriguanos and probably accelerated these types of conflicts on the frontier and its hinterlands. Shawn Austin has called this custom cuñadazgo, from the Spanish term *cuñado*, meaning brother-in-law, and applied it to his analysis of Spanish-Guaraní relations in colonial Paraguay. It appears that the same or similar relationships existed on the nineteenth-century Bolivian frontier. The pattern of using women to create interethnic alliances was widespread in the Americas, as Julianne Barr showed for colonial Texas and others have shown for the French fur traders in North America, where their marriages with indigenous women opened access to hunting grounds and the furs of their tribes.[27]

To summarize, the relationship of the karai landlords to the Chiriguano people was much more complex than scholars have previously realized. Complicating the common narrative of submission of indigenous villages to the conquering hacendados, some internal documents from the haciendas show different relations even among the indigenous peoples who were subsumed into the haciendas. These relationships probably varied according to the relative strength of each Chiriguano group versus the settlers. Thus, evidence suggests that, at least in some cases, indigenous villagers maintained a relatively autonomous existence on the hacienda. They had rights to territory for a village where they could not be molested, as well as to fields that they freely farmed, without the kinds of mandatory labor obligations that were common on highland haciendas. That there may have been schools for indigenous children on the haciendas is another interesting data point, though unfortunately the information is only suggestive. It is likely that when native society on the frontier was militarily dominant in the early republican period, the terms of settling on an hacienda were relatively favorable to the Indians; after all, the landlord immediately gained valuable allies and protection for his estate, as Octavio Padilla did. In other cases, landlords paired with the daughters of powerful capitanes to gain access to Indian resources.

The evidence from internal hacienda documents thus reveals a different reality than the one reproduced in very many official pronouncements. Chiriguanos played a much more complex role along the frontier than generally acknowledged, many of them being far from the savages or invaders that writers claimed they were. Landlords at the beginning of the republican period had to rely on good relations with the Indians to survive. They entered into mutually beneficial alliances, where the great Indian chiefs protected the landlords. At times, the voluntary resettlement on the haciendas of indigenous refugees who formed their own autonomous villages under their own capitanes led to a number of privileges for the landlord, who received labor power and, particularly in the early period, a source of protection for the landed estate. This scenario was far from the image of the savage invader who stole from hapless settlers. Indeed, alliances were crucial for understanding the development of the Chiriguano frontier.

CHIRIGUANO VILLAGERS FIGHT BACK: TAKING CONTROL OF THE LAND GRANT PROCESS

The villages that allied with the karai were fundamental to the eventual conquest of the Chiriguanía, which occurred by the end of the nineteenth century. Only the Franciscan missions were more important because they created permanent alliances with the Bolivian government and, by the last quarter of the nineteenth century, constituted the largest population of Chiriguanos on the frontier. Be that as it may, throughout the struggles in the Chiriguanía during the republican period, the vast majority of combatants on both sides of any conflict on the frontier, up to and including the defeat at Kuruyuki in 1892, were indigenous.[28]

The harsh rhetoric against the Chiriguanos conceptually limited the ability of the Indians to maintain their own lands. After all, if the Indians were barbarous, savage invaders who killed settlers and stole their livestock, they did not deserve to have rights to the land they occupied. Although some nineteenth-century laws included the general principle that even frontier indigenous peoples had rights to their own territory, these laws remained mainly theoretical, with just a few exceptions.[29] The land grant legislation, which evolved over the nineteenth century and had crystallized by the 1870s and 1880s, conceived of a process that gave lands to settlers rather than preserving territories for indigenous peoples who presumably had been conquered.[30]

For the Chiriguanía, the most important land grant legislation explicitly focused on partitioning the territories opened up by warfare was enacted in 1874 and 1877, in the aftermath of the Huacaya War. As described, Octavio Padilla and many others who claimed that they had aided national forces obtained large tracts of lands in the heart of the indigenous rebel territory. Indeed, one of the most important allies during the war, the great chief Buricanambi of Ingre, saw his valley divvied up among the español-americano victors. Buricanambi had been so powerful earlier that in 1864 the national legislature recognized his authority and authorized him to sell a piece of property to an español-americano.[31] This decision was made despite the fact that

Buricanambi had run afoul of some frontier authorities in Tarija that year, when he had raided another allied indigenous village and had made off with cattle and women and children. However, he had the support of authorities from Santa Cruz, so was able to get away with the assault.[32] Neither his friendship with Santa Cruz authorities nor his having fought with Bolivian frontier militia forces against the Huacaya alliance was enough to save his land however. Buricanambi disappeared from historical records as the Ingre Valley went to the militia captains he had helped. As the Franciscan missionary Angélico Martarelli noted, "Very late, the poor Ingre [Indians thus] got to know that the loyalty and friendship with the cristianos would cost them exile and the loss of all of their lands and their independence.[33]

The official rhetoric about the Indians' barbarism and the fate of the Ingre Chiriguano communities suggest that the Bolivian conquest and the subsequent land grant process would have doomed the frontier Indians to lose their land unless they chose to be protected by the Franciscan missionaries. The land grant process was meant to divide up indigenous lands among settlers precisely because of the Indians' lack of legal standing as barbarians who were beyond the pale of republican laws. By the late nineteenth century, hacienda owners simply took over lands from the Indians, whether or not these lands were settled by indigenous peoples. Several land grants indeed showed indigenous settlements on land that was supposed to be vacant, such as the land grant San Ramón de Ñaguambaruzú, solicited by Ramón Sanabria (see figure 11.1). There, the small penciled-in houses and the labeling of "casas de indígenas" on the land grant map gave away the fact that Sanabria had appropriated territory that included the residences of indigenous people.

The narrative of the usurpation of indigenous lands and scholars' assumptions that the Chiriguanos' only options were to succumb to the hacienda regime or permit the establishment of a mission is, however, incorrect. I have identified at least seven relatively large Chiriguano communities that were able to use the land grant process intended to take away their land for their own purposes and successfully gain rights to their own territories.[34] Of these, I was able to gather substantial information on four of them: Caraparirenda, Caipipendi, San Miguel, and Iti/Itimiri. Each one had a somewhat different story of how the Indians were able to turn the land grant process in their favor and, despite legal assaults and other incidents, maintain their territories intact into the twentieth century.

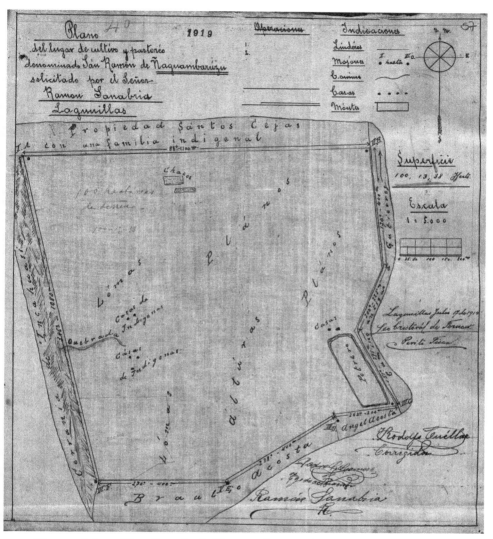

Fig. 11.1. Map of San Ramón de Ñaguambaruzú (Lagunillas, 1914). (ABNB, Sección Colonización, IC909_0057)

255

Caraparirenda

The Caraparirenda community has the longest paper trail regarding the issue of lands, in part because neighboring landlords were eager to dismember this community. It was close to two major español-americano urban centers, Sauces and Sapirangui. Yet the community persevered, maintained documents, and fought back successfully in the courts. A lengthy legajo of the Colonization Institute documents this case.[35]

The Caraparirenda Valley contained eleven different Chiriguano settlements, each with its own capitán. In 1860, it encompassed about three square leagues. The oldest document dates from 1859, when the capitanes complained that a karai was trying to acquire a piece of their community as vacant land to pasture cattle. The Indian chiefs argued that if the settler were to prevail, "where we with our soldados occupy ourselves with growing corn with which to feed ourselves; such that perhaps we will be in the position to abandon our fields and our pueblos." Given the threat of abandonment, local authorities moved this petition to higher levels in the government, claiming that the Caraparirenda people were their allies, that they "aid us with their work [*fuerzas*] in our enterprises [*labores*] and with all types of services," and that if they had their land taken away it would cause "a number of contrasts that would lead to loss of some lives."[36] The petition went all the way up to the Minister of Hacienda, who claimed that there was no law that permitted the taking of vacant lands and that therefore the rancher could not usurp the fields.[37] This initial decree enabled the community to stave off other ranchers in 1868.

By 1885, the authority structure within Caraparirenda had changed. Rather than eleven capitanes, one capitán, Bata, appeared in the documentation as the main leader. In that year he received a printed certificate from President Gregorio Pacheco, giving him the title of "Capitán of his tribe" because of his services as an ally.[38] Bata that year also took a karai to court for usurping land. He requested the measurement of Caraparirenda; the community won the case because according to the Indians' information, only their surveyor showed up and did the measurements. For some reason, the surveyor for the rancher did not appear, so the rancher did not participate to press his claims.[39]

Bata formally requested a land grant for his community in 1893, which the government granted a year later. The document asserted that, citing the 1859 disposition, "all the political authorities of that Province have made our rights respected as first occupiers deserving the possession of these properties, according to various legislative and administrative dispositions that are in force [but] that are too tiresome to cite."[40] In other words, the document claimed that all the local authorities agreed with the Indians' application. The land grant cited the 1890 Reglamento de Colonias, whose article 8 stated that the natives' lands should be measured and marked to preserve their rights.[41]

The petition included a map of the Caraparirenda Valley subject to the land grant (see figure 11.2). Compared to other land grant maps, its style looks less precise, with no measurements attached to it, but with copious details on the physical characteristics of the valley and the names of the different *quebradas* (riverbeds), and with small houses marking where the Chiriguano settlements were. Given its unique characteristics, the map appears to have been drawn with the help of the indigenous people who provided information that a land surveyor would not include (unlike the map of San Ramón de Ñaguambaruzú). The limits were not drawn in straight lines, but rather they appeared to correspond to the hills surrounding the various canyons where the settlements could be found. Compared to typical colonial maps, this style was more visual and followed more the contours of what an observer would see when in the valleys.

To sum up, the Caraparirenda Indians were able to gain legal access to their land after a long, drawn-out process during which they used local officials to help them preserve their land. At times, they were more astute than potential usurpers of their land, hiring lawyers and land surveyors to protect their land. They based their arguments for preserving their land on their value as Indian allies to local authorities, a fact that undoubtedly aided them when ranchers attempted to take their fields. They emphasized and received the support of the national government, as for example, when Bata received certificates from two different presidents in the late nineteenth century, cementing his position as an official Indian ally and supporting his claim to be the most powerful capitán among the chiefs in Caraparirenda. When the government approved land grants for settlers, Bata and his people successfully took advantage of this legislation to press their own case. The ability of the Caraparirenda Chiriguano to maneuver in the legal thicket of the land grant process was a testament to their ability to hire outside specialists and gain the support of local Bolivian frontier authorities. Later, in the early twentieth century, when other landlords threatened the territorial integrity of the *capitanía*, the Indians were able to fight back and preserve their lands.[42]

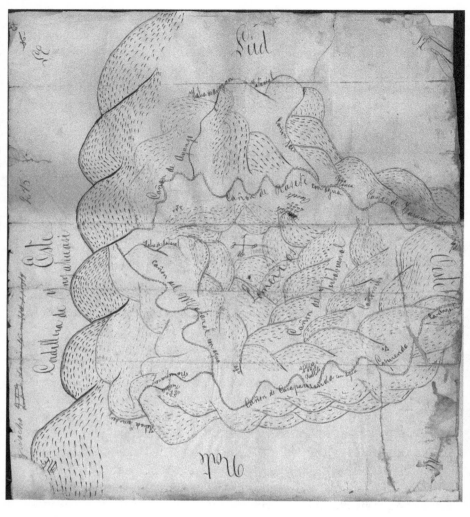

Fig. 11.2. Map of Caraparirenda (1896). (ABNB, Sección Colonización, IC587_0067)

Caipipendi

The Caraparirenda Indians left the longest documentary trail, but by far the largest community to benefit from the land grant legislation was the Capitanía of Caipipendi, located in a long north-south valley where about sixteen Chiriguano settlements were situated along the two streams that bisected it.

Since the colonial period, Caipipendi Valley had been one of the most populous and powerful capitanías in Chiriguano territory. It consisted of more than a dozen villages, all under the hegemony of one family, which produced the leading tubicha.[43] As in Caraparirenda, the tubichas of Caipipendi maintained mostly friendly relations with the local authorities of Cordillera Province, and the valley was able to maintain its independence. For example, as a sign of friendship with the karai, in 1853 Güirakota I had two of his sons baptized in Lagunillas. In 1870 his son, Güirakota II, who was one of the sons baptized in 1853, received a certificate from the president of Bolivia (like the one Bata from Caraparirenda had), naming him "Capitán Grande" of Yuti, a settlement at the southern end of the Caipipendi Valley. He also had led some of his men to work in Caraparicito, which meant that he probably had the support of the powerful Octavio Padilla as well.[44]

Two leaders from Yuti, José Ignacio Aireyu and Bernardino Güirakota, were accused of inciting the 1892 rebellion. Local authorities imprisoned Aireyu before hostilities broke out, so he remained out of the insurrection. However, Güirakota, also known as Chaparilla, was one of the leaders of the rebellion. He presented himself to the authorities after the Chiriguano defeat at the battle of Kuruyuki and was executed with other leaders in 1892. Padilla, with his Indian militia, razed the village of Yuti.[45]

After the rebellion was suppressed, Aireyu was permitted to take in many of the Indian prisoners, but the karai did not trust him. Fray Angélico Martarelli, who was a witness to the rebellion and its aftermath, surmised that the authorities did not execute Aireyu because they were afraid doing so would incite another rebellion.[46] Aireyu passed away in 1897, still the tubicha of his people.

Perhaps it was for this reason that the Caipipendi Indians did not request a land grant until 1915, when José Santos Aireyu had become tubicha.[47] Aireyu based the claim to lands on the fact that "the tribes of Caipipendi, Carabaicho and other names in possession of the lands since time immemorial occupy [them] as their original [primitivos] settlers, which today are detained by our neighbors." He cited the 1905 law that "makes it possible for the government to reserve lands that it might find necessary for distribution among the Indians."[48] In other words, the legal basis for the land grant request was not the Caipipendi residents' role as allies to the government, but simply the fact that the territory had always been indigenous land. Perhaps because it was by far the largest remaining Chiriguano territory and because local landlords and authorities depended on the Indians' labor, many local landlords supported his case. In fact, it is likely that the tubicha played off different landlords and authorities against each other in a situation where nobody wanted anyone else to monopolize this huge labor reserve. This scenario made it possible for the Caipipendi Indians to prevent the permanent takeover of their land by neighboring hacendados. In the end, Aireyu was able to obtain a land grant that incorporated around thirty-six settlements in an area that encompassed more than 58,000 hectares (143,000 acres), the largest land grant of any along the frontier (see figure 11.3).[49]

San Miguel

In other cases, national authorities—and even local ones—confused the nomenclature of the frontier with that of the Andean highlands. The capitanía of San Miguel, which claimed its lands in 1906, consisted of Itembeguazu, Itembemi, Guiraguarenda, and Curuguaca, in Cantón Gutiérrez, in Cordillera Province (Santa Cruz). Its representatives, with the Spanish names Miguel Montenegro and Inosencio Rojas, called themselves alcaldes (mayors), as Andean indigenous authorities were sometimes called. The lawyer who petitioned for the land grant described the members of the communities as "Indians of the Ayllus" and asserted that "these have possessed [the territory] since time immemorial, forming small ayllus, or centers of population."[50] "Ayllu" is a purely Andean term that is used in the highlands to distinguish kinship groups in indigenous communities.[51] Perhaps using the terms familiar to national authorities from the highlands, was a strategy the petitioners used to show their higher degree of civilization compared to the category of frontier savages. Likewise, naming their land grant for a saint was meant to convey that the Indians were civilized because of their presumed association with the Catholic missions.

The San Miguel Indians initiated the land grant process when a neighboring settler claimed their lands under the "false concept that they were vacant."[52] The government conceded the land to the Indians on a different basis than applied to the rest of the indigenous land grants examined so far. The lawyer

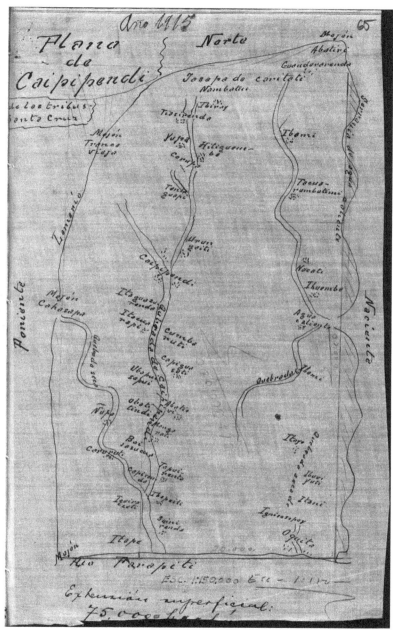

Fig. 11.3. Map of Caipipendi (1915). (ABNB, Sección Colonización, IC909_0065)

261

for the San Miguel Indians, Carmelo Saucedo, asserted that the community was entitled to request more than the 10,000 hectares (61,060 acres) he was petitioning for because the law of 1890 permitted each Indian to ask for one square league per family, plus a square mile for each male son over the age of fourteen. However, he was not doing so because "there isn't enough free land with which to amplify the solicitation."[53] Instead, he petitioned to have 25 hectares (62 acres) of land granted to each of the 120 Chiriguano inhabitants who were listed in the land grant document, for a total of 3,000 hectares (7,413 acres). This is what occurred; the land surveyor demarcated exactly 3,000 hectares. However, because of the constraints of the 25-hectare rule, the surveyor remarked that "some of the fields have remained outside of the line of demarcation, which is not of great importance because, being nonirrigated crops, after harvesting them, [the Indians] can transfer their fields to the place that they own, where they have sufficient plots for their labors."[54]

Despite this odd mixture of invoking highland Andean categories together with the mission-like denomination of "San Miguel," in the end the land grant was adjudicated in typical liberal form, in accord with the Liberal government then in power. Each male member of the capitanía received a plot based on an arbitrary number that parceled out the land, though in the end the two tubichas were the representatives who received the land in the name of their capitanía. This did mean that some of the land the Indians had farmed was outside their land grant; whether they continued to claim it or farm it without legal backing is not known. The grant conformed to the European aesthetic of straight lines and rectangles, imposing on the round and ragged landscape a kind of geometry that it did not intrinsically possess. The map that accompanied the land grant did not distinguish individual plots but did show the houses and fields within each of the settlements as a whole. This land grant had a mix of features that only uneasily reflected the reality on the ground along the frontier (see figure 11.4).

Iti and Itimiri

The last type of land grant emerged from a former mission. Iti and Itimiri had been a Franciscan mission in the colonial period. Founded in 1789 by Francisco del Pilar, in 1810 it contained 1,379 souls, more than half of whom were baptized.[55] According to Fr. Antonio Comajuncosa, the settlement was populated by Chané Indians, people of Arawak rather than Tupí-Guaraní ancestry, who had largely been subsumed by the Guaraní-speaking Chiriguanos.

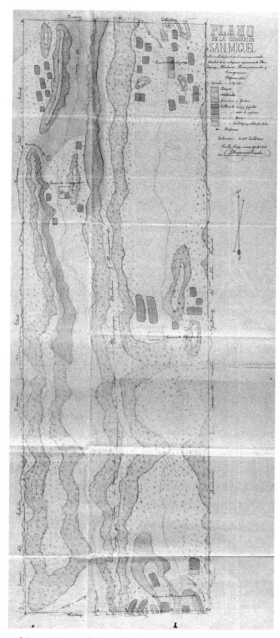

Fig. 11.4. Map of San Miguel (1912). (ABNB, Sección Colonización, IC909_0037)

By the eighteenth century, the Chané spoke Guaraní as well and did not distinguish themselves greatly from the Chiriguanos in cultural practices.[56]

According to the Franciscan chronicler Alejandro Corrado, the independence struggles destroyed Iti and other missions in the region. In 1813 patriot troops from Buenos Aires entered the mission and took the friars prisoner. Later, patriot forces sacked the missions, and the Indians either retook the settlements for themselves or disappeared into the forest. According to Corrado, who wrote in 1880, "The four missions of the frontier of Sauces [which included Iti] were lost completely and no vestige of them remains today. The 2,534 Indians that inhabited them dispersed along the shores of the Acero [River] and in the neighboring forests and ravines; only a small number of their miserable grandchildren stay, without religious instruction and with all of the vices of a semi-barbarous life."[57]

The lost mission continued to exist however. The communities of Iti and Itimiri survived, and the government recognized the lands of these Indians in 1831 and 1863. On the latter date, the judge wrote, "I declare legal the property of the lands [terrenos] possessed since time immemorial by the individuals of the Indian race."[58] The leader of the Iti and Itimiri Indians in the late nineteenth century was Mariano Chanca, who titled himself "Capitán Grande of the allied Chiro-Guaraní forces." Interestingly, Chanca claimed Chiriguano rather than Chané heritage for himself and his people. Chanca hired two lawyers in 1894, in the aftermath of the 1892 rebellion, to process the paperwork for a land grant in the prefectural office in Sucre. In total, he requested 5,000 hectares for Itimiri and 750 hectares for Iti, basing his petition on the 1831 and 1863 confirmations of ownership, as well as on the fact that Iti was "originally a mission established by the Reverend Father Comajuncosa."[59] Indeed, the map of the land grant (see figure 11.5) labeled the village of Iti, tucked in the valley of the Iti River, as the "Pueblo de neófitos [neophytes]," matching the designation of the many Franciscan missions located fewer than one hundred kilometers south of the land grant. The pueblo is also represented in the characteristic mission layout, with a central plaza and blocks of houses arranged neatly around it.

What was unique about this successful petition was that the lawyer for the Iti and Itimiri Indians had some karai neighbors testify in favor of the 1894 petition, to strengthen the case for the granting of the land. Most simply confirmed that the Iti Indians had possessed the land and that the settlers had been permitted to use part of the land, but only with the permission of the Indians. Thus, Nicolás Romero stated that he "sowed there with the previous

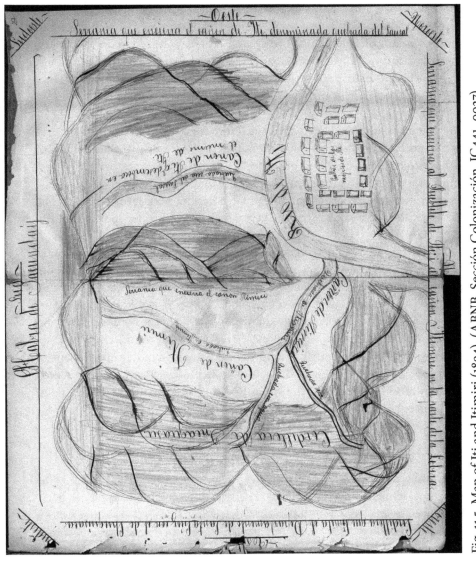

Fig. 11.5. Map of Iti and Itimiri (1894). (ABNB, Sección Colonización, IC441_0027)

consent of the Capitán Grande Mariano Chanca." Another, Napoleón Calvi-montes, testified that he had asked a Señor Villarroel to sow some rice and other products on the property, but that Villarroel refused to do so, "assert-ing that said canyon was occupied by the Indians of Iti and that he did not have the means to dispose of the lands without the previous consent of these naturales." In total, ten karai testified on behalf of the Indians.[60]

Here we have the reverse of the Caraparicito hacienda deal: in Carapari-cito, the Indians constituted a village and were permitted to cultivate part of the land of the estate, but only after agreeing to preserve the land rights of the landlord. The 1894 land grant for Iti and Itimiri contained strikingly similar language about permission to use the land, except that it was the karai who received permission to use the land, but without any land rights. Whether the Indians required the karai to provide labor for the community is unknown.

The land grant map, like its counterpart for Caraparirenda, shows charac-teristics of indigenous conceptions of the land. It confirms the Chiriguano predominance, given that even the Ministry of Colonization accepted a map that was drawn in ways that a regular land surveyor would not have done. Again, the hills, not arbitrary straight lines, constituted the borders of the land grant, and the waterways, especially the Iti River, were prominent in the map. The regularity of the housing, with the houses clustered around a central square, reminded the ministry officials of its mission heritage. The map served as a powerful illustration of the issues that the document itself raised and of the legal basis for the grant.

CONCLUSIONS

The land tenure situation on the Chiriguano frontier was much more com-plex than scholars have thought. It is necessary to make the duality of haci-endas versus missions into a trio in which stable, indigenous communities supported by local authorities, and in many cases even powerful local land-lords, survived. These communities gained legal status through the land grant process, which was principally designed for white settlers, and were able to prevail despite frequent attempts at usurpation by encroaching settlers. Prom-inent landlords availed themselves of the labor of these communities through other means. Despite sparse documentary records of labor relations between landlords and these Chiriguano communities, there were at least three basic ways in which a prominent landlord could gain access to indigenous labor.

One was through "marrying" the daughters of local chiefs and thus, as a son-in-law, claiming Indian labor for his estates. This cuñadazgo relationship, common in the Guaraní regions of colonial Paraguay, continued on the nineteenth-century Bolivian frontier with Guaraní-speaking Indians.

This deal maintained the relative autonomy of these Indian groups in ways that other strategies, such as the Huacaya or Ingre captainships, could not. The Huacaya captainship lost most of its lands after the 1874–77 war, though its refugees largely settled in the Franciscan mission of Boicobó, founded in 1893.[61] The allied villagers from Ingre who did not flee into the Chaco or Argentina were absorbed into haciendas as peons. This is indeed what happened in the southern part of the Chiriguanía south of the Parapetí River, where Franciscan missions proliferated: in the early 1890s in the Chuquisaca and Tarija Departments twelve missions were founded with more than fourteen thousand Indians.[62] In the Department of Santa Cruz of Cordillera Province and in the northern part of Azero Province of Chuquisaca, missions never prospered even though the population of Chiriguanos was just as large as in Tarija and southern Azero in Chuquisaca combined.[63] There, the leaders of a former mission at Iti and Itimiri, rather than seeking to form a mission again, elected to go through the land grant process to gain a measure of security over their lands.

These developments characterize the late nineteenth century. Yet as the documents from Hacienda Caraparicito demonstrate, labor relations varied earlier in the century, even on landed estates owned by the karai. The ownership of large parcels of land was neither valuable nor necessarily secure without people to protect and work that land. It appears that large estates such as Caraparicito also contained "vacant lands" and, therefore, the owner, Octavio Padilla, was willing to allow indigenous people to settle the land and remain autonomous in exchange for written recognition that the land did not belong to them. Of course, that did not preclude having other Indians live on the hacienda as peons. In other words, we must conceive of the frontier haciendas as maintaining different labor regimes that varied over time. Initially, when the Chiriguanos were the most powerful group on the frontier, they were able to negotiate the terms of their labor. As the frontier moved farther east and indigenous groups lost out to settlers and the national state, these terms undoubtedly changed for the worse.

However, many Chiriguano communities that were never part of an hacienda were able to preserve their lands even against colonists' attempts at usurpation. Their role as allies—at least at certain times—and their willingness to provide some labor to the surrounding haciendas and to local officials enabled them to preserve their lands through the land grant process, which had been principally designed to enable white settlers to take indigenous "vacant lands." This mutual benefit was part of the heritage of a relatively integrative frontier, where access to agricultural labor trumped the need for land and where indigenous women served as mediators to access indigenous labor on the great haciendas, thereby making possible the continued autonomy of Chiriguano communities and their chiefly lineages. Even today, most of the leaders of the Asamblea del Pueblo Guaraní, the most powerful indigenous association of what were once called Chiriguanos, consist of descendants of the chiefs that made their peace with the local karai landlords.

NOTES

1. See Gilbert, "Nomadic Territories"; see also his *Nomadic Peoples*.

2. This is what happened in Argentina, for example. See Delrio, *Memorias de expropiación*. For Chile, see Bengoa, *Mapuche, colonos y el estado*.

3. Langer, *Expecting Pears*.

4. See Langer, *Economic Change*, 146–55.

5. For Caraparirenda, see Langer, *Economic Change*, 135–36, 154–55.

6. Much ink has been spilled on the topic of Andean highland tribute and land rights. See, for example, Larson, *Trials of Nation Making*; Platt, *Estado boliviano*.

7. *Karai* in Guaraní describes somebody who, "in their behavior, words, projects, and conquests [is] astute, clever and skilled." Giannecchini, *Diccionario chiriguano-español*, 2. See also De Nino, *Etnografía chiriguana*, 114.

8. See Nordenskiöld, "Guaraní Invasion," 103–21; Sušnik, *Dispersión Tupí-Guaraní*; Clastres, *Land-Without-Evil*; Combès and Saignes, *Alter Ego*.

9. Pifarré, *Historia de un pueblo*, 45–74; Pinckert Justiniano, *La guerra chiriguana*.

10. For the best summary of Chiriguano history, see Pifarré, *Historia de un pueblo*. On mission numbers, see Saignes and Combès, *Historia del pueblo chiriguano*, 248.

11. Corrado and Comajuncosa, *El Colegio Franciscano de Tarija*, 294.

12. Manuel Fernando Bacaflor to Ministro del Interior, Tarija, December 25, 1834, Ministerio del Interior, tomo 51, no. 28, Correspondencia Oficial, Archivo y Biblioteca Nacionales de Bolivia (hereafter ABNB).

13. Martarelli, *El Colegio Franciscano*, 303; Sušnik, *Chiriguanos*, 60.

14. See Langer, *Expecting Pears*, 35–60.

15. There is a large literature on the battle of Kuruyuki, which has become emblematic of lowland indigenous resistance to imposition from the national state. See, for example, Sanabria Fernández, *Apiaguaiqui Tumpa*; Combès, *Kuruyuki*; Langer, "Caciques y poder." We still do not have a history of the Tobas. Some preliminary attempts are Combès, "Como agua y aceite," and Langer and Bass Werner de Ruiz,

Historia de Tarija, 203–330. Curiously, other messianic movements emerged around the same time, such as the Ghost Dance among the Plains Indians of North America. For a recent reassessment, see Warren, *God's Red Son*.

16. Francisco Barrios to Governor of the Province, Corregimiento de Sauces, March 22, 1833, p. 3, MI, t 44, no. 25, ABNB.

17. *Informe del Prefecto*, 25.

18. "1er cuerpo del expediente administrativo organizado por el Departamento de Santa Cruz sobre la posesión de Cuevo é Ibo," ABNB. The document consists of 238 pages. Many thanks to Isabelle Combès, who sent me a copy.

19. See 1901: 14, ff. 92–93, Notaría de Hacienda y Minas, Fondo Prefectural, Chuquisaca Prefecture, Sucre, Bolivia. The owner also had to introduce at least four hundred head of cattle and settle on the estate.

20. "Propiedades del Señor Octavio Padilla: Relación de los títulos de propiedad sobre terrenos que posee el Señor Octavio Padilla en Cordillera, Azero, Tomina y Sucre. San Ysidro de Caraparicito, Marzo 10 de 1897," 21. My thanks to Ronald Larson, who kindly provided me with a photocopy of this invaluable document. It is one of the few internal documents of haciendas from this region I have been able to access.

21. "Propiedades del Señor Octavio Padilla," 46–47. As with many documents cited in this two-hundred-page summary, not all of original paper is cited.

22. "Propiedades del Señor Octavio Padilla," 48–49.

23. "Propiedades del Señor Octavio Padilla," 39–40

24. 1885:2, f. 8; Notaría de Hacienda y Minas, Fondo Prefectural, Chuquisaca Prefecture, Sucre, Bolivia. Padilla purchased six more land grants from other petitioners once he was able to do so legally. See Langer, *Economic Change*, 130.

25. "Propiedades del Señor Octavio Padilla," 41. Pastor Durán's residence is noted in 1859 in the "Padrón jeneral que manifiesta el numero de almas de la Parroquia de Gutierres de casta blanca con [illegible] Patria, ocupación, condición, estado, hijos i edad; incluyendo en él los domésticos de todo [illegible]do por el Presbítero José Miguel Montero cura actual de la Parroquia en la fecha que espresara," p. 20, Archivo Parroquial de Lagunillas. Parapití, which also refers to the river, was located in Cordillera Province.

26. See Langer, *Expecting Pears*, 32–33.

27. Austin, "Guaraní Kinship"; Austin, "Embodied Borderland." For a classic statement of this issue, see Service, "Encomienda in Paraguay"; see also Barr, *Peace Came*. For the fur trade, see Van Kirk, *Many Tender Ties*, and Sleeper-Smith, "Women, Kin, and Catholicism."

28. This fundamental understanding also undermines the rhetoric of Chiriguano otherness and duplicity, since español-americanos or even mestizos were always minorities on any side of any conflict during this period. They always worked with more numerous indigenous allies.

29. See Langer, "Savages and Vassals."

30. See Langer, "Savages and Vassals"; Langer, *Economic Change*, 125–38. The history of frontier land grants merits its own study, which is sadly lacking.

31. "Resolución del 16 de marzo, 1864: adjudicación de terrenos en el Chaco a los chiriguanos y tobas poseedores," in Corvera Zenteno, *Legislación agraria boliviana*, 60–61.

32. "N 100 Juicio criminal que se instruye contra Santiago Buricanambi por el delito de matanza saqueo é incendio en el pueblo de Guacaya," 1866:82, Archivo Judicial de Partido de Entre Ríos, Tarija.

33. Martarelli, *El Colegio Franciscano*, 301.

34. All in Instituto de Colonización, ABNB, Sucre. I also found another three land grants given to Izoceño peoples farther northeast. For the Izozog, see Combès, *Etnohistorias del Isoso*.

35. "Obrados seguidos por el Capitán e indígenas naturales de los terrenos de Caraparirenda, pidiendo la inscripción en el Registro de Colonias del Departamento 1907," IC578, Instituto de Colonización, ABNB. For the number of villages and their sizes, see f. 8. Also see Langer, *Economic Change*, 135–36; 154–55.

36. "Obrados seguidos . . . de Caraparirenda," f. 3v.

37. "Obrados seguidos . . . de Caraparirenda," f. 8.

38. "Obrados seguidos . . . de Caraparirenda," f. 14.

39. "Obrados seguidos . . . de Caraparirenda," ff. 16–18.

40. "Obrados seguidos . . . de Caraparirenda," f. 32.

41. "Obrados seguidos . . . de Caraparirenda," f. 32v.

42. See Langer, *Economic Change*, 135–36; 154–55.

43. Early on, it was actually a Chané polity, but by the nineteenth century the Indians identified themselves as Chiriguano. See Combès "Chindica y Guaricaya."

44. Pifarré, *Historia de un pueblo*, 295–96.

45. Combès has by far the best analysis of this revolt; see *Kuruyuki*. Much of this and subsequent paragraphs are based on her account.

46. Martarelli, quoted in Combès, *Kuruyuki*, 127.

47. According to Combès (*Kuruyuki*, 127), the son of José Ignacio, by the name of Ignacio, became the tubicha. It is not clear whether José Santos was the son or the brother of Ignacio.

48. "Registro Nacional de Tierras, no. 135, 127:887 Año 1949," ff. 143–45; Sección Colonización, ABNB.

49. "Registro Nacional de Tierras," f. 147. On the map, it states that the area was 75,000 hectares; however, in the document itself the grand total of Caipipendi and Carabaicho is listed as 58,869 hectares. This was still the largest single land grant.

50. IC 779, "Títulos de los indígenas comunarios Itembeguazu, Itembemi, Guiraguarenda, y Curuguaca de la concesión denominada 'San Miguel,' ubicada en el Departamento de Santa Cruz, provincia Cordillera, cantón Gutiérrez," ff. 126v–128r, Sección Colonización, ABNB.

51. For a good definition of "ayllu," see Spalding, *Huarochirí*, 28–34.

52. IC 779, "Títulos de los indígenas comunarios," ff. 125f–v.

53. IC 779, "Títulos de los indígenas comunarios," f. 128. Article 42 of the law of 1890 did indeed stipulate the granting of this amount of land to indigenous inhabitants,

although to my knowledge nowhere was this article put into practice. For the 1890 law, see Corvera, *Legislación agrarian boliviana*, 124–37. Article 42 is on p. 135.

54. IC 779, "Títulos de los indígenas comunarios," f. 131.

55. See Comajuncosa, *Manifiesto histórico*, 195–201.

56. There is a large literature concerning the interactions between the Chanés and the Chiriguanos. According to most scholars, the Chanés were conquered by the Guaranís as they moved north from what is now Brazil, intermixing with them and thus creating the Chiriguanos. See, for example, Combès and Saignes, *Alter Ego*; Combès, *Etno-historias del Isoso*; Nordenskiöld, "Guaraní Invasion"; Nordenskiöld, *Changes in the Material Culture*. For Iti and its residents' Chané ethnic origin, see Combès "Chindica y Guaricaya."

57. Corrado, *El Colegio Franciscano*, 288–92; quotation on 292.

58. "Cap. Mariano Chanca. Cañon de Iti y Itimiri, Título Ejecutorial (1916)," Concesiones de toda la República, Lote no. 152, tomo I, Instituto de Colonización, ABNB.

59. "Cap. Mariano Chanca," 36. Of course, Comajuncosa wrote only about Iti; it was Fr. del Pilar who had founded the mission. It would be interesting to find out how the lawyer was able to consult Comajuncosa, or whether this was a legend perpetuated in Iti. In 1894 the only available version of Comajuncosa was the first edition of *El Colegio Franciscano*. Did he get it from the Franciscan convent in Sucre or Tarija?

60. "Cap. Mariano Chanca," 3v–4v.

61. Martarelli, *El Colegio Franciscano*, 186–95.

62. Combès, *Kuruyuki*, 99.

63. In Cordillera Province only three short-lived missions—San Antonio del Parapetí, San Francisco del Parapetí, and Itatiqui—survived more than a few years in the early twentieth century. Landlord opposition (and probably opposition from powerful capitanes, such as from Caipipendi) eliminated the missions by 1915. See de Nino, *Continuación*, 103–33.

Epilogue

ONGOING INDIGENOUS STRUGGLES

Joaquín Rivaya-Martínez

As the chapters in this book exemplify, a growing number of scholars now tell the history of the Western Hemisphere in terms of Native agency and power, problematizing the simplistic teleological sequence of indigenous defeat, submission, and extinction that once dominated the historiography. In the New World, numerous indigenous peoples used a variety of strategies to survive, resist, and even thrive after contact. Long gone are the times when scholars saw Natives merely as passive victims of colonialism. Yet, in the third decade of the twenty-first century, Amerindians across the hemisphere continue to face tremendous challenges.

That indigenous people have played key roles in forging their own destiny and shaping today's world is amply documented. Too often, however, dominant popular and political discourses, in the Americas and elsewhere, tend to reduce Native peoples to historical and contemporary irrelevance. Thus, in the United States, for instance, Native Americans rarely make the headlines unless some major controversy occurs, often having to do with Indian-run casinos, the infringement of indigenous rights, or sports teams' mascots caricaturizing Natives. In some Caribbean countries, as well as in Argentina and other parts of Latin America, dominant historical narratives continue to take for granted the disappearance of "the native," denying many of their citizens their indigenous cultural and biological legacy.

Even in countries where official discourses tend to be ostensibly pro-indigenous, an enormous gap often exists between the politicians' rhetoric and the unsettling reality of many extant Amerindian communities, characterized by disproportionately high rates of unemployment, underpaid jobs, domestic violence, alcoholism, obesity, and subpar education and health services. As I write these lines, the ongoing COVID-19 pandemic has brought to the fore states' abandonment of vulnerable indigenous communities as diverse as the Navajos of the US Southwest and the Yanomami of the Orinoco Basin. Even in states whose national identity rests on a self-proclaimed indigeneity, Native people tend to be portrayed as victims of colonial oppression *in the past* while the inaction of powerful elites perpetuates the discrimination and helplessness of indigenous communities *in the present*. In 2020, for instance, diverse indigenous organizations denounced the Mexican administration for giving priority to the so-called Maya Train megaproject over the resolution of their many grievances and needs, while others rejected the enterprise on sovereignty grounds.

In many regions, the distress of unincorporated Amerindian peoples results partly from a combination of demographic, political, and sociocultural circumstances that render them vulnerable: indigenous populations tend to be relatively small and politically divided into a myriad of groups speaking a babel of tongues. In Brazil, for instance, Amerindians constitute about 0.4 percent of the overall population but there are more than 170 extant aboriginal languages spoken by members of more than 220 distinct indigenous groups.[1] Yet even in areas with much higher densities of Natives, their claims often remain unresolved, as demonstrated by the upsurge in the 2010s, in southern Chile and neighboring regions of Argentina, of the Mapuche demands for greater autonomy, recognition of rights, and recovery of ancestral lands. According to the official 2017 census, more than 1.7 million Chileans—almost 10 percent of the overall population—self-identified as Mapuche.

Oil, gas, and mining interests remain a serious menace to Natives' land rights, threatening public health and endangering fragile environments in places as diverse as the northern Great Plains, Alaska, and the Amazon Basin. Efforts to end the Dakota Access Pipeline—which potentially could contaminate the water supply of the Standing Rock Lakota Reservation and nearby communities in the Dakotas—has elicited unprecedented support from Natives and non-Natives all over the United States, including groups as diverse as environmentalists and military veterans.[2] In the summer of 2020, a district court judge ruled that the pipeline must be shut down and emptied of oil pending a new environmental review, although the shutdown was promptly overturned by a court of appeals. Other recent developments have been more promising, including the 2015 report of the Truth and Reconciliation Commission in Canada, the appointment of Deb Haaland (Laguna Pueblo) as US secretary of the interior—thus making her the first Native American to serve as a cabinet secretary—along with her subsequent appointment of Charles F. "Chuck" Sams III (Cayuse and Walla Walla) as director of the National Park Service, and the ongoing investigations into deaths of Native children at Canadian and US boarding schools. On the other hand, a recent US Supreme Court ruling has severely limited the impact of the landmark 2020 ruling (*McGirt v. Oklahoma*) that implicitly acknowledged an enormous swath of the state of Oklahoma is Indian country.[3]

The long-term consequences of all those ongoing processes and controversies remain to be seen. Still, they remind us that indigenous peoples continue resolutely to influence the course of events in many parts of the Americas, notwithstanding dominant discourses about their purported extinction or irrelevance. Remarkably, all those regions were once, and some arguably continue to be, indigenous borderlands.

NOTES

1. Monteiro, "Indigenous Histories in Colonial Brazil," 408.

2. For an excellent overview of this controversy and the historical roots of Native resistance by a participant, see Estes, *Our History Is the Future.*

3. In a controversial five-to-four vote, the US Supreme Court ruled in *Oklahoma v. Castro-Huerta* that the state of Oklahoma has concurrent jurisdiction and can prosecute non-Natives for crimes occurring on tribal land when the victim is Native.

Bibliography

Adams, David Wallace. *Education for Extinction: American Indians and the Boarding School Experience, 1875–1928.* Lawrence: University Press of Kansas, 1995.

Adams, E. Charles. "Passive Resistance: Hopi Reponses to Spanish Contact and Conquest." In *Columbian Consequences.* Vol. 1 *Archaeological and Historical Perspectives on the Spanish Borderlands West,* edited by David Hurst Thomas, 77–91. Washington, DC: Smithsonian Institution Press, 1991.

Adelman, Jeremy, and Stephen Aron. "From Borderlands to Borders: Empires, Nation-States, and the Peoples in Between in North American History." *American Historical Review* 104, no. 3 (June 1999): 814–41.

Aguilar Meza, Trinidad. "Las trampas para cazar camélidos." In *Llamichos y paqocheros. Pastores de llamas y alpacas,* edited by Jorge Flores Ochoa, 59–65. Cuzco: Centro de Estudios Andinos, 1988.

Albeck, M. E. "Producción y lógica de la red vial incaica en el extremo septentrional del NOA." *Arqueología* 22, no. 1 (2016): 61–79.

Alexander, Rani T. "Isla Cilvituk and the Difficulties of Spanish Colonization in Southwestern Campeche." In *The Postclassic to Spanish-Era Transition in Mesoamerica: Archaeological Perspectives,* edited by Susan M. Kepecs and Rani T. Alexander, 161–81. Albuquerque: University of New Mexico Press, 2005.

Alonso, Ana Maria. *Thread of Blood: Colonialism, Revolution and Gender in Mexico's Northern Frontier.* Tucson: University of Arizona Press, 1995.

Altman, Ida. *The War for Mexico's West: Indians and Spaniards in New Galicia, 1524–1550.* Albuquerque: University of New Mexico Press, 2010.

Álvarez, Salvador. "Agricultores de paz y cazadores-recolectores de guerra: los tobosos de la cuenca del río Conchos en la Nueva Vizcaya." In Hers, Mirafuentes, Soto, and Vallebueno, *Nómadas y sedentarios,* 305–54.

———. "De 'zacatecos' y 'tepehuanes': dos dilatadas parcialidades de chichimecas norteños." In *La Sierra Tepehuana. Asentamientos y movimientos de población,* edited by Chantal Cramaussel and Sara Ortelli, 97–128. Zamora: El Colegio de Michoacán; Universidad Juárez del Estado de Durango—Instituto de Investigaciones Históricas, 2006.

———. *El indio y la sociedad colonial norteña. Siglos XVI–XVIII.* Zamora: IHH/UJED, El Colegio de Michoacán, 2009.

———. "La guerra chichimeca." In *Historia del reino de la Nueva Galicia,* edited by Thomas Calvo and Aristarco Regalado Pinedo, 211–59. Guadalajara, JA: Universidad de Guadalajara, 2016.

Álvarez Palma, Ana María. "Huatabampo: consideraciones sobre una comunidad agrícola prehispánica en el sur de Sonora." *Noroeste de México* 9 (1990): 9–93.

Anderson, David G. *Savannah River Chiefdoms: Political Change in the Late Prehistoric Southeast.* Tuscaloosa: University of Alabama Press, 1994.

———. "Stability and Change in Chiefdom-Level Societies: An Examination of Mississippian Political Evolution on the South Atlantic Slope." In *Lamar Archaeology: Mississippian Chiefdoms in the Deep South*, edited by Mark Williams and Gary Shapiro, 187–213. Tuscaloosa: University of Alabama Press, 1990.

Anderson, David G., and Robbie Ethridge, eds. "Book Forum: On *Chiefdoms and Other Archaeological Delusions*, by Timothy R. Pauketat." *Native South* 2 (2009): 69–132.

Anderson, David G., and Kenneth E. Sassaman. *Recent Developments in Southeastern Archaeology: From Colonization to Complexity.* Washington, DC: Society for American Archaeology Press, 2012.

Anderson, Gary C. *The Conquest of Texas: Ethnic Cleansing in the Promised Land, 1820–1875.* Norman: University of Oklahoma Press, 2005.

———. *Ethnic Cleansing and the Indian: The Crime That Should Haunt America.* Norman: University of Oklahoma Press, 2015.

———. *The Indian Southwest, 1580–1830: Ethnogenesis and Reinvention.* Norman: University of Oklahoma Press, 1999.

Anzaldúa, Gloria. *Borderlands/La Frontera: The New Mestiza.* 4th ed. San Francisco, CA: Aunt Lute Books, 2012.

Arancibia, Ubén G. *Vida y mitos del mundo mataco.* Buenos Aires: Ediciones de Palma, 1953.

Archer, Christon I. "The Deportation of Barbarian Indians from the Internal Provinces of New Spain, 1789–1810." *Americas* 29 (January 1973): 376–85.

Ardren, Traci, Scott R. Hutson, David R. Hixscon, and Justin Lowry. "Connections beyond Chunchucmil." In *Ancient Maya Commerce: Multidisciplinary Research at Chunchucmil*, edited by Scott R. Hutson, 273–97. Boulder: University Press of Colorado, 2017.

Areces, Nidia. "Los guaraní-monteses y los yerbales silvestres en Concepción. Frontera norte paraguaya, durante el gobierno del Dr. Francia." *Andes, Antropología e Historia* 6 (1994): 303–25.

Arenas, Pastor. *Etnografía y alimentación entre los Tobas-Ñachilamole#ek y Wichí-Lhuku'tas del Chaco Central (Argentina).* Buenos Aires: Self-published, 2003.

Armatto de Welti, Zulema. *Diccionario guaraní de usos. Etnolexicología estuctural del guaraní yopará.* Buenos Aires: Editorial Fundación Ross, 1988.

Asselbergs, Florine G. L. *Conquered Conquistadors: The Lienzo de Quauhquechollan: A Nahua Vision of the Conquest of Guatemala.* Leiden: CNWS, 2004.

Atkinson, James R. "The de Soto Expedition through North Mississippi in 1541." *Mississippi Archaeology* 22, no. 1 (1987): 63–68.

———. "A Historic Contact Indian Settlement in Oktibbeha County, Mississippi." *Journal of Alabama Archaeology* 25, no. 1 (1979): 61–82.

Austin, Shawn Michael. *Colonial Kinship: Guaraní, Spaniards, and Africans in Paraguay.* Albuquerque: University of New Mexico Press, 2020.

———. "Embodied Borderland: Colonial Guairá, 1570s–1630s." In *Big Water: The Making of the Borderlands between Brazil, Argentina, and Paraguay,* edited by Jacob Blanc, Federico Freitas, and Zephyr L. Frank, 25–53. Tucson: University of Arizona Press, 2018.

———. "Guaraní Kinship and the Encomienda Community in Colonial Paraguay, Sixteenth and Early Seventeenth Centuries." *Colonial Latin American Review* 24, no. 4 (2015): 545–71.

Awe, Jaime J., and Christophe Helmke. "The Sword and the Olive Jar: Material Evidence of Seventeenth-Century Maya-European Interaction in Belize." *Ethnohistory* 62, no. 2 (April 2015): 333–60. https://doi.org/10.1215/00141801-2854369.

Ayala, Ricardo. "Revisión de las abejas sin aguijón de México (Hymenóptera: Apidae: Meliponini)." *Folia Entomológica Mexicana* 106 (1999): 1–123.

Babcock, Matthew. *Apache Adaptation to Hispanic Rule.* Cambridge: Cambridge University Press, 2016.

———. "Rethinking the Establecimientos: Why Apaches Settled on Spanish-Run Reservations, 1786–1793." *New Mexico Historical Review* 84, no. 3 (Summer 2009): 363–97.

Bahar, Matthew. *Storm of the Sea: Indians and Empires in the Atlantic's Age of Sail.* New York: Oxford University Press, 2018.

Bannon, John Francis. *Bolton and the Spanish Borderlands.* Norman: University of Oklahoma Press, 1964.

Bañuelos, Noemí. "Etnobotánica, una ventana hacia la concepción de los mundos mayo y guarijío." In *Los pueblos indígenas del noroeste. Atlas etnográfico,* edited by José Luis Moctezuma Zamarrón and Alejandro Aguilar Zeleny, 403–7. Hermosillo, SO: Instituto Sonorense de Cultura; Mexico City: INAH, INALI, 2013.

Barba, Fernando Enrique. *Frontera ganadera y guerra con el indio. La frontera y la ocupación ganadera en Buenos Aires entre los siglos XVIII y XIX.* La Plata, Argentina: Editorial de la Universidad Nacional de La Plata, 1997.

Barber, Russell J., and Frances F. Berdan. *The Emperor's Mirror: Understanding Cultures through Primary Sources.* Tucson: University of Arizona Press, 1998.

Barbosa, Pablo Antunha, and Fabio Mura. "Construindo e reconstruindo territórios guarani: dinámica territorial na fronteira entre Brasil e Paraguai (sec. XIX–XX)." *Journal de la Société des Américanistes* 97, no. 2 (2011): 287–318.

Barcelos, Artur H. F. "El saber cartográfico indígena entre los guaraníes de las misiones jesuíticas." In *Saberes de la conversión. Jesuitas, indígenas e imperios coloniales en las fronteras de la cristiandad,* edited by Guillermo Wilde, 191–204. Buenos Aires: Editorial SB, 2011.

———. *O Mergulho no seculum: exploração, conquista e organização espacial jesuítica na América espanhola colonial.* Porto Alegre: Animal, 2006.

Barnett, James Jr. *The Natchez Indians: A History to 1735.* Jackson: University Press of Mississippi, 2007.

Barr, Juliana. "Geographies of Power: Mapping Indian Borders in the 'Borderlands' of the Early Southwest." *William and Mary Quarterly*, 3rd ser., 68, no. 1 (January 2011): 5–46.

———. *Peace Came in the Form of a Woman: Indians and Spaniards in the Texas Borderlands*. Chapel Hill: University of North Carolina Press, 2007.

———. "There's No Such Thing as 'Prehistory': What the Longue Durée of Caddo and Pueblo History Tells Us about Colonial America." *William and Mary Quarterly*, 3rd ser., 74, no. 2 (2017): 203–40.

Barr, Juliana, and Edward Countryman, eds. *Contested Spaces of Early America*. Philadelphia: University of Pennsylvania Press, 2014.

Barrera Monroy, Eduardo. *Mestizaje, comercio y resistencia. La Guajira durante la segunda mitad del siglo XVIII*. Bogota: Instituto Colombiana de Antropología e Historia, 2000.

Baskes, Jeremy. *Indians, Merchants, and Markets: A Reinterpretation of the Repartimiento and Spanish-Indian Economic Relations in Colonial Oaxaca, 1750–1821*. Stanford, CA: Stanford University Press, 2000.

Basso, Keith H. *Wisdom Sits in Places: Landscape and Language among the Western Apache*. Albuquerque: University of New Mexico Press, 1996.

Bateman, Rebecca B. "Africans and Indians: A Comparative Study of the Black Carib and Black Seminole." *Ethnohisotry* 37, no. 1 (Winter 1990): 1–24.

Baud, Michie, and Willem van Schendel. "A Comparative Approach to Borderlands." In *Major Problems in the History of North American Borderlands*, edited by Pekka Hämäläinen and Benjamin H. Johnson, 1–13. Boston, MA: Wadsworth Cengage Learning, 2012.

Bayer, Laura. *Santa Ana: The People, the Pueblo, and the History of Tamaya*. Albuquerque: University of New Mexico Press, 1994.

Bayne, Brandon, *Missions Begin with Blood: Suffering and Salvation in the Spanish Borderlands*. New York: Fordham University Press, 2021.

———. "Willy-Nilly Baptisms and Chichimeca Freedoms: Missionary Disputes and Indigenous Desires in the O'odham Revolt of 1695." *Journal of Early Modern History* 21 (2017): 9–37.

Beck, Robin E. "Consolidation and Hierarchy: Chiefdom Variability in the Mississippian Southeast." *American Antiquity* 68, no. 4 (2003): 641–61.

Beckerman, Stephen. *Datos etnohistóricos acerca de los Barí (Motilones)*. Caracas: Universidad Católica Andrés Bello, 1979.

Bengoa, José. *Mapuche, colonos y el estado nacional*. Santiago: Catalonia, 2014.

Benn Torres, Jada. "Prospecting the Past: Genetic Perspectives on the Extinction and Survival of Indigenous Peoples of the Caribbean." *New Genetics and Society* 33, no. 1 (January 2014): 21–41. https://doi.org/10.1080/14636778.2013.873245.

Benn Torres, Jada, Miguel G. Vilar, Gabriel A. Torres, Jill B. Gaieski, Ricardo Bharath Hernandez, Zoila E. Browne, Marlon Stevenson, et al. "Genetic Diversity in the Lesser Antilles and Its Implications for the Settlement of the Caribbean Basin." [In eng]. *PloS One* 10, no. 10 (2015): e0139192–e92. https://doi.org/10.1371/journal.pone.0139192.

Benton, Bradley. *The Lords of Tetzcoco: The Transformation of Indigenous Rule in Post-conquest Central Mexico.* Cambridge: Cambridge University Press, 2017.

Berdan, Frances F., John K. Chance, Alan R. Sandstrom, Barbara L. Stark, James Taggart, and Emily Umberger. *Ethnic Identity in Nahua Mesoamerica: The View from Archaeology, Ethnohistory, and Contemporary Ethnography.* Salt Lake City: University of Utah Press, 2008.

Bernabéu, Salvador, Chritophe Giudicelli, and Gilles Havard, eds. *La indianización. Cautivos, renegados, "hommes libres" y misioneros en los confines de las Américas, s. XVI–XIX.* Seville: Doce Calles, 2013.

Berrojalbiz, Fernando. *Paisajes y fronteras del Durango prehispánico.* Mexico City: UNAM, 2012.

Bidondo, Emilio A. "Una discusión sobre el asentamiento original de la ciudad de Ledesma (Provincia de Jujuy–República Argentina)." In *Sexto Congreso Internacional de Historia de América,* 311–31. Buenos Aires: Academia Nacional de la Historia, 1982.

Biedma, Luys Hernández de. "Relation of the Island of Florida." In Clayton, Knight, and Moore, *de Soto Chronicles,* 1:221–46.

Birnbaum, Emily. "Poll: 29 Percent See Migrant Caravan as Major Threat to US." *The Hill,* November 19, 2018. https://thehill.com/latino/417454-poll-29-percent-see -migrant-caravan-as-major-threat-to-us.

Blackhawk, Ned. "Currents in North American Indian Historiography." *Western Historical Quarterly* 42 (Autumn 2011): 319–24.

———. *Violence over the Land: Indians and Empires in the Early American West.* Cambridge, MA.: Harvard University Press, 2006.

Blanton, Dennis B. "Tracking an Entrada by Comparative Analysis of Sixteenth-Century Archaeological Assemblages from the Southeast." In Boudreaux, Meyers, and Johnson, *Contact, Colonialism, and Native Communities,* 73–101.

Blitz, John H. *Ancient Chiefdoms of the Tombigbee.* Tuscaloosa: University of Alabama Press, 1993.

———. "Mississippian Chiefdoms and the Fusion-Fission Process." *American Antiquity* 64, no. 4 (1999): 577–92.

———. "New Perspectives in Mississippian Archaeology." *Journal of Archaeological Research* 18 (2010): 1–39.

Block, David. *Mission Culture on the Upper Amazon: Native Tradition, Jesuit Enterprise, and Secular Policy in Moxos, 1660–1880.* Lincoln: University of Nebraska Press, 1994.

Bloom, Lansing Bartlett. "New Mexico under Mexican Administration, 1821–1846." *Old Santa Fe: A Magazine of History, Archaeology, Genealogy and Biography* 1, no. 1 (July 1913): 3–47.

Blyth, Lance R. *Chiricahua and Janos: Communities of Violence in the Southwestern Borderlands.* Lincoln: University of Nebraska Press, 2012.

Boccara, Guillaume. "Génesis y estructura de los complejos fronterizos euro-indígenas: Repensando los márgenes americanos a partir (y más allá) de la obra de Nathan Wachtel." *Memoria Americana* 13 (2005): 21–52.

———. *Guerre et ethnogenèse Mapuche dans le Chili colonial: L'invention du soi.* Paris: Editions L'Harmattan, 1998.

———. *Los vencedores. Historia del Pueblo Mapuche en la época colonial.* San Pedro de Atacama: Universidad Católica del Norte, 2007.

———. "Mundos nuevos en las fronteras del Nuevo Mundo." *Nuevo Mundo Mundos Nuevos* (2001). https://doi.org/10.4000/nuevomundo.426.

Boidin, Capucine. "Textos de la modernidad política en guaraní (1810–1813)." *Corpus. Archivos Virtuales de la Alteridad Americana* 4, no. 2 (2014). https://doi.org/10.4000/corpusarchivos.1322.

Bolton, Herbert E. *The Spanish Borderlands: A Chronicle of Old Florida and the Southwest.* New Haven, CT: Yale University Press, 1921.

Borrero Silva, María del Valle, and Jesús Dénica Velarde Cadena. "Los indios auxiliares: las compañías de ópatas de la provincia de Sonora." In *Indios, españoles y mestizos en zonas de frontera, siglos XVII–XX,* edited by José Marcos Medina Bustos and Esther Padilla Calderón, 95–116. Hermosillo: El Colegio de Sonora; Zamora: El Colegio de Michoacán, 2013.

Boudreaux, Edmond A. III, Charles R. Cobb, Emily Clark, Chester B. DePratter, James Legg, Brad R. Lieb, Allison M. Smith, and Steven D. Smith. "The Early Contact Period in the Black Prairie of Northeast Mississippi." In Boudreaux, Meyers, and Johnson, *Contact, Colonialism, and Native Communities,* 35–56.

Boudreaux, Edmond A. III, Stephen G. Harris, Allison M. Smith, Emily L. Clark, Jay K. Johnson, Brad R. Lieb, and John W. O'Hear. "Archaeological Investigations in the Chickasaw Homeland: A Report on Fieldwork at Two Sites in Northeast Mississippi." Report prepared for the Chickasaw Nation Department of Culture and Humanities, Ada, OK, by the Center for Archaeological Research, University of Mississippi, 2017.

Boudreaux, Edmond A. III, Maureen Meyers, and Jay K. Johnson, eds. *Contact, Colonialism, and Native Communities in the Southeastern United States.* Gainesville: University Press of Florida, 2020.

Bowden, J. J. "Antonio Ortiz Grant." *New Mexico History,* accessed July 15, 2013. http://www.newmexicohistory.org/filedetails.php?fileID=24816.

Bowes, John P. *Exiles and Pioneers: Eastern Indians in the Trans-Mississippi West.* Cambridge: Cambridge University Press, 2007.

———. *Land Too Good for Indians: Northern Indian Removal.* Norman: University of Oklahoma Press, 2017.

Bowne, Eric E. *Mound Sites of the Ancient South: A Guide to the Mississippian Chiefdoms.* Athens: University of Georgia Press, 2013.

Bracamonte y Sosa, Pedro. *La conquista inconclusa de Yucatán: Los mayas de las montañas, 1560–1680.* Collección Peninsula. Mexico City: Centro de Investigaciones y Estudios Superiores en Antropología Social, Universidad de Quintana Roo, 2001.

Bracco, Diego. *Charrúas, guenoas y guaraníes: interacción y destrucción: indígenas en el Río de la Plata.* Montevideo: Linardi y Risso, 2004.

Brand, Donald D. "The Honey Bee in New Spain and Mexico." *Journal of Cultural Geography* 9, no. 1 (1988): 71–81.

Braun Wilke, Rolando H., et al. *Carta de aptitud ambiental de la Provincia de Jujuy.* Jujuy: Universidad Nacional de Jujuy, 2001.

Braund, Kathryn E. Holland. "The de Soto Map and the Luna Narratives: An Overview of Other Sixteenth-Century Sources." In Knight, *Search for Mabila*, 45–63. Tuscaloosa: University of Alabama Press, 2009.

Brayer, Herbert O. *Pueblo Indian Grants of the "Rio Abajo," New Mexico.* Albuquerque: University of New Mexico Press, 1938.

Brooks, James F. *Captives and Cousins: Slavery, Kinship, and Community in the Southwest Borderlands.* Chapel Hill: University of North Carolina Press, 2002.

Brosseder, Claudia. *The Power of Huacas: Change and Resistance in the Andean World of Colonial Peru.* Austin: Univesity of Texas Press, 2014.

Brown, James A. "Sequencing the Braden Style within Mississippian Period Art and Iconography." In Reilly and Garber, *Ancient Objects and Sacred Realms*, 213–45.

Brown, Jennifer S. H., and Elizabeth Vibert, eds. *Reading Beyond Words: Contexts for Native History.* 2nd ed. Toronto, ON: University of Toronto Press, 2003.

Brown, Tracy. *Pueblo Indians and Spanish Colonial Authority in Eighteenth-Century New Mexico.* Tucson: University of Arizona Press, 2013.

———. "Tradition and Change in Eighteenth-Century Pueblo Indian Communities." *Journal of the Southwest* 46, no. 3 (Autumn 2004): 463–500.

Bruno, Cayetano. *La evangelización de la Patagonia y de la Tierra del Fuego.* Rosario: Ediciones Didascalia, 1982.

Bushnell, Amy Turner, and Jack P. Greene. "Peripheries, Centers, and the Construction of Early Modern American Empires: An Introduction." In *Negotiated Empires. Centers and Peripheries in the Americas, 1500–1820*, edited by Christine Daniels and Michael D. Kennedy, 1–14. New York: Routledge, 2002.

Bussu, Salvatore. *Mártires sin altar. Padre Juan Antonio Solinas, Don Pedro Ortiz de Zárate y dieciocho cristianos laicos.* Salta: Universidad Católica de Salta, 2003.

Cadogan, León. "Las reducciones del Tarumá y la destrucción de la organización social de los Mbyá-Guaraníes del Guairá (Ka'yguä o Monteses)." In *Estudios antropológicos publicados en homenaje al doctor Manuel Gamio*, 295–303. Mexico City: UNAM, 1956.

Calloway, Colin G. *New Worlds for All: Indians, Europeans, and the Remaking of Early America.* Baltimore, MD: Johns Hopkins University Press, 1997.

Camacho Ibarra, Fidel, "El sol y la serpiente: el *pajko* y el complejo ritual comunal de los mayos de Sonora." Masters thesis, Mexico City, UNAM, 2017.

Cameron, Catherine M., Paul Kelton, and Alan C. Swedlund, eds. *Beyond Germs: Native Depopulation in North America.* Tucson: University of Arizona Press, 2015.

Campos Goenaga, María Isabel. "Sobre tempestades con remolino y plagas de langosta. Siglos XVI al XVIII en la península de Yucatán." *Relaciones* 129 (2012): 125–60.

Candela, Guillaume. "Corpus indígenas en la conquista del Paraguay (siglo XVI). *Corpus* 4, no. 1 (2014): 1–17.

Carballo, David. *Collision of Worlds: A Deep History of the Fall of Aztec Mexico and the Forging of New Spain.* Oxford: Oxford University Press, 2020.

Carlisle, Jeffrey D. "Spanish Relations with the Apache Nations East of the Rio Grande." PhD diss., University of North Texas, 2001.

Carpenter, John. "The Pre-Hispanic Occupation of the Río Fuerte Valley, Sinaloa." In *Building Transnational Archaeologies/Construyendo arqueologías transnacionales*, edited by Elisa Villalpando and Randall H. McGuire 37–52. Tucson: University of Arizona Press, 2014.

Caso Barrera, Laura, and Mario Aliphat Fernández. "Cacao, Vanilla, and Annatto: Three Production and Exchange Systems in the Southern Maya Lowlands, XVI–XVII Centuries." *Journal of Latin American Geography* 5, no. 2 (2006): 29–52.

Castillo Palma, Norma A. *Cholula: sociedad mestiza en ciudad india. Un análisis de las consecuencias demográficas, económicas y sociales del mestizaje en una ciudad novohispana (1649–1796)*. Mexico City: Plaza y Valdés, 2001.

Castro, Hortensia. *Aportes en torno a la discusión población-recursos. El caso de la alta cuenca del río Bermejo, en el noroeste argentino*. Tucumán: Conferencia en Congreso de Investigación Social, 1995.

Castro Gutiérrez, Felipe. "Los ires y devenires del fundo legal de los pueblos indios." In *De la historia económica a la historia social y cultural. Homenaje a Gisela von Wobeser*, edited by María del Pilar Martínez López-Cano, 69–103. Mexico City: Instituto de Investigaciones Históricas, UNAM, 2015.

———. *Los tarascos y el imperio español, 1600–1740*. Mexico City: Instituto de Investigaciones Históricas, UNAM; Universidad Michoacana de San Nicolás Hidalgo, 2004.

Castro Gutiérrez, Felipe, ed. *Los indios y las ciudades de Nueva España*. Mexico City: Instituto de Investigaciones Históricas, UNAM, 2010.

Chamberlain, Kathleen. *Victorio: Apache Warrior and Chief*. Norman: University of Oklahoma Press, 2007.

Charles, John. *Allies at Odds: The Andean Church and Its Indigenous Agents, 1583–1671*. Albuquerque: University of New Mexico Press, 2010.

Chase, Arlen F., and Diane Z. Chase. "Postclassic Temporal and Spatial Frames for the Lowland Maya: A Background." In *The Lowland Maya Postclassic*, edited by Arlen F. Chase and Prudence M. Rice, 9–22. Austin: University of Texas Press, 1985.

Childs, Matt. *The 1812 Aponte Rebellion in Cuba and the Struggle against Atlantic Slavery*. Chapel Hill: University of North Carolina Press, 2006.

Chipman, Donald E. *Moctezuma's Children: Aztec Royalty under Spanish Rule, 1520–1700*. Austin: University of Texas Press, 2005.

Chuchiak, John F. IV. "'Fide, Non Armis': Franciscan Reducciónes and the Maya Mission Experience on the Colonial Frontier of Yucatán, 1602–1640." In *Francis in the Americas: Essays on the Franciscan Family in North and South America*, edited by John Frederick Schwaller, 119–42. Berkeley, CA: Academy of American Franciscan History, 2005.

Churruca Peláez, Agustín, Héctor Barraza Arévalo, Gildardo Contreras Palacios, and Mayela Sakanassi Ramírez. *El sur de Coahuila en el siglo XVII*. Parras: Ayuntamiento de Parras, 1994.

Cipolletti, María Susana. *Sociedades indígenas de la Alta Amazonía. Fortunas y adversidades (siglos XVII–XX)*. Quito: Ediciones Abya-Yala, 2017.

Clark, Jeffrey J., Jennifer A. Birch, Michelle Hegmon, and Barbara J. Mills. "Resolving the Migrant Paradox: Two Pathways to Coalescence in the Late Precontact U.S. Southwest." *Journal of Anthropological Archaeology* 53 (2019): 262–87.

Clarke, Emily. "The Analysis of the Contact-Era Settlements in Clay, Lowndes, and Oktibbeha Counties in Northeast Mississippi." Master's thesis, University of Mississippi, 2017.

Clastres, Hélène. *The Land-Without-Evil: Tupí-Guaraní Prophetism*. Urbana: University of Illinois Press, 1995.

Clayton, Lawrence A., Vernon. J. Knight Jr., and Edward C. Moore, eds. *The de Soto Chronicles: The Expedition of Hernando de Soto to North America in 1539–1543*. 2 vols. Tuscaloosa: University of Alabama Press, 1993.

Clendinnen, Inga. "Yucatec Maya Women and the Spanish Conquest: Role and Ritual in Historical Reconstruction." *Journal of Social History* 15, no. 3 (1982): 427–42.

Clifford, James. "Diasporas." *Cultural Anthropology* 9, no. 3 (August 1994): 302–38.

Cobb, Charles, James Legg, Kimberly Wescott, Brad Lieb, Domenique Sorresso, William Edwards, and Kristin Hall. "Beyond Yaneka: Archaeological Survey in the Protohistoric Chickasaw Settlement Region." Report prepared for the Chickasaw Nation, Ada, OK, by the Florida Museum of Natural History, University of Florida, Gainesville, 2016.

Comajuncosa, Antonio. *Manifiesto histórico, geográfico, topográfico, apostólico y político de lo que han trabajado, entre fieles e infieles los misioneros Franciscanos de Tarija, 1754–1810*. Tarija, Bolivia: Editorial Offset Franciscana, 1993.

Combès, Isabelle. "Chindica y Guaricaya, capitanes chané 'ynfieles de estas montañas.'" *Anuario ABNB* (2004): 223–40.

———. "Como agua y aceite. Las alianzas guerreras entre Tobas y Chiriguanos en el siglo XIX." *Indiana* 31 (2014): 321–49.

———. *De la una y otra banda del río Paraguay. Historia y etnografía de los itatines (siglos XVI–XVIII)*. Cochabamba: Instituto de Misionología/Editorial Itinerarios, 2015.

———. "Etnohistoria, etnocidio y etnogénesis en la frontera: la trayectoria de los itatines." *Memoria Americana* 25, no. 2 (2017): 11–28.

———. *Etno-historias del Isoso. Chané y chiriguanos en el Chaco boliviano (siglos XVI a XX)*. La Paz: Institut Français d'Études Andines; Programa de Investigación Estratégica en Bolivia, 2005.

———. *Kuruyuki*. Cochabamba: Itinerarios Editorial, 2014.

Combès Isabelle, and Thierry Saignes. *Alter Ego: Naissance de l'identité Chiriguano*. Paris: École des Hautes Études, 1991.

Conkey, Margaret W. "Dwelling at the Margins, Action at the Intersection? Feminist and Indigenous Archaeologies, 2005." *Archaeologies* 1, no. 1 (August 2005): 9–59.

Connell, William F. *After Moctezuma: Indigenous Politics and Self-Government in Mexico City, 1524–1730*. Norman: University of Oklahoma Press, 2011.

Conrad, Paul. *The Apache Diaspora: Four Centuries of Displacement and Survival.* Philadelphia: University of Pennsylvania Press, 2021.

———. "Captive Fates: Displaced American Indians in the Southwest Borderlands, Mexico, and Cuba." PhD diss., University of Texas at Austin, 2011.

———. "Empire through Kinship: Rethinking Spanish-Apache Relations in Southwestern North America in the Late Eighteenth and Early Nineteenth Centuries." *Early American Studies* 14, no. 4 (Fall 2016): 626–60.

———. "Indians, Convicts, and Slaves: An Apache Diaspora to Cuba at the Beginning of the Nineteenth Century." In *Linking the Histories of Slavery: North America and Its Borderlands*, edited by Bonnie Martin and James F. Brooks, 67–95. Santa Fe, NM: School for Advanced Research Press, 2015.

Cook, Curtis, and Juan D. Lindau, eds. *Aboriginal Rights and Self-Government: The Canadian and Mexican Experience in North American Perspective.* Montreal and Kingston: McGill-Queen's University Press, 2000.

Cook, Sherburne F., and Woodrow Borah. *Essays in Population History: Mexico and the Caribbean.* Vol. 1. Berkeley and Los Angeles: University of California Press, 1974.

Corbeil, Laurent. *The Motions Beneath: Indigenous Migrants on the Urban Frontier of New Spain.* Tucson: University of Arizona Press, 2018.

Corrado, Alejandro María, and Antonio Comajuncosa, *El Colegio Franciscano de Tarija y sus misiones. Noticias recogidas por dos misioneros del mismo colegio.* Quaracchi: Tipografía del Colegio de S. Buenaventura, 1884.

Cortesão, Jaime. *Manuscritos da coleção de Angelis.* Vol. 1. *Jesuítas e bandeirantes no Guairá (1594–1640).* Rio de Janeiro: Biblioteca Nacional, Divisão de Obras Raras e Publicações, 1951.

Corvera Zenteno, Rómulo. *Legislación agraria boliviana: 1824–1926.* La Paz: Talleres Gráficos La Prensa de José L. Calderón, 1926.

Couchonnal, Ana, and Guillermo Wilde. "De la política de la lengua a la lengua de la política. Cartas guaraníes en la transición de la colonia a la era independiente." *Corpus* 4, no. 1 (2014). https://doi.org/10.4000/corpusarchivos.774.

Covey, R. Alan. *Inca Apocalypse: The Spanish Conquest and the Transformation of the Andean World.* New York: Oxford University Press, 2020.

Cramaussel, Chantal. "De cómo los españoles clasificaban a los indios: naciones y encomiendas en la Nueva Vizcaya central." In Hers, Mirafuentes, Soto, and Vallebueno, *Nómadas y sedentarios*, 275–300.

———. "El Bolsón de Mapimí: un hábitat indígena en la época colonial." In *Caminos y vertientes del septentrión mexicano. Homenaje a Ignacio del Río*, edited by Patricia Osante, José Enrique Covarrubias, Juan Domingo Vidargas, and Nancy Leyva, 165–88. Mexico City: Instituto de Investigaciones Históricas, UNAM, 2020.

———. "El exterminio de los chizos, sisimbles, acoclames y cocoyomes del Bolsón de Mapimí." *Revista de Historia* 6 (2014): 35–56.

———. "The Forced Transfer of Indians in Nueva Vizcaya and Sinaloa: A Hispanic Method of Colonization." In *Contested Spaces in Early America*, edited by Edward Countryman and Juliana Barr, 184–208. Philadelphia: University of Pennsylvania Press and Southern Methodist University, 2014.

———. "Indios de paz contra indios de guerra durante las campañas punitivas en el Bolsón de Mapimí, 1652–1653 y 1722–1723." In *El orden social y político en zonas de frontera: Norte de México y Argentina*, edited by José Marcos Medina Bustos, 69–102. Hermosillo: El Colegio de Sonora and El Colegio de San Luis, 2018.

———. "La función de la cartografía colonial a la luz de las representaciones del Bolsón de Mapimí." In *La cartografía del norte de la Nueva España*, edited by José Refugio de la Torre Curiel and Salvador Álvarez, 135–64. Hermosillo: El Colegio de Sonora; Guadalajara: El Colegio de Jalisco, 2020.

———. "La región de San Francisco de Lajas, Dgo., Los tepehuanos audam de la vertiente occidental de la Sierra Madre." *Transición* 35 (2007): 8–27.

———. "La violencia en Chihuahua a mediados del siglo XIX." In *Violencia interétnica pública y privada en territorios fronterizos: representaciones y acciones sociales, siglos XVIII al XX*, edited by José Marcos Medina and Raquel Padilla Calderón, 195–226. Hermosillo: El Colegio de Sonora; Mexicali: Universidad Autónoma de Baja California, 2015.

———. "Poblar en tierras de muchos indios. La región de Álamos en los siglos XVII y XVIII." *Región y Sociedad* 24, no. 53 (2012): 11–53.

———. *Poblar la frontera. La provincia de Santa Bárbara durante los siglos XVI y XVII*. Zamora: El Colegio de Michoacán, 2006.

———. "Population and Epidemics North of Zacatecas." In Levin Rojo and Radding, *Oxford Handbook of Borderlands*, 107–30.

Cramaussel, Chantal, and Celso Carrillo Valdez. *Coahuila o "tierra adentro." Un valle transformado en gobernación (1585–1722)*. Zamora: El Colegio de Michoacán, in press.

———. "Don Santiago Alonso, gobernador de los cabezas y la suerte de los indios de su nación. Bolsón de Mapimí, norte del virreinato de la Nueva España (1645–1724)." *Revista Brasileña de Historia y Ciencias Sociales* 10, no. 19 (2018): 9–31.

———. "El difícil poblamiento de Mapimí y la fundación del presidio en 1711." *Revista de Historia* 8 (2016): 63–93.

Cramaussel, Chantal, and Manuel Rosales Villa. *San Francisco de Conchos. Misión y presidio (1604–1755)*. Zamora: El Colegio de Michoacán, 2019.

Crandall, Maurice. *These People Have Always Been a Republic: Indigenous Electorates in the US-Mexico Borderlands, 1598–1912*. Chapel Hill: University of North Carolina Press, 2019.

Crane, Eva. *The World History of Beekeeping and Honey Hunting*. New York: Routledge, 1999.

Crawford, Suzanne J., and Dennis F. Kelley. "Ceremony and Ritual, Apache." In *American Indian Religious Traditions. An Encyclopedia*, vol. 1, 111–17. Santa Barbara, CA: ABC-CLIO, 2005.

Crewe, Ryan D. *The Mexican Mission: Indigenous Reconstruction and Mendicant Enterprise in New Spain, 1521–1600*. New York: Cambridge University Press, 2019.

Crosby, Alfred W. Jr. *The Columbian Exchange: Biological and Cultural Consequences of 1492*. Westport, CT: Greenwood Press, 1972.

———. "Virgin Soil Epidemics as a Factor in the Aboriginal Depopulation in North America." *William and Mary Quarterly* 33, no. 2 (April 1976): 289–99.

Crumrine, N. Ross. *The Mayo Indians of Sonora: A People Who Refuse to Die.* Tucson: University of Arizona Press, 1977.

Cruz, Enrique N. "La nueva sociedad de frontera. Los grupos sociales en la frontera de San Ignacio de Ledesma, Chaco occidental, finales del siglo XVIII." *Anuario de Estudios Americanos* 58, no. 1 (January–June 2001): 135–60.

———. "Notas para el estudio de las rebeliones indígenas a fines del período colonial. La frontera Tucumana del Chaco en 1781." *Anuario de Estudios Americanos* 64, no. 2 (July–December 2007): 271–86.

———. "Propiedad, producción y mano de obra en el pedemonte surandino. El caso de las haciendas de la familia Zegada en los Valles Orientales de Jujuy, finales del siglo XVIII." *América Latina en la Historia Económica* 8, no. 16 (July–December 2001): 105–21.

Cruz, Pablo. "Monte adentro. Aproximaciones sobre la ocupación prehispánica de la serranía de Calilegua (prov. de Jujuy)." *Intersecciones en Antropología* 11 (2010): 129–44.

Cruz, Pablo, and Rosario Jara. "Por encima de las nubes. Caminos, santuarios y arte rupestre en la serranía de Calilegua (Jujuy, Argentina)." *Comechingonia* 14 (2011): 75–96.

Cuello, José. "The Persistence of Indian Slavery and Encomienda in the Northeast of Colonial Mexico, 1577–1723." *Journal of Social History* 21 (1988): 683–700.

Cunill, Caroline. *Los defensores de indios de Yucatán y el acceso de los mayas a la justicia colonial, 1540–1600.* Mexico City: UNAM, 2012.

Curet, L. Antonio. "The Chief Who Is Dead, Long Live . . . Who? Descent and Succession in the Protohistoric Chiefdoms of the Greater Antilles." *Ethnohistory* 49, no. 2 (2002): 159–280.

Cutter, Charles R. *The Protector de Indios in Colonial New Mexico, 1659–1821.* Albuquerque: University of New Mexico Press, 1986.

Cutter, Donald C., ed. and trans. *The Defenses of Northern New Spain: Hugo O'Connor's Report to Teodoro de Croix, July 22, 1777.* Dallas: Southern Methodist University Press/DeGolyer Library, 1994.

De Jong, Ingrid, ed. *Diplomacia, malones y cautivos en la frontera sur: siglo XIX. Miradas desde la antropología histórica.* Buenos Aires: Sociedad Argentina de Antropología, 2016.

de la Puente Luna, José Carlos. *Andean Cosmopolitans: Seeking Justice and Reward at the Spanish Royal Court.* Austin: University of Texas Press, 2018.

de la Torre Curiel, José Refugio. *Twilight of the Mission Frontier: Shifting Interethnic Alliances and Social Organization in Sonora, 1768–1855.* Stanford, CA: Stanford University Press, 2013.

De Nino, Bernardino. *Continuación de la historia de misiones franciscanas del Colegio de P.P.F.F de Potosí.* 2nd ed. La Paz: Talleres Gráficos "Marinoni," 1918.

———. *Etnografía chiriguana.* La Paz: Tipografía Comercial de Ismael Argote, 1912.

Dean, Warren. *With Broadax and Firebrand: The Destruction of the Brazilian Atlantic Forest.* Berkeley and Los Angeles: University of California Press, 1995.

Deeds, Susan M. *Defiance and Deference in Mexico's Colonial North: Indians under Spanish Rule in Nueva Vizcaya.* Austin: University of Texas Press, 2003.

——. "Labyrinths of Mestizaje: Understanding Cultural Persistence and Transformation in Nueva Vizcaya." In Levin Rojo and Radding, *Oxford Handbook of Borderlands,* 343–70.

——. "Rendering unto Caesar: The Secularization of Jesuit Missions in Mid-Eighteenth Century Durango." PhD diss., University of Arizona, 1981.

——. "Rural Work in Nueva Vizcaya. Forms of Labor Coercion on the Periphery." *Hispanic American Historical Review* 69 (1989): 425–51.

DeLay, Brian E., ed. *North American Borderlands: Rewriting Histories.* New York: Routledge, 2013.

——. *War of a Thousand Deserts: Indian Raids and the U.S.-Mexican War.* New Haven, CT: Yale University Press, 2008.

Delgado, Jessica L. *Laywomen and the Making of Colonial Catholicism in New Spain, 1630–1790.* Cambridge Latin American Studies Series. Cambridge: Cambridge University Press, 2018.

Deloria, Vine Jr. *Custer Died for Your Sins: An Indian Manifesto.* New York: Macmillan, 1969.

Delrio, Walter. *Memorias de expropiación. Sometimiento e incorporación indígena en la Patagonia, 1872–1943.* Buenos Aires: Universidad Nacional de Quilmes, 2005.

Demitropulos, Olga. *Apuntes históricos de Ledesma.* Jujuy: Talleres Gráficos Gutenberg, 1991.

Dempsey, Hugh A. "Blackfoot." In *Handbook of North American Indians.* Vol. 13, *Plains,* edited by Raymond J. DeMallie, 604–28. Washington, DC: Smithsonian Institution, 2001.

Denson, Andrew. *Monuments to Absence: Cherokee Removal and the Contest over Southern Memory.* Chapel Hill: University of North Carolina Press, 2017.

DePratter, Chester B., Charles Hudson, and Marvin T. Smith. "Hernando de Soto Expedition: From Chiaha to Mabila." In *Alabama and the Borderlands: From Prehistory to Statehood,* edited by R. R. Badger and L. A. Clayton, 108–27. Tuscaloosa: University of Alabama Press, 1985.

Díaz Balsera, Viviana. *The Pyramid under the Cross: Franciscan Discourses of Evangelization and the Nahua Christian Subject in Sixteenth-Century Mexico.* Tucson: University of Arizona Press, 2005.

Diel, Lori Boornazian. *The Codex Mexicanus: A Guide to Life in Late Sixteenth-Century New Spain.* Austin: University of Texas Press, 2018.

Din, Gilbert C. *Spaniards, Planters, and Slaves: The Spanish Regulation of Slavery in Louisiana, 1763–1803.* College Station: Texas A&M University Press, 1999.

Din, Gilbert C., and Abraham P. Nasatir. *The Imperial Osages: Spanish-Indian Diplomacy in the Mississippi Valley.* Norman: University of Oklahoma Press, 1983.

Dixon, Benjamin Y. "Furthering Their Own Demise: How Kansa Indian Death Customs Accelerated Their Depopulation." *Ethnohistory* 54, no. 3 (2007): 473–508.

Domínguez, Argelia. "No permitiremos 'invasión' de migrantes: Trump sobre cara-vanas." *Entrelíneas*, November 4, 2018. https://entrelineas.com.mx/mundo/no-permitiremos-invasion-de-migrantes-trump-sobre-caravanas/.

Doolittle, William E. *Pre-Hispanic Occupance in the Valley of Sonora, Mexico: Archae-ological Confirmation of Early Spanish Reports.* Anthropological Papers, University of Arizona, 48. Tucson: University of Arizona Press, 1988.

Doucet, Gastón G. "Acerca de los churumatas con particular referencia al antiguo Tucumán." *Revista Histórica* 17, no. 1 (July 1993): 21–91.

———. "La jornada pobladora de Martín de Ledesma Valderrama al Chaco Gual-amba: dos documentos para su estudio." *Congreso Internacional de Historia Amer-icana* 4, no. 2 (1982): 369–93.

———. "Sobre cautivos de guerra y esclavos indios en el Tucumán. Notas en torno a un fichero documental salteño del siglo XVIII. *Revista de Historia del Derecho* 16 (1988): 59–152.

Drury, Bob, and Tom Clavin. *The Heart of Everything That Is: The Untold Story of Red Cloud, An American Legend.* New York: Simon and Schuster, 2013.

Dubois, Laurent. *Avengers of the New World: The Story of the Haitian Revolution.* Cambridge, MA: Harvard University Press, 2005.

Dueñas, Alcira. "Indian Colonial Actors in the Lawmaking of the Spanish Empire in Peru." *Ethnohsitory* 65, no. 1 (January 2018): 51–73.

Dunlay, Tom. *Wolves for the Blue Soldiers: Indian Scouts and Auxiliaries with the United States Army, 1860–90.* Lincoln: University of Nebraska Press, 1987.

Durán Estragó, Margarita. *Presencia franciscana en el Paraguay.* 2 vols. Biblioteca de Estudios Paraguayos 19, no. 24. Asunción: Universidad Católica Nuestra Señora de la Asunción, 1987.

DuVal, Kathleen. *The Native Ground: Indians and Colonists at the Heart of the Con-tinent.* Philadelphia: University of Pennsylvania Press, 2006.

Dye, David H. "Art, Ritual, and Chiefly Warfare in the Mississippian World." In *Hero, Hawk, and Open Hand: American Indian Art of the Ancient Midwest and South*, edited by Richard F. Townsend and Robert V. Sharp, 191–205. New Haven, CT: Yale University Press in association with the Art Institute of Chicago, 2004.

———. *War Paths, Peace Paths: An Archaeology of Cooperation and Conflict in Native Eastern North America.* Lanham, MD: AltaMira Press, 2009.

Eastman, Scott, and Natalia Sobrevilla Perea, eds. *The Rise of Constitutional Govern-ment in the Iberian Atlantic World: The Impact of the Cádiz Constitution of 1812.* Tuscaloosa: University of Alabama Press, 2015.

Ebright, Malcolm, and Rick Hendricks. *The Witches of Abiquiu: The Governor, the Priest, the Genízaro Indians, and the Devil.* Albuquerque: University of New Mex-ico Press, 2006.

Ebright, Malcolm, Rick Hendricks, and Richard W. Hughes. *Four Square Leagues: Pueblo Indian Land in New Mexico.* Albuquerque: University of New Mexico Press, 2014.

Edmunds, R. David. *The Shawnee Prophet.* Lincoln: University of Nebraska Press, 1983.

———. *Tecumseh and the Quest for Indian Leadership*. New York: Longman, 1984.

Edwards, Tai. *Osage Women and Empire: Gender and Power*. Lawrence: University Press of Kansas, 2018.

Eiselt, B. Sunday. *Becoming White Clay: A History and Archaeology of Jicarilla Apache Enclavement*. Salt Lake City: University of Utah Press, 2012.

Ekberg, Carl J. *Stealing Indian Women: Native Slavery in the Illinois Country*. Urbana: University of Illinois Press, 2010.

Elvas, Gentleman of. "True Relation of the Vicissitudes That Attended the Governor Don Hernando de Soto and Some Nobles of Portugal in the Discovery of the Province of Florida." Translated by James Robertson. In Clayton, Knight, and Moore, *de Soto Chronicles*, 1:25–219.

Erbig, Jeffrey A. Jr. "Borderline Offerings: Tolderías and Mapmakers in the Eighteenth-Century Río de la Plata." *Hispanic American Historical Review* 96, no. 3 (2016): 445–80.

Erbig, Jeffrey A. Jr., and Sergio Latini. "Across Archival Limits: Colonial Records, Changing Ethnonyms, and Geographies of Knowledge." *Ethnohisotry* 66, no. 2 (2019): 249–73.

Escandón, Patricia. "La nueva administración misional y los pueblos de indios." In *Tres siglos de historia sonorense, 1530–1830*, edited by Sergio Ortega Noriega and Ignacio del Río, 321–54. Mexico City: Instituto de Investigaciones Históricas, UNAM, 2010.

Escalante Arce, Pedro. *Los tlaxcaltecas en Centro América*. San Salvador: Biblioteca de Historia Salvadoreña, 2001.

Espinoza Soriano, Waldemar. "Los churumatas y los mitmas chichas orejones en los lindes del Collasuyo. Siglos XV–XX." *Revista Histórica* 35 (1986): 243–97.

Estes, Nick. *Our History Is the Future: Standing Rock versus the Dakota Access Pipeline, and the Long Tradition of Indigenous Struggle*. London: Verso, 2019.

Ethridge, Robbie. "Creating the Shatter Zone: Indian Slave Traders and the Collapse of the Southeastern Chiefdoms." In *Light on the Path: The Anthropology and History of the Southeastern Indians*, edited by Thomas J. Pluckhahn and Robbie Ethridge, 207–18. Tuscaloosa: University of Alabama Press, 2006.

———. "Differential Responses across the Southeast to European Incursions." In Boudreaux, Meyers, and Johnson, *Contact, Colonialism, and Native Communities*, 216–28.

———. *From Chicaza to Chickasaw: The European Invasion and the Transformation of the Mississippian World, 1540–1715*. Chapel Hill: University of North Carolina Press, 2010.

———. "Navigating the Mississippian World: Infrastructure in the Sixteenth-Century Native South." In *Forging Southeastern Identities: Social Archaeology, Ethnohistory, and Folklore of the Mississippian to Early Historic South*, edited by Gregory A. Waselkov and Marvin T. Smith, 62–84. Tuscaloosa: University of Alabama Press, 2017.

Ethridge, Robbie, Kathryn Braund, Lawrence Clayton, George Lankford, and Michael Murray. "A Comparative Analysis of the de Soto Accounts on the Route to and

Events at Mabila." In Knight, *Search for Mabila*, 153–81. Tuscaloosa: University of Alabama Press, 2009.

Ethridge, Robbie, and Sheri M. Shuck-Hall, eds. *Mapping the Mississippian Shatter Zone: The Colonial Indian Slave Trade and Regional Instability in the American South*. Lincoln: University of Nebraska Press, 2009.

Farriss, Nancy M. *Maya Society under Colonial Rule: The Collective Enterprise of Survival*. Princeton: Princeton University Press, 1984.

———. *Tongues of Fire: Language and Evangelization in Colonial Mexico*. New York: Oxford University Press, 2018.

Fenn, Elizabeth A. *Encounters at the Heart of the World: A History of the Mandan People*. New York: Hill and Wang, 2015.

Fernández, Juan Patricio, SJ. *Relación historial de las misiones de indios Chiquitos*. 1726. Jujuy: Universidad Nacional de Jujuy, 1994.

Fernández C., Jorge, ed. *Historia de los indios ranqueles. Orígenes, elevación y caída del cacicazgo ranquelino en la pampa central, siglos XVIII y XIX*. Buenos Aires: Instituto Nacional de Antropología y Pensamiento Latinoamericano, 1998.

Ferreiro, Juan P. "El Chaco en los Andes. Churumatas, Paypayas, Yalas y Ocloyas en la etnografía del Oriente Jujeño." *Población & Sociedad* 2 (1994): 3–24.

Few, Martha. *Women Who Live Evil Lives: Gender, Religion, and the Politics of Power in Colonial Guatemala*. Austin: University of Texas Press, 2002.

Flagler, Edward K. "La política española para pacificar a los indios apaches a finales del siglo XVIII." *Revista Española de Antropología Americana* 30 (2000): 221–34.

Folsom, Raphael. *The Yaquis and the Empire: Violence, Spanish Imperial Power, and Native Resilience in Colonial Mexico*. New Haven, CT: Yale University Press, 2014.

Forbes, Jack D. *Apache, Navaho, and Spaniard*. Norman: University of Oklahoma Press, 1960.

Foucault, Michel. "The Subject and Power." In *Beyond Structuralism and Hermeneutics*, edited by H. Dreyfus and P. Rabinow, 208–26. Chicago: University of Chicago Press, 1983.

Frank, Ross. *From Settler to Citizen: New Mexican Economic Development and the Creation of Vecino Society, 1750–1820*. Berkeley: University of California Press, 2000.

Frank, Ross H. "Review of *The Protector de Indios in Colonial New Mexico, 1659–1821*, by Charles R. Cutter." *American Indian Quarterly* 13, no. 3 (Summer 1989): 290–92.

Freidel, David A. "Terminal Classic Lowland Maya: Successes, Failures, and Aftermaths." In *Late Lowland Maya Civilization: Classic to Postclassic*, edited by Jeremy A. Sabloff and E. Wyllys Andrews V, 409–30. Albuquerque: University of New Mexico Press, 1986.

Furlong, Guillermo. *Antonio Sepp, S.J., y su "gobierno temporal" (1732)*. Buenos Aires: Ediciones Theoria, 1962.

———. *Cartografía jesuítica del Río de la Plata*. Publicaciones del Instituto de Investigaciones Históricas no. 71. Buenos Aires: Universidad de Buenos Aires and Peuser, 1936.

———. *Juan Escandón y su carta a Burriel (1760)*. Buenos Aires: Ediciones Theoria, 1965.

Gabbert, Wolfgang. *Violence and the Caste War of Yucatán*. Cambridge: Cambridge University Press 2019.

Gadelha, Regina Maria A. F. *As missões jesuíticas do Itatim: um estudo das estruturas sócio-econômicas coloniais do Paraguai (séculos XVI e XVII)*. Coleção Estudos Latino-americanos 15. Rio de Janeiro: Paz e Terra, 1980.

Gallaga Murrieta, Emiliano. "An Archaeological Survey of the Onavas Valley, Sonora, Mexico. A Landscape of Interactions during the Late Prehispanic Period." PhD diss., University of Arizona, 2006.

Gallardo Arias, Patricia, and Cuauhtémoc Velasco Ávila, eds. *Fronteras étnicas en la América colonial*. Mexico City: Insituto Nacional de Antropología e Historia, 2018.

Gallay, Alan. *The Indian Slave Trade: The Rise of the English Empire in the American South, 1670–1717*. New Haven, CT: Yale University Press, 2002.

———., ed. *Indian Slavery in Colonial America*. Lincoln: University of Nebraska Press, 2009.

Galloway, Patricia K. *Choctaw Genesis, 1500–1700*. Lincoln: University of Nebraska Press, 1995.

———., ed. *The Hernando de Soto Expedition: History, Historiography, and "Discovery" in the Southeast*. Lincoln: University of Nebraska Press, 1997.

———. "The Incestuous de Soto Narratives." In *The Hernando de Soto Expedition: History, Historiography, and "Discovery" in the Southeast*, edited by Patricia Galloway, 11–44. Lincoln: University of Nebraska Press, 1997.

———. *Practicing Ethnohistory: Mining Archives, Hearing Testimony, Constructing Narrative*. Lincoln: University of Nebraska Press, 2006.

Gálvez, Bernardo de. *Instrucción formada en virtud de Real Orden de S.M., que se dirige al Señor Comandante General de Provincias Internas Don Jacobo Ugarte y Loyola para gobierno y puntual observancia de este Superior Gefe y de sus inmediatos subalternos*. Mexico City, 1786.

Gamboa Mendoza, Jorge Augusto. *El cacicazgo muisca en los años posteriores a la Conquista: del psihipqua al cacique colonial, 1537–1575*. Bogota: Instituto Colombiano de Antro-pología e Historia, 2013.

Gandía, Enrique de. *Cultura y folklore en América*. Buenos Aires: El Ateneo, 1947.

Ganson, Barbara. *The Guaraní under Spanish Rule in the Río de la Plata*. Stanford, CA: Stanford University Press, 2003.

Garavaglia, Juan Carlos. "La guerra en el Tucumán colonial: sociedad y economía en un área de frontera (1660–1760)." *HISLA* 4 (1984): 21–34.

———. *Mercado interno y economía colonial*. 1st ed. Mexico City: Grijalbo, 1983.

García, Bartholomé. *Manual para administrar los santos sacramentos de penitencia, eucharistia, extrema-uncion y matrimonio a los indios a las naciones pajalates, orejones, pacaos, pacóas, tilijayas, alasapas y otras muchas diferentes*. Mexico City: Da. María de Rivera, 1760.

Garcia, Elisa Frühauf. *As diversas formas de ser índio: políticas indígenas e políticas indigenistas no extremo sul da América portuguesa*. Prêmio Arquivo Nacional de

Pesquisa 26. Rio de Janeiro: Arquivo Nacional, Casa Civil, Presidência da República, 2009.

García Bernal, Manuela Cristina. "Desarrollos indígena y ganadero en Yucatán." *Historia Mexicana* 43, no. 3 (1994): 373–400.

———. "El gobernador de Yucatán Rodrigo Flores de Aldana." In *Economía, política y sociedad en el Yucatán colonial*, 141–260. Mérida: Ediciones de la Universidad Autónoma de Yucatán, 2005.

———. "La visita de fray Luis de Cifuentes, obispo de Yucatán." *Anuario de Estudios Americanos* 29 (1972): 229–60.

———. *Población y encomienda en Yucatán bajo los Austrias*. Seville: Publicaciones de la Escuela de Estudios Hispano-Americanos de Sevilla, 1978.

García Martínez, Valentina. "Poblamiento y colonización en el noreste novohispano, siglos XVI y XVII." PhD diss., Centro de Estudios Históricos, El Colegio de México, 2002.

Garcilaso de la Vega, the Inca. "La Florida." Translated by Charmion Shelby. In Clayton, Knight, and Moore, *de Soto Chronicles*, 2:25–560.

Gauderman, Kimberly. *Women's Lives in Colonial Quito: Gender, Law, and Economy in Spanish America*. Austin: University of Texas Press, 2003.

Gelo, Daniel J. *Indians of the Great Plains*. Boston, MA: Pearson, 2012.

Gentry, Howard Scott. *Río Mayo Plants: A Study of the Flora and Vegetation of the Valley of the Rio Mayo, Sonora*. Washington, DC: Carnegie Institution, 1942.

Gerhard, Peter. *The North Frontier of New Spain*. Norman: University of Oklahoma Press, 1993.

———. *The Southeast Frontier of New Spain*. Princeton, NJ: Princeton University Press, 1993.

Giannecchini, Doroteo. *Diccionario chiriguano-español*. Tarija: n.p., 1916.

Gibson, Arrell Morgan. *The Kickapoos: Lords of the Middle Border*. Norman: University of Oklahoma Press, 1963.

Gilbert, Jérémie. "Nomadic Territories: A Human Rights Approach to Nomadic Peoples' Land Rights." *Human Rights Law Review* 7, no. 4 (January 2007): 681–716.

———. *Nomadic Peoples and Human Rights*. New York: Routledge, 2014.

Ginzberg, Eitan. *The Destruction of the Indigenous Peoples of Hispano America. A Genocidal Encounter*. Brighton, UK: Sussex Academic Press, 2018.

Giudicelli, Christophe, ed. *Fronteras movedizas. Clasificaciones coloniales y dinámicas socioculturales en las fronteras americanas*. Zamora: Centro de Estudios Mexicanos y Centroamericanos, El Colegio de Michoacán, 2010.

———. "Indigenous Autonomy and the Blurring of Spanish Sovereignty in the Calchaquí Valley, Sixteenth to Seventeenth Century." In Levin Rojo and Radding, *Oxford Handbook of Borderlands*, 317–42.

Gonzales, Moises. "The Genizaro Land Grant Settlements of New Mexico." *Journal of the Southwest* 56, no. 4 (Winter 2014): 583–602.

Gonzales, Richard. "Trump Says He'll Send as Many as 15,000 Troops to the Southern Border." National Public Radio, October 31, 2018. https://www.npr.org/2018/10

/31/662735242/trump-says-hell-send-as-many-as-15-000- troops-to-the-southern
-border.

González, Julio Cesar. "Un informe del gobernador de misiones, don Francisco Bruno
de Zavala, sobre el estado de los treinta pueblos (1784)." *Boletín del Instituto de
Investigaciones Históricas* 25 (1941): 159–87.

González-Acereto, Jorge A. "La importancia de la meliponicultura en México, con
énfasis en la península de Yucatán." *Bioagrociencias* 5, no. 1 (2012): 34–41.

González Rodríguez, Luis. "Los tobosos, bandoleros y nómadas. Experiencias y tes-
timonios históricos (1583–1849). In Hers, Mirafuentes, Soto, and Vallebueno,
Nómadas y sedentarios, 370–72.

Gradie, Charlotte M. *The Tepehuan Revolt of 1616: Militarism, Evangelism, and Colonialism in Seventeenth-Century Nueva Vizcaya.* Salt Lake City: University of Utah
Press, 2005.

Grant, Mary Lee, and Nick Miroff. "Citizen Militia Groups Head to Border, Stirred
by Trump's Call to Arms." *Washington* Post, November 3, 2018. https://www
.washingtonpost.com/world/national-security/us-militia-groups-head-to
-border-stirred-by-trumps-call-to-arms/2018/11/03/ff96826c-decf-11e8-b3f0
-62607289efee_story.html.

Graubart, Karen B. *With Our Labor and Sweat: Indigenous Women and the Formation of Colonial Society in Peru, 1550–1700.* Stanford, CA: Stanford University Press,
2007.

Greer, Allan. *Mohawk Saint: Catherine Tekakwitha and the Jesuits.* Oxford: Oxford
University Press, 2005.

———. *Property and Dispossession: Natives, Empires, and Land in Early Modern
North America.* New York: Cambridge University Press, 2018.

Griffen, William B. *Apaches at War and Peace: The Janos Presidio, 1750–1858.* Norman: University of Oklahoma Press, 1988.

———. *Culture Change and Shifting Population in Central Northern Mexico.* Tucson:
University of Arizona Press, 1969.

———. *Indian Assimilation in the Franciscan Area of Nueva Vizcaya.* Tucson: University of Arizona Press, 1979.

Guaman Poma de Ayala, Felipe. *Nueva corónica y buen gobierno.* Vol. 1. Lima: Fondo
de Cultura Económica, [1615], 1993.

Güereca Durán, Raquel. *Milicias indígenas en la Nueva España.* Mexico City: IIJ-
UNAM, 2016.

Guevara, José. *Historia del Paraguay, Río de la Plata y Tucumán.* 1764. Buenos Aires:
Plus Ultra, 1969.

Guiteras Mombiola, Anna. "Los indígenas benianos en el acceso a la propiedad de la
tierra y la constitución de una sociedad de frontera en la Bolivia republicana, 1842–
1915." *Boletín Americanista* 60, no. 1 (2010): 67–89.

Gullón Abao, Alberto. *La frontera del Chaco en la Gobernación del Tucumán (1750–
1810).* Cádiz: Universidad de Cádiz, 1993.

Gunnerson, Dolores A. *The Jicarilla Apaches: A Study in Survival.* DeKalb: Northern
Illinois University Press, 1974.

Gunnerson, James, and Dolores Gunnerson. *Ethnohistory of the High Plains.* Denver: Colorado State Office, Bureau of Land Management, 1988.

Guy, Donna J., and Thomas E. Sheridan, eds. *Contested Ground: Comparative Frontiers on the Northern and Southern Edges of the Spanish Empire.* Tucson: University of Arizona Press, 1998.

Hackel, Steven W. *Children of Coyote, Missionaries of Saint Francis: Indian-Spanish Relations in Colonial California, 1769–1850.* Chapel Hill: University of North Carolina Press, 2005.

Hadley, Diana, Thomas H. Naylor, and Mardith R. Schuetz-Miller, eds. *The Presidio and Militia on the Northern Frontier of New Spain: A Documentary History,* vol. 2, pt. 2. Tucson: University of Arizona Press, 1997.

Hahn, John H. *A History of the Timucua Indians and Missions.* Gainesville: University Press of Florida, 1996.

Hall, G. Emlen. "Juan Estevan Pino, 'Se los coma': New Mexican Land Speculation in the 1820s." *New Mexico Historical Review* 57, no. 1 (January 1982): 27–42.

Hall, G. Emlen, and David J. Weber. "Mexican Liberals and the Pueblo Indians, 1821–1829." *New Mexico Historical Review* 59, no. 1 (January 1984): 5–32.

Hally, David J. *King: The Social Archaeology of a Late Mississippian Town in Northwestern Georgia.* Tuscaloosa: University of Alabama Press, 2008.

———. "The Nature of Mississippian Regional Systems." In *Light on the Path: The Anthropology and History of Southeastern Indians,* edited by Thomas J. Pluckhahn and Robbie Ethridge, 26–42. Tuscaloosa: University of Alabama Press, 2006.

———. "Platform Mound Construction and the Instability of Mississippian Chiefdoms." In *Political Structure and Change in the Prehistoric Southeastern United States,* edited by John Scarry, 92–127. Gainesville: University Press of Florida, 1996.

———. "The Territorial Size of Mississippian Chiefdoms." In *Archaeology of Eastern North America: Papers in Honor of Stephen Williams,* edited by James A. Stoltman, 143–68. Archaeological Report No. 25. Jackson: Mississippi Department of Archives and History, 1993.

Hally, David J., and John F. Chamblee. "The Temporal Distribution and Duration of Mississippian Polities in Alabama, Georgia, Mississippi, and Tennessee." *American Antiquity* 84, no. 3 (2019): 420–37.

Hally, David J., Marvin T. Smith, and James B. Langford Jr. "The Archaeological Reality of de Soto's Coosa." In *Columbian Consequences.* Vol. 2, *Archaeological and Historical Perspectives on the Spanish Borderlands East,* edited by David Hurst Thomas, 121–38. Washington, DC: Smithsonian Institution, 1990.

Hämäläinen, Pekka. *El imperio comanche.* Barcelona: Península, 2011.

———. *The Comanche Empire.* New Haven, CT: Yale University Press, 2008.

———. "The Rise and Fall of Plains Indian Horse Cultures." *Journal of American History* 90, no. 3 (Dec. 2003): 833–62.

Hämäläinen, Pekka, and Benjamin H. Johnson. "What Is Borderlands History?" In *Major Problems in the History of North American Borderlands,* edited by Pekka Hämäläinen and Benjamin H. Johnson, 1–2. Boston, MA: Wadsworth Cengage Learning, 2012.

Hämäläinen, Pekka, and Samuel Truett. "On Borderlands." *Journal of American History* 98, no. 2 (September 2011): 338–61.

Hamill, Hugh M., ed. *Caudillos: Dictators in Spanish America.* Norman: University of Oklahoma Press, 1992.

Hanke, Lewis. *Do the Americas Have a Common History? A Critique of the Bolton Theory.* New York: Alfred A. Knopf, 1964.

Hannes, Schroeder, Martin Sikora, Shyam Gopalakrishnan, et al. "Origins and Genetic Legacies of the Caribbean Taino." *Proceedings of the National Academy of Sciences of the United States of America* 115, no. 10 (March 2018): 2341–46.

Harriss Clare, Claudia Jean. *"Hasta aquí son todas las palabras." La ideología lingüística en la construcción de la identidad entre los guarijío del alto mayo.* Chihuahua: PIALLI, Instituto Chihuahuense de Cultura, 2012.

Hassig, Ross. *Mexico and the Spanish Conquest.* Norman: University of Oklahoma Press, 2006.

Havard, Gilles. *Empire et métissages. Indiens et Français dans le Pays d'en Haut, 1660–1715.* 2nd ed. Québec and Paris: Septentrion, Presses de l'Université de París-Sorbonne, 2017.

———. *Histoire des coureurs de bois. Amérique du Nord, 1600–1840.* Paris: Les Indes Savantes, 2016.

Heaney, Christopher. "The Conquests of Peru." In *Oxford Research Encyclopedia of Latin American History,* edited by William H. Beezley. Oxford: Oxford University Press, 2016. DOI: 10.1093/acrefore/9780199366439.013.61

Heidler, David S., and Jeanne T. Heidler. *Indian Removal.* New York: W. W. Norton, 2007.

Hemming, John. *Red Gold: The Conquest of the Brazilian Indians.* Clerkenwell, UK: Pan, 2004.

Hers, Marie-Areti, José Luis Mirafuentes, Maria de los Dolores Soto, and Miguel Vallebueno, eds. *Nómadas y sedentarios en el norte de México. Homenaje a Beatriz Braniff.* Mexico City: UNAM, 2000.

Hickerson, Nancy P. *The Jumanos: Hunters and Traders of the South Plains.* Austin: University of Texas Press, 1994.

Hidalgo, Alex. *Trail of Footprints: A History of Indigenous Maps from Viceregal Mexico.* Austin: University of Texas Press, 2019.

Hill, Jonathan. *History, Power, and Identity: Ethnogenesis in the Americas, 1492–1992.* Iowa City: University of Iowa Press, 1996.

Hoffman, Paul E. "Introduction: The de Soto Expedition, a Cultural Crossroads." In Clayton, Knight, and Moore, *de Soto Chronicles,* 1:1–17.

Hornborg, Alf, and Jonathan D. Hill, eds. *Ethnicity in Ancient Amazonia: Reconstructing Past Identities from Archaeology, Linguistics, and Ethnohistory.* Boulder: University Press of Colorado, 2011.

Hoyo, Eugenio del. *Esclavitud y encomiendas de indios en el reino de Nuevo León, siglos XVI y XVII.* Monterrey: Archivo General del Estado de Nuevo León, 1985.

Hu-Dehart, Evelyn, *Adaptación y resistencia en el yaquimí.* Mexico City: Centro de Investigaciones y Estudios Superiores en Antropología Social, Instituto Nacional Indigenista, 1995.

Hudson, Charles M. Introduction to *The Transformation of the Southeastern Indians, 1540–1760*, edited by Robbie Ethridge and Charles M. Hudson, ii–xvi. Jackson: University Press of Mississippi, 2002.

——, ed. *The Juan Pardo Expeditions: Exploration of the Carolinas and Tennessee, 1566–1568*. 2nd ed. Tuscaloosa: University of Alabama Press, 2005.

——. *Knights of Spain, Warriors of the Sun: Hernando de Soto and the South's Ancient Chiefdoms*. Athens: University of Georgia Press, 1997.

——. *The Southeastern Indians*. Knoxville: University of Tennessee Press, 1976.

Hudson, Charles M., Marvin T. Smith, and Chester B. DePratter. "The de Soto Expedition: From Apalachee to Chiaha." *Southeastern Archaeology* 19, no. 1 (1987): 18–28.

Hudson, Charles M., Marvin T. Smith, Chester B. DePratter, and Emilia Kelley. "The Tristán de Luna Expedition, 1559–1561." *Southeastern Archaeology* 8, no. 1 (1989): 31–45.

Hunt, Marta Espejo-Ponce. "The Processes of the Development of Yucatan, 1600–1700." In *Provinces of Early Mexico: Variants of Spanish American Regional Evolution*, edited by Ida Altman and James Lockhart, 33–62. Los Angeles: UCLA Latin American Center Publications, 1976.

Informe del Prefecto del Departamento de Chuquisaca. Sucre: Tipografía Excelsior, 1897.

Ingold, Tim. *The Perception of the Environment: Essays in Livelihood, Dwelling, and Skill*. London: Routledge, 2000.

Isenberg, Andrew C. *The Destruction of the Bison: An Environmental History, 1750–1920*. Cambridge: Cambridge University Press, 2000.

Iverson, Peter. *Diné: A History of the Navajos*. Albuquerque: University of New Mexico Press, 2002.

Jackson, Robert H. *From Savages to Subjects: Missions in the History of the American Southwest*. Armonk, NY: M. E. Sharpe, 2000.

——. "La raza y la definición de la identidad del "indio" en las fronteras de la América española colonial." *Revista de Estudios Sociales* 26 (2007): 116–25.

——. *Missions and Frontiers of Spanish America: A Comparative Study of the Impact of Environmental, Economic, Political, and Socio-Cultural Variations on the Missions in the Río de la Plata Region and on the Northern Frontier of New Spain*. Scottdale, AZ: Pentacle Press, 2005.

——. "The Population and Vital Rates of the Jesuit Missions of Paraguay, 1700–1767." *Journal of Interdisciplinary History* 38, no. 3 (2008): 401–31.

——. "Una mirada a los patrones demográficos de las misiones jesuitas." *Fronteras de la Historia* 9 (2004): 129–78.

Jacoby, Karl. *Shadows at Dawn: A Borderlands Massacre and the Violence of History*. New York: Penguin, 2008.

Jaffary, Nora E., ed. *Gender, Race, and Religion in the Colonization of the Americas*. Aldershot, UK: Ashgate, 2007.

Jenkins, Ned J. "Tracing the Origins of the Early Creeks, 1050–1700 CE." In Ethridge and Shuck-Hall, *Mapping the Mississippian Shatter Zone*, 188–249.

Jenkins, Ned J., and Craig T. Sheldon. "Late Mississippian/Protohistoric Ceramic Chronology and Cultural Change in the Lower Tallapoosa and Alabama River Valleys." *Journal of Alabama Archaeology* 62, nos. 1 and 2 (2016): 69–121.

Jennings, Francis. *The Ambiguous Iroquois Empire: The Covenant Chain Confederation of Indian Tribes with English Colonies.* New York and London: W. W. Norton, 1984.

John, Elizabeth A. H. *Storms Brewed in Other Men's Worlds: The Confrontation of Indians, Spanish, and French in the Southwest, 1540–1795.* Norman: University of Oklahoma Press, 1996.

Jolís, José, SJ. *Ensayo sobre la historia natural del Gran Chaco.* 1789. Resistencia: Universidad Nacional del Nordeste, 1972.

Jones, Grant D. "Agriculture and Trade in the Colonial Period Southern Maya Lowlands." In *Maya Subsistence: Studies in Memory of Dennis E. Puleston*, edited by Kent V. Flannery, 275–93. New York: Academic Press, 1982.

———. *Maya Resistance to Spanish Rule: Time and History on a Colonial Frontier.* Albuquerque: University of New Mexico Press, 1989.

Jones, Oakah L. Jr. *Nueva Vizcaya: Heartland of the Spanish Frontier.* Albuquerque: University of New Mexico Press, 1988.

———. *Pueblo Warriors and Spanish Conquest.* Norman: University of Oklahoma Press, 1966.

Julien, Catherine. "Alejo García en la historia." *Anuario de Estudios Bolivianos, Archivísticos y Bibliográficos* 11 (2005): 223–66.

Kates, Adrienne. *The Persistence of Maya Autonomy: Global Capitalism, Tropical Environments, and the Limits of the Mexican State, 1880–1950.* Washington, DC: Georgetown University Press, 2018.

Kavanagh, Thomas W. *Comanche Political History: An Ethnohistorical Perspective, 1706–1875.* Lincoln: University of Nebraska Press, 1996.

Kepecs, Susan M. "Mayas, Spaniards, and Salt: World Systems Shifts in Sixteenth-Century Yucatán." In *The Postclassic to Spanish-Era Transition in Mesoamerica: Archaeological Perspectives*, edited by Susan M. Kepecs and Rani T. Alexander, 117–37. Albuquerque: University of New Mexico Press, 2005.

———. "Native Yucatán and Spanish Influence: The Archaeology and History of Chikinchel." *Journal of Archaeological Method and Theory* 4, nos. 3–4 (1997): 307–29.

Kersten, Ludwig. *Las tribus indígenas del Gran Chaco hasta fines del siglo XVIII. Una contribución a la etnografía histórica de Sudamérica.* Resistencia: Universidad Nacional del Nordeste, 1968.

Kessell, John L. *Kiva, Cross, and Crown: The Pecos Indians and New Mexico.* Washington, DC: National Park Service, US Department of the Interior, 1979.

———. *Miera y Pacheco: A Renaissance Spaniard in Eighteenth-Century New Mexico.* Norman: University of Oklahoma Press, 2013.

———. *Pueblos, Spaniards, and the Kingdom of New Mexico.* Norman: University of Oklahoma Press, 2008.

Kleinpenning, Jan. *Paraguay 1515–1870: A Thematic Geography of Its Development.* 2 vols. Madrid: Iberoamericana; Frankfurt: Vervuert, 2003.

Knaut, Andrew L. *The Pueblo Revolt of 1680: Conquest and Resistance in Seventeenth-Century New Mexico.* Norman: University of Oklahoma Press, 1995.

Knight, Vernon James Jr. "Farewell to the Southeastern Ceremonial Complex." *Southeastern Archaeology* 25, no. 1 (2006): 1–5.

———. *Mound Excavations at Moundville: Architecture, Elites, and Social Order.* Tuscaloosa: University of Alabama Press, 2010.

———. "Moundville as a Diagrammatic Ceremonial Center." In *Archaeology of the Moundville Chiefdom,* edited by Vernon James Knight Jr., and Vincas P. Steponaitis, 44–62. Tuscaloosa: University of Alabama Press, 2007.

———. "Puzzles of Creek Social Organization in the Eighteenth and Nineteenth Centuries. *Ethnohistory* 65, no. 3 (2018): 373–89.

———, ed. *The Search for Mabila: The Decisive Battle between Hernando de Soto and Chief Tascalusa.* Tuscaloosa: University of Alabama Press, 2009.

Krauthamer, Barbara. *Black Slaves, Indian Masters: Slavery, Emancipation, and Citizenship in the Native American South.* Chapel Hill: University of North Carolina Press, 2015.

Krippner-Martínez, James. *Rereading the Conquest: Power, Politics, and the History of Early Colonial Michoacán, Mexico, 1521–1565.* University Park: Penn State University Press, 2001.

La Vere, David. *Contrary Neighbors: Southern Plains and Removed Indians in Indian Territory.* Norman: University of Oklahoma Press, 2000.

Lahti, Janne. *Wars for Empire: Apaches, the United States, and the Southwest Borderlands.* Norman: University of Oklahoma Press, 2017.

Lamana, Gonzalo. *Domination without Dominance: Inca-Spanish Encounters in Early Colonial Peru.* Durham, NC: Duke University Press, 2008.

Landa, Diego de. *Relación de las cosas de Yucatán.* Barcelona: Red Ediciones, 2011.

Landavazo, Marco Antonio, ed. *Territorio, frontera y región en la historia de América: siglos XVI al XX.* San Nicolás de Hidalgo: Universidad Michoacana de San Nicolás de Hidalgo and Editorial Porrúa, 2003.

Landers, Jane. *Black Society in Spanish Florida.* Urbana: University of Illinois Press, 1999.

Langberg, Emilio. "Inspección de las colonias militares de Chihuahua." *Boletín de la Sociedad Mexicana de Geografía y Estadística* 3 (1852): 19–25.

Langebaek Rueda, Carl Henrik. *Los muiscas. La historia milenaria de un pueblo chibcha.* Bogota: Debate, 2019.

Langer, Erick D. "Caciques y poder en las misiones franciscanas entre los Chiriguanos durante la rebelión de 1892." *Siglo XIX: Revista de Historia* 15 (January–June 1994): 82–103.

———. "The Eastern Andean Frontier (Bolivia and Argentina) and Latin American Frontiers: Comparative Contexts (19th and 20th Centuries)." *The Americas* 59, no. 1 (July 2002): 33–63.

———. *Economic Change and Rural Resistance in Southern Bolivia, 1880–1930.* Stanford, CA: Stanford University Press, 1989.

———. *Expecting Pears from an Elm Tree: Franciscan Missions on the Chiriguano Frontier in the Heart of South America, 1830–1949.* Durham, NC: Duke University Press, 2009.

———. "Savages and Vassals: Comparing Bolivian State Policies and Indigenous Responses to Indian Land (Nineteenth and Early Twentieth Centuries)." Unpublished manuscript.

Langer, Erick D., and Zulema Bass Werner de Ruiz, eds. *Historia de Tarija: corpus documental.* Vol. 5. Tarija: Universidad Juan Misael Saracho, 1988.

Langfur, Hal. *The Forbidden Lands: Colonial Identity, Frontier Violence, and the Persistence of Brazil's Eastern Indians, 1750–1830.* Stanford, CA: Stanford University Press, 2006.

———. "Native Informants and the Limits of Portuguese Dominion in Late-Colonial Brazil." In Levin Rojo and Radding, *Oxford Handbook of Borderlands,* 209–34.

Lankford, George E. "How Historical are the de Soto Chronicles?" In Knight, *Search for Mabila,* 31–44. Tuscaloosa: University of Alabama Press, 2009.

———. *Looking for Lost Lore: Studies in Folklore, Ethnology, and Iconography.* Tuscaloosa: University of Alabama Press, 2008.

———. "Some Cosmological Motifs in the Southeastern Ceremonial Complex." In Reilly and Garber, *Ancient Objects and Sacred Realms,* 8–28.

Lankford, George E., F. Kent Reilly III, and James F. Garber, eds. *Visualizing the Sacred: Cosmic Visions, Regionalism, and the Art of the Mississippian World.* Austin: University of Texas Press, 2011.

Lara, Jaime. *Christian Texts for Aztecs: Art and Liturgy in Mexico.* Notre Dame, IN: University of Notre Dame Press, 2008.

Lara Cisneros, Gerardo. *El cristianismo en el espejo indígena. Religiosidad en el occidente de la Sierra Gorda, siglo XVIII.* 2nd ed. Mexico City: Instituto de Investigaciones, UNAM; Instituto de Investigaciones Históricas, Universidad Autónoma de Tamaulipas, 2009.

———. *¿Ignorancia invencible? Superstición e idolatría ante el Provisorato de Indios y Chinos del Arzobispado de México en el siglo XVIII.* Mexico City: UNAM, 2014.

Larson, Brooke. *Trials of Nation Making: Liberalism, Race, and Ethnicity in the Andes, 1810–1910.* Cambridge: Cambridge University Press, 2008.

Lastarria, Miguel. *Colonias orientales del río Paraguay o de la Plata.* Documentos para la Historia Argentina. Buenos Aires: Compañía Sud-Americana de Billetes de Banco, 1914.

Lefebvre, Henri, *The Production of Space.* Oxford: Blackwell, 1991.

Legg, James B., Dennis B. Blanton, Charles R. Cobb, Steven D. Smith, Brad R. Lieb, Edmond A. Boudreaux, III. "An Appraisal of the Indigenous Acquisition of Contact-Era European Metal Objects in Southeastern North America." *International Journal of Historical Archaeology* 23 (2018): 81–102. https://doi.org/10.1007/s10761-018-0458-1.

Lentz, Mark. "Castas, Creoles, and the Rise of a Maya Lingua Franca in Eighteenth-Century Yucatan." *Hispanic American Historical Review* 97, no. 1 (2017): 29–61.

León Portilla, Miguel. *Visión de los vencidos.* Mexico City: UNAM, 2003.

León Solís, Leonardo. *Los señores de la cordillera y las pampas. Los pehuenches de Malalhue, 1770–1800.* Mendoza, Argentina: Universidad de Congreso and Universidad de Malargüe, 2001.

———. *Maloqueros y conchavadores en Aracucanía y las Pampas, 1700–1800.* Temuco: Ediciones Universidad de la Frontera, 1990.

Leonhardt, Carlos, ed. *Cartas anuas de la provincia del Paraguay, Chile y Tucumán, de la Compañía de Jesús (1615–1637).* Vol. 20 of *Documentos para la historia Argentina.* Buenos Aires: Instituto de Investigaciones Históricas, Facultad de Filosofía y Letras, Universidad de Buenos Aires, and Peuser, 1929.

Lerma Rodríguez, Enriqueta, "'El nido heredado.' Estudio sobre cosmovisión, espacio y ciclo ritual de la tribu yaqui." PhD diss., Mexico City, UNAM, 2011.

Levaggi, Abelardo. *Diplomacia hispano-indígena en las fronteras de América: Historia de los tratados entre la monarquía española y las comunidades aborígenes.* Madrid: Centro de Estudios Políticos y Constitucionales, 2002.

———. *Paz en la frontera. Historia de las relaciones diplomáticas con las comunidades indígenas en la Argentina (siglos XVI–XIX).* Buenos Aires: Universidad del Museo Social Argentino, 2000.

Levillier, Roberto. *Gobernación del Tucumán: correspondencia de los cabildos en el siglo XVI. Documentos del Archivo de Indias.* Madrid: Sucesores de Rivadeneyra, 1918.

Levin Rojo, Danna. "'Indian Friends and Allies' in the Spanish Imperial Borderlands of North America." In Levin Rojo and Radding, *Oxford Handbook of Borderlands,* 131–62.

———. *Return to Aztlan: Indians, Spaniards, and the Invention of Nuevo México.* Norman: University of Oklahoma Press, 2014.

Levin Rojo, Danna, and Cynthia Radding. "Introduction: Borderlands, A Working Definition." In Levin Rojo and Radding, *Oxford Handbook of Borderlands,* 1–27.

———., eds. *The Oxford Handbook of Borderlands of the Iberian World.* New York: Oxford University Press, 2019.

Levinton, Norberto. "La micro-región: espacio y tiempo en la cartografía producida por la interacción jesuítico-guaraní." *Anuario de Estudios Americanos* 67, no. 2 (2010): 577–604. https://doi.org/10.3989/aeamer.2010.v67.i2.520.

Lewis, Laura A. *Hall of Mirrors: Power, Witchcraft, and Caste in Colonial Mexico.* Durham, NC: Duke University Press, 2003.

Lewis, Oscar. *The Effects of White Contact upon Blackfoot Society, with Special Reference to the Role of the Trade.* Monographs of the American Ethnohistorical Society 6. Seattle: University of Washington Press, 1942.

Liebmann, Matthew. *Revolt: An Archaeological History of Pueblo Resistance and Revitalization in Seventeenth-Century New Mexico.* Tucson: University of Arizona Press, 2012.

Lipman, Andrew. *The Saltwater Frontier: Indians and the Contest for the American Coast.* New Haven, CT: Yale University Press, 2017.

Livi-Bacci, Massimo, and Ernesto Maeder. "The Missions of Paraguay: The Demography of an Experiment." *Journal of Interdisciplinary History* 35 (2004): 185–224.

Livingood, Patrick. "The Many Dimensions of Hally Circles." In *Archaeological Perspectives on the Southern Appalachians: A Multiscalar Approach*, edited by Ramie A. Gougeon and Maureen S. Meyers, 245–62. Knoxville: University of Tennessee Press, 2015.

Lockhart, James. *The Nahuas after the Conquest: A Social and Cultural History of the Indians of Central Mexico, Sixteenth through Eighteenth Centuries*. Stanford, CA: Stanford University Press, 1992.

———. *We People Here: Nahuatl Accounts of the Conquest of Mexico*. Berkeley: University of California Press, 1994.

López Castillo, Gilberto. *Composición de tierras y tendencias de poblamiento hispano en la franja costera. Culiacán y Chiametla, siglos XVII y XVIII*. Culiacán: Centro INAH Sinaloa, 2014.

———. *El poblamiento en tierra de indios cáhitas*. Mexico City: Siglo XXI and El Colegio de Sinaloa, 2010.

López de Cogolludo, Diego. *Historia de Yucatán*. Barcelona: Linkgua Ediciones, 2007.

Lorandi, Ana M. "La frontera oriental del Tawantinsuyu: el Umasuyu y el Tucumán. Una hipótesis de trabajo." *Relaciones de la Sociedad Argentina de Antropología* 14, no. 1 (1980): 147–64.

———. "Las rebeliones indígenas." In *Nueva historia argentina*, edited by Enrique Tandeter, 285–329. Buenos Aires: Editorial Sudamericana, 2000.

———. "Pleito de Juan Ochoa de Zárate por la posesión de los indios Ocloyas. ¿Un caso de verticalidad étnica o un relicto de archipiélago estatal?" *RUNA* 14 (1984): 125–44.

Lorenz, Karl G. "The Natchez of Southwest Mississippi." In *Indians of the Greater Southeast: Historical Archaeology and Ethnohistory*, edited by Bonnie G. McEwan, 142–77. Gainesville: University Press of Florida, 2000.

Lovell, W. George, Christopher H. Lutz, and Wendy Kramer. *Strike Fear in the Land: Pedro de Alvarado and the Conquest of Guatemala, 1520–1541*. Norman: University of Oklahoma Press, 2020.

Lozano, Pedro, SJ. *Descripción corográfica del Gran Chaco Gualamba*. 1773. Tucumán: Universidad Nacional de Tucumán, 1989.

Lucaioli, Carina P. *Abipones en las fronteras del Chaco. Una etnografía histórica sobre el siglo XVIII*. Buenos Aires: Sociedad Argentina de Antropología, 2011.

MacLeitch, Gail D. *Imperial Entanglements: Iroquois Change and Persistence on the Frontiers of Empire*. Philadelphia: University of Pennsylvania Press, 2011.

MacLeod, Murdo. *Spanish Central America: A Socioeconomic History, 1520–1720*. Berkeley: University of California Press, 1973.

Madley, Benjamin. *An American Genocide: The United States and the California Indian Catastrophe, 1846–1873*. New Haven, CT: Yale University Press, 2016.

Maeder, Ernesto J. A. "El modelo portugués y las instrucciones de Bucareli para las misiones guaraníes." *Revista de Historia del Derecho* 14 (1986): 309–25.

———. "La población de las misiones de guaraníes (1641–1682). Reubicación de los pueblos y consecuencias demográficas." *Estudios Iberoamericanos* 15 (1989): 49–68.

———. "Las encomiendas en las misiones jesuíticas." *Folia Histórica del Nordeste* 6 (1984): 119–37.

———. *Misiones del Paraguay. Conflictos y disolución de la sociedad guaraní (1768–1850)*. Colección Realidades Americanas 11. Madrid: Editorial MAPFRE, 1992.

———. *Misiones del Paraguay. Construcción jesuítica de una sociedad cristiano guaraní (1610–1768)*. Resistencia: Instituto de Investigaciones Geohistóricas and CONICET, 2013.

Maeder, Ernesto, and Alfredo Bolsi. "Evolución y características de la población guaraní de las misiones jesuíticas. 1671–1767." *Historiografía. Revista del Instituto de Estudios Historiográficos* 2 (1976): 113–50.

———. "La población guaraní de la provincia de Misiones en la época post-jesuítica (1768–1810)." *Folia Histórica del Nordeste* 5 (1982): 60–106.

Magaña Mancillas, Mario Alberto. *Población y misiones de Baja California. Estudio histórico demográfico de la misión de Santo Domingo de la Frontera, 1775–1850*. Tijuana: El Colegio de la Frontera Norte, 1998.

Mandrini, Raúl J., ed. *Vivir entre dos mundos. Conflicto y convivencia en las fronteras del sur de la Argentina, siglos XVIII y XIX*. Buenos Aires: Taurus, 2006.

Mandrini, Raúl J., and Carlos D. Paz, eds. *Las fronteras hispanocriollas del mundo indígena latinoamericano en los siglos XVIII–XIX. Un estudio comparativo*. Tandil: Centro de Estudios de Historia Regional, Universidad Nacional del Comahue, 2003.

Marcheco-Teruel, Beatriz, Esteban J. Parra, Evelyn Fuentes-Smith, Antonio Salas, Henriette N. Buttenschøn, Ditte Demontis, María Torres-Español, et al. "Cuba: Exploring the History of Admixture and the Genetic Basis of Pigmentation Using Autosomal and Uniparental Markers." *PLOS Genetics* 10, no. 7 (2014): e1004488. https://doi.org/10.1371/journal.pgen.1004488.

Mariluz Urquijo, José María. "Los guaraníes después de la expulsión de los jesuitas." *Estudios Americanos* 6, no. 25 (1953): 323–30.

Maroukis, Thomas C. *The Peyote Road: Religious Freedom and the Native American Church*. Norman: University of Oklahoma Press, 2012.

Martarelli, Angélico. *El Colegio Franciscano de Potosí y sus misiones*. 2nd ed. La Paz: Talleres Gráficos Marinoni, 1918.

Martin, Bonnie, and James F. Brooks, eds. *Linking the Histories of Slavery: North America and Its Borderlands*. Santa Fe, NM: School of Advanced Research Press, 2015.

Martin, Cheryl. *Governance and Society in Colonial Mexico: Chihuahua in the Eighteenth Century*. Stanford, CA: Stanford University Press, 1996.

Martínez, Oscar J. *Troublesome Border*. Tucson: University of Arizona Press, 2006.

Martínez Baracs, Andrea. *Un gobierno de indios. Tlaxcala 1519–1750*. Mexico City: Fondo de Cultura Económica, 2008.

Martínez Baracs, Rodrigo. *Convivencia y utopía. El gobierno indio y español de la "ciudad de Mechuacan" 1521–1580*. Mexico City: Fondo de Cultura Económica, 2005.

Mathers, Clay. "War and Peace in the Sixteenth-Century Southwest: Object-Oriented Approaches to Native-European Encounters and Trajectories. In *Material Encounters and Indigenous Transformations in the Early Colonial Americas*, edited by Corinne L. Hofman and Floris W. M. Keehnen, 308–32. Leiden: Koninklijke Brill, 2019.

Matorras, Gerónimo de. "Diario de la expedición hecha en 1774 a los países del gran Chaco desde el fuerte del Valle por D. Gerónimo Matorras gobernador del Tucumán." 1774. In *Colección de obras y documentos relativos a la historia antigua y moderna de las provincias del Río de la Plata*, edited by Pedro de Angelis, 127–53. Buenos Aires: Librería Nacional de J. Lajoune, 1910.

Matthew, Laura E., and Michel R. Oudijk, eds. *Indian Conquistadors: Indigenous Allies in the Conquest of Mesoamerica*. Norman: University of Oklahoma Press, 2007.

May-Itzá, William de Jesús, José Javier G. Quezada Euán, Luis A. Medina, Eunice Enríquez, and Pilar de la Rúa. "Morphometric and Genetic Differentiation in Isolated Populations of the Endangered Mesoamerican Stingless Bee *Melipona Yucatanica* (Hymenoptera: Apoidea) Suggest the Existence of a Two-Species Complex." *Conservation Genetics* 11, no. 5 (October 2010): 2079–84.

McComb Sanchez, Andrea. "Resistance through Secrecy and Integration: Pueblo Indians, Catholicism, and the Subversion of Colonial Authority." *Religion* 50, no. 2 (2020): 196–214.

McDonnell, Michael. *Masters of Empire: Great Lakes Indians and the Making of America*. New York: Hill and Wang, 2015.

McEnroe, Sean F. *From Colony to Nationhood in Mexico: Laying the Foundations, 1560–1840*. Cambridge: Cambridge University Press, 2014.

———. "The Indian Garrison Colonies of New Spain and Central America." In Levin Rojo and Radding, *Oxford Handbook of Borderlands*, 163–82.

———. "A Sleeping Army: The Military Origins of Interethnic Civic Structures on Mexico's Colonial Frontier." *Ethnohistory* 59, no. 1 (Winter 2011): 109–39.

McKillop, Heather I. "Development of Coastal Maya Trade: Data, Models, and Issues." In *Coastal Maya Trade*, edited by Heather I. McKillop and Paul F. Heal, 1–17. Occasional Papers in Anthropology. Peterborough, ON: Trent University, 1989.

———. *Salt: White Gold of the Ancient Maya*. Gainesville: University Press of Florida, 2002.

McMillen, Christian W. *Making Indian Law: The Hualapai Land Case and the Birth of Ethnohistory*. New Haven, CT: Yale University Press, 2007.

Meadows, William C. *Kiowa, Apache, and Comanche Military Societies*. Austin: University of Texas Press, 1999.

———. *Kiowa Ethnogeography*. Austin: University of Texas Press, 2008.

Medina Bustos, José Marcos. "Cambio político y las rebeliones de indígenas ópatas y yaquis (1819–1827)." In *Violencia interétnica en la frontera norte novohispana y mexicana. Siglos XVII–XIX*, edited by José Marcos Medina Bustos and Esther Padilla Calderón, 157–93. Hermosillo: El Colegio de Sonora, 2015.

Medina Bustos, José Marcos, and Ignacio Almada Bay. "Inter-Ethnic War in Sonora: Indigenous Captains General and Cultural Change, 1740–1832." In Levin Rojo and Radding, *Oxford Handbook of Borderlands*, 183–208.

Medina Bustos, José Marcos, and Esther Padilla Calderón, eds. *Indios, españoles y mestizos en zonas de frontera, siglos XVII–XX*. Hermosillo: El Colegio de Sonora; Zamora: El Colegio de Michoacán, 2013.

———, eds. *Violencia interétnica en la frontera norte novohispana y mexicana. Siglos XVII–XIX*. Hermosillo: El Colegio de Sonora, 2015.

Melià, Bartomeu. *El guaraní conquistado y reducido. Ensayos de etnohistoria*. Asunción: CEADUC, 1986.

———. *La lengua guaraní del Paraguay: historia, sociedad y literatura*. Colección Lenguas Y Literaturas Indígenas 6. Madrid: Editorial MAPFRE, 1992.

———. *La lengua guaraní en el Paraguay colonial. La creación de un lenguaje cristiano en las reducciones de los guaraníes en el Paraguay*. Asunción: CEPAG, 2003.

Melià, Bartomeu, Georg Grünberg, and Friedl Grünberg. *Los Paî-Tavyterã: etnografía guaraní del Paraguay contemporáneo*. Asunción: Centro de Estudios Antropológicos, Universidad Católica Nuestra Señora de la Asunción, 1976.

Mendoza, Blanca, Virginia García-Acosta, Victor Velasco, Ernesto Jáuregui, and Rosa Díaz-Sandoval. "Frequency and Duration of Historical Droughts from the 16th to the 19th Centuries in the Mexican Maya Lands, Yucatan Peninsula." *Climatic Change* 83 (2007): 151–68. https://doi.org/10.1007/s10584-006-9232-1.

Mendoza, Marcela. "The Bolivian Toba (Guaicuruan) Expansion in Northern Gran Chaco, 1550–1850." *Ethnohistory* 66, no. 2 (April 2019): 275–300.

Merrell, James H. *The Indians' New World: Catawbas and Their Neighbors from European Contact to the Era of Removal*. Chapel Hill: University of North Carolina Press, 1989.

Merrill, William L. "Cultural Creativity and Raiding Bands in Eighteenth-Century Northern New Spain." In *Violence, Resistance, and Survival in the Americas*, edited by William Taylor and Franklin Pease. Washington, DC: Smithsonian Institution Press, 1994.

Metcalf, Alida C. *Go-Betweens and the Colonization of Brazil, 1500–1600*. Austin: University of Texas Press, 2006.

Meyers, Albert, ed. *Fuerte de Samaipata*. Santa Cruz de la Sierra: Biblioteca de Museo de Historia and UAGRM, 2015.

Mihesuah, Devon A. *Indigenous American Women: Decolonization, Empowerment, Activism*. Lincoln: University of Nebraska Press, 2003.

Mikecz, Jeremy M. "Beyond Cajamarca: A Spatial Narrative Reimagining of the Encounter in Peru, 1532–1533." *Hispanic American Historical Review* 100, no. 2 (2020): 195–232.

Miles, Tiya. *Ties That Bind: The Story of an Afro-Cherokee Family in Slavery and Freedom*. Oakland: University of California Press, 2015.

Miller, Douglas K. *Indians on the Move: Native American Mobility and Urbanization in the Twentieth Century*. Chapel Hill: University of North Carolina Press, 2019.

Miller, Michael. "Land, Violence and Death: The Bartolome Baca Grant." Accessed July 15, 2013. https://newmexicohistory.org/2015/07/21/land-violence-and-death-the-bartolome-baca-grant/

Milne, George. *Natchez Country: Indians, Colonists, and the Landscapes of Race in French Louisiana.* Athens: University of Georgia Press, 2015.

Minor, Nancy McGown. *The Light Gray People: An Ethno-History of the Lipan Apaches of Texas and Northern Mexico.* Lanham, MD: University Press of America, 2009.

———. *Turning Adversity to Advantage: A History of the Lipan Apaches of Texas and Northern Mexico, 1700–1900.* Lanham, MD: University Press of America, 2009.

Mirafuentes Galván, José Luis. *Movimientos de resistencia y rebeliones indígenas en el norte de México (1680–1821).* 2 vols. Mexico City: UNAM, 1989, 1993.

———. "Relaciones interétnicas y dominación colonial en Sonora." In Hers, Mirafuentes, Soto, and Vallebueno, *Nómadas y sedentarios,* 591–612.

Miroff, Nick, and Missy Ryan. "Army Assessment of Migrant Caravans Undermines Trump's Rhetoric." *Washington Post.* November 2, 2018. https://www.washingtonpost.com/world/national-security/army-assessment-of-migrant-caravans-undermines-trumps-rhetoric/2018/11/02/78b9d82a-dec0–11e8-b3f0-62607289efee_story.html?utm_term=.50b53fcbb34b.

Mishkin, Bernard. *Rank and Warfare among the Plains Indians.* Lincoln: University of Nebraska Press, 1992.

Missale Romanum Ex Decreto Concilii Tridentini. 28th ed. Vatican City: Juxta Typicam Vaticanam, 1920.

Moctezuma Zamarrón, José Luis, and Alejandro Aguilar Zeleny, eds. *Los pueblos indígenas del noroeste. Atlas etnográfico.* Mexico City: INAH, INALI, Instituto Sonorense de Cultura, 2013.

Moctezuma Zamarrón, José Luis, Hugo López, and Claudia Harriss, "Los territorios del noroeste." In *Los pueblos indígenas del noroeste. Atlas Etnográfico,* edited by José Luis Moctezuma Zamarrón and Alejandro Aguilar Zeleny, 253–76. Mexico City: INAH, INALI, Instituto Sonorense de Cultura, 2013.

Molina, Raúl. "La obra franciscana en el Paraguay y Río de la Plata." *Missionalia Hispanica* 11, no. 33 (1954): 485–522.

Montanez-Sanabria, Elizabeth, and María Ximena Urbina Carrasco. "The Spanish Empire's Southernmost Frontiers: From Arauco to the Strait of Magellan." In Levin Rojo and Radding, *Oxford Handbook of Borderlands,* 717–39.

Monteiro, John M. "Indigenous Histories in Colonial Brazil: Between Ethnocide and Ethnogenesis." In Levin Rojo and Radding, *Oxford Handbook of Borderlands,* 397–408.

———. *Negros da terra: índios e bandeirantes nas origens de São Paulo.* São Paulo: Companhia das Letras, 1994.

Moorhead, Max L. *The Apache Frontier: Jacobo Ugarte and Spanish-Indian Relations in Northern New Spain, 1769–1791.* Norman: University of Oklahoma Press, 1968.

Morandi, Steven J. "Xibun Maya: The Archaeology of an Early Spanish Colonial Frontier in Southeastern Yucatan." PhD diss., Colgate University, 2010.

Moreno-Estrada, Andrés, Simon Gravel, Fouad Zakharia, Jacob L. McCauley, Jake K. Byrnes, Christopher R. Gignoux, Patricia A. Ortiz-Tello, et al. "Reconstructing the Population Genetic History of the Caribbean." [In eng]. *PLoS Genetics* 9, no. 11 (2013): e1003925–e25. https://doi.org/10.1371/journal.pgen.1003925.

Morey, Nancy C., and Robert V. Morey. "Foragers and Farmers: Differential Consequences of Spanish Contact." *Ethnohistory* 20, no. 3 (Summer 1973): 229–46. https://
doi.org/10.2307/481445.

Morillo, Francisco. "Diario del viaje al río Bermejo por Fray Francisco Morillo del
orden de San Francisco." 1780. In *Colección de obras y documentos relativos a la
Historia Antigua y Moderna de las Provincias del Río de la Plata*, edited by Pedro
de Angelis, 203–15. Buenos Aires: Librería Nacional de J. Lajoune, 1910.

Morris, John Miller. *El Llano Estacado: Exploration and Imagination on the High
Plains of Texas and New Mexico*. Austin: Texas State Historical Association, 1997.

Moutoukias, Zacarías. "Gobierno y sociedad en el Tucumán y el Río de la Plata, 1550–
1800." In *Nueva Historia Argentina*. Vol. 2, *La sociedad colonial*, edited by Enrique
Tandeter, 355–411. Buenos Aires: Sudamericana, 2000.

Mulroy, Kevin. "Mixed Race in the Seminole Nation." *Ethnohistory* 58, no. 1 (2011):
113–41.

———. *The Seminole Freedmen: A History*. Norman: University of Oklahoma Press,
2007.

Mumford, Jeremy. *Vertical Empire: The General Resettlement of the Indians in the
Colonial Andes*. Durham, NC: Duke University Press, 2012.

Muñoz Arbeláez, Santiago. *Costumbres en disputa. Los muiscas y el imperio español
en Ubaque, siglo XVI*. Bogota: Universidad de los Andes, Facultad de Ciencias
Sociales, Departamento de Historia, Ediciones Uniandes, 2015.

Mura, Fabio, and Rubem Ferreira Thomaz de Almeida. "Historia y territorio entre
los Guaraní de Mato Grosso do Sul, Brasil." *Revista de Indias* 64 (2004): 55–66.

Murray, N. Michelle, and Akiko Tsuchiya, eds. *Unsettling Colonialism: Gender and
Race in the Nineteenth-Century Global Hispanic World*. Albany: State University
of New York Press, 2019.

Nacuzzi, Lidia, ed. *Funcionarios, diplomáticos, guerreros. Miradas hacia el otro en
las fronteras de pampa y patagonia (siglos XVIII y XIX)*. Buenos Aires: Sociedad
Argentina de Antropología, 2002.

———. *Identidades impuestas. Tehuelches, aucas y pampas en el norte de la Patagonia*. Buenos Aires: Sociedad Argentina de Antropología, 2005.

Navarro García, Luis. *Don José de Gálvez y la Comandancia General de las Provincias
Internas del norte de Nueva España*. Seville: Escuela de Estudios Hispanoameri-
canos, 1964.

Naylor, Celia. *African Cherokees in Indian Territory: From Chattel to Citizens*. Chapel
Hill: University of North Carolina Press, 2008.

Necker, Louis. *Indios guaraníes y chamanes franciscanos: las primeras reducciones del
Paraguay, 1580–1800*. Biblioteca Paraguaya de Antropología 7. Asunción: Centro de
Estudios Antropológicos, Universidad Católica Nuestra Señora de la Asunción, 1990.

———. "La réaction des Indiens Guarani à la Conquête espagnole du Paraguay, un
des facteurs de la colonisation de l'Argentine à la fin du XVIe siècle." *Bulletin de
la Société Suisse des Américanistes* 38 (1974): 71–79.

Nelson, Al B. "Juan de Ugalde and Picax-andé Ins-Tinsle, 1787–1788." *Southwestern
Historical Quarterly* 43 (April 1940): 438–64.

Neumann, Eduardo. "A escrita dos guaranis nas reduções: usos e funções das formas textuais indígenas. Século XVIII." *Topoi* 8 (2007): 48–79.

———. *Letra de indio. Cultura escrita, comunicação e memória indígena nas Reduções do Paraguai*. São Bernardo do Campo: Nhanduti, 2015.

———. "Razón gráfica y escritura indígena en las reducciones guaraníticas." In *Saberes de la conversión. Jesuitas, indígenas e imperios coloniales en las fronteras de la cristiandad*, edited by Guillermo Wilde, 99–130. Buenos Aires: Editorial SB, 2011.

Neumann, Eduardo, and Guillermo Wilde. "Escritura, poder y memoria en las reducciones jesuíticas del Paraguay: trayectorias de líderes indígenas en tiempos de transición." *Colonial Latin American Historical Review* 2 (2014): 353–80.

Newell, Quincy D. *Constructing Lives at Mission San Francisco: Native Californians and Hispanic Colonists, 1776–1821*. Albuquerque: University of New Mexico Press, 2009.

Newson, Linda A. "Piety, Beeswax, and the Portuguese African Slave Trade to Lima, Peru, in the Early Colonial Period." *Atlantic Studies* 16, no. 2 (2018): 144–62 .https://doi.org/10.1080/14788810.2018.1434284.

Nielsen, Axel E. *Celebrando con los antepasados*. Jujuy: Mallku Ediciones, 2010.

Nordenskiöld, Erland. *The Changes in the Material Culture of Two Indian Tribes under the Influence of New Surroundings*. Göteborg: Erlander, 1920.

———. "The Guaraní Invasion of the Inca Empire in the Sixteenth Century: An Historical Migration." *Geographical Review* 4 (1917): 103–21.

Obregón, Baltasar de. *Historia de los descubrimientos antiguos y modernos de la Nueva España escrita por el conquistador en el año de 1584*. Edited by Mariano Cuevas. 1584. Mexico City: Editorial Porrúa, 1988.

Obregón Iturra, Jimena Paz. *Des Indiens rebelles face à leurs juges: Espagnols et Araucans-Mapuches dans le Chili colonial, fin XVIIe siècle*. Rennes: Presses Universitaires de Rennes, 2015.

Obregón Iturra, Jimena Paz, Andrés Castro Roldán, and Christophe Giudicelli. *Revers de conquête et résistances amérindiennes: Les confins de l'Amérique du Sud espagnole au XVIe siècle*. Paris: Belin/Humensis, 2019.

Ochoa, Margarita R., and Sara V. Guenguerich, eds. *Cacicas: The Indigenous Women Leaders of Spanish America, 1492–1825*. Norman: University of Oklahoma Press, 2021.

O'Conor, Hugo de. *Informe de Hugo de O'Conor sobre el estado de las Provincias Internas del Norte*. Mexico City: Editorial Cultura, 1952.

Oland, Maxine Heather. "Long-Term Indigenous History on a Colonial Frontier: Archaeology at a 15th–17th Century Maya Village, Progresso Lagoon, Belize." PhD diss., Northwestern University, 2009.

Oland, Maxine Heather, and Joel W. Palka. "The Perduring Maya: New Archaeology on Early Colonial Transitions." *Antiquity* 90, no. 350 (April 2016): 472–86.

Oliveto, Lía Guillermina, and Beatriz N. Ventura. "Dinámicas poblacionales de los valles orientales del sur de Bolivia y norte de Argentina, siglos XV–XVII. Aportes etnohistóricos y arqueológicos." *Población y Sociedad* 16 (2009): 119–50.

———. "Final de la jornada al Chaco de Ledesma Valderrama en 1631. Análisis y nuevas perspectivas a partir de documentación inédita." *Relaciones de la Sociedad Argentina de Antropología* 42, no. 2 (December 2017): 257–80. http://www .saantropologia.com.ar/wp-content/uploads/2017/12/3-Olivetto-y-Ventura-C .pdf.

Opler, Morris Edward. *An Apache Life-Way: The Economic, Social, and Religious Institutions of the Chiricahua Indians*. Lincoln: University of Nebraska Press, 1996.

———. "The Apachean Culture Pattern and Its Origins." In *Handbook of North American Indians*. Vol. 10, edited by Alfonso Ortiz, 368–92. Washington, DC: Smithsonian Institution, 1983.

Ortega Ricaurte, Enrique. *Los inconquistables. La guerra de los Pijaos, 1602–1603*. Bogota: Archivo Nacional de Colombia; Ministerio de Educación Nacional, 1949.

Ortelli, Sara. "Enemigos internos y súbditos desleales: La infidencia en Nueva Vizcaya en tiempos de los Borbones." *Anuario de Estudios Americanos* 61 (2004): 467–89.

———. *Trama de una guerra conveniente. Nueva Vizcaya y la sombra de los apaches (1748–1790)*. Mexico City: El Colegio de México, 2007.

Ortiz, Gabriela, and Beatriz Ventura, eds. *La mitad verde del mundo andino. Investigaciones arqueológicas en la vertiente oriental de los Andes y las Tierras Bajas de Bolivia y Argentina*. Jujuy: Universidad Nacional de Jujuy, 2003.

Ostler, Jeffrey. *The Lakotas and the Black Hills: The Struggle for Sacred Ground*. New York: Viking, 2010.

———. *The Plains Sioux and U.S. Colonialism from Lewis and Clark to Wounded Knee*. New York: Cambridge University Press, 2004.

———. *Surviving Genocide: Native Nations and the United States from the American Revolution to Bleeding Kansas*. New Haven, CT: Yale University Press, 2019.

Owensby, Brian P. *Empire of Law and Indian Justice in Colonial Mexico*. Stanford, CA: Stanford University Press, 2008.

Pacheco de Oliveira, Joao. "¿Una etnología de los indios misturados? Situación colonial, territorialización y flujos culturales." In *La antropología brasileña contemporánea. Contribuciones para un diálogo latinoamericano*, edited by Alejandro Grimson, Gustavo Lins Ribeiro, and Pablo Semán. Buenos Aires: Prometeo, 2004.

Page, Carlos. "Las reducciones-fuertes de los jesuitas en el Chaco. Historia y tipología de un emplazamiento urbano devenido en legado inmaterial." Actas del Congreso Electrónico: el patrimonio de culto al servicio de la difusión de las creencias. Grupo Patrimonio: Rosario, 2012. http://www.carlospage.com.ar/wp-content/2008 /06/PAGE-C-Las-reducciones-fuertes-de-los-jesuitas-en-el-Chaco-Historia-y -tipolog-ia-de-un-emplazamiento-urbano-devenido-en-legado-inmaterial -Mesa_3.pdf.

Pailes, Richard A. "An Archaeological Reconnaissance of Southern Sonora and Reconsideration of the Río Sonora Culture." PhD diss., University of Southern Illinois. Carbondale, 1972.

———. "An Archeological Perspective on the Sonora Entrada." In *The Coronado Expedition to Tierra Nueva. The 1540–1542 Route across the Southwest*, edited by

Richard Flint and Shirley Cushing Flint, 147–57. Boulder: University Press of Colorado, 2004.

———. "Relaciones culturales prehistóricas en el noroeste de Sonora. In *Sonora: antropología del desierto*, Edited by Beatriz Braniff and Richard S. Felger, 117–22. Noroeste de México 12. Hermosillo: Centro INAH, 1994.

Paleari, Antonio. *Jujuy: diccionario general.* Jujuy: Ediciones del Gobierno de la Provincia de Jujuy, 1992.

Pardo, Osvaldo F. *The Origins of Mexican Catholicism: Nahua Rituals and Christian Sacraments in Sixteenth-Century Mexico.* Ann Arbor: University of Michigan Press, 2004.

Paso y Troncoso, Francisco del. "Epistolario de Nueva España, 1505–1818." In *Biblioteca histórica mexicana de obras inéditas*. Vol. 5. Mexico City: José Porrúa e Hijos, 1939.

Patch, Robert W. "The (Almost) Forgotten Plants of Yucatán." In *The Lowland Maya Area: Three Millennia at the Human-Wildland Interface*, edited by Arturo Gómez-Pompa, Michael F. Allen, Scott L. Feddick, and Juan J. Jiménez-Osornio, 561–69. Binghamton, NY: Haworth Press, 2003.

———. *Indians and the Political Economy of Colonial Central America, 1670–1810.* Norman: University of Oklahoma Press, 2012.

———. *Maya and Spaniard in Yucatan, 1648–1812.* Stanford, CA: Stanford University Press, 1993.

Pauketat, Timothy R. *Chiefdoms and Other Archaeological Delusions.* Lanham, MD: AltaMira Press, 2007.

Paz, Gustavo L. "La liquidación de las instituciones corporativas coloniales en tiempos de la independencia: la Reducción de San Ignacio de los Tobas, Jujuy." *Mundo Agrario* 17 (2016). http://www.mundoagrario.unlp.edu.ar/article/view/MAe017.

Paz, Gustavo L., and Gabriela B. Sica. "La frontera oriental del Tucumán en el Río de la Plata (siglos XVI–XVIII)." In *Las fronteras en el mundo atlántico (siglos XVI–XIX)*, edited by Susana Truchuelo and Emir Reitano, 293–330. La Plata: Universidad Nacional de La Plata, 2017. http://libros.fahce.unlp.edu.ar/index.php/libros/catalog/book/85.

Paz Reverol, Carmen Laura. *El pueblo Wayuu. Rebeliones, comercio y autonomía: una perspectiva histórica-antropológica.* Quito: Editorial Abya-Yala, 2017.

Peirotti, Leonor. Familia, haciendas y negocios. Concentración y fragmentación de la propiedad de la tierra en el Oriente Jujeño (1780- 1890). Licenciatura thesis, Universidad Nacional de Jujuy, 2005.

Penry, Elizabeth. *The People Are King: The Making of an Indigenous Andean Politics.* New York: Oxford University Press, 2019.

Perdue, Theda. *Slavery and the Evolution of Cherokee Society, 1540–1866.* Knoxville: University of Tennessee Press, 1979.

Perego, Ugo A., Hovirag Lancioni, Maribel Tribaldos, Norman Angerhofer, Jayne E. Ekins, Anna Olivieri, Scott R. Woodward, et al. "Decrypting the Mitochondrial Gene Pool of Modern Panamanians." [In eng]. *PloS One* 7, no. 6 (2012): e38337. https://doi.org/10.1371/journal.pone.0038337.

Pérez de Ribas, Andrés. *Historia de los triunfos de nuestra santa fe entre gentes las más bárbaras y fieras del Nuevo Orbe.* Madrid: Alonso de Paredes, 1645.

Pérez Garzón, Juan Sisinio. *Las Cortes de Cádiz. El nacimiento de la nación liberal (1808–1814).* Madrid: Síntesis, 2008.

Peterson, Jeanette Favrot, and Kevin Terraciano, eds. *The Florentine Codex: An Encyclopedia of the Nahua World in Sixteenth-Century Mexico.* Austin: University of Texas Press, 2019.

Picon, François René. *Pasteurs du Nouveau Monde. Adoption de l'élevage chez les indiens guajiros.* Paris: Maison des Sciences de l'Homme, 1983.

Pifarré, Francisco. *Historia de un pueblo: Los Guaraní-Chiriguano.* La Paz: CIPCA, 2015.

———. *Los Guaraní-Chiriguano.* Vol. 2, *Historia de un pueblo.* La Paz: Centro de Investigación y Promoción del Campesinado, 1989.

Pike, Ruth. "Penal Servitude in the Spanish Empire: Presidio Labor in the Eighteenth Century." *Hispanic American Historical Review* 58, no. 1 (1978): 21–40.

Pinckert Justiniano, Guillermo. *La guerra chiriguana.* Santa Cruz: Talleres Gráficos Los Huérfanos, 1978.

Pinto de Medeiros, Ricardo. "Política indigenista do período pombalino e seus reflexos nas Capitanias do norte da América portuguesa." In *Novos olhares sobre as Capitanias do Norte do Estado do Brasil,* edited by Carla Mary S. Oliveira and Ricardo Pinto de Medeiros, 125–59. João Pessoa: Editora Universitária/UFPB, 2007.

Pinto Rodríguez, Jorge, ed. *Araucanía y Pampas. Un mundo fronterizo en América del Sur.* Temuco: Ediciones Universidad de la Frontera, 1996.

———. *La formación del estado y de la nación y el pueblo mapuche: de la inclusión a la exclusión.* Santiago de Chile: Direccion de Biblioteca, Archivos y Museos, 2003.

Pizzigoni, Caterina. *The Life Within: Local Indigenous Society in Mexico's Toluca Valley, 1650–1800.* Stanford, CA: Stanford University Press, 2012.

Platt, Tristan. *Estado boliviano y ayllu andino: tierra y tributo en el norte de Potosí.* 2nd ed. La Paz: Biblioteca del Bicentenario de Bolivia, 2016.

Poderti, Alicia. *San Ramón de la Nueva Orán: una ciudad, muchas historias.* Salta: Fundación Banco del Noroeste, 1995.

Poenitz, Edgar, and Alfredo Poenitz. *Misiones, Provincia Guaranítica: defensa y disolución.* Posadas: Editorial Universitaria, Universidad Nacional de Misiones, 1993.

Porras Muñoz, Guillermo. *Iglesia y estado en Nueva Vizcaya (1562–1821).* Mexico City: UNAM, 1980.

———. *La frontera con los indios de Nueva Vizcaya en el siglo XVII.* Mexico City: Banamex, 1980.

Powell, Philip Wayne. *Mexico's Miguel Caldera: The Taming of America's First Frontier, 1548–1597.* Tucson: University of Arizona Press, 1977.

———. *Soldiers, Indians, and Silver: The Northward Advance of New Spain, 1550–1600.* Berkeley: University of California Press, 1952.

Powers, Karen Vieira. *Women in the Crucible of Conquest: The Gendered Genesis of Spanish American Society, 1500–1600.* Albuquerque: University of New Mexico Press, 2005.

Presta, Ana M. "La población de los valles de Tarija, siglo XVI. Aportes para la solución de un enigma etnohistórico en una frontera incaica." In *El Tucumán colonial y Charcas*, edited by Ana M. Lorandi, 163–75. Buenos Aires: Universidad de Buenos Aires, 1997.

Presta, Ana M., and Mercedes del Río. "Reflexiones sobre los churumatas del sur de Bolivia." *Histórica* 17, no. 2 (December 1993): 223–37.

Price, Catherine. *The Oglala People, 1841–1879: A Political History.* Lincoln: University of Nebraska Press, 1998.

Priestly, Herbert I., ed. and trans. *The Luna Papers: Documents Relating to the Expedition of Don Tristan de Luna y Arellano for the Conquest of La Florida in 1559–1561.* 2 vols. Deland: Florida State Historical Society, 1928.

Pugh, Timothy W. "Maya Sacred Landscapes at Contact." In *Maya Worldviews at Conquest*, edited by Leslie Cecil and Timothy W. Pugh, 317–34. Boulder: University Press of Colorado, 2009.

Qiu, Linda. "Trump's Evidence-Free Claims about the Migrant Caravan." *New York Times*, October 22, 2018. https://www.nytimes.com/2018/10/22/us/politics/migrant-caravan-fact-check.html

Quezada, Sergio. *Maya Lords and Lordship: The Formation of Colonial Society in Yucatán, 1350–1600.* Translated by Terry Rugeley. Norman: University of Oklahoma Press, 2014.

———. "Tributos, limosnas, y mantas en Yucatán, siglo XVI." *Ancient Mesoamerica* 12, no. 1 (2001): 73–78.

Quezada Euán, José Javier G. *Biología y uso de las abejas sin aguijón de la península de Yucatán, México (Hymenoptera: Meliponini).* Tratados 16. Mérida: Ediciones de la Universidad Autónoma de Yucatán, 2005.

Quijada, Mónica, ed. *De los cacicazgos a la ciudadanía. Sistemas políticos en la frontera, Río de la Plata, siglos XVIII–XX.* Berlin: Gebr. Mann Verlag, 2011.

Radding, Cynthia. *Landscapes of Power and Identity: Comparative Histories in the Sonoran Desert and the Forests of Amazonia from Colony to Republic.* Durham, NC: Duke University Press, 2006.

———. *Wandering Peoples: Colonialism, Ethnic Spaces, and Ecological Frontiers in Northwestern Mexico, 1700–1850.* Durham, NC: Duke University Press, 1997.

Raffino, R., A. Nielsen, and R. Alvis. "El dominio Inka en dos secciones del Kollasuyu: Aullagas y Valle Grande (Altiplano de Bolivia y Oriente de Humahuaca)." *Comechingonia* 9 (1991): 99–151.

Ramírez, Susan E. *The World Upside Down: Cross-cultural Contact and Conflict in Sixteenth-Century Peru.* Stanford, CA: Stanford University Press, 1996.

Ramos, Gabriela. *Death and Conversion in the Andes: Lima and Cuzco, 1532–1670.* Notre Dame, IN: University of Notre Dame Press, 2010.

Ramsey, William L. *The Yamasee War: A Study of Culture, Economy, and Conflict in the Colonial South.* Lincoln: University of Nebraska Press, 2010.

Rangel, Rodrigo. "Account of the Northern Conquest and Discovery of Hernando de Soto." Translated by John E. Worth. In Clayton, Knight, and Moore, *de Soto Chronicles*, 1:246–306.

Readman, Paul, Cynthia Radding, and Chad Bryant. "Introduction: Borderlands in a Global Perspective." In *Borderlands in World History, 1700–1914*, edited by Paul Readman, Cynthia Radding, and Chad Bryant, 1–26. New York: Palgrave Macmillan, 2014.

Record, Ian. *Big Sycamore Stands Alone: The Western Apaches, Aravaipa, and the Struggle for Place*. Norman: University of Oklahoma Press, 2008.

Reed, Nelson A. *The Caste War of Yucatán*. Stanford, CA: Stanford University Press, 2001.

Reff, Daniel T. "The 'Predicament of Culture' and Spanish Missionary Accounts of the Tepehuan and Pueblo Revolts." *Ethnohistory* 42, no. 1 (Winter 1995): 63–90.

Regnier, Amanda L. *Reconstructing Tascalusa's Chiefdom: Pottery Styles and the Social Composition of Late Mississippian Communities along the Alabama River*. Tuscaloosa: University of Alabama Press, 2014.

Reilly, F. Kent, III. "People of Earth, People of Sky: Visualizing the Sacred in Native American Art of the Mississippian Period." In *Hero, Hawk, and Open Hand: American Indian Art of the Ancient Midwest and South*, edited by Richard F. Townsend and Robert V. Sharp, 125–38. New Haven, CT: Yale University Press in association with the Art Institute of Chicago, 2004.

Reilly, F. Kent, III, and James F. Garber, eds. *Ancient Objects and Sacred Realms: Interpretations of Mississippian Iconography*. Austin: University of Texas Press, 2007.

Reséndez, Andrés. "Borderlands of Bondage." In Levin Rojo and Radding, *Oxford Handbook of Borderlands*, 571–82.

———. *The Other Slavery: The Uncovered Story of Indian Enslavement in America*. Boston, MA: Houghton Mifflin Harcourt, 2016.

Restall, Matthew. *The Black Middle: Africans, Mayas, and Spaniards in Colonial Yucatan*. Stanford, CA: Stanford University Press, 2009.

———. *Maya Conquistador*. Boston, MA: Beacon Press, 1998.

———. *The Maya World: Yucatec Culture and Society, 1550–1850*. Stanford, CA: Stanford University Press, 1997.

Restall, Matthew, and Florine Asselbergs. *Invading Guatemala: Spanish, Nahua, and Maya Accounts of the Conquest Wars*. University Park: Penn State University Press, 2007.

Richards, John F. *The Unending Frontier: An Environmental History of the Early Modern World*. Berkeley and Los Angeles: University of California Press, 2003.

Richter, Daniel K. *The Ordeal of the Longhouse: The Peoples of the Iroquois League in the Era of European Colonization*. Chapel Hill: University of North Carolina Press, 1992.

Rindfleisch, Bryan C. *George Galphin's Intimate Empire: The Creek Indians, Family, and Colonialism in Early America*. Tuscaloosa: University of Alabama Press, 2019.

Río, Ignacio del. "El noroeste novohispano y la nueva política imperial española." In *Tres siglos de historia sonorense, 1530–1830*. 2nd ed. Edited by Sergio Ortega Noriega and Ignacio del Río, 243–82. Mexico City: Instituto de Investigaciones Históricas, UNAM, 2010.

Rivaya-Martínez, Joaquín. "Diplomacia interétnica en la frontera norte de Nueva España. Un análisis de los tratados hispano-comanches de 1785 y 1786 y sus consecuencias desde una perspectiva etnohistórica." *Nuevo Mundo, Mundos Nuevos*, November 30, 2011. http://nuevomundo.revues.org/62228.

———. "Incidencia de la viruela y otras enfermedades epidémicas en la trayectoria histórico-demográfica de los indios comanches, 1706–1875." In *El impacto demográfico de la* viruela. *De la época colonial al siglo XX*, edited by Chantal Cramaussel and David Carbajal López, 63–80. Zamora: El Colegio de Michoacán, 2010.

———. "Reflexión historiográfica sobre los genízaros de Nuevo México, una comunidad pluriétnica del septentrión novohispano." In *Familias pluriétnicas y mestizaje en la Nueva España y el Río de la Plata*, edited by David Carbajal López, 271–308. Guadalajara, JA: Universidad de Guadalajara, 2014.

———. "Trespassers in the Land of Plenty: Comanche Raiding across the U.S.-Mexico Border, 1846–1853." In *These Ragged Edges: Histories of Violence along the U.S.-Mexico Border*, edited by Andrew Torget and Gerardo Gurza Lavalle, 48–73. Chapel Hill: North Carolina University Press, 2022.

Rivera y Villalón, Pedro de. *Diario y derrotero de lo caminado, visto y observado en el discurso de la visita general de presidios, situados en las provincias internas de la Nueva España (1736)*. Edited by Vito Alessio Robles. Mexico City: Taller Autográfico, 1946; reprint: Málaga, Algazara, 2007.

Robins, Nicholas A. *Native Insurgencies and the Genocidal Impulse in the Americas.* Bloomington and Indianapolis: Indiana University Press, 2005.

Robinson, Sherry. *I Fought a Good Fight: A History of the Lipan Apaches.* Denton: University of North Texas Press, 2013.

Rodríguez-Sala, María Luisa. *La expedición militar-geográfica a la junta de los ríos Conchos y Grande del norte y al Bolsón de Mapimí.* Mexico City: UNAM, 1999.

Roller, Heather F. *Amazonian Routes: Indigenous Mobility and Colonial Communities in Northern Brazil.* Stanford, CA: Stanford University Press, 2014.

Rollings, Willard H. *The Osage: An Ethnohistorical Study of Hegemony on the Prairie-Plains.* Columbia: University of Missouri Press, 1992.

Romero Frizzi, María de los Ángeles. "The Power of the Law: The Construction of Colonial Power in an Indigenous Region." In *Negotiation within Domination: New Spain's Indian Pueblos Confront the Spanish State*, edited by Susan Kellogg, 107–35. Boulder: University Press of Colorado, 2010.

Rosenthal, Nicolas G. *Reimagining Indian Country: Native American Migration and Identity in Twentieth-Century Los Angeles.* Chapel Hill: University of North Carolina Press, 2012.

Ross, Richard Jeffrey, and Brian Philip Owensby, eds. *Justice in a New World: Negotiating Legal Intelligibility in British, Iberian, and Indigenous America.* New York: New York University Press, 2018.

Rossi, Juan José. *Los Wichí ("Los Mataco").* Buenos Aires: Galerna-Búsqueda Ayllu, 2003.

Roubik, David W. "Nest and Colony Characteristics of Stingless Bees from Panamaa (Hymenoptera: Apidae)." *Journal of the Kansas Entomological Society* 56, no. 3 (June 1983): 327–55.

Roulet, Florencia. *La resistencia de los guaraní del Paraguay a la conquista española, 1537–1556.* Posadas: Editorial Universitaria, Universidad Nacional de Misiones, 1993.

Roys, Ralph L. *The Political Geography of the Yucatan Maya.* Washington, DC: Carnegie Institution of Washington, 1957.

Rugeley, Terry. *Rebellion Now and Forever: Mayas, Hispanics, and Caste War Violence in Yucatan, 1800–1880.* Stanford, CA: Stanford University Press, 2009.

———. *Yucatán's Maya Peasantry and the Origins of the Caste War.* Austin: University of Texas Press, 1996.

Ruiz de Montoya, Antonio. *Arte y bocabulario de la lengua guaraní.* Iuan Sanchez: Madrid, 1640.

———. *Tesoro de la Lengva Gvarani por Antonio Ruiz de Montoya publicado nuevamente sin alteración alguna por Julio Platzmann. Arte, Bocabulario, Tesoro y Catecismo de la lengva gvarani.* Vol. 3. Leipzig: B. G. Teubner Impr. W. Drugulin, 1639.

Ruiz-Esquide Figueroa, Andrea. *Los indios amigos en la frontera araucana.* Santiago de Chile: Dirección de Bibliotecas, Archivos y Museos, 1993.

Ruiz Medrano, Ethelia, and Susan Kellogg, eds. *Negotiation within Domination: New Spain's Indian Pueblos Confront the Spanish State.* Boulder: University Press of Colorado, 2010.

Rushforth, Brett. *Bonds of Alliance: Indigenous and Atlantic Slaveries in New France.* Chapel Hill: University of North Carolina Press, 2012.

Saeger, James Schofield. *The Chaco Mission Frontier: The Guaycuruan Experience.* Tucson: University of Arizona Press, 2000.

———. "Warfare, Reorganization, and Readaptation at the Margins of Spanish Rule— The Chaco and Paraguay (1573–1882)." In *The Cambridge History of the Native Peoples of the Americas.* Vol. 3: *South America,* edited by Frank Salomon and Stuart B. Schwartz, 257–86. Cambridge: Cambridge University Press, 1999.

Saeler, James. "Survival and Abolition: The Eighteenth-Century Paraguayan Encomienda." *The Americas* 38 (1981): 59–85.

Saignes, Thierry. *Ava y Karai: Ensayos sobre la frontera chiriguano (siglos XVI–XX).* La Paz: Hisbol, 1990.

———. *Historia del pueblo chiriguano.* Lima and La Paz: Instituto Francés de Estudios Andinos, Embajada de Francia en Bolivia, 2007.

Salas, Mario Alberto. *El Antigal de Ciénaga Grande (Quebrada de Purmamarca, Provincia de Jujuy).* Buenos Aires: Museo Etnográfico, 1945.

Sanabria Fernández, Hernando. *Apiaguaiqui Tumpa.* La Paz: Amigos del Libro, 1972.

Sánchez Bramdam, Sandra. "'Se hace camino al andar.' Tupac Amaru en Jujuy: una reinterpretación." Master's thesis, Universidad de Chile, 2002.

———. "Un viaje entre la historia y la memoria. Los 'ossa' jujeños." *Anuario de Estudios Americanos* 55, no.1 (January 2003): 41–76.

Sánchez Bramdam, Sandra, and Gabriela Sica. "La frontera oriental de Humahuaca y sus relaciones con el Chaco (1595–1650)." *Boletín del IFEA* 19, no. 2 (1990): 469–97.

————. "Por ser gente de otra ley Tobas, Mocovies y Ojotaes reducidos en el Valle de Jujuy. Prácticas y discursos (siglos XVII y XVIII)." *Journal de la Société des Américanistes* 83 (1997): 59–82.

Santamaría, Daniel J. *Chaco Gualamba. Del monte salvaje al desierto ilustrado.* Jujuy: Cuadernos del Duende, 2007.

————. *Del tabaco al incienso. Reducción y conversión en las misiones jesuítas de las selvas sudamericanas, siglos XVII y XVIII.* Jujuy: CEIC, 1994.

————. "La sociedad indígena." In *Nueva Historia de la Nación Argentina.* Vol. 2, *Período Español (1600–1810)*, 183–206. Buenos Aires: Planeta, 1999.

————. "Paz y asistencialismo vs. guerra y esclavitud. La política reformista del gobernador Gerónimo de Matorras en el Chaco Centro-Occidental, 1769–1775." *Folia Histórica del Nordeste* 14 (1999): 7–31.

————. "Población y economía interna de las poblaciones aborígenes del Chaco en el siglo XVIII." *Andes* 9 (1998): 173–95.

Santamaría, Daniel J., and Marcelo A. Lagos. "Historia y etnografía de las tierras bajas del Norte Argentino. Trabajo realizado y perspectivas." *Anuario del IEHS* 7 (1992): 74–92.

Santiago, Mark. *A Bad Peace and a Good War: Spain and the Mescalero Apache Uprising of 1795–1799.* Norman: University of Oklahoma Press, 2018.

————. *The Jar of Severed Hands: Spanish Deportation of Apache Prisoners of War, 1770–1810.* Norman: University of Oklahoma Press, 2011.

Sarreal, Julia. "Caciques as Placeholders in the Guaraní Missions of Eighteenth-Century Paraguay." *Colonial Latin American Review* 23 (2014): 224–51.

————. *The Guaraní and Their Missions: A Socioeconomic History.* Stanford, CA: Stanford University Press, 2014.

Sauer, Carl O. *Aboriginal Population of Northwestern Mexico.* Ibero-Americana no. 10. Berkeley: University of California Press, 1935.

————. *Aztatlán.* Edited by Ignacio Guzmán Betancourt. Mexico City: Siglo XXI, 1998.

————. *The Road to Cíbola.* Ibero-Americana 1. Berkeley: University of California Press, 1932.

Saunt, Claudio. *A New Order of Things: Property, Power, and the Transformation of the Creek Indians, 1733–1816.* Cambridge: Cambridge University Press, 1999.

Scholes, France V., and Eleanor B. Adams. *Documents Relating to the Mirones Expedition to the Interior of Yucatan, 1621–1624.* Translated by Robert D. Wood. Culver City, CA: Labyrinthos, 1991.

————., eds. *Don Diego Quijada, alcalde mayor de Yucatán 1561–1565: Documentos sacados de los archivos de España y publicados por France V. Scholes y Eleanor B. Adams.* Vol. 2. Biblioteca Historica Mexicana de Obras Ineditas 14. Mexico City: Antigua Librería Robredo, de José Porrúa e Hijos, 1938.

Scholes, France V., and Ralph L. Roys. *The Maya Chontal Indians of Acalan-Tixchel: A Contribution to the History and Ethnography of the Yucatan Peninsula.* Washington, DC: Carnegie Institute of Washington, 1948.

Schroeder, Susan, Stephanie Wood, and Robert Haskett, eds. *Indian Women of Early Mexico.* Norman: University of Oklahoma Press, 1997.

Schwaller, Robert C. "Contested Conquests: African Maroons and the Incomplete Conquest of Hispaniola, 1519–1620." *The Americas* 75, no. 4 (2018): 609–38.

Scott, James C. *The Art of Not Being Governed: An Anarchist History of Upland Southeast Asia*. New Haven, CT: Yale University Press, 2009.

Secoy, Frank R. *Changing Military Patterns of the Great Plains Indians*. 1953. Lincoln: University of Nebraska Press, 1992.

Service, Elman R. "The Encomienda in Paraguay." *Hispanic American Historical Review* 31, no. 2 (1951): 230–52.

Shapard, Bud. *Chief Loco: Apache Peacemaker*. Norman: University of Oklahoma Press, 2010.

Shefveland, Kristalyn Marie. *Anglo-Native Virginia: Trade, Conversion, and Indian Slavery in the Old Dominion, 1646–1722*. Athens: University of Georgia Press, 2016.

Sheldon, Craig T. Jr. "The Present State of Archaeological Survey and the Site File Data for the Alabama River and Adjacent Regions. In Knight, *Search for Mabila*, 107–28. Tuscaloosa: University of Alabama Press, 2009.

Sheridan Prieto, Cecilia. *Fronterización del espacio hacia el norte de la Nueva España*. Mexico City: CIESAS–Instituto Mora, 2015.

———. "Reflexiones en torno a las identidades nativas en el noreste colonial." *Relaciones* 92 (2002): 77–106.

Shoemaker, Nancy, ed. *Negotiators of Change: Historical Perspectives on Native American Women*. New York: Routledge, 1995.

Shorter, David Delgado. *We Will Dance Our Truth: Yaqui History in Yoeme Performances*. Lincoln: University of Nebraska Press, 2009.

Shuck-Hall, Sheri Marie. *Journey to the West: The Alabama and Coushatta Indians*. Civilization of the American Indian 256. Norman: University of Oklahoma Press, 2008.

Sica, Gabriela B. "Maíz y trigo: molinos y conanas; mulas y llamas. Tierras, cambio agrario y participación mercantil indígena en los inicios del sistema colonial (siglo XVII)." In *Jujuy. Arqueología, historia, economía y sociedad*, edited by Daniel J. Santamaría, 106–23. Jujuy: Cuadernos del Duende, 2005.

Siegel, Peter E., ed. *Ancient Borinquen: Archaeology and Ethnohistory of Native Puerto Rico*. Tuscaloosa: University of Alabama Press, 2005.

Skinner, Claiborne. *The Upper Country: French Enterprise in the Colonial Great Lakes*. Baltimore, MD: Johns Hopkins University Press, 2008.

Sleeper-Smith, Susan. *Indian Women and French Men: Rethinking Cultural Encounter in the Western Great Lakes*. Amherst: University of Massachusetts Press, 2001.

———. "Women, Kin, and Catholicism: New Perspectives on the Fur Trade." *Ethnohistory* 47, no. 2 (2000): 423–52.

Sluyter, Andrew. "The Ecological Origins and Consequences of Cattle-Ranching in Sixteenth-Century New Spain," *Geographical Review* 86, no. 2 (April 1996): 161–77.

———. "From Archive to Map to Pastoral Landscape: A Spatial Perspective on the Livestock Ecology of Sixteenth-Century New Spain." *Environmental History* 3, no. 4 (October 1998): 508–28.

Smith, Allison Meriwether. "Sherds with Style: A Ceramic Analysis from a Proto-historic Site in Okitbbeha County, Mississippi." Master's thesis, University of Mississippi, 2017.

Smith, F. Todd. *From Dominance to Disappearance: The Indians of Texas and the Near Southwest, 1786–1859*. Lincoln: University of Nebraska Press, 2005.

Smith, Linda Tuhiwai. *Decolonizing Methodologies: Research and Indigenous Peoples*. London: Zed Books, 1999.

Smith, Marvin T. *Coosa: The Rise and Fall of a Mississippian Chiefdom*. Gainesville: University Press of Florida, 2000.

Smith, Marvin T., and David J. Hally. "Chiefly Behavior: Evidence from Sixteenth-Century Spanish Accounts." *Archaeology Papers of the American Anthropological Association* 3, no. 1 (1992): 99–109.

Smith, Victoria. *Captive Arizona, 1851–1901*. Lincoln: University of Nebraska Press, 2009.

Smoak, Gregory E. *Ghost Dances and Identity: Prophetic Religion and American Indian Ethnogenesis in the Nineteenth Century*. Berkeley: University of California Press, 2006.

Snyder, Christina. *Slavery in Indian Country: The Changing Face of Captivity in Early America*. Cambridge, MA.: Harvard University Press, 2010.

Soler Lizarazo, Luisa C., and Enrique N. Cruz. "Un proyecto innovador en una hacienda de añil del Tucumán (fines del siglo XVIII)." *Boletín Americanista* 72, no. 1 (2016): 155–77.

Solís, Eduardo Tello. *La vida en Yucatán durante el gobierno del Conde de Peñalva. Verdades y trebejos*. Mérida: Ediciones de la Universidad Autónoma de Yucatán, 1998.

Solís Robleda, Gabriela, and Paola Peniche, eds. *Documentos para la historia indígena de Yucatán*. Vol. 1: *Idolatría y sublevación*. Mérida: Universidad Autónoma de Yucatán, 1996.

Sousa, Lisa. *The Woman Who Turned into a Jaguar and Other Narratives of Native Women in the Archives of Colonial Mexico*. Stanford, CA: Stanford University Press, 2017.

Spalding, Karen. *Huarochirí: Indian Society under Inca and Spanish Rule*. Stanford, CA: Stanford University Press, 1984.

Spicer, Edward H. *Cycles of Conquest: The Impact of Spain, Mexico, and the United States on the Indians of the Southwest, 1533–1960*. Tucson: University of Arizona Press, 1962.

———. *The Yaquis: A Cultural History*. Tucson: University of Arizona Press, 1980.

Spielmann, Katherine A., ed. *Farmers, Hunters, and Colonists: Interaction between the Southwest and the Southern Plains*. Tucson: University of Arizona Press, 1991.

Stavig, Ward. *The World of Túpac Amaru: Conflict, Community, and Identity in Colonial Peru*. Lincoln: University of Nebraska Press, 1999.

Steponaitis, Vincas P. "Contrasting Patterns of Mississippian Development." In *Chiefdoms: Power, Economy, and Ideology*, edited by Timothy K. Earle, 193–228. Cambridge: Cambridge University Press, 1991.

———. "Location Theory and Complex Chiefdoms: A Mississippian Example." In *Mississippian Settlement Patterns*, edited by Bruce Smith, 417–53. New York: Academic Press, 1978.

Stern, Steve J. "The Age of Andean Insurrection, 1742–1782: A Reappraisal." In *Resistance, Rebellion, and Consciousness in the Andean Peasant World, 18th to 20th Centuries*, edited by Steve J. Stern, 34–93. Madison: University of Wisconsin Press, 1987.

———. *Peru's Indian Peoples and the Challenge of the Spanish Conquest: Huamanga to 1640*. 2nd ed. Madison: University of Wisconsin Press, 1982.

———. "The Rise and Fall of Indian-White Alliances: A Regional View of 'Conquest' History." *Hispanic American Historical Review* 61, no. 3 (August 1981): 461–91.

———. *The Secret History of Gender: Women, Men, and Power in Late Colonial Mexico*. Chapel Hill: University of North Carolina Press, 1995.

Stoler, Ann Laura. *Along the Archival Grain: Epistemic Anxieties and Colonial Common Sense*. Princeton, NJ: Princeton University Press, 2009.

———. *Carnal Knowledge and Imperial Power: Race and the Intimate in Colonial Rule*. Berkeley: University of California Press, 2002.

———. "Tense and Tender Ties: The Politics of Comparison in North American History and (Post) Colonial Studies." *Journal of American History* 88, no. 3 (December 2001): 829–65.

Stratton, Billy J. *Buried in Shades of Night: Contested Voices, Indian Captivity, and the Legacy of King Philip's War*. Tucson: University of Arizona Press, 2013.

Sušnik, Branislava. *Chiriguanos*. Vol. 1. Asunción: Museo Etnográfico Andrés Barbero, 1968.

———. "Dimensiones migratorias y pautas culturales de los pueblos del Gran Chaco y de su periferia (enfoque etnológico)." *Suplemento Antropológico* 7 (1972): 85–106.

———. *Dispersión Tupí-Guaraní prehistórica*. Asunción: Museo Etnográfico Andrés Barbero, 1975.

———. *Etnohistoria de los guaraníes: época colonial*. Los aborígenes del Paraguay 2. Asunción: Museo Etnográfico Andrés Barbero, 1979.

———. *El indio colonial del Paraguay*. 2 vols. Asunción: Museo Etnográfico Andrés Barbero, 1965–66.

———. *Una visión socio-antropológica del Paraguay del siglo XIX*. Asunción: Museo Etnográfico Andrés Barbero, 1992.

———. *Una visión socio-antropológica del Paraguay del siglo XVIII*. Asunción: Museo Etnográfico Andrés Barbero, 1990.

Sušnik, Branislava, and Miguel Chase-Sardi. *Los indios del Paraguay*. Madrid: Mapfre, 1992.

Svriz Wucherer, Pedro Miguel Omar. *Resistencia y negociación: milicias guaraníes, jesuitas y cambios socioeconómicos en la frontera del imperio global hispánico (ss. XVII–XVIII)*. Rosario: Prohistoria Ediciones, 2019.

———. *Un levantamiento indígena en las fronteras imperiales. La rebelión de Arecayá (1660)*. Saarbrücken: Editorial Académica Española, 2017.

Sweeney, Edwin R. *From Cochise to Geronimo: The Chiricahua Apaches, 1874–1886*. Norman: University of Oklahoma Press, 2010.

——. *Mangas Coloradas: Chief of the Chiricahua Apaches.* Norman: University of Oklahoma Press, 1998.

Taiaiake, Alfred. *Peace, Power, and Righteousness: An Indigenous Manifesto.* Oxford: Oxford University Press, 2009.

Takeda, Kazuhiza. "Cambio y continuidad del liderazgo indígena en el cacicazgo y en la milicia de las misiones jesuíticas: análisis cualitativos de las listas de indios guaraníes." *Tellus* 12 (2012): 59–79.

——. "Los padrones de indios guaraníes de las misiones jesuíticas (1656–1801): análisis dinámico y comparativo desde la óptica de los cacicazgos." *Surandino Monográfico* 5 (2016): 65–107.

Talavera Ibarra, Oziel Ulises. *Historia del pueblo de indios de San Francisco Uruapan.* Morelia, MI: Morevallado Editores, 2008.

Tamarón y Romeral, Pedro de. "Descripción del vastísimo obispado de la Nueva Vizcaya." In *Viajes pastorales y descripción de la diócesis de la Nueva Vizcaya*, edited by Mario Hernández Sánchez-Barba, 947–1062. Biblioteca Indiana 2. Madrid: Aguilar, 1958.

Taylor, Alan. *The Divided Ground: Indians, Settlers, and the Northern Borderland of the American Revolution.* New York: Vintage, 2006.

Taylor, William B. "Cochití Lands and the Disputed Sale to Luis María Cabeza de Baca, 1805." In US Congress. Senate. *Pueblo de Cochiti Lands Bill: Hearing before the Select Committee on Indian Affairs, United States Senate.* 98th Cong. (1984): 31–78

Taylor, William B., and Franklin G. Y. Pease, eds. *Violence, Resistance, and Survival in the Americas: Native Americans and the Legacy of Conquest.* Washington, DC: Smithsonian Institution Press, 1994.

Telesca, Ignacio. *Tras los expulsos: cambios demográficos y territoriales en el Paraguay después de la expulsión de los jesuitas.* Biblioteca de Estudios Paraguayos 76. Asunción: Universidad Católica Nuestra Señora de la Asunción, 2009.

Telesca, Ignacio, and Guillermo Wilde. "Antiguos actores de un nuevo régimen: indígenas y afrodescendientes en el Paraguay de la independencia." *Journal de la Société des Américanistes* 97 (2011): 175–200.

TePaske, John Jay. "Integral to Empire. The Vital Peripheries of Colonial Spanish America." In *Negotiated Empires: Centers and Peripheries in the Americas, 1500–1820*, edited by Christine Daniels and Michael D. Kennedy, 29–42. New York: Routledge, 2002.

Terán, Silvia, and Christian H. Rasmussen. *La milpa de los mayas. La agricultura de los mayas prehispánicos y actuales en el noreste de Yucatán.* Mérida: Danida, 1994.

Terraciano, Kevin. *The Mixtecs of Colonial Oaxaca: Ñudzahui History, Sixteenth through Eighteenth Centuries.* Stanford, CA: Stanford University Press, 2001.

——. "Three Texts in One: Book XII of the Florentine Codex." *Ethnohistory* 57, no. 1 (2010): 51–72.

Teruel, Ana A. "Las tierras bajas. Una historia de fronteras, azúcar y olvidos. In *Jujuy, arqueología, historia, economía y sociedad*, edited by Daniel J. Santamaría, 200–15. Jujuy: Cuadernos del Duende, 2005.

———. "Zenta y San Ignacio de los Tobas. El trabajo en dos misiones del Chaco occidental a fines de la colonia." *Anuario del IEHS* 9 (1994): 247–48.

Teruel, Ana A., and Víctor O. Jerez, eds. *Pasado y presente de un mundo postergado. Estudios de antropología, historia y arqueología del Chaco y pedemonte surandino.* Jujuy: Universidad Nacional de Jujuy, 1998.

Thomas, David Hurst. "Columbian Consequences: The Spanish Borderlands in Cubist Perspective." In *Columbian Consequences.* Vol. 1 *Archaeological and Historical Perspectives on the Spanish Borderlands West,* edited by David Hurst Thomas, 1–14. Washington, DC: Smithsonian Institution Press, 1991.

Thomson, Sinclair. "Sovereignty Disavowed: The Tupac Amaru Revolution in the Atlantic World." *Atlantic Studies* 13, no. 3 (2016): 407–31.

———. *We Alone Will Rule: Native Andean Politics in the Age of Insurgency.* Madison: University of Wisconsin Press, 2002.

Thornton, Russell. *American Indian Holocaust and Survival: A Population History since 1492.* Norman: University of Oklahoma Press, 1987.

Thun, Harald. "La hispanización del guaraní jesuítico en ´lo espiritual´ y en ´lo temporal.´ Primera parte: El debate metalingüístico." In *Kenntnis und Wandel der Sprachen. Beiträge zur Postdamer Ehrenpromotion für Helmut Lüdtke,* edited by Thomas Stehl, 217–40. Tübingen: Gunter Narr Verlag Tübingen, 2008.

Tissera, Ramón. *Chaco Gualamba. Historia de un nombre.* Resistencia: Ediciones Cultural Nordeste, 1972.

Tomichá Charupá, Roberto. *La primera evangelización en las reducciones de Chiquitos, Bolivia (1691–1767).* Cochabamba: Editorial Verbo Divino, 2002.

Tommasini, Gabriel. *El Convento de San Francisco de Jujuy, en la historia y en la cultura cristiana.* Córdoba: Imprenta de la Universidad Nacional, 1934.

———. *La civilización cristiana del Chaco (1554–1810).* Buenos Aires: Librería Santa Catalina, 1937.

———. *Los indios ocloyas y sus doctrineros en el siglo XVII.* Jujuy: Universidad Nacional de Jujuy, 1990.

Torkel Karlin U., L. Catalán, and R. Coirini. *La naturaleza y el hombre en el Chaco Seco.* Salta: Proyecto GTZ, 1994.

Townsend, Camilla. *Annals of Native America: How the Nahuas of Colonial Mexico Kept Their History Alive.* New York: Oxford University Press, 2017.

———. *Fifth Sun: A New History of the Aztecs.* New York: Oxford University Press, 2019.

Townsend, Richard F., and Robert V. Sharp, eds. *Hero, Hawk, and Open Hand: American Indian Art of the Ancient Midwest and South.* New Haven, CT.: Yale University Press in association with the Art Institute of Chicago, 2004.

Twinam, Ann. *Public Lives, Private Secrets: Gender, Honor, Sexuality, and Illegitimacy in Colonial Spanish America.* Stanford, CA: Stanford University Press, 1999.

Twitchell, Ralph Emerson. *The Spanish Archives of New Mexico.* Vol. 1. Cedar Rapids, IA: Torch Press, 1914.

Urbina Carrasco, María Ximena. *La frontera de arriba en Chile colonial. Interacción hispano-indígena en el territorio entre Valdivia y Chiloé e imaginario de sus bordes geográficos, 1600–1800*. Valparaíso: DIBAM; Centro de Estudios Diego Barros Arana, Ediciones Universitarias de Valparaíso, PUCV, 2009.

US Congress. House. *New Mexico—Private Land Claim of the Heirs of Luis Maria C. de Baca*. 36th Cong., 2nd Sess. (1861), House of Representatives Ex. Doc. No. 58, 2–5.

Valdés, Carlos Manuel. *La gente del mezquite. Los indios del noreste en la época colonial*. Mexico City: CIESAS, 1995.

———. *Los bárbaros, el rey, la iglesia. Los nómadas del noreste novohispano frente al estado español*. Saltillo: Universidad Autónoma de Coahuila, 2017.

———, ed. *Sociedades y culturas en el río Nadadores a través del tiempo*. Saltillo: Universidad Autónoma de Coahuila, Municipios de Nadadores, San Buenaventura, Santa Rosa, Museo Biblioteca Harold Pape, and Archivo Histórico Parroquial de Santiago, 2015.

Van de Logt, Mark. *War Party in Blue: Pawnee Scouts in the U.S. Army*. Norman: University of Oklahoma Press, 2010.

Van Deusen, Nancy. *Global Indios: The Indigenous Struggle for Justice in Sixteenth-Century Spain*. Durham, NC: Duke University Press, 2015.

Van Kirk, Sylvia. *Many Tender Ties: Women in Fur-Trade Society, 1670–1870*. Norman: University of Oklahoma Press, 1983.

Van Valen, Gary. "In Search of Juan Antonio Ignacio Baca, a Pueblo Participant in the Shifting Politics of Nineteenth-Century New Mexico." In *Transnational Indians in the North American West*, edited by Clarissa Confer, Andrae Marak, and Laura Tuennerman, 65–88. College Station: Texas A&M University Press, 2015.

———. *Indigenous Agency in the Amazon: The Mojos in Liberal and Rubber-Boom Bolivia, 1842–1932*. Tucson: University of Arizona Press, 2013.

Van Veen, J. W., and H. G. Arce. "Nest and Colony Characteristics of Log-Hived *Melipona beecheii* (Apidae: Meliponae)." *Journal of Apicultural Research* 38, nos. 1–2 (1999): 43–48.

Vassberg, David E. "The *Tierras Baldías*: Community Property and Public Lands in 16th-Century Castile." *Agricultural History* 48, no. 3 (July 1974): 385–86.

Vázquez Cienfuegos, Sigfrido, and Antonio Santamaria García. "Indios foráneos en Cuba a principios del siglo XIX: historia de un suceso en el contexto de la movilidad poblacional y la geoestrategia del imperio español." *Colonial Latin American Historical Review*, 2nd ser., 1, no. 1 (Winter 2013): 1–34.

Velasco Ávila, Cuauhtémoc. *La frontera étnica en el noreste mexicano. Los comanches entre 1800–1841*. Mexico City: CIESAS, INAH, 2012.

———. *Pacificar o negociar: los acuerdos de paz con apaches y comanches en las Provincias Internas de Nueva España, 1784–1792*. Mexico City: Instituto Nacional de Antropología e Historia, 2015.

Velasco Murillo, Dana. *Urban Indians in a Silver City: Zacatecas, Mexico, 1546–1810*. Stanford, CA: Stanford University Press, 2016.

Velasco Murillo, Dana, Mark Lentz, and Margarita R. Ochoa, eds. *City Indians in Spain's American Empire: Urban Indigenous Society in Colonial Mesoamerica and Andean South America, 1530–1810*. Brighton, UK: Sussex Academic Press, 2012.

Velázquez, María del Carmen. *La frontera norte y la experiencia colonial.* Mexico City: Secretaría de Relaciones Exteriores, 1982.

Venegas Delgado, Hernán, and Carlos Manuel Valdés Dávila. *La ruta del horror. Prisioneros indios del noreste novohispano llevados como esclavos a La Habana, Cuba (finales del siglo XVIII y principios del XIX).* Mexico City: Plaza y Valdés, Universidad Nacional Autónoma de Coahuila, 2013.

Ventura, Beatriz, and A. C. Scambato. "La metalurgia de los valles orientales del norte de Salta, Argentina." *Boletín del Museo Chileno de Arte Precolombino* 18, no. 1 (2013): 85–106.

Vergara, Miguel A. *Don Pedro Ortiz de Zárate. Jujuy, tierra de mártires (siglo XVII).* Rosario: Imprenta del Colegio Salesiano San José, 1966.

Viau, Roland. *Enfants du néant et mangeurs d'âmes. Guerre, culture et société en Iroquoise ancienne.* 2nd ed. Montreal: Boréal, 2000.

Viedma, Francisco de. "Descripción geográfica y estadística de la provincia de Santa Cruz de la Sierra." In *Colección de obras y documentos relativos a la historia antigua y moderna de las provincias del Río de la Plata.* Vol. 3. Buenos Aires, Imprenta del Estado, 1836. https://www.cervantesvirtual.com/obra/descripcion-geografica -y-estadistica-de-la-provincia-de-santa-cruz-de-la-sierra--0.

Villagutierre Sotomayor, don Juan de. *History of the Conquest of the Province of the Itza: Subjugation and Events of the Lacandon and Other Nations of Uncivilized Indians in the Lands from the Kingdom of Guatemala to the Provinces of Yucatan in North America.* Edited by Frank E. Comparato. Translated by Br. Robert D. Wood. Culver City, CA: Labyrinthos, 1983.

Villalobos R., Sergio. *Los pehuenches en la vida fronteriza: investigaviones.* Santiago de Chile: Ediciones Universidad Católica de Chile, 1988.

———. *Relaciones fronterizas en la Araucanía.* Santiago de Chile: Ediciones Universidad Católica de Chile, 1982.

———. *Vida fronteriza en la Araucanía. El mito de la Guerra de Arauco.* Barcelona: Editorial Andrés Bello, 1995.

Villella, Peter B. *Indigenous Elites and Creole Identity in Colonial Mexico, 1500–1800.* Cambridge Latin American Studies Series 101. Cambridge: Cambridge University Press, 2016.

Viñuales, Graciela María. "El territorio y la ilustración. La fortificación de la frontera chaco-tucumana." In *Estudios sobre el territorio iberoamericano,* 207–31. Seville: Junta de Andalucía, 1996.

Vitar, Beatriz. *Guerra y misiones en la frontera chaqueña del Tucumán (1700–1767).* Madrid: Consejo Superior de Investigaciones Científicas, 1997.

Vitar, María B. *Tucumán y el Chaco en el siglo XVIII: milicia, jesuitas y fronteras.* PhD diss., Universidad Complutense de Madrid, 1988.

Wade, Maria F. *Missions, Missionaries, and Native Americans: Long-Term Processes and Daily Practices.* Gainesville: University Press of Florida, 2008.

———. *The Native Americans of the Texas Edwards Plateau, 1582–1799.* Austin: University of Texas Press, 2003.

Wagner, John. "Trump Highlights Days-Old Violent Clash between Caravan and Mexican Authorities." *Washington Post*, October 31, 2018. https://www .washingtonpost.com/politics/trump-highlights-days-old-violent-clash-between -caravan-and-mexican-authorities/2018/10/31/f3e56f74-dcf3-11e8-85df-7a6b4d 25cfbb_story.html.

Walker, Charles F. *The Tupac Amaru Rebellion.* Cambridge, MA: Harvard University Press, 2016.

Wallace, Anthony F. C. *The Death and Rebirth of the Seneca.* New York: Vintage Books, 1972.

Wallace, Geoffrey H. "The History and Geography of Beeswax Extraction in the Northern Maya Lowlands, 1520–1700." PhD diss., McGill University, 2020.

Wallace, Henry D. "The Strange Case of the Panucho Plugs: Evidence of Pre-Columbian Apiculture on Cozumel." Unpublished manuscript, 1978.

Warren, Louis S. *God's Red Son: The Ghost Dance Religion and the Making of Modern America.* New York: Basic Books, 2017.

Warren, Stephen. *The Worlds Shawnees Made: Migration and Violence in Early America.* Chapel Hill: University of North Carolina Press, 2014.

Waselkov, Gregory A., Linda Derry, and Ned J. Jenkins. "The Archaeology of Mabila's Cultural Landscape." In Knight, *Search for Mabila,* 227–44.

Weaver, John C. *The Great Land Rush and the Making of the Modern World, 1650–1900.* Montreal: McGill-Queen's University Press, 2003.

Weber, David J. *Bárbaros: Spaniards and Their Savages in the Age of Enlightenment.* New Haven, CT: Yale University Press, 2005.

———. "John Francis Bannon and the Historiography of the Spanish Borderlands: Retrospect and Prospect." *Journal of the Southwest* 29, no. 4 (1987): 331–63.

———. *The Mexican Frontier, 1821–1848: The American Southwest under Mexico.* Albuquerque: University of New Mexico Press, 1982.

———. "The Spanish Borderlands, Historiography Redux." *History Teacher* 39, no. 1 (November 2005): 43–56.

———. "The Spanish Borderlands of North America: A Historiography." *Magazine of History* 14, no. 4 (Summer 2000): 5–11.

———. *The Spanish Frontier in North America.* New Haven, CT: Yale University Press, 1992.

Webster, Laurie D., Maxine E. McBrinn, and Eduardo Gamboa Carrera, eds. *Archaeology without Borders: Contact, Commerce, and Change in the U.S. Southwest and Northwestern Mexico.* Boulder: University Press of Colorado; Chihuahua: CONACULTA, INAH, 2008.

Weisiger, Marsha L. *Dreaming of Sheep in Navajo Country.* Seattle: University of Washington Press, 2009.

Wesson, Cameron B. "Chiefly Power and Food Storage in Southeastern North America." *World Archaeology* 31, no. 1 (1999): 145–64.

West, Elliot. *Contested Plains: Indians, Goldseekers, and the Rush to Colorado.* Lawrence: University Press of Kansas, 1998.

———. *The Last Indian War: The Nez Perce Story.* Oxford: Oxford University Press, 2010.

West, Robert C. *The Mining Community in Northern New Spain: The Parral Mining District.* Berkeley: University of California Press, 1949.

———. *Sonora: Its Geographical Personality.* Austin: University of Texas Press, 1993.

Whigham, Thomas. "Paraguay's *Pueblos de Indios*: Echoes of a Missionary Past." In *The New Latin American Mission History*, edited by Erick Langer and Robert Jackson, 157–88. Lincoln: University of Nebraska Press, 1995.

White, Richard. *The Middle Ground: Indians, Empires, and Republics in the Great Lakes Region, 1650–1815.* Cambridge: Cambridge University Press, 1991.

———. "The Winning of the West: The Expansion of the Western Sioux in the Eighteenth and Nineteenth Centuries." *Journal of American History* 65 (1978): 319–43.

Whitehead, Neil L. *Lords of the Tiger Spirit: A History of the Caribs in Colonial Venezuela and Guyana, 1498–1820.* Dordrecht and Providence: Foris, 1988.

Whitmore, Thomas M. "Population Geography of Calamity: The Sixteenth- and Seventeenth-Century Yucatán." *International Journal of Population Geography* 2 (1996): 291–311.

Wilde, Guillermo. "Cacicazgo, territorialidad y memoria en las reducciones jesuíticas del Paraguay." In *Reducciones. La concentración forzada de las poblaciones indígenas en el Virreinato del Perú*, edited by Akira Saito and Claudia Rosas Lauro, 555–97. Lima: Fondo Editorial de la Pontificia Universidad Católica del Perú; National Museum of Ethnology, 2017.

———. "De las crónicas jesuíticas a las 'etnografías estatales': realidades y ficciones del orden misional en las fronteras Ibéricas." *Nuevo Mundo Mundos Nuevos* (2011). https://doi.org/10.4000/nuevomundo.62238.

———. "Entre las tipologías políticas y los procesos sociales: elementos para el análisis situacional de los liderazgos indígenas en una frontera colonial." *Años 90* 19, no. 34 (2011): 19–54.

———. "Frontier Missions in South America: Impositions, Adaptations, and Appropriations." In Levin Rojo and Radding, *Oxford Handbook of Borderlands*, 545–60.

———. "Orden y ambigüedad en la formación territorial del Río de la Plata a fines del siglo XVIII." *Horizontes Antropológicos* 19, no. 19 (2003): 105–35.

———. *Religión y poder en las misiones de guaraníes.* Buenos Aires: Editorial SB, 2009.

———., ed. *Saberes de la conversión. Jesuitas, indígenas e imperios coloniales en las fronteras de la cristiandad.* Buenos Aires: Editorial SB, 2011.

Wilde, Guillermo, and Fabián R. Vega. "De la diferencia entre lo temporal y lo eterno. Élites indígenas, cultura textual y memoria en las fronteras de América del Sur." *Varia Historia* 35, no. 68 (2019): 461–506.

Williams, Jerry L., ed. *New Mexico in Maps.* 2nd ed. Albuquerque: University of New Mexico Press, 1986.

Witgen, Michael. *An Infinity of Nations: How the Native New World Shaped Early North America.* Philadelphia: University of Pennsylvania Press, 2012.

Wood, Stephanie. "The *Fundo Legal* or Lands *Por Razón de Pueblo*: New Evidence from Central New Spain." In *The Indian Community of Colonial Mexico: Fifteen*

Essays on Land Tenure, Corporate Organizations, Ideology, and Village Politics, edited by Arij Ouweneel and Simon Miller, 117–29. Amsterdam: CEDLA, 1990.

Worcester, Donald E. "The Significance of the Spanish Borderlands to the United States." *Western Historical Quarterly* 7, no. 1 (January 1976): 5–18.

Yannakakis, Yanna. *The Art of Being In-between: Native Intermediaries, Indian Identity, and Local Rule in Colonial Oaxaca*. Durham, NC: Duke University Press, 2008.

Yannakakis, Yanna, and Martina Schrader-Kniffki. "Between the 'Old Law' and the New: Christian Translation, Indian Jurisdiction, and Criminal Justice in Colonial Oaxaca." *Hispanic American Historical Review* 96, no. 3 (2016): 517–48.

Yarbrough, Fay. *Race and the Cherokee Nation: Sovereignty in the Nineteenth Century*. Philadelphia: University of Pennsylvania Press, 2007.

Yaremko, Jason M. Colonial Wars and Indigenous Geopolitics: Aboriginal Agency, the Cuba-Florida-Mexico Nexus, and the Other Diaspora. *Canadian Journal of Latin American and Caribbean Studies/Revue canadienne des études latino-américaines et caraïbes* 35, no. 70 (2010): 165–96.

———. "Indigenous Diaspora, Bondage, and Freedom in Colonial Cuba." In Levin Rojo and Radding, *Oxford Handbook of Borderlands*, 817–39.

———. *Indigenous Passages to Cuba, 1515–1900*. Gainesville: University Press of Florida, 2016.

Yetman, David A. *Conflict in Colonial Sonora: Indians, Priests, and Settlers*. Albuquerque: University of New Mexico Press, 2012.

———. *The Ópatas: In Search of a Sonoran People*. Tucson: University of Arizona Press, 2010.

Yetman, David A., and Thomas R. Van Devender. *Mayo Ethnobotany: Land, History, and Traditional Knowledge in Northwest Mexico*. Berkeley: University of California Press, 2002.

Yurrita, Carmen L., Miguel A. Ortega-Huerta, and Ricardo Ayala. "Distributional Analysis of Melipona Stingless Bees (Apidae: Meliponini) in Central America and Mexico: Setting Baseline Information for Their Conservation." *Apidologie* 48, no. 2 (March 2017): 247–58.

Zappia, Natale. *Traders and Raiders: The Indigenous World of the Colorado River Basin, 1540–1859*. Chapel Hill: University of North Carolina Press, 2014.

Zarley, Jesse. "Between the Lof and the Liberators: Mapuche Authority in Chile's Guerra a Muerte (1819–1825)." *Ethnohisotry* 66, no. 1 (January 2019): 118–39.

Zavala Cepeda, José Manuel. *Los mapuches del siglo XVIII. Dinámica interétnica y estrategias de resistencia*. Santiago de Chile: Editorial Universidad Bolivariana, 2008.

Zavala, Silvio. *Los esclavos indios en la Nueva España*. Mexico City: Colegio Nacional Luis González Obregón, 1967.

Zavala Cepeda, José Manuel, and Tom Dillehay. "El 'Estado de Arauco' frente a la conquista española: estructuración sociopolitica y ritual de los araucanos-mapuches en los valles nahuelbutanos durante los siglos XVI y XVII." *Chungara, Revista de Antropología Chilena* 42, no. 2 (2010): 433–50.

Źrałka, Jarosław, Christophe Helmke, Laura Sotelo, and Wiesław Koszkul. "The Discovery of a Beehive and the Identification of Apiaries among the Ancient Maya." *Latin American Antiquity* 29, no. 3 (2018): 514–31. https://doi.org/10.1017 /laq.2018.21.
Zuloaga Rada, Marina. *La conquista negociada. Guarangas, autoridades locales e imperio en Huaylas, Perú, 1532–1610.* Lima: IFEA; IEP, 2012.

Contributors

Paul Conrad is Associate Professor of History and English at the University of Texas at Arlington, where he teaches courses on Native American history and literature. His research focuses on indigenous peoples' confrontations with colonialism in North America across the longue durée, with particular interest in questions of captivity, forced migration, and enslavement. He is also interested in collaborative, community-based interdisciplinary work. His research has been supported by grants and fellowships from organizations such as the McNeil Center for Early American Studies, the Phillips Fund for Native American Research, and the Clements Center for Southwest Studies. His book *The Apache Diaspora: Four Centuries of Displacement and Survival* was published by the University of Pennsylvania Press in 2021.

Chantal Cramaussel holds a BA in social anthropology from the Escuela Nacional de Antropología e Historia in Mexico City and a PhD in history from the École des Hautes Études en Sciences Sociales in Paris. Ranked at the highest level within the Mexican Sistema Nacional de Investigadores, she is currently a professor and researcher (*profesora investigadora*) at the Centro de Estudios Históricos of the Colegio de Michoacán, where she coordinates the Seminario Permanente sobre el Norte de México y Sur de Estados Unidos. She is also a founding member of the Mexican Red de Historia Demográfica. She specializes in the history and the anthropology of northern Mexico. She has authored and edited ten books, including *Poblar la frontera: La provincia de Santa Bárbara durante los siglos XVI y XVII* (Zamora: El Colegio de Michoacán, 2006), and more than one hundred scholarly articles and book chapters. In the past few years her scholarship has focused on the history and anthropology of the indigenous peoples of the Sierra Tepehuana and the Bolsón de Mapimí, the presidios of the Camino Real de Tierra Adentro, and the demographic history of Nueva Vizcaya.

Antonio Cruz Zárate holds a BA in history from the Universidad Autónoma Metropolitana, Unidad Iztapalapa, at Mexico City. He is currently obtaining an MA in humanities at the same institution while serving as a research assistant at the Dirección de Etnohistoria of the Instituto Nacional de Antropología e Historia. He coauthored the essay "'El escándalo de la república' de la misión de Vizarrón, 1757–1788," published in *Fronteras étnicas en la América Colonial* (Secretaría de Cultura–INAH, 2018), and is the author of "El presidio de San Antonio de Béxar a través de una causa criminal en 1730" (in *Sin Dios ni ley: transgresiones en los territorios españoles americanos, siglos XVI-XVIII*, Secretaría de Cultura–INAH) and "La vida escandalosa de don Pedro de Güemes en la villa de Altamira, Nuevo Santander (1792–1793)," in *Historias*, both of which are in press.

Enrique Normando Cruz holds a PhD from the Universidad de Sevilla. A researcher affiliated with Argentina's Research Council (CONICET), he is currently a professor at the Universidad Nacional de Jujuy in the same country. He was a posdoctoral fellow at University of Bonn in Germany and Universidade Federal de Goiás and Universidade Salgado de Oliveira in Brazil. He specializes in colonial South America and the indigenous peoples of Argentina. His recent publications include "El fandango como performance de Antiguo Régimen (Jujuy, siglos XVIII–XIX)" (*Relaciones Estudios de Historia y Sociedad*, 2020, coauthored with G. K. Koeltzsch); "Un líder que no fue héroe: José Quiroga en el contexto de la rebelión de Tupac Amaru en la Argentina" (in *El otro héroe: Estudios sobre la producción social de memoria al margen del discurso oficial en América Latina*, Vandenhoeck & Ruprecht, 2021); and "Horadando la frontera: Soldados de fuertes entre los siglos XVIII y XIX (Jujuy en el Tucumán)" (in *En Vivir en los márgenes: Fronteras en América colonial*, IIH-UNAM, 2021).

Robbie Ethridge is Professor Emeritus of Anthropology at the University of Mississippi. She is the recipient of numerous awards, including an American Philosophical Society Mellon Fellowship, a grant from the National Endowment for the Humanities, the Robert C. Anderson Memorial Award for Outstanding Research and Creative Scholarship from the University of Georgia Research Foundation, and the College of Liberal Arts Award for Research, Scholarship, and Creative Achievement from the University of Mississippi. She is the founding editor of the journal *Native South*, and she served from 2013 to 2020 as North American editor of the journal *Ethnohistory*. Her first monograph, *Creek Country: The Creek Indians and Their World, 1796–1816*, is a social and environmental history of the Creek Indians just prior to Removal.

Author of numerous articles and book chapters and coeditor of four anthologies, she is best known for her work on the early colonial disruptions in the American South from the commercial trade in Indian slaves and the resultant "shatter zone" that transformed the Southern Indians. She has published the anthology *Mapping the Mississippian Shatter Zone: The Colonial Indian Slave Trade and Regional Instability in the American South* and the Mooney Award–winning monograph *From Chicaza to Chickasaw: The European Invasion and the Transformation of the Mississippian World, 1540–1715*. She, with coauthor Robert Miller, has a forthcoming book from the University of Oklahoma Press examining the bombshell US Supreme Court case *McGirt v. Oklahoma*, which confirmed the Muscogee (Creek) reservation. Her current research reconstructs the seven hundred–year history of the Mississippian world and the rise of the precolonial Mississippian chiefdoms, the transformation sparked by European contact, and the restructuring of Native societies that occurred as they became an instrumental part of the colonial South.

Erick D. Langer is Professor of Latin American History in the Edmund A. Walsh School of Foreign Service and in the History Department at Georgetown University, where he has taught since 1999. He received his PhD at Stanford University and taught fourteen years at Carnegie Mellon University. Dr. Langer has published eight books and over fifty scholarly articles. He served as Director of the Center for Latin American Studies at Georgetown from 2009 to 2013. He specializes in the history of the Andes in the nineteenth and early twentieth centuries, with an emphasis on economic history, indigenous peoples, frontiers, and Catholic missions. Among other books, he has authored *Expecting Pears from an Elm Tree: Franciscan Missions on the Chiriguano Frontier in the Heart of South America, 1830–1949* (Duke University Press, 2009) and coedited with Miléna Santoro *Hemispheric Sovereignties: Native Identity and Agency in the Andes, Mesoamerica, and Canada* (University of Nebraska Press, 2018). Dr. Langer is the History Commission Chair for the Pan American Institute of Geography and History, part of the Organization of American States. He has received multiple awards, including four Fulbright Research and Lecturing Awards, two Social Science Research Council Awards, two National Endowment for the Humanities Research Awards, and the Orden de la Universidad Central de Venezuela. He was elected Honorary Member of the Academia Boliviana de Historia in 2016.

Cynthia Radding is the Gussenhoven Distinguished Professor of History and Latin American Studies at the University of North Carolina, Chapel Hill. Her scholarship is rooted in the imperial borderlands of the Spanish and Portuguese American empires and emphasizes the role of indigenous peoples and other colonized groups in shaping those borderlands, transforming their landscapes, and producing colonial societies. She is past President of the Conference on Latin American History (2011–13), affiliated with the American Historical Association; she served as book review editor of *Hispanic American Historical Review* (*HAHR*; 2012–17); on the editorial boards of *American Historical Review, HAHR*, and *The Americas*. Dr. Radding is President of the Board of Directors of the Americas Research Network and is coeditor, with Danna A. Levin Rojo, of *The Oxford Handbook of Borderlands of the Iberian World*. In addition to numerous journal articles, her publications include *Landscapes of Power and Identity: Comparative Histories in the Sonoran Desert and the Forests of Amazonia from Colony to Republic* (Duke University Press, 2005); *Wandering Peoples: Colonialism, Ethnic Spaces, and Ecological Frontiers (Northwestern Mexico, 1700–1850)* (Duke University Press, 1997); *Borderlands in World History*, coedited with Chad Bryant and Paul Readman (Palgrave, 2014); and *Bountiful Deserts: Sustaining Indigenous Worlds in Northern New Spain* (University of Arizona Press, 2022).

Joaquín Rivaya-Martínez is Associate Professor of History at Texas State University. He earned a PhD in anthropology at the University of California, Los Angeles, in 2006 and was a postdoctoral fellow at the Clements Center for Southwest Studies at Southern Methodist University in 2007–8. His scholarly interests include ethnohistory, Plains Indians, captivity, and Spanish-indigenous relations. His research has been funded by the Wenner-Gren Foundation, the American Philosophical Society, the Newberry Library, the Philips Fund for Native American Research, the University of California Institute for Mexico and the United States (UC MEXUS), UCLA's Institute of American Cultures, and Mexico's CONACyT, among other institutions. He specializes in the eighteenth- and nineteenth-century history of the indigenous peoples of the US-Mexico borderlands and the southern Great Plains. He has authored numerous scholarly essays, including "A Different Look at Native American Depopulation: Comanche Raiding, Captive Taking, and Population Decline" (in the journal *Ethnohistory*, 2014); and "*Progresarán infinitamente en civilización:* El efímero asentamiento comanche de San Carlos de los Jupes, 1787–1788," in *Fronteras étnicas en la América colonial*, edited by Patricia Gallardo Arias and Cuauhtémoc Velasco Ávila (INAH, 2018). He is currently working on several book projects on the history of the Comanches and the US-Mexico Borderlands.

Gary Van Valen is Professor of History at the University of West Georgia. He holds a BA in history from Montclair State University in in New Jersey, an MA in Latin American history from the University of South Carolina, and a PhD in Latin American history from the University of New Mexico. After teaching classes for the University of New Mexico, he served as a visiting assistant professor at Roanoke College before joining the faculty at the University of West Georgia. He teaches courses on Latin American, indigenous, Atlantic, and world history. His primary interests are in Latin American indigenous history and the frontiers of Latin America, with particular emphasis on Bolivia and New Mexico. In both places, his research has centered on the ethnohistory and cultural contact of frontiers. He is the author of *Indigenous Agency in the Amazon: The Mojos in Liberal and Rubber-Boom Bolivia*, which won the American Society for Ethnohistory's Erminie Wheeler-Voegelin Award. He has contributed to the edited volume *Transnational Indians in the North American West* and to the *Anuario de Estudios Bolivianos, Archivísticos y Bibliográficos;* the *Diccionario histórico de Bolivia;* the *World History Bulletin;* the *SECOLAS Annals;* *The Middle Ground Journal: World History and Global Studies;* and *Voices: The Journal of New York Folklore.*

Cuauhtémoc Velasco Ávila has been a full-time researcher for the Mexican Instituto Nacional de Antropología e Historia (INAH) since 1975, and a member of the Sistema Nacional de Investigadores since 2012. He is currently the director of the the INAH's ethnohistory branch. He served as subdirector for modern history at the INAH's Dirección de Estudios Históricos from 1989 to 1996. He specializes in the history of the indigenous peoples of northeastern Mexico and New Spain. He is the author of numerous scholarly works on that subject, including the books *En manos de los bárbaros* (Breve Fondo Editoria1, 1996), *La frontera étnica en el noreste mexicano: Los comanches entre 1800 y 1841* (CIESAS-INAH, 2013), and *Pacificar o negociar: Los acuerdos de paz con apaches y comanches en las Provincias Internas de Nueva España, 1784–1792* (INAH, 2014).

Geoffrey H. Wallace is a professional cartographer and historic geographic information systems (H-GIS) specialist in Durham, England. Dr. Wallace's

PhD thesis, "The History and Geography of Beeswax Extraction in the Northern Maya Lowlands, 1540–1700" (McGill University) won the American Society for Environmental History's 2020 Rachel Carson Prize for best dissertation in the field. His maps, produced under the trade name G. Wallace Cartography & GIS, have appeared in more than a hundred journal articles, websites, cultural institutions, and books. His thirty-four maps will provide historical and geographical context for the New York Metropolitan Museum of Art's renovated Americas, Oceania, and Africa galleries when they open in 2024.

Guillermo Wilde holds a PhD in anthropology from the Universidad de Buenos Aires. A researcher affiliated with Argentina's CONICET, he is currently Professor of Anthropology at the Universidad Nacional de San Martín. He has received grants and fellowships from the Alexander von Humboldt Foundation at the Universities of Colonia and Hamburg, the Wenner Gren Foundation for Anthropological Research, the Fulbright Commission, the British Council, Brown University, and the Betty Meggers Program of the Americas Research Network, among other institutions. He has been an invited professor at Université Paris III and the École des Hautes Études en Sciences Sociales in Paris, Japan's National Museum of Ethnology, and the Museu Nacional of Brazil in Rio de Janeiro. He is the author of numerous scholarly works on indigenous peoples and ethnogenesis processes in Latin America, Iberian-American frontiers, religious conversion, and colonial art and music, including *Religión y Poder en las Misiones Guaraníes* (Sb Editorial, 2009), which won the 2010 Premio Iberoamericano Book Award from the Latin American Studies Association; and the anthology *Saberes de la conversión: Jesuitas, indígenas e imperios coloniales en las fronteras de la Cristiandad* (Sb Editorial, 2011).

Index

References to maps or other illustrations appear in italic type.

Africans: Afro-Yucatecans, 64–65; Black Seminoles, 21; enslaved, 173, 175, 177, 179, 196, 214; runaway African slaves (maroons), 7, 21, 33n57, 170, 174, 176–79

agriculture: agricultural labor, 9, 50, 192; and Çinaloas, 38, 44–45; crops grown, 38, 43, 47, 48, 50, 63, 84–85, 88, 102, 214, 228, 233, 244, 247, 256; granary surplus, 88–89; and indigenous communities, 38, 39, 84; and indigenous peoples, 19, 22, 43–44, 46, 47, 48, 59, 88–89, 102, 112, 143, 151, 161, 192, 196, 222, 235, 244, 251, 262; irrigation, 48, 222, 262; land devoted to, 38, 41, 47–48, 49, 50, 162, 193, 199, 200, 235, 236, 250, 262; in New Mexico, 222; and peoples of Yaqui, Mayo, and Fuerte basins, 35, 38; and possession of land, 233, 242; and *rancherías* (bands), 133n5

Aldana, Rodrigo Flores de, 68, 75n19

Altamira, Viceroy Marqués de, 149

Álvarez, Salvador, 144

Americas: aboriginal peoples of, 15, 23, 24; and American republics, 8; borderlands in, 1, 3, 4, 5, 8, 15–16, 18, 73, 81, 158–59, 274; and caciques, 107n53; Caribbean, 21, 107n53; and Caste War of Yucatan, 16; and Central America, 20, 158; and communal lands (*tierras sobrantes*), 225; conquests, 3, 81; frontiers in, 2, 9, 57; fur and brazilwood trade in, 57; and Great Lakes area, 16; history of, 3, 4, 6–9, 8, 9, 11n12, 20, 24; indigenous groups in, 1, 8, 9, 9n1, 18–19, 20, 24, 28; and Kingdom of Guatemala, 63; languages of, 19, 23, 24, 25–26; Latin America, 9, 73, 237n1, 242, 272; Mesoamerica, 23, 26; New Mexico, 8–9, 16, 18, 221–37; North America, 2, 5, 18, 252; Panama, 75n22; South America, 5, 8, 185; Spanish America, 9n1, 57, 224–225; and *tierras baldías* (empty territories), 242, *246*; Western Hemisphere, 9n1. *See also* North America; South America; United States

Anderson, Gary, 110

Anza, Juan Bautista de, 112

Anzaldúa, Gloria, 27, 158, 179

Apachería, 5, 111, 124, 130, 131, 169

archaeology, 22–23, 27, 34n64, 36, 38–39, 51. *See also* United States

Argentina: Asunción de Paraguay, Corrientes, 210, 212; Bermejo River, 210; Calchaquí Valleys of, 21; colonization of, 238n1; haciendas and cattle estates in, 212, 213, 214, 215; indigenous peoples, 24, 214, 267; Jujuy region of, 8, 207, 208–10, *211*, 212, 213; Mapuches, 17, 273; *mercedes de tierra* (land grants), 210; nation-state of, 186; native peoples of, 272; Potosí mines, 212; Río Blanco, 210; San Francisco River, 210; Santiago de Guadalcázar, 210; Tucumán district in, 8, 16, 207, 208, 215

Ayucú, Miguel, 200

Balthasar, Juan Antonio, 47
Barr, Juliana, 252
Barrio, Pedro, 131
Basso, Keith, 26
Bautista Pino, Pedro, 228
beeswax industry: areas of production,
    59–62, *61*, 63, 64; barter, 56, 63–64;
    Bishop Escalante's report on,
    61–62; in Calkiní, 65; Chancenote,
    67; contraband trade, 54, 56,
    64–67; decline of, 74n9; enclave
    of Ixpimienta, 64; forest bees, 58,
    72; and Franciscan order, 70; and
    frontiers, 75n25; isolation from
    Spanish control, 57, 62; and Juan
    Chan, 67, 70; and La Pimienta, 65,
    66; *limosnas*, 68–69, 70, 72, 75n19,
    78n71; Maya role, 4, 6, 55–66, 67,
    70–73; Peru, 74n10; and *repartimiento*
    system, 58–62, *60*, *61*, 65–73, 74n6,
    74n16, 75n18, 77n57, 78n71; Spaniards,
    64, 65, 66, 67, 70, 71, 72, 73, 74n6;
    Spanish province of Yucatán, 4, 6,
    20, 32n49, 54–73, 74n6, 74n10,
    75n18; stingless bees, 56, 57–58, 59,
    74n6, 75n22; town of Sayab, 69, 70;
    trade routes, 4, 6, 57, 62, 63, 64–65,
    66; Tucolahnexmo, 55; and wax
    extraction, 58–62, 69, 73, 75n21, 75n25,
    77n59; wax smuggling, 70–71, 72;
    Yucatec Maya borderlands, 4, 56–57,
    63. *See also* labor
Berdan, Frances, 23
Berroterán, Don Joseph de, 163, 164, 165,
    167, 169, 171
Bié, Cristóbal, 200
Biedma, Luys Hernández de, 81, 83, 95,
    96, 97, 99
Bolivia: abolishment of communal
    lands, 244; and alcaldes (mayors),
    260; alliances with indigenous
    groups, 252–53, 260, 267–68;
    Amazonia, 11n18; and Andean
    region, 243, 244, *246*, 260, 268n6;

Aquio lands, 249; and Arawak, 262;
    archives in Sucre, Santa Cruz, and
    Tarija, 243; Asamblea del Pueblo
    Guaraní, 268; Azero Province in,
    267; Caipipendi, *254*; Caipipendi
    people, 254, 259–60; and Caiza, 245;
    Cantón Ticucha, 243, 248; capitán
    Bata, 256, 257, 259; and Capitán
    Grande Mariano Chanca, 264, 266;
    capitanes Jaropa and Yacaire, 250;
    Caraparirenda community, 243, 254,
    256–58, *258*, 259, 266; cattle trade,
    244; Chaco region of, 208, 244, 267;
    Chanes, 262, 264, 271n56; chief
    Buricanambi of Ingre, 253–54; and
    Chiriguanos, 9, 242–45, 247–53, 254,
    256–57, 259, 260, 262, 264, 266,
    267–68, 271n56; Chuquisaca and
    Tarija Departments, 247, 248–49,
    254, 267; climate of, 244; conquest
    of Chiriguanía, 253; Cordillera
    Province (Santa Cruz), 251, 260, 267,
    271n63; Cuevo and Ivo territory,
    249; department of Beni, 11n18;
    Franciscans in, 245, 247, 254, 262,
    264, 267; and Fr. Angelico Martarelli,
    247, 254, 259; frontiers, 242, 243, 244,
    245, 247, 249, 251–53, 254, 260,
    266–68; Güirakota I and II, 259;
    Huacaya War, 247, 251, 253; and
    Huacayas, 267; and Ingre, 253–54,
    267; Ingre Valley, 247; Iti and Itimiri
    community, 254, 262, *265*, 266, 267;
    Iti River, 264, 266; and José Ignacio
    Aireyu, 259; and José Padilla, 250;
    and Juan Agustín Terán, 249; karai
    landlords, 268; karai settlers, 249,
    264; karai villages, 245, 247; and
    Kuruyuki, 248, 253, 259, 268n15; land
    grants, 9, 243, 249, 251, 253, 254,
    256–57, 259–60, 262, 264, 266, 267,
    268, 269n30, 270–71n53; land rights,
    243, 244, 248–49, 250, 266, 268n6;
    land tenure, 244, 266; latifundio

Caraparicito, 249, 250, 266, 267; and Manuel P. Durán, 250, 251; mining industry, 207, 244, 247; missions, 242, 245, 247, 248, 250, 253, 262, 264, 266, 267, 271n63; and Octavio Padilla, 249, 250, 251, 252, 253, 259, 267; Parapetí River, 247, 249, 251; people of Ibeyeca, 250; Potosí mining center, 207, 244; President Gregorio Pacheco, 256; and Ramón Sanabria, 254; and Rev. Father Comajuncosa, 264; San Miguel, 254, 263; San Miguel people, 260, 262; and San Ramon de Naguambaruzu, 254, 255, 257; Santa Cruz Department, 248–49, 254; Sapirangui, 248, 249, 256; Sauces in, 249, 256, 264; Tarija (town), 245; Toba Indians, 247; in twentieth century, 1; and Viceroy Francisco de Toledo, 244; and Yuti leaders, 259
borderlands: Apache, 7, 131–32, 162–66; and Bolsón, 143; Calchaquí Valleys, 21; and center-periphery dichotomy, 2, 9n2; and Chaco de Jujuy, 210; colonial, 180n6; cultural, 4, 44; definitions, 2, 10n4, 10n5, 10n8, 158; digital mapping of, 34n68; establishment of boundaries, 8, 27, 46; ethnic lines, 46–47; fluvial, 39; formation of, 11n12; and frontiers, 2, 8, 10n3, 10n8, 27, 40, 52n1, 55, 56, 57, 60, 65, 66, 67, 68, 70, 72, 97, 163, 165, 167, 195, 208; Guaraní, 5, 8, 18, 19, 32n35; indigenous, 1, 2–4, 5, 6, 7, 8, 10n8, 15–16, 18–19, 21, 22, 24, 27, 34n68, 35–36, 50–51, 57, 73, 111, 131–32, 174, 179, 207, 208, 209, 216, 274; and indigenous communities, 27–28, 35–36, 51; and indigenous peoples, 3, 42, 47, 51, 67–68, 104, 174, 178–79; indigenous-Spanish relations, 162–68; Jesuit missionaries, 44–45, 51; maroon, 21, 33n57; Mississippian, 5, 6; North American, 158–59, 177; of Parana and Uruguay Rivers, 188, 189;

plural sovereignty, 160; population centers, 165; Pueblo, 5; pueblo boundaries, 51; and Sahcabchén, 68–73; scholarship on, 11n11, 21–28, 81, 179, 180n2, 181n26; Sierra Gorda, 21; Spaniards and, 67, 76n35, 104–5; Spanish, 10n3; and Spanish borderlands, 179, 185; and states or empires, 2, 8, 10n5, 10n7, 11n11; and stereotypes, 160–61, 178–79; and town of Hopelchén, 64, 65, 66; and US-Mexican region, 27; in Western Hemisphere, 3, 21; and Yoreme borderlands, 40; and Yucatec Maya borderlands, 4, 56–57. *See also* beeswax industry; Cuba; Nueva Vizcaya, Kingdom of
Bracamonte y Sosa, Pedro, 71
Brazil, 8, 186, 194, 212, 218n27, 244
Brooks, James, 223
Brown, Tracy, 223, 226

Cabeza de Vaca, Álvar Núñez, 39
Calloway, Colin, 15
Cámara, Diego de la, 64, 67
Canche, Pedro, 62
Carballo, David, 23
Caribbean islands, 11n16, 149, 163, 172, 173, 174, 272. *See also* colonization; Cuba; Spain
Chan, Juan, 54, 55, 56, 63, 64, 66. *See also* beeswax industry; labor
Chance, John, 23
Chile, 16, 273
Cifuentes, Luis de, 59
Cochise, 18
Colombia, 16, 19, 22–23
colonization: Amerindian adaptations, 28, 51, 82; Anglophone colonies, 238n1; Apache-Spanish relations, 162–66; Cainguás, 199; Captain Ventura, 147; Caribbean, 21; *Carta Anua* report, 192; cattle ranching, 247; of Chaco, 209, 213; Coahuila

colonization (*continued*)
mission, 152; colonial law and
sources, 41, 42; *composición*, 41,
52n19; conquistadors, 144, 187;
encomienda system, 209; and
epidemics, 63, 104, 187; ethnic
denominations, 202; ethnification,
189–90; European, 3–4, 7–9, 15–16, 17,
18, 19, 20–21, 26, 40, 41, 47, 51, 54, 55,
57, 66, 68, 94, 104, 130, 141–43, 144,
146, 159, 160, 161, 199, 201–2, 209,
247, 252; extermination of native
peoples, 146; and Franciscan
missions, 187, 262; and Francisco
Bruno de Zavala, 192, 193; frontier
governance, 130, 215; Guajardo
Fajardo, 148; Haitian Revolution, 160,
174, 183n42; independent regions, 63;
indigenous communities, 42, 47, 104;
indigenous peoples, 7, 11n11, 15, 16–20,
26, 32n34, 47, 104, 130, 143, 146–48,
152–53, 161, 187–88, 216n2, 272; Jesuit
missionaries, 187, 213; Jesuit missions,
40–41, 47, 51, 146; labeling of native
groups, 7, 8, 147, 148, 150–53, 212; labor
extraction, 19, 151–52; landownership,
19, 41, 52n17, 52n19, 160; of Mexico,
237n1; mining industry, 40, 46, 47,
212, 247; mission system, 151, 212, 216;
missionaries, 31n32, 43–46, 213–14,
216n2; in New Spain, 35–36, 41, 47,
150–53; Oaxaca, 20, 25; Portuguese in
South America, 8, 197; presidio of
Ledesma, 214, 215; *pueblos de misión*
(mission villages), 8, 197; race and
gender, 26–27; *realengas*, 41, 52n18;
reducciones (mission settlements),
213–16; rhetoric of barbarians and
invaders, 248–49; royal land grants,
214; of South America, 8, 185, 186–88,
196–97, 207–10, 212–16; Spaniards, 8,
10n3, 20, 25, 40–41, 47, 56–57, 147,
150–53, 161–62, 163, 166, 168, 169, 171,
177, 187, 194, 207, 208, 209, 210, 212,

215, 216, 237n1, 244–45; Spanish
government, 223; Spanish in Tucumán,
207, 209, 210; taxation, 58, 163; in
Texas, 252; Tobosos, 146; violence
of conquest, 213; and war against
Apaches, 167; and wars of fire and
blood, 144, 149; Yucatán, 4, 6, 54–57,
58, 63. *See also* Americas; Cuba;
Mexico; New Spain; Nueva Vizcaya,
Kingdom of
Concha, Fernando de la, 131, 137n84
Conkey, Margaret, 27
Coosa, Chief, 90, 92, 98
Coronado, Francisco Vázquez de, 39
Cortés, Hernán, 17
Cortes of Cádiz, 9, 11n17, 224–225, 228,
232, 237
Costa Rica, 75n22
Couoh, Pedro, 64
Coy, Pablo, 66, 67
Craddock, Jerry, 25
Cramaussel, Chantal, 7, 162
Cuba, 5; alliances of indigenous groups,
21; Apache captives in, 173–74, 175, 177,
179; borderlands, 178–79; crimes and
livestock raids, 174, 175, 176; de Soto's
expeditions, 82; deportations to, 7,
160, 172–75, 177–79, 183n42; Diego José
Navarro, 172; Governor Someruelos,
175, 177, 178; Havana, 160, 172, 173,
174, 175, 176, 177, 178, 179, 184n59;
indigenous peoples, 24, 160, 161,
172–79; interethnic alliances, 204n33;
Josef de Aguilar, 175, 177; Lieutenant
Malvar, 176, 177; Pinar del Río, 175, 177;
racial and ethnic stereotypes, 174, 177,
178; and Veracruz, 179

de Soto, Hernando: army of, 82, 83,
88–89, 90, 92, 97, 98, 99, 101, 102, 103;
battle of Mabila, 101, 102; and Chief
Tascalusa, 82, 92–101, 102, 104; death
of, 83; and elites from Tascalusa, 89,
90, 92; expeditions of, 6, 81, 82–83, 84,

87, 88, 89, 90, 92, 96–101, 103–4, 105–6n12, 105n11; food supplies, 88–89, 101, 102, 103; and Garcilasco de la Vega, 83; and Gentleman of Elvas, 83, 93, 95, 97, 99, 100; gifts, 90, 99; and Juan Ortiz, 89; Mississippian world, 88–89, 96–104; in Nicaragua, 82; in Peru, 82; route through Alabama, 90, *91*; Tampa Bay, Florida, 83, 89; and women, 95, 96
Diaz, Captain Domingo, 112, 115, 131
Don Quijote (Cervantes), 154n18

Ecueracapa, 131
Edwards, Tai, 27
El Chico, 175, 176, 178, 183n50
El Grande, 175, 176, 178, 183n50
Elguezábal, Juan Bautista, 112
El-lite (Quemando), 123, 124, 125, 127
ethnic identity, 23, 27, 28, 160, 186, 189–90. *See also* native peoples
Europeans: alliances with indigenous groups, 17–18, 30n18, 31n29, 82; and Amerindians, 1, 6, 18–21, 26, 81–82; Baltasar de Gallegos, 100; battle of Mabila, 101; Bolivia, 245; colonization, 3–4, 8, 9, 17–21, 82, 144; conquests, 4, 16, 17, 26, 30n18, 81; diplomatic encounters, 132; economic partners, 17, 20, 82; gifts, 110; and indigenous peoples, 7, 15, 17–19, 20, 23, 25–26, 81–82, 110, 144; mapping, 24; Mesoamerican trade, 35; military action, 82; missionaries, 18, 19, 25, 26; as political allies, 17–18; political systems, 3–4, 20; Spaniards, 6, 8, 9, 16, 17, 18, 19, 20, 22, 25, 30n18, 31n29, 39, 110–15, 117–20, 224; territories claimed, 2, 8, 9, 15–16; Tristan de Luna y Arellano expedition, 102

Farriss, Nancy, 25–26
Fenn, Elizabeth, 22
Flórez, Manuel Antonio, 115, 127, 129, 130, 133n21, 134n30

Gálvez, José de, 130
Gavilán, José, 175–76, 177
genetics, 23, 24
geographic information system (GIS) technology, 4, 5, 23–24
Gran Chaco, 5, 198; Andes, 208, 217n4; Argentina, 208–13; Bermejo River, 212; Bolivia and Brazil, 208; borderlands, 21, 208, 216; Calchaquís, 210; Chaco de Jujuy, 207, 208–10, 212–16, 217n4; Charcas, 209; Chiquitano territory, 208; Chiriguanos of, 16, 209, 212; city of Córdoba, 209; city of Corrientes, 218n27; city of Cuiabá, 218n27; city of Jujuy, 209–10, 212; city of Salta, 209; city of Tucumán, 209, 210, 218n27; climate of, 208, 217n4; conquered peoples, 208–9; Cuzco, 217n12; estancias in, 219n44; 220n57; Governor Esteban de Urízar y Arespacochaga, 213; and Governor Francisco de Viedma, 215; and Governor Martínez de Tineo, 213; and Governor Matías de Anglés y Gortari, 213; Guaycuruans, 16; haciendas and farms, 213, 215, 216, 219n48; Inca settlers, 218n15; indigenous borderland of, 209, 216; indigenous people of, 210, 212, 213, 215, 216, 218n15, 218n26; Itaú River, 212; Jesuits in, 218n26; Juan José Ortiz, 215; jurisdiction of San Salvador de Jujuy (Xuxui), 207; Nuestra Señora de los Dolores del Río Negro, 213–14; Paraguay River, 208; Paraná River, 208; Pilcomayo River, 212; Potosí, 210; San Francisco River, 212; San Ignacio reduction, 213, 214–16, 220n57; Santa Cruz de la Sierra, 209; Tawantinsuyu, 208, 209, 217n12; trade routes, 218n27; Tucumán frontier, 208, 209, 213, 216, 216n2
Green, Michael, 105
Griffen, William, 143, 144, 148

Grimarest, Enrique, 49
Guaca, Pedro, 200
Guarapy, Antonio, 200
Guasé, Esteban, 200
Güemes, Juan Vicente de (Viceroy
  Revillagigedo), 130, 131, 136n78,
  137n84
Guzmán, Nuño Beltrán de, 39

*Historia de los triunfos de nuestra santa
  fe* (Pérez de Ribas), 44

Ibarra, Francisco de, 39
Imaz, Padre Patricio, 47, 48, 49, 51, 53n34
Inca Empire, 207, 208, 209, 244

Jones, Grant D., 56–57, 64, 66, 67
Julián, Antón, 55, 64

labor: agricultural, 9, 48, 50, 248, 268;
  community, 194, 196; construction of
  houses, 193; and *criados*, 223; in Cuba,
  178; elite control, 88, 173; *encomienda*
  system, 58, 144, 147, 150–53, 156n54,
  156n56, 185, 186, 187–89; forced labor,
  68, 69, 151, 170, 172, 173, 174, 178, 179,
  215; on haciendas, 214, 215, 216, 242,
  267–68; indigenous people, 40, 46, 47,
  48, 49, 50, 68, 69, 71, 88, 144, 147,
  151–52, 156n54, 160, 161, 170, 172, 173,
  178, 179, 185, 187–88, 196, 212–15, 223,
  243, 247, 250, 251, 252–53, 260, 266–68;
  and Juan Chan, 73n3; Julime and
  Mamite, 145; mining industry, 40,
  46, 47, 48, 49, 151, 243; patterns of
  extraction, 19, 23, 58–59; peoples of
  Yaqui, Mayo, and Fuerte basins, 35,
  36, 40; *repartimiento* system, 40, 58,
  59–61, 68, 150, 151, 152, 153, 187, 188; and
  Salineros of Tizonazo, 146; and Santa
  María de los Tobosos, 144; and slave
  labor, 20–21, 29n1, 45, 172, 209; Spanish
  demands for, 44, 172; of women,
  32n46, 58, 173. *See also* slavery

Lafora, Nicolás de, 147, 152
language/languages: Algonquian, 89;
  Apaches, 111, 159, 161; Arawak, 244;
  Athapaskan-speaking peoples, 161;
  Audam speakers, 154n7; and
  Bartholomé Garcia, 148; of Bolsón,
  143; of Brazil, 273; Caddoan, 89;
  Coahuiltecan speakers, 148, 172;
  Concho, 154n11; Conchos, 143, 144–45;
  conchos, tepehuanes del desierto, and
  coahuiltecas, 143; and culture, 28; Fray
  Juan Lario, 148; Ge, 189; Guarani, 19,
  186, 190, 196, 197, 200, 202, 208, 218n15,
  244, 262, 264; Guaycurú, 218n15; and
  "Indians of Chiriuana, Tucuman y
  Parauay," 208; indigenous, 42, 43, 89,
  143, 194; and indigenous peoples, 39,
  144, 172; Iroquoian, 89; language
  contact with natives, 25–26, 89; Latin,
  26; *lengua chuíta*, 49, 50, 53n41;
  linguistic diversity, 3, 26; linguistic
  methodology, 4, 22, 23, 24–26; Maya,
  19; meaning of Coahuila, 148;
  meaning of *odame*, 148; meaning of
  "Toboso," 154n18; Mesoamerican
  tradition, 22, 26, 33n59; Mississippian
  world, 89; Mixtec, 26; Muskogean,
  89, 94, 105n5; Nahuatl, 17, 23, 26,
  43, 147, 176; Oaxaca, 26; Odami,
  154n7; O'odham speakers, 154n7;
  Otomanguean languages, 25; of
  Petalán, 43; Quechua, 208, 209;
  religious missionaries, 19, 25, 26;
  Roman alphabet, 22; Siouan, 89;
  Spanish, 25, 49, 89, 172, 194, 197, 202,
  223; standard language (*lengua
  general*), 189; Taino, 107n53; Timucuan,
  89; Toboso, 154n11; toponyms, 26,
  41; translations, 24–25, 89, 94;
  Tupí-Guaraní, 189; Wichí, 218n15;
  Yoeme and Yaqui, 53n41; Yucatec
  Maya, 66; Zapotec, 19, 25–26
Lockhart, James, 22–23
Luzero, Alférez Joseph, 166

Mangas Coloradas, 18
May, Francisco, 54
Mboacati, Ignacio, 200
Medrango, Diego, 146
Menchaca, José, 111, 115, 116, 120
Méndez, Pedro, 45, 46
Merrell, James, 15
Mexico: Antonio Ortiz, 232; Audiencia of Mexico's General Indian Court, 229; Bolsón de Mapimí region, 7, 21; *cartas anuas* (annual letters) of Jesuits, 42, 43–44, 52n20; Central, 17, 22–23, 33n62, 75n19, 149; Chichimecas, 16; Chihuahua, 20, 39, 141, 144, 150, 159, 160; Coahuila, 16, 20, 141, 144, 160; Diputación Provincial, 232; Durango, 20, 39, 141; El Vado, 233; Francisco Ignacio de Madariaga, 232; Francisco Ortiz, 232; Fuerte River, 44; Gallinas River, 232; Governor Baptista, 45; Governor Diego Martínez de Hurdaide, 45, 46; Governor Jefe Político Facundo Melgares, 232; independence of, 232; land grants, 224, 232; Maya Train megaproject, 273; Mayo and Cedros drainages, 44; Mayo nation, 45; meaning of "Toboso," 154n18; Mescalero Apaches, 127; Mexico City, 130, 165, 171, 172, 179, 181n26, 184n60, 229, 235; mission of Ocoroni, 44; New Mexico, 221–37; northern, 10n3, 16, 20, 110; Ostimuri in, 44, 46, 48; Pecos Pueblo, 232; pre-Hispanic frontier of, 52n1; private landholding, 225; Pueblo of Abiquiu, 232; Salinas del Rey, 144; San Miguel del Bado, 232; Sile rancho, 232; Sinaloa province, 43, 44, 45, 46, 48; Spanish expansion, 17, 45–47; Spanish *vecinos*, 224; Tovoropa, 44; Veracruz, 160; Vicente Villanueva, 232; Viceroy Álvaro Manrique de Zúñiga, 45; Villa de Sinaloa, 43, 44, 45; and Yucatecan wax, 57, 75n19

Mirones, Francisco de, 66
Mis, Francisco, 54

Nandabú, Lorenzo, 200
native peoples: Abipones, 212; Acoclames, 144, 145, 146–49, 151, 152, 153; agency of, 8, 17, 26, 82, 167, 179, 182n29, 199, 216, 221, 237, 272; Alabamas, 104; and Alegre, 123, 124, 125, 128, 129; alliances through matrimony, 132, 135n54, 161; alliances with indigenous groups, 92, 98, 111, 112, 129, 145, 148, 161, 187, 269n28; Amazonia, 16, 23, 24; Amerindians, 1, 3, 4, 9n1, 15–20, 27, 28, 119, 177; in Andean regions, 17, 18, 21, 22–23; and Antonio Jaulesgua, 226; Apaches, 6–7, 11n16, 16, 18, 20, 29n7, 30n26, 31n30, 110–32, 134n26, 134n30, 135n45, 135n54, 147, 151–53, 157n71, 159–75, 177–78, 180n5, 180n11, 182n28, 182n29, 182n35, 182n36, 182n38, 184n60, 222, 223; as *apóstatas* (apostates), 147, 164; Arapahos, 18; assimilation, 8, 151, 153, 154n7, 185–86, 194; Auchanes, 151; autonomy of groups, 2–3, 8, 9, 15, 17, 21, 57, 71, 73, 94, 98, 131, 164, 192, 193, 199, 243, 251, 252, 267, 268; Azamatas, 209; battle of Mabila, 100–102; Blackfoot, 17, 30n20; Bolsón de Mapimí region, 7, 8, 141–53, 164; Borrados, 151; Cabezas, 145, 146, 147, 148, 156n44; Cacalotes, 150, 156n57; Cachu-ende, 118, 134n30; cacique Malaquí, 147, 148; caciques, 23, 44, 76n34, 94, 107n53, 147, 148, 150, 190–94, 200–201, 251; Caddos, 20; Cainguás, 198, 199; Calaxtrin, 169, 170, 182n30; Calchaquís, 210; Caraparirendas, 256–57, 259–60; Carlanas, 111, 112; Catawbas, 104; Chacoan natives, 208; challenges faced by, 9, 22, 104, 272–73; Chanés, 9, 244, 262, 264, 270n43, 271n56;

native peoples (*continued*)
Cherokees, 21; Cheyennes, 18;
Chichimecas, 16; as "Chichimecos,"
173; Chichitames, 151; Chickasaws,
21, 104; chiefdoms, 8, 20–21, 84–86,
90, 92, 94, 95–98, 100–104, 106n16;
Chihenes, 180n10; Chinipas, 45;
Chiricahuas, 162, 166, 170, 180n10;
Chiriguanos, 9, 16, 29n5, 209, 210,
248, 251–54, 256–60, 262, 264, 265–68,
268n10, 269n28, 270n43, 271n56;
Chiriguanos (Ava Guaraní), 242–43;
Chizos, 144, 145, 147, 148, 149, 150, 151;
Choctaws, 21, 104; Cholomes, 151, 153,
166; Chontales, 65; Churumatas, 209;
Cibolos, 145, 147, 149, 150, 151, 152,
154n18; and citizenship, 199, 201;
Coahuiltecans, 148–49, 153, 155n40,
156n49; Cochiti Pueblo, 225–232;
Cocoyomes, 146, 148, 149, 152, 153;
colonial classification of, 7, 8, 148, 150,
151, 152, 153; Comanches, 6, 16, 17, 18,
20, 29n8, 31n29, 110, 111, 112, 113, 114,
116, 118–22, 128–32, 153, 162, 167, 222,
223, 225; communication as *indios
poblados*, 71; community lands, 224,
225, 243; Conchos, 144–53, 154n10,
156n57, 157n64; "Conchos Tobosos,"
144, 146, 152; Conicaris, 38, 45, 46;
conquest, 15, 17, 26, 27, 66, 73, 167, 207;
construction of indigenous others, 2,
168, 207–8, 269n28; Creeks, 21, 104;
criados, 223; Cuicatomes, 151; culture,
1, 3, 4, 6, 7, 9, 15, 19, 20, 23, 24, 27–28,
32n46, 38, 39, 47, 51, 88, 104, 119, 125,
126, 132, 207, 210, 213, 214, 216, 242,
245, 264, 269n15; decentralized
polities of, 88, 159, 161; deportations,
127, 149–50, 156n51, 160–62, 171–74,
179, 180n5, 183n42; Dine (Navajos), 19;
and diplomacy, 19, 20, 35, 92, 131;
diseases, 15, 22, 28n1, 46, 104, 187;
documentary sources, 22, 36, 47,
146–49, 151, 152, 153, 168, 171, 174, 178,
190, 191, 197, 198, 199, 207–8, 209,
216n2, 248–49, 252, 259, 264, 266;
Domingo, 226; Dominican Republic,
24; ethnic identity, 208, 212, 223;
extermination of, 2, 15, 146, 149, 153;
Felipe Santiago, 226; and firearms,
16, 17, 164; folklore and testimonies
of, 28, 36; food stores, 94, 102–3,
215–16; forced relocation of, 11n16,
129, 159, 163–64, 171–74, 177, 179;
Gavilanes, 147, 148, 149; Gaypetes, 209;
Genízaros, 8–9, 222–26, 232, 233, 234,
237; gifts, 96, 99, 113, 114, 115; Gileños,
119; of Greater Antilles, 24; Guahibos
(Sikuani), 19; Guajira Peninsula, 16;
Guamalcas, 209; Guaranís, 18, 29n6,
186, 190–191, 268; Guarijios, 38, 45;
Guaycurúes, 186, 212; Guazapares,
45, 46; Gueleleas, 209; Hopis, 16;
and horses, 16, 17, 20, 90, 95, 112, 113,
114, 115, 117, 119, 120, 121, 125, 126, 128,
129, 131, 142–43, 145, 166, 168, 245;
Huacayas, 247, 251, 254; Huichols
and Coras, 154n7; Huites, 45; as
hunter-gatherers, 19, 38, 39, 43, 44,
84, 88, 112, 131, 133n5, 143, 151, 212, 215;
Hurumatas, 209; Ilhíos, 45; imagined
threats from, 159, 161, 170–71, 174, 178;
Incas, 17, 30n18, 208–9; "Indians of
the Ayllus," 260; indigenous
communities, 38–39, 41–44, 46, 47,
49–50, 51, 66, 75n19, 83–86, 94–95,
102, 125, 162–63, 185, 187, 192–94, 196,
223, 224, 243, 247, 249, 251, 253,
256–66, 272–73; indigenous-Hispano
relations, 180n11, 198, 223, 237; as
indios bárbaros, 7, 160, 168; Ingre
Indians, 254; Iroquois, 17, 30n19; Iti
and IItimiri people, 264; Itza Mayas,
65, 72; Jesuit missionaries, 43–45, 47,
48, 51, 204n341; Jicarillas, 111, 129, 131;
Jocomes, 151; José Archibeque, 226;
Juan José Quintana, 226, 227;
Julimes, 148–51, 156n57, 157n64;

Jumanos, 152, 154n10, 157n64; Kejaches, 65, 77n66; Kickapoos, 16; kinship networks, 8, 19, 32n35, 88, 94, 95, 144, 150, 159, 161, 243; Kiowas, 16, 29n8; Laguneros, 155n40; Lakotas, 17, 18, 30n25; and land, 1, 3, 6, 8–9, 15, 17, 18, 19, 21, 24, 26, 35, 36, 41–42, 47, 48, 50, 51, 95, 96, 97, 102, 110–11, 113, 114, 143, 146, 160, 161, 163, 170, 179, 192, 197, 199–201, 202, 217n12, 221–37, 238n1, 242, 243–45, 247–49, 253, 254, 256–66, 264, 267, 268, 273; land rights, 238n1, 242, 248–49, 253; Lipan Apaches, 7, 110, 111–19, 112–24, 126, 127, 128, 129, 131, 132, 162, 166; and livestock, 16, 19, 47, 48, 50, 51, 59, 159, 160, 162, 163, 166, 167, 168, 170, 171, 192, 196, 215, 253; Llanero (Lipiyán) Apaches, 6–7, 110, 111–26, 128, 129, 131, 132, 134n30; looting expeditions of, 16, 159, 162, 168, 171; Macoyagüis, 38, 48; Mandans, 22; Mapuches, 17, 30n21; Matacos (Mataguayos), 209, 210, 212, 214, 216; Matacos (Wichís), 212, 245, 248; Maya, 4, 6, 54–67, 70, 71, 72–73, 75n19, 77n66; Mayos, 45–46; Mbayás, 209; Mescalero Apaches, 7, 110, 111, 112, 113, 114, 115, 116, 117, 118, 120–29, 131, 132, 134n30, 135n45, 162, 170; and Mesoamerican claims, 21; mestizos, 169, 213, 214, 215, 224, 245, 269n28; Mexicas (Aztecs), 17, 23, 26; Mezquites, 150, 156n57; Miamis, 18; micos (Mississippian leaders), 84, 86, 88, 90, 92, 94–101, 103, 105n5; migration, 16, 24, 26, 46, 57, 159, 162, 163, 164, 187, 189, 196, 201, 212; military campaigns against, 216n2; Mingos, 18; and mining industry, 40, 187; mission Indian pueblos, 160, 164, 167, 267; and mission system, 242, 243; Mississippian world, 20–21, 89, 92, 95; Mitimaes, 217n12; mitote (dance) of, 116; Mixtecs, 17; Mocovíes

(Mocobíes), 209, 210, 212, 213; Muiscas, 22–23; multiethnic confederacy of, 18; naciones (nations), 148, 161–62, 189; Natagé Apaches, 111, 112, 121, 131, 132; Navajos, 19, 20, 129, 161, 222, 223, 233, 273; Nit-ajende (Faraón Apaches), 118, 134n30; Noctenes, 212; and nonnatives, 1–2, 3, 8–9, 16, 17–18, 19, 20–21, 35, 83, 111, 113, 117, 131, 132, 144, 145, 146, 161–62, 187, 198; Nonojes, 147, 151; Nonolat massacre, 146, 149; of North American Great Plains, 16, 17; Ocloyas, 209, 210, 213; Ocoronis, 44; ódames, 155n40; Odawas (Ottawas), 18; Ojotaes, 210, 213; Opatas, 18, 31n28; Oposmes, 150, 156n57; oral traditions of, 27, 28, 38; oratas, 94–95, 97, 100; Orinocan Llanos, 19; in Orinoco Basin, 16; Osages, 17, 27; Osas, 209; of Ostimuri, 47; Otomis, 17; Panama, 24; Paypayas, 209, 210; Pecos people, 235; Pehuenches, 18, 31n29; Pelones, 152; and peoples of New Spain, 38, 141–53; peoples of Yaqui, Mayo, and Fuerte basins, 4, 35–36, 38; Pijaos, 16; Pimas, 18, 31n28; Plains Indians, 29n7, 222, 234; Plains military societies of Plains Indians, 34n82; Poclames, 150, 156n57; population, 15, 46, 50, 59, 84, 98, 100, 150, 163, 164, 186, 187–89, 191, 192, 193, 197–98, 201–2, 224, 273; Posalmes, 150, 156n57; Pottawatomis, 18; and power, 6, 10n3, 10n8, 17, 18, 26, 30n15, 66, 85, 86, 88, 89, 96, 98, 100, 103, 111, 117, 118, 125, 127, 167, 179, 180n2, 201, 272; principales (leaders), 45, 46; and privatization of public land, 9, 224–25; Pueblos, 8–9, 16–20, 23, 43, 161–62, 222–26, 228–229, 230, 231, 237; Puerto Ricans, 24; Purépechas (Tarascans), 17; Quintarsas (Quintanas), 228; raids of haciendas,

native peoples (*continued*)
212–13, 216; rancherias (bands), 36, 41, 50, 51, 111, 112, 127–31, 133n5, 135n54, 145, 147, 159, 214, 216; Raramuris, 38; rebellions of, 16, 23, 29n12, 31n27, 46, 47, 67–68, 69, 70, 71, 103, 126, 127, 144–45, 146, 147, 149–50, 153, 161–62, 171, 174, 187, 214, 216n2, 248, 259, 264, 270n45; removal of tribes, 11n16, 21, 33n53, 129, 149–50, 159, 173; resilience of, 1–2, 4, 47; resistance, 6, 8, 9, 15, 16–18, 29n6, 31n32, 56–57, 70, 73, 81, 97, 185, 186, 188, 199, 207, 208, 209, 210, 212, 215, 216, 222, 237, 242, 247, 248, 268n15, 272, 274n2; rhetoric of barbarians and invaders, 253, 254; rituals, 18, 36, 38, 46, 116, 120; Salineros, 145, 146, 147, 149, 152, 153, 155n27, 155n40; San Ignacio reduction, 214, 215; Seminoles, 21; Sende Apaches, 118, 119, 125, 134n30; Seris, 155n27; Shawnees, 18; *sinaloas*, 43–47; Sisimbles, 147, 149, 151; social organization of, 6, 19, 24, 36, 39, 84, 85–86, 88, 104, 189, 190–94, 199, 202, 214, 256; as soldiers in forts, 212, 213, 216; of Southeast Asian mainland, 27–28; of Southern Cone, 11n14, 17, 20; sovereignty, 1, 8, 17–18, 20, 21, 26, 197, 273; and Spanish citizens, 224; and Spanish intrusion, 6, 17, 19, 20, 21, 132, 243; Spanish naming of, 141, 143–48, 150–53, 180n10, 203n13, 212, 222; Spanish policies, 11n11, 48, 185–86, 194; spiritual beliefs, 19, 45–46, 110, 115–18, 125–26, 128, 129, 132, 177; and states or empires, 8, 21, 27–28, 35, 44, 45, 46, 48, 73, 106n16, 111, 179, 199, 201, 202, 222, 242–44, 267, 268n15; Sumas, 166, 167; Tainos, 24; Taños, 210; Tapacolmes, 150, 151, 156n57; Tarahumaras, 151, 154n7, 167–71, 182n28, 182n35; Tehuecos, 44; Temoris, 45; Tepagüis, 38, 45, 46, 47,

48; Tepehuanes, 16, 147–49, 152, 154n7; Terocodames, 149; Tewas, 18; Tlaxcallans, 17, 149; Tobas, 209, 210, 212, 213, 214, 216, 245, 247, 248, 268n15; Tobatines, 198; Tobosos, 144–49, 151, 152, 153, 164, 165; Tohono O'odhams, 20; Tomatas, 209; Tosimoras, 149; Totonacs, 17; trade, 20, 38, 39, 56–57, 65, 71–73, 82, 85, 111, 112, 131, 162–67, 169, 170, 187, 208, 233; tributes, 69, 71, 116, 132, 151, 185, 213, 217n12, 243–44; Tripas Blancas, 149; Tucumán, 16; urban, 3, 10n9, 11n18; use of animal skins, 108n77; Utes, 20, 222, 223; vassals, 191, 192, 200; Vejoz, 212; warfare, 16, 23, 31n30, 45, 86, 92, 98, 99, 100–102, 109n90, 113, 114, 131, 132, 144, 145, 146, 148, 149, 162, 170, 182n36, 245, 248, 251; Wayuu (Guajiros), 16, 19; Wichitas, 18, 20, 31n29; women, 19, 20, 22, 26–27, 32n46, 34n75, 43, 45, 46, 58, 68, 90, 94, 96, 99, 118, 123, 125, 127, 166, 168, 170, 172, 173, 213, 243, 251–52, 254, 266, 268; Wyandots, 18; Yalas, 209; Yamasees, 104; Yanomamis, 273; Yapanatas, 209; Yaquis, 20, 35–36, 38, 44, 46, 49; Yoeme/Yaquis, 44, 47, 49, 50, 51, 53n41; Yoes/Choix, 45; Yoreme, 4, 38, 42, 44, 47, 51; Yucatec Mayas, 54–68, 70–73, 73n3, 76n34; Yutas, 129; of Zapato Tuerto, 112; Zapotecs, 17; Zizimble nation, 144; Zizimbres, 149; Zuaques, 44. *See also* Bolivia; language; spirituality; United States

New Mexico: Alcalde José García de la Mora, 233; *alcaldía* of Belen, 233; Anacleto de Miera y Pacheco, 226; Antonio, 226; Antonio Alonso, 227; Antonio José Ortiz, 226, 228, 230; Antonio Quintana, 229; Bernardo Bonavia, 228; Cacique José Antonio Saya, 229; and Chihuahua, 227; Cochiti Pueblo measurement, 229–32, 237; Colorado Plateau, 222;

Comandante General Bernardo Bonavía, 228; common lands, 233, 234–37; community lands, 229, 231, 236, 239n30; don Felipe Sandoval, 226–27, 230, 231; don Joaquín Pérez Gavilán, 225; don Mariano de la Peña, 228; don Santiago Coris, 226, 229; Dr. Franciso Antonio de Landa, 229; Durango, 228, 229; environment of, 222; Estancia Springs, 233; Francisco, 229; Francisco Ignacio de Madariaga, 235; Franciso Caiso, 226; frontiers, 221, 222, 223, 233, 237; *fundo legal*, 223, 229, 230, 239n30; Gallinas River, 233; Governor Alberto Maynez, 227, 228, 229; Governor Fernando de la Concha, 226, 228; Governor Jefe Político Bartolomé Baca, 221, 233, 234, 235, 236, 237; Governor Jefe Político Facundo Melgares, 233; Governor Joaquín del Real Alencaster, 225, 226, 227, 228; Governor José Manrique, 227, 228; Governor Juan Antonio Ignacio Baca, 227, 228; Governor Juan José Martinez, 227; Governor Manuel Armijo, 237; Governor Pedro Fermin de Mendinueta, 230, 231; Governor Pedro María de Allande, 229–30; Guadalajara, 227, 229, 231, 239n30; Hacienda de San Juan Bautista del Ojito del Río de las Gallinas, 234; Ignacio María Sánchez Vergara, 231, 232; importance of water in, 222; Jefe Político y Militar Antonio Narbona, 234, 235, 236; Jemez Pueblo, 228; José Cota, 236; José de Miera, 227; José Francisco Ortiz, 236; José Joaquín Reyes, 229; José Miguel de la Peña, 230; Juan Antonio Cabeza de Baca, 227; Juan Diego Coris, 230; Juan Diego Sena, 236; Juan Domingo Carnero, 226; Juan Estaban Pino, 234, 236; Juan Ignacio Montoya, 227; Juan José Gutierrez, 227, 228, 230; Juan José Quintana, 227, 229, 231; Juan Roque Yurena, 226; Juana Baca, 231; land of Peña Blanca, 225–29; land grants, 223, 228, 233, 234, 237; land rights, 223–24, 225; land rush in, 221, 224, 225, 233, 235, 236–37, 237n1; landownership, 221, 223, 225, 234, 235–36; lawyer Rafael Brancho, 229; legal proceedings against Spaniards, 226; Lieutenant Governor Baltazar Domínguez, 227; livestock, 222; "Lo de Basquez," 230; Los Fernández, 230, 231; Luis María Cabeza de Baca, 225, 226, 227, 228, 229–32; Manuel Antonio Baca, 234; Manuel Domingo, 229; Manzano Mountains, 233; Nambé Pueblo, 236, 237; Nemesio Salcedo, 226; Nereo Antonio Montoya, 230, 231; *New Mexico Historical Review* (Hall and Weber), 234; Ogito de Agua, 226, 229; Ojo del Espíritu Santo, 228; Pecos Pueblo, 234–37; Pecos River, 222, 226, 233, 234; Pedro Bautista Pino, 226, 231, 233; Preston Beck Grant, 233; privatization of land, 233, 237; public land, 223, 234, 237; Pueblo of Santo Domingo, 226, 227–31, 236, 237; Río Abajo region, 233; Río Grande, 222, 223, 228, 230, 231, 233, 234; San Felipe Pueblo, 230, 231, 236, 237; San Fernando, 233; San Juan Pueblo, 18, 236, 237; San Miguel del Bado, 234; Santa Ana Pueblo, 228; Santa Cruz, 231; Santa Fe, 226, 228, 233; Santiago Ulibarri, 234; Sile property, 228, 229, 230; Spanish elite, 221, 224, 225; Spanish rule in, 223–24; Spanish *vecinos*, 222, 223, 225, 226, 230, 231, 232, 237; Supreme Government in Mexico City, 235; *tierras baldías* (public land), 223; Tomé in, 233; Vicente Villanueva, 230, 231; Zia Pueblo in, 228

New Spain: Aguaverde Presidio, 111; Apache leader Pascual, 164; Atotonilco, 144, 147; Baroyeca, 40; Batacosa, 47, 48; Beneficios Altos district, 59–60, 62, 63, 72, 77n59; Bishop Pedro de Tamarón y Romeral, 149; Bolsón de Mapimí region, 5, 8, 114, 141–43, *142*, 144–50, 152–53, 155n23, 162, 164; Californias, 115; *camino real de tierra adentro*, 145, 146, 148; Camino Real region, 61, 64, 75n18; Campeche region, 54–56, 61, 66, 70, 73n1; Casas Grandes in Paquime, Chihuahua, 39, 144; Cedros River, 47; Central Mexico, 224; Chalchihuites, 39; Chancenote, 75n18; Chiametla, 41; Chihuahua, 148, 154n7, 162, 168, 169–70, 171, 172, 181n26, 182n28; Chinarras, 145; Cifuentes visita, 69, 77n57; Coahuila in, 112, 113, 115, 121, 126, 130, 143, 146, 147, 148, 151, 152, 162, 163, 164, 165, 166, 167; Colorado River, 112, 113, 121; *composición*, 41; Concheria, 144; Conchos Presido, 144, 147, 149, 163, 164; Conchos River, 141, 144, 147, 150, 151; crimes and raiding in, 171; de Soto's expeditions, 83; Durango, 49, 146, 154n7, 165; Dzacabuchen, 69, 70; eastern Internal Provinces of, 6, 110, 115, 129, 130; El Pasaje, 149; El Paso, 131, 165, 166; environment of, 35–36, 38, 39–42, 47, 48, 50, 51, 59, 63, 68, 112, 113, 141–42; epidemics, 68; forest region of *montaña*, 54, 55, 63, 64, 66, 67–68, 70, 71, 77n59; frontier of, 222; Fuerte River, 4, 39; Gila and Santa Cruz River valleys, 39; Governor Antonio de Cortaire, 75n19; Governor Antonio de Oca y Sarmiento, 145; Governor Diego Guajardo Fajardo, 145; Governor Diego Martinez de Hurdaide, 114; Governor Fayni, 169; Governor

Fernando de la Concha, 114; Governor Francisco de Escobedo, 71, 72; Governor José Antonio de Ecay y Múzquiz, 152; Governor Juan Manso, 161; Governor Lope de Sierra Osorio, 145; governorship of Sonora-Sinaloa, 41; gulf coast, 40, 172; Gulf of California, 36, 49; Hecelchakan in, 64; history of, 238n7; history of Mission Conicari, 47, 53n34; Hohokam in, 39; Huatabampo, 39; indigenous communities, 41, 42–43, 45–47, 49; indigenous landscapes, 38–39; indigenous peoples, 142, 143–53, 159–72, 176; Ixpimienta, 66; Janos region, 151; Jesuit missionaries, 49, 53n34; José Berroterán, 149; Julimes mission, 151; La Aduana, 40; La Pimienta in, 64, 65, 66; land of, 41, 42, 152, 224; lands of marquis of Aguayo, 146; Las Canas, 147; Las Vacas Pass, 122; livestock ranching, 41; local goverance in, 36, 49, 64, 68, 75n19, 76n34; Los Arenales in, 128, 130; Los Frailes in, 40; Los Nogales, 147; Manuel Antonio San Juan, 165; Mayo River, 4, 39, 40, 45, 47; Merida in, 54, 55, 59, 73n3; Milpitas arroyo in, 114; mining industry in, 40, 41, 47, 48, 51, 74n10, 141, 145, 146, 147, 151, 162; mission of San Francisco de Bizarrón, 167; Mission Santa Rosa de Viterbo de los Nadadores, 148, 149, 152; missionaries' letters and reports, 42, 47, 48, 49, 51, 52n20; Mocorito Valley in, 38; Monclova, 148, 149, 152; Monterrey in, 147; Namiquipa, 144; Nazas River basin, 141; New Mexico, 115, 118, 120, 121, 129, 131, 135n45, 137n84, 147, 166, 222; Nonolat hill, 145; northeastern region of, 110, 146, 152, 172; northern region of, *37*, 49, 50–51, 145, 147–48, 150, 151, 162–64, 167, 170–72, 174, 178, 179; northwestern region of, 53n34; Nueces River, 111; Nuestra Señora de la Asunción de Tepagüi, 47, 48; Nuevo Leon, 115, 130, 146, 147, 150; Nuevo Santander, 146; Onavas Valley, 39; Ostimuri in, 4, 5, 35, 36, 39, 40, 41, 42, 47, 48, 49, 51; Oxkutzcab, 64, 66; *parajes* (places), 41; Parral in, 40, 144, 145, 147, 149, 152, 155n40, 163; Parras, 147–148, 149, 163; Pecos Pueblo, 111, 112, 131; Pecos River, 6, 111, 112, 122; people of Sinaloa river basin, 38; peoples of Yaqui, Mayo, and Fuerte basins, 4, 35–36, 38; Petalán, 36, 51; Piedras Verdes, 40; Pimeria Alta, 49; population by Mexicans and US nationals, 143; Presidio del Norte ("El Norte") in, 112, 114, 115, 121, 123, 127, 129, 131, 135n45, 165; Presidio La Bahía, 166, 167; presidio of San Franciso de Conchos, 144; private property, 41; Promontorios, 40; province of Xalisco, 49; real de minas, 142–143, 150, 162; Reales de los Alamos, 40; Río Chico, 40; Río Grande, 7, 111, 120, 129, 141, 147, 148, 150, 151, 152, 154n18, 156n57, 163, 164, 171; river valleys in, 35, 39, 40, 42, 45, 49; Sacramento, 166; Sahcabchén, 65–73, 78n71; Salado River, 146; Salinas del Machete, 144, 147; Saltillo region, 151, 163, 172; San Antonio de Béxar, 120; San Bartolomé, 145, 151, 152, 156n57; San Buenaventura Mission, 144, 149; San Diego River, 120, 123; San Felipe de Real de Chihuahua, 145, 162, 181n26; San Fernando in, 117; San Franciso de Conchos mission, 144, 145, 147, 151, 152; San Francisco, 120; San Ignacio, 40; San Ildefonso, 40; San José de Parral, 144, 150, 151; San Miguel Arcángel, 40; San Miguel de Macoyagüi, 47, 48; San Pedro River,

114; San Rodrigo River, 119, 124; Santa Barbara Province, 145, 147, 150, 152; Santa Catalina, 147; Santa Cruz de los Auchanes, 151; Santa Rosa, 117, 119, 120, 121, 122, 123, 124, 127, 128, 129, 167; Santander, 115; Sierra de Guadalupe, 112; Sierra del Carmen, 112; Sierra district of, 54, 59, 60, 61, 62, 63, 64, 72, 73, 75n18, 148; Sierra Madre, 39, 40, 45, 47, 141, 143, 144, 154n7, 163, 168; Sierra Mojada, 147; Sinaloa province, 35, 36, 39, 40, 41, 42, 47, 48, 49, 51, 151; Sonora, 5, 18, 35, 39, 40, 41, 49, 51, 115, 151; Spanish alliances with native groups, 18, 20, 117; Spanish naming criteria, 141, 143; Spanish *vecinos*, 41, 47, 48, 49; Tacupeto in, 40; Tarahumara pueblos, 163; taxation, 163, 165; Tepagüis, 47–48; Texas, 115, 118, 146, 147, 166, 167; Tizimín, 59, 60, 61, 62, 72, 75n18; Tizonazo, 146, 149; town of Dzibalchen, 78n78; town of Hopelchén, 78n78; transfrontier trade, 55, 76n36; Tucolahnexmo community, 54, 55; urban and trade centers of, 39, 60; Valladolid region, 75n18; Villa de Sinaloa, 40, 42; village of Conicari, 47, 48; war against Apaches, 166, 171, 181n23; wax repartimientos, 60; western provinces of, 41; Yaqui River, 4, 39, 40; Yaqui Valley, 38, 49, 50; Yucatán, 4, 5, 16, 19, 30n12, 54–62, 63, 68, 70, 75–76n27, 75n18, 75n19, 75n22

Niza, Marcos de, 39
North America, 5; during nineteenth century, 10n7, 18; Apache Wars, 18; Beaver Wars, 17; Canada, 274; captive traffic in, 32n50; European colonization, 82, 159, 161; frontiers, 2, 161; Great Plains of, 16, 17, 111; indigenous violence, 182n29, 182n38; Iroquois, 17; native peoples' control of, 159; nomadic groups of, 16; Pecos

North America (*continued*)
River, 110; Plains Indians of,
269n15; Plains Wars, 18; private
landownership, 9; Rio Grande Basin,
16, 18; trade of furs, hides, and horses,
20, 252. *See also* native peoples;
United States
Nueva Vizcaya, Kingdom of, 41, 49; and
Acoclames, 146–47; and Apaches, 7,
129, 160, 164, 166, 168, 174, 179, 182n29;
Berroterán report, 181n14; Bolsón de
Mapimí region, 162; Cabezas in, 147;
Chief Picax-andé Ins-tinsle, 112;
Chihuahua, 160; Coahuila in, 160;
crimes in, 168–71; districts of Saltillo
and Parras, 115; Durango, 160, 182n30;
encomienda Indians, 150–51, 152;
Indian nations, 149; indigenous-
settler relations, 166, 167, 170;
interethnic alliances, 204n33;
mestizaje (mixing) in, 20; mines in,
40; occupation of *realengas*, 41;
Parral in, 40; Parras, 163; Salineros,
146; Spanish naming of native
peoples, 143, 147; Spanish *vecinos*, 41;
taxes in, 163; Tobosos, 145; war on
Apache groups, 144, 160

O'Conor, Hugo, 111, 171, 172, 183n39

Paraguay: Antonio Ruiz de Montoya,
190, 191; Antonio Sepp, 192;
bandeirante attacks, 188, 189, 201,
203n9, 203n10; cacicazgos, 199, 201,
202; citizenship for indigenous
people, 199; city of Asuncion, 197;
Corpus Christi, 189, 201; Diaz Tano,
190; Encarnación de Itapua, 189;
encomienda system, 156n56, 185–90,
196, 202; epidemics, 204n32;
Franciscan friars in, 188; Francisco
de Alfaro, 188; Governor Hernando
Arias de Saaedra, 188; Gran Chaco,
208, 209; Guaraní borderlands, 8,

186, 267; Guaranís of, 16, 186, 190–91,
196–99, 200, 201; Guaycurúes, 186;
Itapúa in, 201; Itatín region of, 189,
203n10; Jesuits in, 19, 187–89, 190,
192, 193–94, 202, 203n10, 203n28,
204n35, 204n341; Jose Gervasio
Artigas, 197; Juan Escandón, 193;
maps by villagers, 200–201; *naciones
infieles* (unconverted nations) in, 185;
Nuestra Señora de la Concepcion, 192,
199; Nuestra Señora de la Natividad
del Acaray, 189; Nuestra Señora de
Santa Fe, 198, 203n10; Paraná River,
188, 189, 198; population, 189, 193,
197–98; President Carlos Antonio
López, 199; *reducciones* (mission
settlements), 188–89, 191–94, 196–99,
202, 203n28, 204n35; regions of
Guairá, Ilatín, and Tape, 188; San
Ignacio del Paraná, 203n10; Santa
María de Iguazú, 189; Santiago de
Jerez, 203n10; Tarumá region of,
198–99; Tobatines, 198, 204n341;
Uruguay River, 189; Viceroy Gabriel
de Avilés, 196; village of Caray,
201; War of the Triple Alliance,
186, 199. *See also* Gran Chaco;
settlements
parlamentos (peace talks), 20
Patagui, Nicolás, 200
Perdue, Theda, 105
Peru, 30n18, 74n10, 82, 207, 213
Picax-andé Ins-tinsle (chief): agreement
with Ugalde, 114–15, 129; and captain
Alegre, 123, 124, 125, 131; and captain
Daunica-Jate, 122; and captain
Xat-ys-an, 130; and captain Zaragate,
123, 124, 125; and Casimiro Valdés,
126, 127–29, 134n39; encounters with
Colonel Ugalde, 113–14, 117–20, 122,
132; gifts from Spaniards, 114, 115, 116,
119, 122, 123, 124, 132; incursions
against Spanish, 135n54; letters to
Ugalde, 120–21, 134n39; and Lipan

captain Dabegsil-sete, 124–26, 128;
and Llanero/Lipiyán Apaches, 132n4;
as main *caudillo* (leader), 6–7, 110, 111,
113, 114, 115–17, 118, 119, 121–29, 132,
137n84; and Mescalero Apaches, 122,
124, 131, 132, 135n45; name of, 112, 118,
130, 131, 134n30, 135n45, 137n84; and
Nataehé, 128; peace attempts, 131,
135n45; power, 117, 118, 123, 127, 131; and
San Sabás Presidio, 121; as warrior,
121–22; wife of, 124, 125, 126, 129
Pirapepó, Claudio, 200

Queipo de Llano, Pedro, 168, 169, 170,
182n29, 182n35

Rangel, Rodrigo, 83, 90, 91, 93, 97, 99
Restall, Matthew, 65, 66
Retana, Juan Fernández de, 147
Rivera, Pedro de, 147, 149

Sánchez Cerdán, Francisco, 54, 56, 73n1
Scott, James, 27–28
settlements: Acaponeta, 39; Agualeguas
and Sabinas, 146; Atotonilco mission,
147; cattle ranching, 269n19;
Chiriguano, 256, 257; city of Asunción,
187, 190, 191; in Coahuila, 148; colonial,
37, 46, 47, 142, 146, 151, 154n7, 210; of
Culiacán, 39; distribution of, 51;
establecimientos (settlements), 18;
of Euro-Americans, 19; Franciscans,
71; haciendas in Bolivia, 252; of
Huacareta and Pirirenda, 248;
independent, 70; of indigenous
peoples, 18, 35, 36, 37, 39, 40–41, 46,
49, 50, 151, 198, 210, 214, 222–23, 245,
254, 262; La Cañada de Cochiti, 231;
land grants, 260, 262; in Mabila,
98–99; mestizo towns, 248; patterns
of, 208; Pueblo de Nuestra Señora del
Rosario de Indios Tobas, 215; *pueblos
de reducciones* (Spanish-supervised
communities), 185, 186, 187;

rancherías, 36, 41, 50, 51; *reducciones*
(mission settlements), 19, 189, 191–94,
210, 213–14; San Miguel del Bado,
232–33; sizes of, 39, 46; Spanish, 39,
40, 41–42, 45–47, 114, 142, 162, 163, 165,
170, 174, 189, 191–92, 209–10, 213–14,
216, 223; Viceroy Francisco de Toledo,
244; Yuti, 259
Sheridan, Cecilia, 152, 156n49
Sitting Bull, 18
slavery: Amerindians, 15, 20–21, 29n1,
32n50, 82, 97, 104, 125; in Cuba, 178–79,
184n59; European model of, 33n53;
and Haitian Revolution, 160; and
indigenous peoples, 144, 145, 149, 160,
161, 187, 188, 209–10, 213, 216, 222, 243;
and intertribal wars, 20–21; Janissaries,
222; and Juan Ortiz, 89; legalization of,
210; and native societies, 104; runaway
African slaves, 7, 160; slave hunters,
188, 189; slave traffic, 33n52, 104, 173,
222; Spanish involvement, 45, 144, 150,
172, 222; and women, 97, 173; and
Yucatan Peninsula, 63
South America: Amazon Basin, 20 21,
273; Andes, 30n18; Argentina, 8, 21,
186; Brazil, 8, 186, 194; Chaco region,
16, 18, 21; Charcas, 208; Chiriguanos
(Ava Guaraní), 16, 29n5; Ciudad Real,
187; colonization of, 185, 207–8;
Cuzco, 209; deterritorialization,
194–99; *encomienda* system, 187–88;
epidemics, 188, 194, 196; governor of
Buenos Aires Francisco de Paula
Bucareli, 194; Guaranís of, 18, 29n6,
186–87; indigenous peoples, 159, *195*;
Paraguay, 8, 185–90; and Pedro
Lozano, 209, 218n26; Peru, 30n18;
pueblos de indios (Indian towns), 187;
Rio de la Plata region, 185, 186, 209;
rubber trade, 20; Santiago de Jerez,
187; Sao Paulo, 188; Villa Rica del
Espíritu, 187. *See also* Argentina;
Bolivia; Brazil; Paraguay

Spain: colonization, 41, 172, 185–86, 194; conquest of Incan Empire, 244; conquest of Tah-Itza, 76n35; empire of, 11n11, 35, 157n63, 172, 185, 186, 187, 223; founding of Jujuy, 207, 209; Hispaniola (island), 174; and indigenous peoples, 71, 114, 151, 185; king of, 18, 127, 130, 131, 136n77, 145, 150, 151, 163, 185, 188, 210, 213, 215, 216; land grants, 224; missionaries, 245; Napoleonic occupation of, 224; PARES database of, 25, 34n72; Spanish Caribbean, 180n5; Spanish citizens, 224; Spanish Constitution of 1812, 11n17; Spanish-Aztec war of 1519–21, 23; and tribute, 75n19; Venezuela in, 19; village in La Mancha, 154n18; wax from Maya towns, 75n19; Yucatan's bishop, 64. *See also* Caribbean islands

spirituality: alms (*limosnas*), 58; Archbishop Juan de Palafox y Mendoza, 156n62; beliefs and practices, 19, 20, 26, 43, 45–46, 48, 49, 50, 57, 58, 73, 74n10, 77n59, 85, 103, 115–17, 118, 152, 163, 177, 194, 197, 210, 259; Catholicism, 17, 26, 46, 54, 110, 118, 172, 186, 242; chiefdoms, 103; Christianity, 45–46, 49, 50, 151, 167, 193, 223; and colonization, 104, 150, 151; conversion, 45, 46, 53n32, 193; Diocese of Guadiana, 49; divine favor, 103; Dominicans, 26, 49, 194; *enramadas* (arbors), 36; evangelization, 210, 215; Franciscan missionaries/missions, 49, 58, 74n16, 156–57n62, 194, 196, 213, 253, 254, 262, 264, 267; Francisco del Pilar, 262; indigenous peoples, 49, 82, 115–17, 151, 164, 191–92, 194, 210; Jesuit missionaries, 35, 40, 41, 42, 43, 44–46, 47, 48, 49, 51, 189, 213; Jesuit missions, 157n62, 194, 245; Mayos, 46; Mercedarians, 194;

missionary-indigenous relations, 31n32, 43–45, 46, 48, 51, 155n35; missions of Bolivia, 245; *monumento* (memorial), 69, 77n67; and nature, 36; *pajko* (ceremonial dances), 46; Pedro Ortiz de Zárate, 210; peoples of Yaqui, Mayo, and Fuerte basins, 35; Picax-andé Ins-tinsle, 115–17, 118, 125–26, 128, 129, 132; power of *diye*, 134n26; religious authority, 85–86; religious instruction, 187, 264; religious missions, 49, 82, 151, 242; religious revitalization, 82; religious syncretism, 32n42; rituals, 17, 20, 46, 51, 85, 134n26; and salt lakes, 233; San José del Tizonazo, 155n35; of the Santa Cruz Department, 245; secularization, 156–57n62; shamans, 18; Villa de Sinaloa, 40; and Yaquis, 46; Zapotec texts, 26

Sumey, Pedro, 200

Sušnik, Branislava, 190, 196, 204n35, 247

Tapia, P. Gonzalo de, 43, 44

Tascalusa (chief): alliances with indigenous groups, 98, 104, 109n90; battle of Mabila, 96, 98, 100–102; capital of Atahachi, 92, 94, 95, 97, 102; chiefdom of, 6, *87*, 89, 96, 97, 100–104; encounter with de Soto, 6, 82, 83, 89, 92–93, 95–101, 102, 104–5; family of, 92, 93, 101; and land, 90; leadership, 81, 90, 92, 96, 100–102; and Luis de Moscoso, 92; as *mico* (principal chief), 81, 89, 90, 92, 93, 94, 95, 96, 100, 101, 105n5; and Mississippian chiefdoms, 97; power of, 83, 89, 90, 92, 95, 96, 98, 100–102; and resistance, 6, 104–5; and Spanish Army, 83, 98; stature of, 6, 81, 90, 93, 95–96; vassals of, 90, 95, 98

Tecumseh, 18, 30n24

Tenskwatawa, 18, 30n24

Tun, Antonio, 54–55

Túpac Amaru II, 18, 31n27
Túpac Katari, 18

Ugalde, Juan de: attacks on Apaches, 112, 129–30; and captains Chul-ul and Caballada, 128; and Casimiro Valdés, 128–29; charges against, 130, 131; and chiefs Zapato and Patule, 127; as commander in chief, 6, 110, 112, 113, 114, 115, 117–20, 124–28, 135n45; encounters with Picax-andé Ins-tinsle, 113–114, 117–120, 122, 132, 132n4; and Mescalero Apaches, 121, 122, 123, 127, 128, 129; and native peoples, 114, 134n30, 134n39; and Provincias Internas de Oriente, 110, 115; and Spaniards, 129; troops of, 112, 113, 114, 127, 130
Ugarte y Loyola, Jacobo de, 112, 115, 121, 129, 130, 131. *See also* Picax-andé Ins-tinsle (chief)
United States: Alabama, 6, 81, 90, 108n77, 160; Alabamas, 104; Alabama River, 92, 97, 98–99; Alaska, 273; Anilco, 102; Arizona, 16, 39, 159, 160, 162; Arkansas, 89, 102; Cahokia in, 83, 84, 106n16; Californias, 18; captive traffic in, 33n51; Casqui, 103; Charlotte Thompson site, 92, 102; chiefdom of Cofitachequi, 96, 103; chiefdom of Coosa (Cosa), 90, *91*, 96, 98, 103, 104, 109n90; chiefdom of Mabila, 98, 100; chiefdom of Quigualtam, 96; chiefdom of Tascalusa, 6, 95–98, 100–104; chiefdom of Utiangue, 89; Colorado River, 6, 20; Dakota Access Pipeline, 273; and Deb Haaland, 274; earthen mounds in, 83, 84, *85*, 92, 93, 94, 95, 99, 102; Florida, 21, 83, 89, 90, 102, 172; Georgia, 104; Great Plains, 20, 22, 83, 273; indigenous peoples' land, 237; indigenous rights, 272; Kansas, 159; land grant acreage, 224; Los

Arenales, 111–12; Mabila, *91*, 95–104, 108n77, 109n92; Midwest, 83; migrants, 158–59; Mississippi, 6, 82; Mississippian Period, 83–84, 88, 101; Mississippian chiefdoms, 20–21, 84–86, 88, 89, 95–96, 102–3; Mississippian world, 83–89, *87*, 92, 94, 102–4; Moundville, *85*, *86*, 88; Muscogee (Creek) Confederacy, 104; Napituca, 102; Native Americans in US Army, 18; Navajos, 273; New Mexico, 18, 111, 112, 161, 162, 221; North Carolina, 90; Ohio River, 18; Oklahoma, 237n1, 274, 274n3; Pánfilo de Narváez expedition, 89; Piachi in, 95, 97, 98, 100, 103; polity of Chicaza, 82, 102, 103, 104; population of, 158–59; President Donald J. Trump, 158; Quigualtam, 104; removal of tribes to Indian Territory, 21, 159, 33n53; reservations in, 19; Santa Fe, 160; South Carolina, 90; Southeastern Indians, 89; and Spaniards, 10n3, 81–82; Spanish frontiers in, 10n3; St. Louis, 83; Talisi, 90, *91*, 92, 95, 98, 100, 103; Tallapoosa and Coosa Rivers, 92, 104; Tascalusa province, 81, 82, *87*, 90, *91*, 92, 95, 102; Tennessee, 90, 104; Texas, 6, 110, 111, 150, 159; unemployment, 273; upper Missouri River, 22; South, 1, 6, 16, 19–22, 81, 82, 83, 84, *87*, 92, 94, 98, 103, 11n12, 33n51, 33n52, 105n11, 273; US Supreme Court, 274, 274n3

Valdés, Carlos, 148
Valdés, Casimiro, 116, 120, 121, 122–23, 124, 125. *See also* Picax-andé Ins-tinsle (chief)
Valdez, Curate Br. Francisco Joaquín, 49–50, 51
Vélez Cachupín, Tomás, 111

Yaguarendí, Melchor, 200

Printed in the USA
CPSIA information can be obtained
at www.ICGtesting.com
LVHW041249101023
760695LV00005B/33

9 780806 191935